Workflow Handbook 2002

Workflow Handbook
2002

Published in association with the
Workflow Management Coalition

Edited by

Layna Fischer

Future Strategies Inc., Book Division
Lighthouse Point, Florida

Workflow Handbook 2002

Copyright © 2002 by Future Strategies Inc.

ISBN 0-9703509-2-9

03 02 01 1 2 3 4 5 6

Published by Future Strategies Inc., Book Division

2436 North Federal Highway, #374
Lighthouse Point FL 33064 USA
954.782.3376 fax +1 954 782 6365
books@wfmc.org

Cover design by Pearl & Associates
160 West Camino Real
Boca Raton, FL 33432, USA
561.338.0380 fax 561.338.9460

Publisher's Cataloging-in-Publication Data

Library of Congress Control Number: 2002100620

Workflow Handbook 2002:
/Layna Fischer

p. cm.

Includes bibliographical references, glossary, appendices and index.

ISBN 0-9703509-2-9

1. Workflow Management. 2. Technological Innovation. 3. Business Process Management. 4. Information Technology. 5. Total Quality Management. 6. Organizational Change 7. Management Information Systems. 8. Office Practice_Automation. 9. Business Process Technology. 10. Electronic Commerce. 11. Process Analysis

Fischer, Layna J

Table of Contents

TABLE OF CONTENTS

Foreword

Jon Pyke, WfMC Chair and CTO, Staffware, UK

It does not seem that long ago that I welcomed you to the 2001 WfMC Official Workflow Handbook. Now I have the honor and pleasure of welcoming you to this latest edition.

Since I first introduced the Handbook, the world in which we all work has changed beyond recognition. The general economic slowdown has also had a dramatic effect on the prospects for business process automation. The increasing need to reduce costs, improve business efficiencies and business flexibility has pushed the concept of business process technology to the forefront of an organization's consciousness.

But it is not just the impact of the economic slowdown that is driving interest in business process automation. The extended supply chain—or value chain as some have termed it—is a key business driver. The much vaunted eBusiness revolution is now a reality. The over hyped Dot Com sector, with its focus on the consumer market, may not have been the new business paradigm many where expecting, but what has rapidly become a reality has been the revolution in the business-to-Business sector. eBusiness is here to stay.

The drive to reduce business costs has also spawned a new opportunity for workflow vendors—the Business Process Management market—or BPM.

Organizations across the globe are now actively looking at outsourcing entire business processes which do not lie at the core of their business. Finance, invoicing, manufacturing, procurement and customer service are among a host of business processes that are already being outsourced to specialist organizations.

Whatever way you look at it, business processes such as these need automating whether they still reside within an organization or whether they are outsourced. Avoiding—or even shedding—non-core business processes, as well as reducing costs are the key drivers in this. However, given the events of September 2001, the protection of mission-critical business processes, ensuring 24x7 data availability in this eBusiness world, has also come to the fore.

Never has the time been more opportune to define and manage the business processes within and beyond and organization through the use of workflow.

The accelerating adoption of new technologies such as the Internet, is causing shifts in the way people work and their working environment. The Workflow Management Coalition is chartered with keeping pace with these advances and you will see a number of these issues addressed in this book.

Importantly WfMC has worked strenuously for the adoption of standards throughout the industry. So where, in this rapidly expanding market, do industry standards fit in?

Standards allow organizations that have more than one workflow system to connect them easily. They provide a fertile environment for workflow component development to grow and flourish, giving a rich array of options for user organizations. Most importantly, standards provide an infrastructure for inter-organizational process automation. The term 'inter-workflow' was first used by a working party in the Japan Standards Association to describe this scenario.

Since its formation the WfMC has made significant progress in establishing vendor-independent workflow standards.

The WfMC has made significant progress in the past year; the release of the new interoperability (Interface 4) based on XML technology (Wf-XML 1.1) is particularly pleasing; and the WfMC would like to extend its thanks to all involved, but especially to Michael Rossi, Rainer Weber and Mike Marin of the WG4 working group, together with Dave Hollingsworth, the Technical Committee Chair for their dedicated efforts in turning the standard into a reality.

With such a broad range of applicability, it is easy to understand why the WfMC membership comprises a highly diverse group of workflow product vendors, analysts, universities, government organizations and corporations; all touched by workflow technology. For the same reasons, it should not be surprising that different approaches are chosen for managing workflow. Combined with the eBusiness revolution workflow has become a rich and diverse technology.

The members of the Workflow Management Coalition hope you enjoy the Workflow Handbook in its latest edition and find it useful as you explore workflow and its many benefits.

Jon Pyke, WfMC Chair and CTO, Staffware Plc.

Introduction

Layna Fischer, General Manager
Workflow Management Coalition

Welcome to the Workflow Handbook 2002. This Handbook offers you four sections:

- **SECTION 1: The World of Workflow** covers a wide spectrum of viewpoints and discussions by experts in their respective fields. Papers range from an Introduction to Workflow through to XML workflow architectures and integrating Business Process Technology with EAI and BPM.

- **SECTION 2**, **Workflow Standards**, deals with the importance of standards, and details the new Wf-XML 1.1 binding recently published by the Coalition's Technical Committee.

- **SECTION 3** offers selected **Case Studies** from the annual Global Excellence in Workflow awards of 2001 and 2002.

- **SECTION 4:** The WfMC Glossary, an explanation of the structure of the Workflow Management Coalition and references comprise the last section, **Directory and Appendices**, including a membership directory.

SECTION 1—THE WORLD OF WORKFLOW
- *Introduction to Workflow.*
  Charles Plesums, CSC
  Evolving from the Executive Briefing presentation, this paper is vendor independent and includes:
    - What is (automated) workflow?
    - What does Work Management accomplish?
    - Benefits
    - Technology and Standards
    - Success stories
    - How to get started.
- *Workflow Application Architectures—Classification and Characteristics of workflow-based Information Systems:*
  Prof. Dr. Jörg Becker and Michael zur Muehlen, University of Muenster, Department of Information Systems, and Dr. Marc Gille, Carnot AG, Engineering Division.
  This paper outlines different architectural approaches to information systems that rely on workflow technology. Based on the granularity of application components as well as on the specifications of the workflow system used, they develop a framework that helps designers and users of workflow applications identify the system type suitable for their specific application. In the organizational dimension, they distinguish between workflow applications at the inter-and intra-organizational level. In the technical dimension they differentiate

between workflow-driven applications, such as Enterprise Application Integration projects, and workflow-based applications, such as systems that rely on embedded workflow components. For each of the four resulting classes of workflow applications they describe typical applications, the role of standards as well as guidelines for successful project management.

- ***The Impact of Business Performance Monitoring on WfMC Standards.***
  Carolyn McGregor, Faculty of Information Technology, University of Technology, Sydney.
  Workflow Management Systems provide a unique vehicle for the organization to capture and analyse a rich set of information about the business processes as they are enacted by the organization. Such information would include, but is not limited to, volume analysis, product mix analysis, service level attainment and resource productivity. The existing assumptions for monitoring workflow enactment do not provide organizations with the ability to use this information for business performance monitoring also. To ensure maximum benefit from their Workflow Management investment, organizations must not only consider the enactment of the business process steps, but also the use of the information captured during these enactments that facilitate organizational performance measurement, together with the delivery of this information to management. This paper evaluates the data flow requirements to enable workflow process definition and workflow audit data to be captured in a decision support system to enable business performance monitoring. The key contribution of this research is an amended WfMC reference model that incorporates business performance monitoring needs.

- ***Workflow as a Web Application—the Grand Unification.***
  Heinz Lienhard, ivyTeam, Switzerland. This paper proposes the direct way from process (be it a business, government or technical one) to the web application in two step: first a design, modeling and prototyping step followed by automatic upload on a suitably prepared web server. The program logic of a Web application is naturally defined and implemented by a graphical *process model*; i.e. the process model eventually controls the application's behavior. If the process is modeled by an appropriate modeling and simulation tool, its simulator can be transformed during upload to the application controlling engine—actually the workflow engine.

- ***Peer-To-Peer Architectures And Collaborative Work Management And Workflow: The Implications Of "Napster" For Document Management.***
  B. John Masters, IMC.
  The much-ballyhooed convergence of digital and wireless technologies will increase the dissemination and distribution of

information processing activities. One model for this is 'peer-to-peer' (e.g., Napster or Groove.net), where information is published locally, and distributed searching algorithms replace central control constructs like directories. Collaboration in this environment will be characterized by participants who grow ever more 'distant': separated by location, responsibilities, domain knowledge, and expertise.

- *An XML based Architecture for Collaborative Process Management:*
  David Hollingsworth, ICL/Fujitsu, UK
  This paper discusses the background to XML and provides a classification of the various diverse standards now defined within the XML framework. Their relevance to workflow architectures is discussed in general terms using the Workflow Reference Model and Web Services Architecture as background. An assessment is made of existing XML based standards with direct applicability to collaborative workflow along with potential areas for further standardization. The paper concludes with a view of a consolidated architecture for workflow applications based on the range of existing and potential XML standards.

- *Process Management: A Fundamental Component of Successful Web Service Execution.*
  Michael Rossi, CSC—PMJCALS.
  This paper describes the role of process management in the Web Services environment. While there are several important facets of a Web Service, such as discovery, description and collaboration protocol agreement, one equally important facet is the ability to control the execution of a desired service. That is to say that there must be a way to request that the service be initiated, to monitor its status (if it is long-lived), to suspend or terminate its execution on demand and to be made aware of its completion. Not only must such a mechanism exist, but it also must be sufficiently standardized so as to be uniformly accessible by all service requesters. It must be a part of the Web Service infrastructure.

- *Business Process Technology—from EAI and Workflow to BPM*
  Mike Marin, FileNET
  Business process technology goes from simple component assembly technology to very complex workflow technology. The challenge for an organization is to easily classify the technology, and apply it to the right problem space. In today's business environments problems often require the integration of several business process technologies to address different areas of the complex problems faced by the organization. This paper describes and classifies the different types of business process technology. It can be seen as a complement to last year's paper by Martin Ader. Martin's paper described the trends; this paper describes how those trends are giving birth to business process

management. It also answers the question of what is the difference between business process management and workflow.

SECTION 2—WORKFLOW STANDARDS

- ***The Value of Standards.***
  Betsy Fanning, AIIM.
  Ms Fanning provides an overview of standardization and explains that industry standards and specifications are developed as the result of members of a given industry identifying a need for standardization and then developing the standard or specification to fill that need. She shows specifically why workflow standards make sure the essential criteria the users ask for has been met, which reduces the risk in implementing the workflow software in their enterprises.

- ***Wf-XML Challenge—Interoperability Demo by SAP and Staffware.***
  Justin Brunt, Staffware, and Rainer Weber, SAP.
  In the fall of 2000, the WfMC issued a challenge to its members to demonstrate their support for the latest XML based version of the interoperability standard—Wf-XML 1.0. SAP and Staffware accepted the challenge:because they shared common aims: SAP software drives the ERP, CRM and B2B components in most blue chip companies and Staffware is the leading independent Workflow/Business Process Management solution provider.

- ***Workflow Standard–Interoperability Wf-XML 1.1 Binding (Document Number WFMC-TC-1023).*** Edited and coordinated on behalf of the WfMC by Program Manager, Joint Computer-aided Acquisition and Logistic Support (JCALS) with technical support from Computer Sciences Corporation (CSC), this document represents a specification for an XML language designed to model the data transfer requirements set forth in the Workflow Management Coalition's Interoperability Abstract specification (WFMC-TC-1012). This language will be used as the basis for concrete implementations of the functionality described in the abstract in order to support the WfMC's Interface 4 (as defined by the workflow reference model).

SECTION 3—GLOBAL EXCELLENCE IN WORKFLOW AWARDS

The prestigious ***Global Excellence in Workflow Awards,*** now in their twelfth year are highly coveted by organizations that seek recognition for their achievements. These awards not only provide a spotlight for companies that truly deserve recognition, but also provide tremendous insights for organizations wishing to emulate the winners' successes.

The WfMC, Giga Information Group and the Workflow And Reengineering International Association (WARIA) joined forces to honor organizations that have demonstrably excelled in implementing innovative solutions to meet strategic business objectives.

To be recognized as winners, companies must address three critical areas: excellence in *innovation*, excellence in *implementation* and excellence in strategic *impact* to the organization. Further information is available at www.waria.com.

While successes in these categories are prerequisites for winning a *Global Excellence in Workflow* Award, it would reward all companies to focus on excelling in innovation, implementation and impact when installing workflow technologies. Without doing so, they will not achieve the full potential that workflow offers.

These companies profiled in this section recognized that implementing innovative technology was useless unless they had a successful implementation approach that delivered—and even surpassed—the anticipated benefits.

- Dutch-based medical insurance firm **Anova**, part of the Agis Group, completely overhauled and updated its document management and workflow system with software and consultancy from **Staffware**, with dramatic long-term benefits to the organization and its competitiveness. Since implementation, Anova has seen an improvement of 93 percent in outstanding work-in-progress jobs. The number of calls to the call center has reduced by 44 percent (with the nature of calls changing from mainly problem solving to mainly information dissemination) and 75 percent of Anova's jobs are now processed within a single day.

- *The City of Salzburg* municipal authority set itself the challenging tasks of putting customer-oriented administration at the top of its priorities to re-emerge as a strong business center in the future. Working with **Unisys** and **Fabasoft**, their productivity improvements included the building permission process being reduced from 150 days to approximately 50 days and paper mail traffic dropped by 60 to 80 percent. Their real achievement, however, was taming the "jungle of signs" which involved the legally obliged two-yearly approval of 20,000 road signs and elimination approximately 6000 redundant traffic signs with a total cost saving of 1.320.000 Euro.

- Every document that enters *Dubai Police* from the outside passes through the general administration department. Their daily volume is over 700 cases with average of 30 papers each. Using the latest communications technology and networking enables the managers to administer their documents through workflow and daily work not only from the offices but also from their houses and cars. Integrator **Emirates Computers** used **IeStream**WMS software imaging and workflow to successfully implement a paperless management solution for the Dubai Police that is considered the first and largest workflow enterprise for the region.

- A bilingual province of Canada, the *Government of New Brunswick* generates a large volume of documents to be translated. These translation activities are in keeping with complex assignment, management, and budgetary charge processes all of which are regulated by extremely tight deadlines, and are thus assigned to a large number of in-house Translators and Freelancers. **GENER-X** developed a **JetForm** solution enabling the user to submit, via the Internet, documents to be translated by including all essential parameters to be performed automatically, in real time and within a collaborative context on the Internet. This solution enables in-house Translators and Freelancers to not only improve the processing time, but reduce costs thanks to the retrieval of existing contents as well as follow project progress, improve quality using automated validation phases and evolve within a fully computerized environment.

- *iJET Travel Intelligence* embedded Fujitsu's i-Flow workflow engine into its WorldcuePro content management system. The application went to production rapidly, only taking three months. The combined products provide a continuous stream of updates that reflect the latest travel information from more than 3,000 sources worldwide, on topics ranging from health, security and transportation to entry/exit rules and communications. The workflow component of the content management system enables editorial and approval processes, ensuring the efficient verification of up-to-the-second travel intelligence. By providing timely, accurate and personalized information, the application helps travelers to circumvent potential travel difficulties and enhance the quality of their travel experiences.

- *R.R. Donnelley & Sons Company*, a leading North American printer, communications services, and logistics company required that their Graphics Management division produce custom educational projects with greater complexity than projects produced in previous years, resulting in the division to experience a challenge in managing their expanded workload. By developing PRISM, a web-based project management system using **ActionWorks Metro**, the Graphics Management team is on track to attain productivity gains in the 14 to 16 percent range. Prior to PRISM, Account Management Specialists could handle approximately 6 to 10 complex components; now with the help of PRISM, process improvement and training, AMS members work in teams and can work with more than 24 different components, and manage more projects at once.

- *Taylor-Nelson Sofres* is the French leader for market surveys, polls and consultancy. After implementing a set of quality processes from **W4**, and deploying the Intranet infrastructure and the groupware tools, they implemented a workflow solution allowing their employees to control the consistency of a highly critical, complex process driving their core business: surveys production. The application was developed according to the spiral methodology, in close collaboration with the employees involved, and deployed step by step within the company.

- **Triumph International Japan** (TIJ), a leading apparel maker with sales of US$400 Million in Japan, and 1800 Japanese staff operating 1,300 manned stores with a total of almost 10,000 outlets, has introduced a unique Integrated Workflow System utilizing ActiveModeler/ActiveFlow from **KAISHA-Tec** and supported by **NEC Corporation**. These innovations are considered to be at the forefront of Workflow technology, and fully cater to the demanding requirements of Japanese work practices. The integration includes 600 Head Office PCs, UNIX backend database systems and more recently CE devices in 1,300 shops and also NTT Docomo I-Mode mobile telephones. Substantial productivity cost savings, increased revenues, and increased productivity overall have been achieved.

- Lockheed Martin Mission Systems Data Capture System 2000 (DCS 2000) utilized barcode, digital imaging, optical recognition and **Staffware** workflow technologies to check-in and extract the data from 151.4 million forms. This is the equivalent of 1.5 billion 8.5" x 11" pages processed for the **United States 2000 Decennial Census**. Seventy percent of the data was extracted automatically with an accuracy of over 99 percent. Lockheed Martin estimates that the integration of commercial off-the-shelf packages, compared to writing the software from scratch, saved $1 million. The generic application interface for COTS integration has saved development time through reuse and reduced administration.

SECTION 4—DIRECTORY AND APPENDICES

The WfMC Glossary, Document Status—Issue 3.0, Feb 99, is available on our website at www.wfmc.org. Compiled by Dave Hollingsworth, chair of the WfMC Technical Committee, it contains technical definitions for terms used in the workflow management coalition specifications and discussions. The Workflow Reference Model, published in last year's Handbook can also be downloaded from the WfMC website.

- The **Authors' Appendix** provides the contact details and biographies of the contributors to this book. You may contact them if you wish to pursue a discussion on their topic.

- The chapters listing the Officers and Fellows together with the section on the **WfMC Structure and Membership** describe the Coalition's background, achievements and membership structure and sets out the contractual rights and obligations between members and the Coalition

- **WfMC Member Directory**: All members in good standing as of December 2001 are listed here. Funding members are permitted to include details on their products or services.

The WfMC invites you to delve into the information presented in whatever manner suits your reading or research style and knowledge level.

Our thanks and acknowledgements extend to not only the authors whose works are published in this Handbook, but also to the many more that could not be published due to lack of space.

Selected papers and case studies are available for free download from our sister website www.e-workflow.org if you wish to continue your reading and research on the topic of workflow.

Section 1

The World
of Workflow

Introduction to Workflow

Charles Plesums
Computer Sciences Corporation, Financial Services Group

WHAT IS WORKFLOW?

In the Middle Ages, monks sat at tables carefully copying the scriptures. The father superior would make the assignments, perhaps giving the illuminated first page of a section to the most skilled artist, perhaps assigning the proofreading tasks to the elderly scholar with trembling hands.

Little has changed in centuries—supervisors assign work, perhaps based on training, skills, and experience, to various resources. At first the resources were only people, eventually supported by tools such as typewriters, printed forms, and adding machines. Eventually some of the steps were automated—the invoices were automatically totaled and printed, but only after people sorted the punched cards, or entered the data. Even though the performance of the work was at least partially automated, the management of the work had changed little—supervisors assigned work and monitored performance. Clerks passed the work from station to station. Lists were made to track the work—to find it when it went astray, and to measure the productivity. And an army of expediters searched for the problems and errors in the routing, and kept it moving.

In the last 15 years or so we finally have developed tools to not only do the work, but to manage the workflow. More than just procedural documents, that workflow process is defined formally in the workflow computer system. *The process is managed by a computer program that assigns the work, passes it on, and tracks its progress.*

The workflow process is traditionally defined in office terms—moving the paper, processing the order, issuing the invoice. But the same principles and tools apply to filling the order from the warehouse, assembling documents, parts, tools, and people to repair a complex system, or manufacturing the complex device.

With the automated workflow management system:
- Work doesn't get misplaced or stalled—expediters are rarely required to recover from errors or mismanagement of the work.
- The managers can focus on staff and business issues, such as individual performance, optimal procedures, and special cases, rather than the routine assignment of tasks. The army of clerks is no longer required to deliver and track the work.

- The procedures are formally documented and followed exactly, ensuring that the work is performed in the way planned by management, meeting all business and regulatory requirements.
- The best person (or machine) is assigned to do each case, and the most important cases are assigned first. Users don't waste time choosing which item to work on, perhaps procrastinating on important but difficult cases.
- Parallel processing, where two or more tasks are performed concurrently, is far more practical than in a traditional, manual workflow.

With the best person doing the most important work following the correct procedures, not only is the business conducted more effectively, but also costs are lowered and the service to the customers is generally better. With the work equitably distributed and the confidence that they are always working on the "right" thing, users are happier. Therefore workflow is good for the company, good for the customers, and good for the users.

WHY BOTHER?

Work done by the best participant

A simple workflow system could evenly distribute work among all the available resources[1], or follow a simple algorithm such as giving the waiting work to the resource with the shortest queue, or implement assignments made manually by a supervisor. However, there are often significant benefits when the system can optimize the assignment of the work.

In order to do the assignment, the workflow management system must know who or what is available to perform the work, and have a profile about each user. This might include what work the resource is qualified to do, how good they are at that type of work (can they do only routine processing or can they handle the toughest cases), and whether the supervisor wants the work to be assigned to them.

A supervisor may bias an automatic assignment for many reasons. A person many nominally be qualified for a type of work, but has made a large number of errors recently—the cause needs to be found and corrected. A person that is not feeling well may be able to handle fewer or simpler cases rather than "taking a sick day." A person who will be going on vacation may be given simpler work that can be completed before they leave, or may not be given any

---

[1] Although most people talk of moving work between people, it could also be moving work between machines, between departments, or even between enterprises. Therefore the more general terms "resource" or "participant" are sometimes used to describe the person, group, or machine that is performing the work.

new work at all, so they can finish any cases "in process." These exceptions don't prevent the majority of work from being automatically assigned, with optimization, in most shops.

In addition to knowing the qualification of each resource, the system also needs to know about the work waiting to be assigned. What types of work are waiting? What needs to be done for each item (what skills or tools)? Is some type of work more important than another? Generally a priority is calculated, based on the type of work and how long it has been waiting to be processed.

"Assembly Line" or "Once and Done"

Much work, even office procedures, can be processed in an assembly line, where there each step in the process is simple and specialized. One person may enter data. The next person may check the data. The next may retrieve the customer's credit bureau rating. A computer may automatically retrieve the current customer status—recent orders, accounts receivable, etc. When all of the information has been consolidated, a specialist may evaluate whether to extend the credit and accept the order. And so forth. Most of the steps are simple. Training is minimized. Staffing is often flexible, because few steps require specialized skills, authority, or licensing. However, an effort is required to move the work between steps, time is lost waiting at each step, and there are more chances that the work will be lost or misplaced.

The other approach, equally popular among the experts, is to have highly trained staff handle the complete process, once and done. Far more training is required, with corresponding delegation of authority, but there is far less overhead in the work process itself.

When the work is managed manually, once and done is generally superior, because there is less overhead and chance for error. But with an automated work management system, either approach can be used. The work management system tracks the work, dramatically reducing the overhead of the assembly line process, with one remaining disadvantage. The elapsed time to complete the work (as seen by the customer) may be longer with the assembly line if a queue is allowed to build at each step in the process. Therefore in practice, a blend seems to be best—separate people to enter data and proofread, to reduce the chance of errors, with total automation of any step where that is practical. But minimize the number of steps where practical, to reduce the time waiting in queue, and thus reduce the total time of service.

Once there is a system that tracks the multiple steps, perhaps not all of the steps need to be done sequentially. Manual systems often include a checklist or routing slip that accompanies the work, thus sequential processing is the easiest way, by far. The limitations of the checklist go away with an automated workflow system. Thus most systems allow multiple tasks to be assigned and performed concurrently, with a function to determine when all the parallel paths are complete, so the consolidated part of the workflow can continue.

Rendezvous

One of the tougher steps in the paper-processing world is waiting for a supporting document to arrive. For example, an application may be received, but a medical or credit report must be ordered and received before the application can be considered. In a small organization the application may be held on the desk of the person who will make the decision. In larger organizations the problem is harder since the recipient cannot remember every case, or there may be multiple people who could make the final decision. The documents need to be filed, and each arriving document that could satisfy a requirement needs to be checked that something isn't waiting for it. A list must be maintained—a tickler system—to trigger a follow up, if the missing information doesn't arrive in a timely manner.

Most automated work management systems support the automatic matching of incoming information to the work that is suspended, waiting for the arrival of that information. The systems also manage the follow-up processing when the information does not arrive on time. The most common name is probably "rendezvous" but some systems call the process "marriage" or other terms.

Distribution

There are a variety of methods to distribute the work to the participants. Work may be pre-assigned, and then selected from the "in-box" by the user. The user may look through a common queue and "pull" the desired work. The user may ask the system to select and assign the most appropriate piece of work—to "push" an item of work. Or the work may be assigned based on "time." Why would each of these be considered?

If someone receives a telephone call, "I sent you a letter last week, and I need to change..." the work needs to be found. It doesn't matter whether it has been completed, it is waiting to be processed, or someone is working on it. (Remember the difficulty of finding the letter when it could have been on someone's desk—especially if there are hundreds of people who could have handled the letter?) Once it is found, the work must be assigned to someone qualified and authorized to handle it—normally to the telephone representative who "pulls" the work.

The ideal way to distribute work is to let the work management system assign the work, following the rules to optimize that distribution. Sometimes called "Send Work." "Get Work," or "Assign Work," in each case the system pushes work to the participant. Some people argue that work should be manually assigned—for example, so that a premium customer always gets their favorite representative. However, if that representative is unavailable (or too busy), the premium customer gets poorer service. The work management system can automatically track the availability and backlog of each participant, and should be set up to optimize even these cases.

Many organizations want to use an "inbox" paradigm because it is familiar—it was used for years with paper. Placing all "new" work in someone's inbox is far from optimum—the systems that have used this approach usually have complex procedures for removing the work when someone else "pulls" it or is idle and available to process it. However, it does make sense for specialists who are the *only* person who can handle a case, or who must complete processing that they have already started on a larger case (such as an insurance claim).

Sometimes work is driven by time—"I will be out of my meeting at 3 pm—please call me back then." The work needs to be suspended, but wake up and be assigned at 3 pm, whether it is pushed to the next available participant, returns to the person who suspended the work, or is simply an alarm to someone reviewing his or her inbox.

Vertical Workflow

One function of a workflow system is to get the work to the right person or process—to move the work through the organization. This is sometimes called "horizontal" workflow. Normally a case consists of multiple tasks—programs, portions of programs, or manual steps—performed at each step in the workflow. Therefore another possible workflow function is to see that all the tasks are completed—the "vertical" workflow.

A senior person might be given the assignment, "review this order" without detailed instructions on how the review should be performed. A beginner may need to be given the assignment, "to review this order, perform the following 10 steps. 1) Look up the customer using…." While managing the individual tasks at each step in the workflow, some systems automatically invoke the various computer systems that are used. Some workflow systems even change the way the tasks are assigned based on the experience of the person performing the work.

Completion

When the work is completed, the normal conclusion is to change the status (from waiting for decision to either approved or rejected, or from waiting for input to ready for checking). Each workflow product has its unique way to move the work to the next step in the process—not all use the term "status."

But what if the processing isn't complete? The work may need to be suspended for the arrival of more information (triggered by an outside event) or for a follow up (try calling again this afternoon). Most workflow systems also allow the workflow to be changed to accommodate exceptions. To pass the work to someone else for a consultation or special approval, and then resume the normal workflow.

Information easily accessible

As work is processed, computer systems and other data are often accessed. It is critical that the information necessary to complete the processing is easily accessible. It doesn't do much good to optimize the assignment of work to a person, then have that person spend hours looking for the associated data. With electronic assignment possible across multiple locations, the data may even be in a different city! Therefore it is common for a work management system to:

- interface to existing computer databases and systems
- invoke complex computer systems, possibly through terminal emulation
- link to document images, fax servers, e-mail, or other "external" sets of data
- extract key information to move with the workflow—for example, the items in an order, a credit limit, the limits of an insurance policy, or the current shipping address. (The workflow system should not try to replicate all the primary data, or be a substitute for a normal database.)

Interface to the data systems

Many organizations are concerned with the complexity of interfacing the workflow system to the business application, or even feel the need to integrate workflow with the application. On the contrary, there are many levels of potential interface.

Workflow can be used with no interface to the legacy processing systems. These systems were often built in the days when work would be delivered by a clerk, as a stack of paper, in an in-box. No interface to the in-box was required for processing. If a work management system rather than a clerk controls the work, there is still no requirement for an interface. As each item is processed, the system is routinely invoked. The legacy processing system is used "side-by-side" with the work management system.

The work management system must know the key identification of the work, such as the contract number, so that items of work can be located and special conditions can be honored. When the users know that a particular type of work always starts by invoking the same program, and entering the same data, and the work management system has that information, it seems like extra work is required—the users are unhappy. In practice, a **minimal interface,** to invoke particular programs and enter key data (perhaps using techniques as simplistic as screen scraping) is popular with users, inexpensive to implement, and contributes to productivity.

A number of business application vendors have seen the advantage of workflow, and want to be sure that advantage is available to the users of their product. Therefore they have embedded a basic work-flow in the business application. As discussed later, if the users only process a single application, it is possible that the **embedded work-flow** approach, where the application drives the workflow, is sufficient.

In practice, most users today must support multiple applications—perhaps an order entry system (or several systems for different product lines), a billing and accounts receivable system, a customer information system, a correspondence system, and others. Therefore it may be more practical to have a workflow system that invokes the appropriate legacy computer system, rather than having one legacy system invoke workflow. In that case, the **independent workflow system will drive the applications**, rather than the application driving the workflow system. EAI, or Enterprise Application Integration, the consolidation of numerous application systems, is often directly or indirectly involved in workflow.

Image systems

Work management systems are often installed in conjunction with document image systems. If there are paper documents involved in the workflow, it doesn't do much good to make an assignment and then have to search for the paper. On the other hand, if the necessary information is available in another form, there is no requirement for an image system with every work management system.

Likewise, image systems often are installed in conjunction with work management systems. If the paper is scanned and only the image is used, there needs to be some way to identify the documents that need processing, when, and by whom. Those are the functions of the associated work management system, although for the simplest cases, the sophistication of a work management system may not be required.

Therefore we should conclude that although image and work management systems often go together, and often bring synergistic benefits to the other, neither requires the other in all cases.

Logging and tracking

Workflow systems typically record the processing history, and provide the opportunity for the users to enter comments.

The history typically includes the date, time, person where each step was performed, including the disposition of the step—for example, was the process approved and moved on in the workflow, or was the work suspended for later processing.

If the work is suspended, documentation of why it is suspended is needed. For example, "More information is required, and I called and got their voice mail" has far different implications than "I went to lunch." Once this special capability is provided, then there are numerous other things this can be used for, such as explanations of variances and special circumstances.

The automated log of who/how/when the work was processed is a substantial advantage, improving the record of what was done and when, while eliminating the manual logs that are often used to find documents and recover from routing errors.

Search for work in process

Messages are often received—"What is the status?" or "Change my request" or "Cancel the order." A work management system must not only manage the work in process, but must also identify the work so that it can be found. Not only must it know that this is a queue of 200 orders, but it must be able to find a specific order in that queue. And once the order has been found, we must be able to determine the status of that work.

If it has been completed, should we start some reversing action? For example, do we need to reverse the transaction or authorize a return?

If it is currently being processed, should the call be transferred? Or is it idle but in mid-process, such as waiting for a credit report? Maybe it is not appropriate to disclose all the details, but at least we know what is happening.

If it has not yet been processed, am I qualified to handle the case (probably yes, or I wouldn't have taken the phone call). Therefore should I "pull" the work (as discussed above), select it to be assigned to myself (so that somebody doesn't start processing while I am working on it), and complete the process while working with this customer?

Control

One of the big advantages of an automated work management system is the control of the process, manifest by the procedures that are implemented by the system, and the record keeping to report on the process.

In some systems the control is focused in the users—the work is largely table driven, with the tables maintained or controlled by user-oriented staff—perhaps supervisors, senior users, or others with a user background.

In other systems the workflow application is tailored to the requirements of the organization by a programming staff, in the information technology area. The customized workflow system is optimized for the application, at the expense of flexibility for "instant" changes.

In either case, the user profiles—qualifications, assignments, absences, vacations, training, and other factors are maintained by the system. Managers need to be able to manually assign work to an individual—perhaps because they made an error and need to fix it,

or perhaps because it is a special case that they are uniquely qualified to fix. Priorities must be adjusted to move critical work to the
head of the list.

Monitoring

Practically all systems include reporting and analysis such as the
total work accomplished—the volume, and the turn-around time
(the response time as seen by the customer). The systems also
maintain data to report the productivity of the individuals, teams,
and groups. A few systems even maintain data about the number
and types of errors that are caught and corrected for each type of
process and user.

Work management systems allow managers to examine the backlog
of work throughout the day—in real time—so that they can schedule
staff as required, adjust assignments if necessary to meet deadlines,
and in general, manage their teams. A few systems even let the
managers set alarms—for example, "notify me if the number of
complaints exceeds 3, or if the total number of items to be processed is greater than 450." This is far better than the clerk having to
constantly count the unassigned work, or noticing that the stacks
are getting too big. The automated work management system provides far better management control of the work.

MEASURING THE BENEFITS

The benefits of a work management system can be put into three
categories. The direct cost savings are readily measured and recognized. But there is another set of benefits that are real and valuable
but very difficult to measure, sometimes called the hidden savings.
And still more benefits where the value cannot be quantified—the
intangible benefits.

Direct Cost Savings

These are the readily measured benefits. Often they involve better
use of staff, or reduction of the staff. How much clerical time is involved in sorting and delivering the work? How much clerical or supervisor time is spent assigning the work to particular individuals?
And how much of the processing is really logging that a particular
piece of work was received at a certain time, or that it was completed and sent on to...?

Less training is required. An automated work management system
can move information through an organization, without an employee
having to understand the entire organization, or even the whole
work process—only their part. And a vertical work manager—a task
management system—can guide a user through a series of steps
and programs, reducing training needs even farther.

With the control of a work management system, the work can always be found. It can't be buried in a desk drawer, when it is a

tough case that "I'd rather handle later." It can't "accidentally" be discarded, without a record of who touched it last. If it is accidentally sent to a wrong place, it can still be located and recovered. A staff of "expediters" to find the missing work and move it through the organization is not required.

The direct savings from installing a work management system (or an image system with a work management system) are primarily related to the reduction of the support staff. Those savings can be substantial, but often don't quite cover the cost of the system. We need to look farther.

Hidden Savings

The hidden savings are actual cash savings, but those that are far harder to measure. For example, better control of the work, savings of manager time, improved productivity of the professional staff, and the opportunity for process improvement.

Control

What is it worth to have the best person handle each item? Remember that the best person for a simple task may be the newest (lowest level) person in the department. One of the problems of manual work management was that the most experienced people were also expert at finding the easy work, making their productivity look even higher. Yet they are the ones who should be handling the hardest cases that a beginner might struggle with for a long time.

Have you ever searched the paper in your in-basket, to see what was waiting for you? And after processing the first item (probably not the top item), have searched again for that "other interesting case?" Have you ever skipped an item that you will "come back to later?" And has "later" ever become the next day? A work management system that pushes work, one item at a time, assures that the first item presented is the most important. If it needs to be deferred, fine, but the history of the transaction will show that it was deferred, and perhaps record the reason.

Experts in workplace satisfaction and time management emphasize that the best way to work is to put one item on your desk, do it to completion if possible, then move to the next. An automated work management system can present work in this way. The most important work is done first. The hard cases can't get buried. And experience has shown that users can find working with such a system very satisfying. How much does it improve productivity? How many problems are eliminated because important work is done first, and hard cases aren't deferred? Those are hard to measure, but the benefit is real.

Management

What do your managers do today? Do they make every work assignment? Do they review work for quality? Do they report on the quantity and timeliness of the work performed? Do they have time to counsel employees, or even process the tough cases themselves? With the automated assignment of work, automated data collection for reporting, and fewer problems such as lost work, one group was able to expand the span of a supervisor's control from eight people to 20 people. And the supervisor was able to spend more of her time counseling the employees, improving their skills, and helping with the tough cases, rather than routine reporting and assignments.

Professional productivity

By many definitions, professional work cannot be measured—it is work that varies from case to case, requiring judgment, rather than a routine operation. How can we estimate productivity, much less project a productivity improvement?

One of the earliest workflow systems involved credit card adjudication—investigation of whether a charge could be valid. After collecting data from the cardholder, the record is examined for clerical errors, and then the merchant is contacted to provide evidence. After the merchant responds, the expert decides whether to enforce the bill, or to issue a credit (recovering the funds from the merchant). Every case is different—a different story, different evidence, and different judgments. Prior to a work management system, the experts averaged 10 cases per hour. Six weeks after installing a work management system, the experts were averaging 13 cases per hour. Certainly individual cases could take a variable amount of time, but averaging a large number of transactions indicated a 30 percent productivity improvement.

Considering a large number of workflow installations, the 30 percent productivity improvement is pretty common. After quoting that figure many times, some companies were disappointed to only get 28 percent (even though that is a great improvement, and very close to 30 percent), so a conservative number might be 20 percent improvement, just due to the automation.

Poor procedures are often characterized by many steps for no apparent reason, or lots of logging to prove innocence (assign blame), or lots of expeditors to keep things moving and handle special cases. Workflows like this have obvious process improvements that often lead to professional productivity improving 50 percent or more. And with a thorough redesign or reengineering of a bad process, 100 percent improvement—doubling the amount of work processed—is not unusual.

Process Improvement Opportunity

Sometimes a process should be completely taken apart and redesigned—reengineered. This is an expensive process and traumatic for the users but has the potential of the greatest improvements—like tearing down a house and rebuilding it. More often, an existing process can be dramatically improved—even though the changes may

may be substantial, the users can usually recognize the process and migrate to the new process with far less training.

With dramatic process improvement or reengineering, a work management system may allow new procedures that would not be possible in a manual system. For example, mail entered early in the morning on the East Coast of the United States might be ready for processing by the time U.S. West Coast users arrive. And the work left by the West Coast users can be migrated to Asia and Europe for further processing by morning. Tasks that were sequential to be manageable can now be processed in concurrent parallel steps.

Intangible Benefits

There are a number of benefits of work management that most people cannot quantify. Unlike the hidden benefits that are real and, with enough effort, can be quantified, it is rare that a cash value can be assigned to improved service, employee satisfaction, organizational options, security, and privacy. If any of the areas have a quantified value in your company, great—that factor can simply be added to the direct or hidden savings listed above.

Improved Service

If the most important work is distributed to the first available qualified person, and they have access to all the information required to handle the case, this service is as good as it can get. With manual work management, the user might casually select a work item, and struggle to find the data, get any necessary authorization, and perhaps procrastinate—saving the tough case for later.

Employee satisfaction

In the early work management systems, there was fear that the users would be oppressed by being directed by a computer—being told what to do. The actual experience was just the opposite—users were more satisfied. Workplace experts recognized that the optimum work environment was to select the one most important piece of work (doing the right thing), and complete it (feeling a sense of accomplishment), before moving on to the next item. At the same time, the employees were given some control—if they received a huge task at quitting time, they could save it until morning; if they didn't understand or weren't qualified to handle something, it could be passed on to a supervisor to be reassigned. The employees have been given that ideal environment, and enjoyed it.

Organizational options

A business that was an early user of workflow wanted to decentralize for a variety of reasons, but was concerned about how the work would be processed. There could be tax advantages by performing certain work in a particular location, while economies of scale dictated that other work should be done centrally. A new, smaller office might lack the size to absorb peak loads among a small number of specialists. Management was concerned about the difficulty of moving work between offices—and how much would be "in the pouch" in transit to the other office whenever it was needed. The automated work management system gave them the confidence to proceed.

In the same organization, a year or so later, the central management noticed that there were many thousands of letters waiting for processing in the regional office. It didn't matter whether it was because of inadequate staffing, too many trainees, or an exceptional peak in their workload, much of that work could be handled by "anyone." The home office staff members were assigned to do the routine work from the field office, as time allowed, along with their regular work. The regional office concentrated on the work that required their special knowledge. Within one week, with no overtime, the entire backlog of work was caught up. Many felt that the savings in overtime and employee stress from events like that alone might have justified the work management system.

A different company was growing rapidly, and realized that they would soon be out of space—just before their seasonal peak. Half the people needed to be moved to a new location, miles away. Since work could be routed to specialists at either location, all the support organizations did not need to be replicated. The facilities were procured, furniture, computer, and network were installed, and the staff transferred in only a few months. Their management credited the work management system with making the move possible in record short time, with minimal disruption.

Privacy and Security

Only authorized users can access work and the associated data. High profile customers (such as celebrities or even other employees) can be handled by a small group of selected representatives. Medical records can be secured, and only routed to those with a need to know, without extraordinary office procedures to protect the documents.

If a user is assigned a hard case, they must handle it—or pass it to someone who can. Work cannot just disappear. The automated audit trail (history) leaves an indelible record of who had been assigned each step in the work, when, and what happened to it. One company (that checked the trash to be sure no work was discarded) noticed a decrease in plumbing problems after the workflow system was implemented.

WORKFLOW TECHNOLOGY

For many years, business analysts and authors categorized workflow systems. Although such categories have fallen into disfavor, they are still instructive—they may help understand the differences between various systems.

Ad hoc

Ad hoc, or collaborative, workflow is often used in the professional and administrative areas of an organization. It is characterized by negotiation, and a new workflow defined for each use. One group decided that there were four steps to doing any piece of work

1. Negotiation—for example, "can you review my document by Friday?"

2. Acceptance—for example, "no, but how about by Monday afternoon?"

3. Assignment—delegating the work to the reviewers. There might be multiple people doing the review concurrently, and as soon as all of them approved the document, it might be routed to the next step—perhaps management or legal.

4. Review—was all the work done and approved. If not, how do I handle rejections or incomplete processing (reviews)?

This type of workflow is tremendously convenient, and provides good control of the process (what is the status of each step, who did what when, where is the work now). The ad-hoc workflows are often built on an e-mail platform (using mail messages to deliver the work). However, if the mailroom gets 500 insurance claims today, we don't want the mailroom to negotiate with the claims adjusters about who should handle each claim.

Production

A production workflow is pre-defined and prioritized, and thus supports high volumes—there are no negotiations about who will do the work or how it will be handled. However, there may be additional tasks or workflows defined and added to the overall process. (Some writers claim that production workflow cannot be used when all the steps are not known in advance—not true.) For example; settling a claim following an auto accident will have some basic steps that are part of most claims—identifying all the parties, confirming policy coverage, ordering copies of police reports. There will likely be other tasks (each of which may be a kind of workflow in itself, that become part of the larger workflow), such as:

- Appraise the damage and arrange for the repair of each vehicle.
- Handle any bodily injury for each party involved.
- Settle any property damage, such as repairs to the fence that was hit.
- Salvage—sell what is left of the car that was totaled.
- Subrogation—get the party that actually caused the accident to pay the losses.

The production workflow can be very simple (deposit these funds) or complex like the auto claim described above. They can be completely predefined, or follow a general procedure, with additional steps and processes added as required. They can be altered for consultations. Normally it has a dedicated delivery channel, rather than using e-mail to deliver the work. Overall the production workflow system provides control of the process, and substantial productivity—thus it save costs.

Administrative

A third type of workflow is sometimes listed, called administrative workflow. This is a cross between the ad-hoc and production. The flow is pre-defined, such as the steps required to place an order or approve an expense report. Sometimes the flow can be reviewed in advance or even altered (add a note asking my boss to endorse the exceptional expense). The delivery may be a blend between e-mail (to professional staff who only have a few cases each day, and are largely driven by the mail), and a custom delivery mechanism (the clerks in purchasing or accounts payable who do this work all day).

Horizontal vs. Vertical

Another useful segmentation of the workflow technology is sometimes called horizontal vs. vertical workflow.

Horizontal workflow moves the work through the organization—from person to person, or to different departments or systems. Some people call the horizontal workflow "routing." It is the most common type of workflow.

Once the work gets to a point in the organization, there may be several steps that are performed. The vertical workflow directs the processing at each step. It may automatically invoke computer programs, enter key data (known to the workflow system, such as account number), and may provide guidance for each step of the process—at least for beginners if not for everyone. If the system can invoke a program and enter data, couldn't it also do the entire process in some cases? The answer is obviously yes, in what some systems call "robotic" or "straight through" processing. For example, a change of address may be read by an optical character recognition system. When it is compared against the postal database of valid addresses, if there is a match, the confidence in the process may be so high that there may be no need for human intervention, or at most, there is a human "quality assurance" step.

Free-standing or within application

Embedded

In some cases the workflow process is part of the business application. As previously noted, the value of workflow may be so great for an application that the vendor of that application includes workflow, so that "everyone" has it. Many of the embedded workflow systems are simple, but optimized for that particular type of use, so may be adequate. Since it is within the application, the user can't generally choose a different workflow, and sometimes find it difficult to dis-able the built-in workflow. In those few cases where somebody only works with one program, this may be the best solution.

Autonomous (stand-alone)

If users deal with many applications (as seems to be the normal case) then a separate stand-alone workflow application may be a better solution, rather than one built into an application. This separate system can be optimized for the total business requirement, rather than just one application. These separate systems support many business applications, and many types of use—for example, the workflow that may be installed on "most" desktops for order processing may also be useful for personnel records work, even though the requirements of personnel processing would not justify a separate workflow system.

WORKFLOW STANDARDS

The Workflow Management Coalition exists to increase the value of a user's investment in workflow technology, decrease the risk of using workflow products, and expand the workflow market by increasing awareness. In addition to educational and publicity programs, another key function of the coalition is the development of international standards for interoperability of the various components of workflow.

The workflow standards exist at three levels. The *Reference Model* is the big picture of how the standards fit together. The *Abstract Specifications* identify each of the functions required and what data is involved. The *Bindings* are the details of how the specification is implemented with a particular set of tools, formats, and protocols. For example, WF/XML is an XML *binding* of the Interoperability *specification* that is Interface 4 of the WfMC *Reference Model*

The workflow reference model has identified five interfaces to the workflow engine:

1. Process definition. The procedures that are followed in implementing the workflow, and the resources (people, systems, groups) that perform the work. Sometimes the workflow is defined in separate modeling and simulation tools, and then the workflow is loaded into the engine through Interface 1. This also allows the workflow to be moved from one system to another. The WfMC Working Group 1 manages the interface for the process, and a separate Working Group 9 handles the resources—people, facilities, and inventory.

2. Client interfaces—the way an application program invokes workflow, such as a request to get the next piece of work, or to complete the existing work.

3. Invoked applications—programs that may be invoked by the workflow system (as contrasted to programs that invoke the

workflow)
The Workflow Application Programming Interface, WAPI, combines the WfMC interface 2, where applications invoke workflow, and WfMC interface 3, where workflow invokes applications. This includes interfaces to and between legacy data systems—EAI or Enterprise Application Integration. It also often includes image systems, document management systems, and mail systems.

4. External workflow services—the interoperability between independent workflow systems, whether from one or several vendors, within a single company, or between multiple companies. The WfMC interface 4 initially used a MIME binding—defined the interface for use with e-mail tools and technology. As XML emerged, the Wf/XML binding was created using XML technology. The intent is that this interface can be used for
   - Macroscopic processes, such as ordering a product or service from another organization, including placing, tracking, and completing or canceling the order.
   - Microscopic processes, such as picking the individual items that constitute an order, either through an external manual system, or by interface to an automated warehouse system.

5. Administration and monitoring involves both the history of each case and the monitoring of the total work performed.
   - Individual cases might include the person/processor that was assigned the work, with the date, time, and disposition. This would be used for reporting and auditing, but could also be used for process control, such as the situation where two approvals, by different people, are required. (The process would need to check the history to be sure that the request for a second approval was not sent to the same person who had given the first approval.)
   - Overall workload includes the "snapshot in time" of the amount of work waiting to be processed and the status of the system, as well as the "history" that is used to report on overall productivity.

SUCCESS STORIES

A major financial services firm with about one million customers had 613 employees providing customer service, and procedures that involved 630 steps, many of them logging and tracking. The typical processing time for a request was one week.

After implementing workflow, the number of steps was reduced from 630 to 270, the number of employees was reduced from 613 to 406, the number of customers increased slightly, and the typical processing time dropped from a week to a day. Far more important than the

34 percent staff savings were the customer satisfaction ratings that rose from one of the lowest in the industry to the top rating, where they stayed for several years.

Another firm refused to comment, because workflow gave them a competitive advantage. However, they told *Computerworld* that they estimated their work management system returned $8 million per year, because their client base was growing over 20 percent per year, with no increase in staff. This gave them one of the lowest costs of service in the industry.

An international insurance firm used workflow as a standard solution that they applied across all their subsidiaries. One division reduced their staff 40 percent while handling a greater volume of claims. At the same time they reduced the errors (improved quality) and improved the speed of service (thus virtually eliminating callbacks).

Another division of the same international firm had a growth rate from 40 percent to 70 percent per year, compounded over several years. They could not hire and train the people or build the office space required fast enough to sustain that growth, so installed a work management system, and were able to dramatically reduce the need for staff and training.

A company in South Africa had a goal of providing service in 7-12 days, but was only meeting that goal about 90 percent of the time. When they installed the work management system, they reduced their staff by 33 percent, set their goals at 3-5 days, and met their goals nearly all the time.

A company in the United Kingdom had a simple way to calculate professional processes—the number of new business applications per year per employee. Before workflow, they averaged 600 applications per employee per year. After workflow, they averaged 1,600 applications per employee per year.

A company in Denver expected a staff reduction of 25 percent in the first year, and was disappointed when they did not achieve it. However, they did process a 50 percent increase in business volume with no increase in staff.

GETTING STARTED

Establish goals

There may be a variety of reasons to implement a work management system.

Improvement of internal processes is the traditional first purpose. This might be to increase capacity (the amount of business processed) without increasing the costs. It might be to improve the quality of service. Or it might be to reduce costs in an industry that is not growing rapidly. It is important to know what you are trying to achieve—for example, increase work performed by existing staff, or reduce staff to do the same amount of work. However, it is rare that reducing staff means direct lay-off, since normal staff turnover is often comparable to the pattern of productivity improvement, as people become expert in using the workflow system.

Managing processes between organizations is another potential use of workflow—issuing and tracking the orders for products and services from a second company, perhaps integrated with processes within the first company. Some of the new facilities for e-commerce have been established and integrated with work management tools.

Project Organization

Information Services (the technical staff) start and manage some workflow projects. Users drive other projects. Either might be fine, depending on the corporate culture. However, in either case, executive sponsorship is important, both for the corporate commitment to organizational change, and the commitment to support the cost of the project.

Workflow Implementation

Most people consider the simplest approach to workflow to automate the current process, exactly as it exists. This may be a good starting point for discussion, and if the process has recently been analyzed, it may work well. However, generally it isn't the best, since there are typically a lot of activities that are no longer required, like logging and batching.

Process improvement, at least to some degree, is usually in order when going to an automated workflow. Eliminate the record keeping of date stamping, logging, and tracking work. Cut out the effort looking for particular items. And take advantage of the ability to suspend work, automate the follow-up, run parallel processes, etc. Utilize the automatic assignment and optimization of the work—considering the priority of the work (based on type and age), and the qualifications of the workers.

Full scale reengineering should probably not be considered just because a workflow system will be installed—most of the benefits could be achieved by simpler process improvements. On the other hand, if a process needs to be reengineered (because of the process, not because of workflow systems), then workflow is a great tool to include as part of the reengineering.

CONCLUSION

Go for it! An automated work management system

- Improves control of the process, with far less management intervention, and far less chance for delays or misplaced work

- Improves the quality of service, by responding more quickly, with the best person available.
- Lowers the cost of training staff, since the work can be guided through complex procedures.
- Lowers the cost of management, allowing a far wider span of control, while allowing the managers to concentrate on nurturing the employees and handling special cases rather than routine reporting and distribution.
- Improves user satisfaction, by giving the user confidence that they are doing "the best item" and giving them the satisfaction of completing that work with fewer conflicting requirements.

Altogether that means that an automated work management system is good for the company, good for the customer, and good for the user.

Workflow Application Architectures: Classification and Characteristics of Workflow-based Information Systems

Prof. Dr. Jörg Becker and Michael zur Muehlen
University of Münster, Germany

Dr. Marc Gille
CARNOT AG, Germany

ABSTRACT

Workflow management systems have come a long way from the first office automation prototypes of the late 1970s. Today, workflow systems are deployed in a variety of situations, ranging from the coordination of document-centric processes in office environments to the automation of application data flow in enterprise application integration scenarios. The variety of applications as well as the diversity of the workflow systems available easily leads to confusion, when the most suitable system for a specific setting has to be identified.

In this paper we present a classification for workflow application architectures. Based on the specifics of the process to be supported, we develop a framework that helps designers and users of workflow applications identify the system type suitable for their specific application. The coordination features and integration requirements of workflow applications serve as guidelines throughout this approach.

Within the organizational dimension, we distinguish between workflow applications at the inter- and intra-organizational level. Within the process dimension we differentiate between workflow-driven software processes, workflow-supported organizational processes, and hybrid processes that combine features of the other two.

FROM OFFICE AUTOMATION TO PROCESS COORDINATION

From Process Thought to Workflow Support

The structuring of organizations along their processes has been a common theme since the 1930s. Authors like NORDSIECK and HENNING in Germany, as well as CHAPPLE and SAYLES in the United States were among the first to point out the potential benefits of a well-managed workflow (see e. g. [3, 11, 17]). Despite these early efforts, a functional separation of tasks, and the resulting functional or divisional structures dominated the corporate practice until the 1980s, when changing market conditions and increasing competition led companies to investigate the efficiency of their process

---

39

structures. Following the Total Quality Management movement of the 1980s, numerous process-related management practices emerged in the 1990s, most notably Process Improvement [10], Business Process Innovation [4], and Business Process Redesign [7-9]. Each of these approaches noted the enabling role of information technology for the restructuring of organizations. Consequently, enterprises that engaged in these activities sought adequate information system support for the management of their processes. Workflow management technology is designed to support this exact problem.

Despite claims that the development of workflow applications is tightly interwoven with the business process reengineering movements of the early 1990s (see e. g. [6]), the origins of workflow technology can be traced back to the late 1970s. One of the first concepts of an information system to support organizational processes was described by ZISMAN in his account of the SCOOP system, an office automation system that used Petri-nets to represent business processes [21]. Research in office automation, which flourished between 1975 and 1985, laid the groundwork for the development of industrial workflow applications through the analysis of technology support for administrative processes [5, 13]. While the research interest in office automation vanished by the middle of the 1980s [19], two developments spun off that were targeted beyond the boundaries of traditional office automation: Groupware and workflow management. While research in groupware focuses on the support of unstructured, collaborative activities, research in workflow management focuses on the coordination of activities along a common process model, without the automation of the activities themselves.

Workflow Management Systems as Coordination Tools

From a conceptual perspective, the purpose of a workflow management system is the coordination of all entities involved in the execution of a (business or software) process. Coordination can be defined as the management of dependencies between activities [14], and workflow management systems address two kinds of coordination problems: Data dependencies between activities (i.e.: one activity relies on the results of one or more other activities), which are managed through control and data flows, and shared resources (i.e.: one resource such as a workflow participant can only perform one task at a time), which are managed through scheduling and staff resolution mechanisms. Through the automation of these coordination functions, workflow management systems support several efficiency goals of the enterprise (see *table 1*).

Efficiency Goal	Description	WfMS Support
Process efficiency	Optimization of process criteria such as processing time (to be minimized) or faithfulness to deadlines (to be maximized)	Coordination of activities through control flow, deadlines etc.
Resource efficiency	Efficient use of the resources (human resources as well as application systems) available for the execution of processes.	Staff resolution and reminder in case of escalations
Market efficiency	The proper positioning of the enterprise in its relation to market partners. This includes a reliable prediction of delivery times, transparent communication with suppliers and customers and optimized procurement and distribution processes.	Well defined process interfaces for web services (defined external behavior), predictable internal behavior through standardized processes
Delegation efficiency	Adequate use of the competencies of superior (greater scope of vision along the process) and subordinate (detailed knowledge about single activities) organizational units.	Coordination of staff assignment, role concepts
Motivation efficiency	Motivation of staff to act in a way congruent to the business goals of the enterprise.	Guidance to perform activities along a workflow model, monitoring of progress and explanation of previous activities

Table 1: Efficiency goals and workflow support (modified from [1])

It is apparent that the benefits of workflow applications increase with the number of coordination tasks that can be automated through the system. The number of coordination tasks varies with the granularity of the components controlled through the workflow system as well as with the type of the process controlled through the workflow system.

Figure 1 shows a classification scheme for workflow applications based on specific attributes relating to their implementation. The participants of a workflow application can be humans, machine resources (e. g. if production processes are automated) or software components (e. g. if workflow is used for application integration purposes). The structure of the processes automated can be predefined or flexible (ranging from production workflow to ad-hoc workflow applications). The scope of the processes automated can be restricted to a single application in case of an embedded workflow system, or extend beyond the boundaries of a single organization in case of a B2B application. The granularity of data objects handled within the workflow can be either coarse (if documents or entire objects are passed along the process) or fine (if single attributes are passed between activities). Finally, the granularity of applications invoked within the workflow can be either coarse (e. g. if web services are used in a B2B implementation) or fine (e. g. if single method calls on application components are used).

Attribute	Possible Values		
Participants	Humans	Machines (Hardware)	Software
Process Structure	Ad-hoc Process and Activities	Pre-defined Activites, Ad-hoc Process	Pre-defined Process
Process Scope	Between organizations (B2B)	Within an organization	Within an application
Data Granularity	Documents, Objects		Attributes
Application Granularity	Process-level (e. g. web services)	Application-level (e. g. programs)	Function-level (e. g. method calls)

Figure 1: Classification of workflow attributes

Using the participant attribute, we can distinguish three major process types, which can be supported through workflow technology:

Organizational processes are business processes with a high degree of human involvement. They typically occur in office environments and consist of a number of human participants working autonomously on activities using applications that may or may not be invoked by the workflow system. The overall process structure is typically coarse and well defined (if the process is well understood, the separation of activities may lead to a finer granularity). A typical workflow application within this category is the routing of document images along a workflow model.

Software processes are automated processes within application systems. Within this category, workflow systems are used to "glue" disparate application system components together and to automate the exchange of data between software components, in case they don't share the same database. Often, the human element in software processes is restricted to the initiation of the process and the presentation of the results.

Hybrid processes combine the characteristics of organizational and software processes. In this case, the workflow system can work as an intermediary between the human participants and a (functionally oriented) application system, guiding the work of participants within single activities.

In the following section we take a closer look at the functions and benefits of workflow systems for the three process types described above.

WORKFLOW SUPPORT CLASSIFIED BY PROCESS TYPE

Workflow for the Coordination of Organizational Processes (Workflow at the Meta Level)

Workflow management systems of the first and second generation have traditionally been applied in administrative settings, supplying office workers with the information necessary to perform clerical tasks, routing the results along the process model to the next participant, and supervising the overall process through the handling of deadlines and escalations.

An important component of workflow management systems for organizational processes is the notification of participants about pending activities. This is done through the concept of a work list, through which all qualified participants can access pending work items and select those they wish to work on.[1] The result is a "pull" model of work assignment, where the workflow system has control over priority and presentment of work items, but the user has the ultimate control about the fact, when s/he performs a particular activity.

Due to this concept, it is difficult for the workflow system to predict processing times of activities and/or processes, because the idle time between the presentment of a work item and the activation through a user can only be estimated (if summarized audit trail information is used, the precision of these estimates may increase, compare e. g. [16, 22]). An important feature of workflow systems for organizational processes is therefore the capability to handle exceptions such as activities exceeding deadlines by notifying the responsible party. If this party is not a frequent user of the workflow system (typically the involvement decreases along the hierarchy of the enterprise), the notification has to be transmitted using a medium used by the recipient (e. g. e-mail or pager).

---

[1] Typically the presentation of work items is integrated into existing messaging applications or user desktops. This is addressed by the WfMC WAPI specification [20]. Under certain conditions it may be desirable to eliminate the user choice of the next work item. For a brokerage application with a high throughput requirement, an American financial institution decided to implement a "next work item" button, which delivered the next work item to the user. The prioritization was done by the workflow system, eliminating "cherry picking" among the participants.

The autonomy of workflow participants is high in organizational processes, and their consent to the use of workflow technology is crucial for the success of a workflow project in this setting. As a consequence, applications are often invoked in a "black-box" fashion, leaving the detailed use of their functionality to the users in order not to micro-manage them. This means that the workflow system has little control over the applications and the data processed therein. Because the use of the applications within the workflow may create changes to data that is used outside of the workflow, these side-effects need to be taken care of in case a workflow needs to be undone. A truly transactional processing of organizational processes thus requires additional effort in terms of compensation activities in case of failure. It is advisable to design the workflow model in such a way that the human participants have the means to perform local trouble-shooting, in case of an error, and not leave this to the workflow system.

Despite these limitations, workflow applications for organizational processes provide a number of benefits. These mainly lie within the controlled assignment of work and the traceability of processes through monitoring and controlling functions.

Workflow for the Coordination of Software Processes (Workflow at the Micro Level)[2]

The emergence of framework-based application system architectures, such as J2EE or .NET leads to an increasing specialization and fragmentation of application system components. While the modular development of applications enables the re-use of components, a software "glue" is necessary, to tie the disparate application components together to form a coherent, enterprise-level application system.

Within this scenario, workflow technology is used to connect application components along a structured process flow. The processes are defined at a fine level of granularity and the workflow component may act in a transactional fashion, controlling the data transfer to and from components and performing data conversions if necessary. Especially in multi-tiered architectures, that combine a web front-end with an application server at the middle tier and database and/or legacy systems at the back-end, the workflow system can be used to implement concepts such as straight-through processing or access to the same functionality through different clients.

The granularity of the process and the application components typically is fine, and the workflow system is located at the center of a hub-and-spoke architecture. A typical application is the integration of back-end data into an application located at the middle-tier of a three-tier architecture, such as the nightly update of a CRM applica-

---

[2]   The term "micro workflow" has been borrowed from MANOLESCU, compare [15].

tion with customer records from a legacy system. Performance considerations play a bigger role in this scenario, since the performance of the workflow component determines the performance of the overall application to a large extent. Idle times are nonexistent, because the workflow component invokes other programs or object methods that are executed right away, resulting in a push-distribution of work items.

The benefits of workflow technology at the micro level lie within the reuse of application components in different processes, the integration of front- and back-end systems along controlled processes and the changeability of applications in case the enterprise processes change.

Workflow for the Coordination of Hybrid Processes (Workflow at the Macro Level)

Companies wishing to streamline their business processes are often faced with an existing information technology infrastructure that has been developed to support the "traditional" functional way of work. Since a new development of existing functionality is costly, companies often strive to retrofit existing applications into new process structures. This can be achieved by creating a lightweight user interface that is controlled by an intermediary workflow component, which in turn invokes the relevant functions of the legacy system without the involvement of the user. The workflow system can perform integrity checks on the data entered by the workflow participant, before it is passed on to the back end system. At this level, the workflow system serves as a guide (or "wizard") for the user through a process-oriented application system.

Figure 2 summarizes the key characteristics of workflow applications for the three different process types.

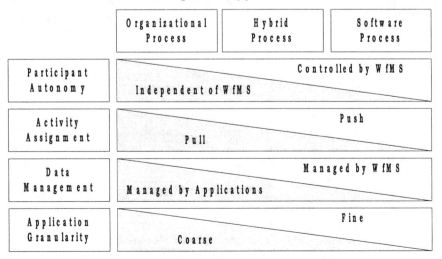

Figure 2: Process Characteristics and Workflow Support

WORKFLOW SUPPORT FOR INTER-ORGANIZATIONAL PROCESSES

The need for companies to expand the automated enactment of their business processes beyond the boundaries of their own organization is driven by the resulting savings in transmission time, gains in data quality and improved monitoring capabilities about processes at the sites of business partners. The current movement toward electronic data interchange is fueled by the relatively inexpensive exchange of business data over the Internet using data encoded in the eXtensible Markup Language (XML), which fosters the development of vendor-independent frameworks that aim to standardize data schemas for common business documents, such as purchase orders, delivery notes, invoices, etc. For a thorough discussion of the role of XML in workflow environments refer to the article by HOLLINGSWORTH [12]. Workflow management systems support inter-organizational processes mainly on the software process level. It should be noted, however, that a number of organizational processes occur at the B2B-level, which may be supported by workflow technology as well.

Software Processes in B2B Settings

For processes across enterprise borders, the significance of automated workflow support at the software process level is high, since many of the interactions between companies are quite standardized (for example the exchange of a purchase order between customer and supplier and the resulting exchange of the purchase order acknowledgement in the other direction, see e. g. [2]). Workflow technology can be used to supervise the correct sequence of documents exchanged, monitor timeouts and supervise the maximum number of retries, in case a message is lost. At the operational level, the workflow system can serve as a gateway to the internal processes of the enterprise. If a standardized message format is used in conjunction with a standardized command set (such as the one defined by Wf-XML), B2B processes can be fully automated, decreasing cycle times and increasing data integrity.

Organizational Processes in B2B Settings

Notwithstanding the benefits of automated B2B processes, the human element in inter-organizational exchanges can also be supported by workflow technology. Since the conversion of data between the internal format of the application of company A, the intermediate format (for example an ebXML document) and the internal format of the application of company B is complex, errors may occur, especially if the overall process has an "optimistic" design, assuming that each company does not modify either its applications or its data formats. The impact of erroneous process instances on the overall economic result should not be underestimated. According to STOHR, each problematic B2B transactions cost 300 percent more than regular transactions (compare [18]). With an increasing automation of transactions, this figure is likely to increase. One possible approach therefore is the handling of erroneous transactions through pre-defined workflows. Within this scenario, the responsible users from both parties are informed about the error and are provided with a structured process to resolve the problem.

INTEGRATION REQUIREMENTS OF WORKFLOW APPLICATIONS

The design of a workflow application creates integration requirements, which can be differentiated into internal and external integration requirements. Internal integration requirements concern those systems a workflow application needs to connect to in order to ensure the functionality of the core workflow system. External integration requirements exist with regard to systems that either invoke the workflow system from the outside (embedded usage) or systems that are invoked by the workflow application.

Internal Integration Requirements

As stated above, a workflow application coordinates participants, data and applications. Consequently, all these elements need to be integrated to ensure the functionality of the workflow systems.

- **Resource integration** is required by the workflow system to keep track of the participants available for work assignment. Since many companies maintain resource information in X.500 directories or similar applications, a fully integrated workflow application would use this information rather than replicate resource data internally.

- **Data integration** is required to make workflow relevant data accessible to the workflow system. This can be achieved by connecting the system to databases using standard connections such as ODBC/JDBC. If the workflow system acts as an enterprise application integration hub, conversion of data types and field values may be necessary.

- **Application integration** describes the ability of the workflow system to invoke external application systems during the enactment of a process. For organizational processes, applications are often called in their entirety (e. g. a word processing application), while for software processes the granularity of application invocation is at the method or function level.

In addition to these three integration requirements, the use of existing security infrastructures is another important feature of workflow applications.

- **Security integration** relates to the use of existing authentication and authorization mechanisms through the workflow system, such as single-sign-on and public key infrastructures.

External Integration Requirements

The external integration of a workflow system relates to the fact, that a workflow system is, after all, an application system in itself. External applications may require calling the services of the work-flow engine from the outside, invoking processes, querying the status of work items or handling resource assignments through ex-ternal scheduling mechanisms. On the other hand, the workflow system may be required to present work to outside parties, which are not participating in the workflow application.

- **External invocation of the workflow engine** is used for example in B2B process integration. The workflow engine can exhibit itself as a service to outside parties, allowing them to invoke a process and pass initial data to the process instance. Examples for the external invocation are e-mail (mail daemon triggers the workflow), the web (a web server triggers the workflow) or other applications, which embed the workflow system (a function within an application results in the start of a workflow).

- **Presentment of information to outside parties** is necessary, if the workflow system has to notify external participants about the status of "their" workflow instance or if system load information is passed on to external system management tools. Also, the use of audit trail information through external applications falls into this category.

Figure 3 summarizes the internal and external integration require-ments of workflow applications.

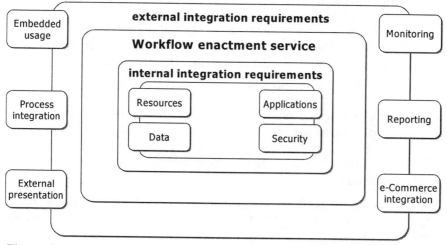

Figure 3: Internal and External Integration Requirements

CONCLUSIONS

Workflow management systems can be deployed in various scenarios, ranging from human-centered organizational processes to autonomous software processes, both confined to or extending beyond the boundaries of an enterprise. Each of these scenarios utilizes the coordination functions provided by the workflow system in different ways and requires integration to a different set of systems. Understanding the differences between these applications and their requirements is an important step for potential users of workflow technology.

Even though the concept of automated workflow management can be traced back for more than 25 years, there are still numerous open research issues, ranging from the organizational impact of workflow technology to integration issues in inter-organizational settings. For the future we expect the coexistence of various types of workflow systems within one organization. Their seamless integration is one of the great challenges of workflow research.

ACKNOWLEDGEMENTS

The authors would like to thank Christoph Bussler (Oracle Corp.), Keith D. Swenson (MS2 Inc.) and the members of the Association for Information Systems Special Interest Group on Process Automation and Management (www.sigpam.org), most notably Prof. Edward A. Stohr and Prof. J. Leon Zhao, for fruitful discussions of the concepts presented in this paper.

REFERENCES

1. Becker, J., von Uthmann, C., zur Muehlen, M. and Rosemann, M., Identifying the Workflow Potential of Business Processes. in *32nd Hawaii International Conference on System Sciences (HICSS 1999)*, (Wailea, HI, 1999), IEEE Publishers.

2. Bussler, C., P2P in B2BI. in *Proceedings of the 35th Hawai'i International Conference on System Sciences (HICSS 2002)*, (Waikoloa, HI, 2002), IEEE.

3. Chapple, E.D. and Sayles, L.R. *The Measure of Management. Designing Organizations for Human Effectiveness*, New York, 1961.

4. Davenport, T.H. *Process Innovation. Reengineering Work through Information Technology*, Boston, 1993.

5. Ellis, C.A. and Nutt, G.J. Office Information Systems and Computer Science. *ACM Computing Surveys, 12* (1). 27-60.

6. Frappaolo, C. The Many Generations of Workflow. in Fischer, L. ed. *Workflow Handbook 2001*, Future Strategies, Lighthouse Point, FL, 2000, 51-60.

7. Hammer, M. *Beyond Reengineering. How the Process-Centered Organization is Changing our Work and our Lives.* HarperBusiness, New York, 1996.

8. Hammer, M. The Superefficient Company. *Harvard Business Review, 79* (8). 82-91.

9. Hammer, M. and Champy, J. *Reengineering the Corporation: A Manifesto for Business Revolution.* HarperBusiness, New York, 1993.

10. Harrington, H.J. *Business Process Improvement. The Breakthrough Strategy for Total Quality, Productivity, and Competitiveness.* McGraw-Hill, New York, 1991.

11. Henning, K.W. *Einführung in die betriebswirtschaftliche Organisationslehre,* Berlin, 1934.

12. Hollingsworth, D. An XML based Architecture for Collaborative Process Management. in Fischer, L. ed. *Workflow Handbook 2002,* Future Strategies, Lighthouse Point, 2002.

13. Mahling, D.E., Craven, N. and Croft, W.B. From Office Automation to Intelligent Workflow Systems. *IEEE Expert, 10* (June). 41-47.

14. Malone, T.W. and Crowston, K. The Interdisciplinary Study of Coordination. *ACM Computing Surveys, 26* (1). 87-119.

15. Manolescu, D.A. Micro-Workflow: A Workflow Architecture Supporting Compositional Object-Oriented Software Development *Department of Computer Science,* University of Illinois, Urbana-Champaign, 2000.

16. McGregor, C. The Impact of Business Performance Monitoring on WfMC Standards. in Fischer, L. ed. *Workflow Handbook 2002,* Future Strategies, Lighthouse Point, FL, 2002.

17. Nordsieck, F. Grundlagen und Grundprinzipien der Organisation des Betriebsaufbaus. *Die Betriebswirtschaft, 24* (6). 158-162.

18. Stohr, E.A., Transaction Resolution Networks: A Case Study. in *Presentation at the 34th Hawai'i International Conference on System Sciences, January 3, 2001,* (Wailea, HI, 2001).

19. Swenson, K.D. and Irwin, K., Workflow Technology: Tradeoffs for Business Process Reengineering. in *Proceedings of the Conference on Organizational Computing Systems (COOCS '95),* (Milpitas, CA, 1995), ACM, 22-29.

20. WfMC. Workflow Management Application Programming Interface (Interface 2 & 3) Specification, Workflow Management Coalition, Winchester, 1998.

21. Zisman, M. Representation, Specification, and Automation of Office Procedures *Wharton Business School,* University of Pennsylvania, Philadelphia, 1977.

22. zur Muehlen, M., Process-driven Management Information Systems Combining Data Warehouses and Workflow Technology. in *Proceedings of the 4th International Conference on Electronic Commerce Research (ICECR-4),* (Dallas, TX, 2001), Southern Methodist University.

The Impact of Business Performance Monitoring on WfMC Standards

Carolyn McGregor, Faculty of Information Technology, University of Technology, Sydney, Australia

ABSTRACT

Workflow Management Systems provide a unique vehicle for the organization to capture and analyze a rich set of information about the business processes as they are enacted by the organization. Such information would include, but is not limited to, volume analysis, product mix analysis, service level attainment and resource productivity. The existing assumptions for monitoring workflow enactment do not provide organizations with the ability to also use this information for business performance monitoring. To ensure maximum benefit from their Workflow Management investment, organizations must not only consider the enactment of the business process steps, but also the use of the information captured during these enactments that facilitate organizational performance measurement, together with the delivery of this information to management.

This paper details a method to capture workflow process definition and workflow audit data in a Decision Support System to enable business performance monitoring. The key contribution of this paper is an amended WfMC reference model that incorporates business performance monitoring needs. A case study is included to provide an example of how to implement this approach.

Keywords: DSS Architecture, Management Information Systems, Business Process Reengineering, Balanced Scorecard, Workflow.

1. INTRODUCTION

The aim of organizations when investing in Workflow Management Systems is to enable seamless integration of the multiple transaction systems to support their business processes. These Workflow Management Systems however, provide a unique vehicle for the organization to capture and analyze a rich set of information about the business processes as they are enacted by the organization. Such information would include, but is not limited to, volume analysis, product mix analysis, service level attainment and resource productivity.

To ensure maximum benefit from their Workflow Management investment, organizations must not only consider the enactment of the business process steps, but also the use of the information captured during these enactments that facilitates organizational performance measurement, together with the delivery of this information to management. (McGregor, 2000)

The existing assumptions for monitoring workflow enactment do not provide organizations with the ability to also use this information for business performance monitoring.

zur Muehlen and Rosemann (2000) similarly state that while Workflow Management Systems facilitate precise and timely analysis of automated business processes through the provision of logged audit trail data, current research does not provide organizations with methods and techniques for analyzing this data in a format suitable for competitive advantage.

This paper describes a method to capture workflow process definition and workflow audit data in a Decision Support System to enable business performance monitoring. The key contribution of this paper is an amended WfMC reference model that incorporates business performance monitoring needs. An additional contribution of this work is a set of recommended functional additions for both Interface 1 and Interface 5 to enable business performance monitoring, for consideration during the XML redefinition of these standards.

The concepts relating to both Decision Support Systems and Workflow are first reviewed. The limitations of the existing WfMC reference model with respect to business performance monitoring are then discussed. An amended WfMC reference model is then proposed, based on the analysis of the WfMC standards and the requirements for business performance monitoring. A case study is then introduced to provide an example of how to implement this approach.

2. BACKGROUND CONCEPTS

2.1 Decision Support Systems

Decision Support Systems provide an organization with a mechanism to track and measure the organization's performance.

Decision Support Systems (DSS) is a term first used by Gorry and Scott Morton in 1971. They developed the Gorry and Scott Morton grid that includes two methods of classifying Decisions—the degree of structure in the underlying problem and the organizational management level at which the decision is made. It is based on Simon's (1960) concept of programmed and non-programmed decisions and Anthony's (1965) management levels (Gorry and Scott Morton, 1971, McLeod, R, 1995, Sprague and Watson, 1980).

Management Levels		
Operational Control	Management Control	Strategic Planning
Accounts Receivable	Budget Analysis engineered costs	Tanker Fleet Mix
Order Entry	Short-term forecasting	Warehouse and Factory location
Inventory Control		
Production Scheduling	Variance Analysis-overall Budget	Mergers and Acquisitions
Cash Management	Budget Preparation	New Product Planning
PERT/COST Systems	Sales and Production	R&D Planning

(Rows grouped by Degree of Problem Structure: Structured, Semistructured, Unstructured)

Figure 1 The Gorry and Scott Morton Grid (Gorry G.A. et al, 1971)

Several of the varied definitions for DSS have been summarized by Sprague and Watson (1980), Turban (1995) and Mallach (1994). Keen and Scott Morton (1978) listed the following three objectives for a DSS:

- Assist managers in making decisions to solve semistructured problems
- Support the manager's judgement rather than trying to replace it.
- Improve the manager's decision-making effectiveness rather than its efficiency.

Sprague and Watson (1980) and Turban (1995) define a DSS as being composed of the following:

- Data Management—including the databases containing the relevant data and the software to manage the data, the Database Management System (DBMS).
- Model Management—A software package including financial, statistical and other qualitative models that provide the system's analytical capabilities.
- Communication Subsystem—through which the user communicates with and controls the DSS.

2.2 Workflow

The Workflow Management Coalition (WfMC, 1994) defines the concept of workflow as: *the computerized facilitation or automation of a business process, in whole or part.* Workflow Management's primary function is the automation of business processes that involve combinations of human and machine based activities, particularly those using IT applications and tools. (WfMC, 1994)

Leymann and Altenhuber (1994) state that the recognition of business processes (and their representation in workflow) as a major asset of an enterprise is becoming more and more accepted. The quality of the business processes will influence the quality of the performance of an enterprise.

Much of the recent research in the area of Workflow has been influenced by the standards that are under development by the Workflow Management Coalition (WfMC).

The WfMC Workflow Reference Model has been developed from the generic workflow application structure by identifying the interfaces within this structure, which enable products to interoperate at a variety of levels. (WfMC, 1994).

Of specific relevance to this research is the work relating to Interface 1 "Process Definition Interchange Process Model" and Interface 5, "Audit Data Specification". Interface 1 details the interaction between the workflow engine(s), executing the workflow instance, and the process definition tool used to define the workflow structure and execution rules. Interface 5 provides the ability to capture and record various events occurring during workflow enactment.

While the Workflow Management Coalition Interface 5 (WfMC, 1998) identifies some elementary information a workflow management system should record about the execution of the workflow instances, it does not advise on how to evaluate this information. Indeed, most of the recent publications in this area relate only to the technical facilities required to log audit trail data. (zur Muehlen and Rosemann, 2000).

3. LIMITATIONS OF THE EXISTING WfMC REFERENCE MODEL

For an organization to develop a Business Performance Monitoring Decision Support System that utilizes data supplied by the enactment of a workflow it must first build knowledge within the Decision Support System about various facets of the definition of the business processes that are being enacted within the workflow. Additionally, in order to enable performance measurement, additional organization goals such as service levels for cycle time and rework levels should also be recorded.

The existing WfMC Reference Model facilitates the provision of information for administration and monitoring via interface 5 only. The current definition of Interface 5 does not supply entities such as service levels for cycle time and rework. Additionally, the format of information within Interface 5 does not provide easy support for the translation of this information to enable organization performance measurement.

To enable the development of business performance measurement using the information supplied during workflow enactment, two options are proposed:

1. Modify Interface 5 to facilitate the additional needs; or
2. Use both interface 1 and 5 together to supply information to the monitoring system

3.1 Option 1: Use Interface 5

This option would involve replicating information currently available within Interface 1 and would change the current functional purpose of Interface 5, which is to capture and record various events occurring during workflow enactment.

3.2 Option 2: Use Interface 1 and Interface 5

This option uses both Interface 1 and 5 together to supply information to the monitoring system. As a result of this option, the definition of Interface 1 would require modification to include the ability to supply cycle time and rework targets, as well as the ability to decompose activities into sub activities.

Interface 5 would also need to be revisited to review the monitoring information that is being supplied to ensure that there is enough information available for the Data Warehouse to be able to construct the necessary summary records to enable organization performance measurement.

Option 2 enables Interfaces 1 and 5 to maintain their functional purpose and hence option 2 is recommended.

4. WfMC STANDARDS AND BUSINESS PERFORMANCE MONITORING

To facilitate workflow monitoring, the WfMC reference model (WfMC, 1994) is modified to include the three layers of a Decision Support System, ie. the Data Subsystem (also known as a Data Warehouse), Model Subsystem and User Interface Subsystem.

The existing WfMC reference model (WfMC, 1994) includes a single entity populated by Interface 5 known as the 'Administration and Monitoring Tools' entity. In Figure 2, the administration tools are still populated via Interface 5, but have been separated from the 'Monitoring Tools' that are now described by the Decision Support System. The audit trail data supplied by Interface 5 will now be used to populate both the Administration and the Data Warehouse within the DSS hence the Interface numbering remains unchanged.

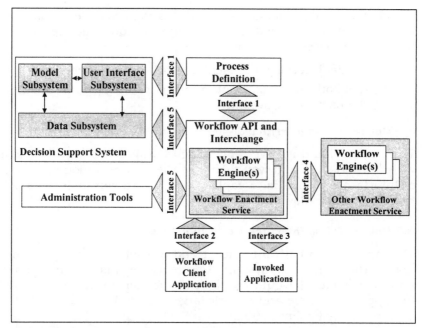

Figure 2 WfMC Reference Model modified to incorporate a Decision Support System

McGregor (2000) details a staged approach to the establishment of a Decision Support System for Business Performance Monitoring—the Design stage and the Implementation stage. Following the Implementation stage, information becomes available to facilitate the Review stage.

During the Design stage, the processes are defined using tools that enable Process Definition.

After the Process Definition or Design stage has been completed, the information collected during this phase is passed onto the Workflow Enactment Service via Interface 1. In addition, Interface 1 should also be used to pass this same information through to the DSS where it will use the information to generate the Data, Model and User Interface structures of the Decision Support System.

During the Implementation and Review stages the Data Warehouse receives log records through Interface 5 as the workflow engine(s) carry out the enactment of the business processes previously defined. Summary records are then created from these audit log records to enable users to view summary information via the User Interface through interactions with both the Model Subsystem and the Data Warehouse.

4.1 Impact on Interface 1

To enable the Decision Support System to construct summary records that provide meaning for business performance monitoring,

Interface 1 needs to incorporate the ability to attach attributes to activities, transitions and participants. The attributes applicable to each are detailed below:

Activities

Name	Description
Cycle Time Service Level	Service level for the cycle time for the activity expressed in time units
Rework target	Identifies the target for the number of process instances that will complete this transition multiple times, expressed as a percentage.
Cost	Cost associated with this activity

Transitions

Name	Description
Transition Level	Identifies if the transition represents a 'summary' transition (value > 0) or a 'leaf' transition (value 0). Only 'leaf' transitions will be utilized by Workflow Management Systems. 'Summary' transitions will enable the DSS to decompose activities into sub activities.
Cycle Time Service Level	Service level for the cycle time for the activity expressed in time units
Volume Target	Identifies the target for the number of process instances to be completed in a given time interval.
Rework target	Identifies the target for the number of process instances that will complete this transition multiple times, expressed as a percentage.

Participants

Name	Description
Productivity Targets	Identifies the target productivity level for each participant, expressed as a percentage.

4.2 Impact on Interface 5

zur Muehlen and Rosemann (2000) describe a process analysis tool (PISA) that analyses workflow audit trail data together with business process modeling data that allows the evaluation of workflow history data using the three perspectives process resource and object. To enable complete business performance monitoring two other perspectives may be required, namely customer and product.

While the majority of workflow management systems generate log records as a result of state changes, these log records need to contain a minimum set of information to enable the Decision Support System to construct summary records that provide meaning for business performance monitoring.

Fields required within this type of log record include:

Name	Description
Object ID	Unique object identifier that is being processed by this instance of the business process
Workflow Instance ID	Instance of the Business Process being enacted
Workflow Process ID	Business Process that is being enacted
Resource ID	Resource that performed the transition
From State ID	Transition from state
To State ID	Transition to state
Timestamp	Time stamp of when transition occurred
Time Zone	Time zone where transition occurred

Additional optional fields that are dependent on the type of workflow include:

Name	Description
Customer Type or Customer ID	Customer identifier for the customer that initiated this enactment of the business process
Product ID	Product associated with this enactment of the business process

5 CASE STUDY

This section presents a case study of an organization in which the introduction of a new product has necessitated the definition of a new business process. The goal is to provide an example of how to implement this approach using a concrete example.

5.1 Introduction

The business case contained in this case study relates to an organization that has chosen to introduce a new product for its customers and thereby requires the development of the business process to support the sale of this product to its customers. Resulting from a strategy review, the organization has decided to offer Unsecured Personal Loans to its customers.

We begin with an assessment of the organization's structure. Examples of the business process rules are then defined. Some examples of the organization's objectives and strategies are introduced. The impact of business performance monitoring on business process design and business process implementation is then detailed. The use of this information during business process review is discussed.

5.2 Organization Structure, Roles and Staff

There are three divisions of the organization that relate to this case study. The three divisions are: *Branch Network, Credit Team and Settlements Team*. For each of these divisions, roles are defined and described as they relate to the business process to be defined. For example, the role of *Sales Person* within the Branch Network division is the responsibility for assisting the customer to complete the application and to carry out follow up contact if the application is declined. Similarly, the *Self Employed Assessment Clerks* within the Credit Team are responsible for assessing applications that have been rejected by the credit check program where at least one of the applicants are self employed.

For each specific role, the organization defines which staff members can perform which roles.

5.3 Business Process Rules

In documenting a business process, each activity must be defined, as must the rules that govern when and where those activities are required. The following examples represent activities and their governing rules:

1. The *Sales Person* collects all the details from the *Customer* and forwards it to the *Credit Team* for approval.

2. All applications received by the *Credit Team* are first fed through a *Credit Check Program* in an attempt to facilitate automatic approval.

3. If the *Credit Check Program* rejects the loan due, say to the person being self-employed then the application is redirected to a *Credit Team Staff Member* who can perform the role of a *Self-Employed Assessment Clerk*.

4. If the *Sales Person* is notified that the loan has been declined, they meet with the client and either adjust the information (eg. reduce the loan amount or add a guarantor) or cease the request for the loan.

5.4 Organization Objectives and Strategies

In addition to the definition of the organization's structure, roles and staff, and the business process rules for the new process, the organization established objectives and strategies, to enable business performance monitoring of this new product and its associated business process. The definition of these objectives and strategies is through the use of a management strategy approach such as the Balanced Scorecard.

The Balanced Scorecard was introduced by Kaplan and Norton in 1992. They identified that "traditional financial accounting measures like return-on-investment and earnings-per-share can give misleading signals for continuous improvement and innovation."

Using the Balanced Scorecard approach is important to organization s when identifying goals because it provides a framework to keep score of a set of items that maintain a balance between short and long-term objectives, financial and non-financial measures, lagging and leading indicators, and external business performance perspectives (Kaplan and Norton, 1996, Martinsons, 1999).

Utilizing the Balanced Scorecard method of management reporting, the following examples of objectives are shown within the four Balanced Scorecard perspectives:

5.4.1 Customer Perspective

Within the Customer Perspective, such questions as "How do our customers see us?" and "How do we become our targeted customers' most valued supplier" are addressed. The following represent examples of objectives relating to customers:

- It will take no more than 24 hours from the completion of the application with the Sales Person, to sending the 'Letter of Offer' if the application is approved.
- It will take no more than 24 hours from the receipt of the completed 'Letter of Offer', for the funds to be released to the customer.

5.4.2 Internal Business Perspective

The Internal Business Perspective focuses on "What processes—both long and short term—must we excel at, to achieve our financial and customer objectives?" The following represent examples of objectives relating to its internal business process:

- It will take no more than four business hours to make a decision about an application, if it was rejected by the Auto Credit Checking program.
- It will take no more to than two business hours for a loan rejected by the *Credit Check Program* to be assessed by a *Self Employed Assessment Clerk*.

5.4.3 *Learning and Growth Perspective*

The Innovation and Learning Perspective provides measurement techniques to determine "How can we continue to improve our processes and systems in order to create value?" The following represent examples of objectives relating to the organization's learning and growth:

- The average time taken by each activity in support of this business process will improve by 10 percent in 3 months time.
- This new product will represent 10 percent or our sales in 3 months time

5.4.4 *Financial Perspective*

The Financial Perspective addresses the need to see "How do we look to our Shareholders?" The following represent examples of objectives relating to the organization's financial position:

- The number of Unsecured Personal Loan applications over the next three months will equal or exceed an average of 5 per week per sales person.

5.5 *Business Process Design*

Currently the business process design stage consists of the documentation of the organization's structure, roles and staff together with the definition of the business process and associated rules. This process culminates in forwarding this business process definition information to workflow enactment software in preparation for workflow enactment.

In addition to the above-mentioned steps, to enable business performance monitoring, the organization's objectives and strategies should also be included within this design and the information also passed onto the Workflow Monitoring Tools that are implemented using Decision Support System principles.

Some of the previously defined organization objectives and strategies are shown below together with the detail demonstrating how these can be represented as part of the business process definition:

- **It will take no more than 24 hours from the completion of the application with the Sales Person, to sending the 'Letter of Offer' if the application is approved.** This represents a 'transition' and as such a service level of '24 hours' would be recorded with the definition of this transition.
- **It will take no more to than two business hours for a loan rejected by the *Credit Check Program* to be assessed by a *Self Employed Assessment Clerk*.** This represents an 'Activity' and as such a service level of '2 hours' would be recorded with the definition of this activity.

The business process definition information would also then be forwarded to the Decision Support System to enable creation of the structure of the Workflow Monitoring Tool, within the Decision Support System. The information supplied through Interface 1, relating to these objectives and strategies could be ignored by the Workflow Enactment Software.

5.6 Business Process Implementation

During the business process implementation stage, the enactment of the workflow commences. As the workflow enacts, information relating to the commencement and completion of activities together with the time that transitions occur is forwarded to the Decision Support System via the workflow audit logs.

The Decision Support System receives the data from the workflow audit logs and stores it in the Data Warehouse. Summary records are then created using the information received from the workflow audit logs together with the information initially received as a result of the business process design stage. This summary information is now available for use during the business process review stage.

5.7 Business Process Review

During the business process review, users access the information contained in the decision support system through the user interface. They are able to then review the performance of the business process based on the performance targets set. In addition, they are also able to assess the performance of the product based on volume throughput information, for example.

6 RELATED WORK

Much of the recent research in the area of Workflow has been influenced by the standards that are under development by the Workflow Management Coalition.

The research detailed in this paper has had an impact on the directions of WfMC Interface 1 research and development. Recent research in relation to Interface 1 highlights its use in providing information not only to workflow enactment software, but also to workflow monitoring tools and workflow simulation tools.

zur Muehlen and Rosemann (2000) state that while Workflow Management Systems facilitate precise and timely analysis of automated business processes through the provision of logged audit trail data, current research does not provide organizations with methods and techniques for analyzing this data in a format suitable for competitive advantage. zur Muehlen and Rosemann (2000) and zur Muehlen (2001) describe a process analysis tool (PISA) that analyses workflow audit trail data together with business process modeling data.

They acknowledge the fact that further developments for Interface 5 are required to enable the development of a generic adaptor that will enable access to all workflow management systems. While their research utilizes information on the business process via a link to ARIS databases, it does not identify the need to extract this information and populate a separate data store via the use of Interface 1. Additionally, the user interface focuses on the support of tactical and operational management functions with little support for strategic, executive usage for business performance monitoring.

A method for utilizing data captured from workflow systems for organization performance measurement was introduced by McGregor (2000).

7 FUTURE WORK

The work in this paper can be extended in several ways for future research. Firstly the architecture is currently being extended to incorporate receiving information from an organization's Balanced Scorecard defined goals and objectives. This information would then be passed through and used during the process definition stage. In addition, the Decision Support System will be able to supply the captured performance information back to the Balanced Scorecard.

Second, information contained within the Decision Support System can be used to make recommendations for amendments to the process definitions.

Third, the architecture described is being further decomposed through detailed design of the Data Warehouse, Model Subsystem and User Interface components.

8 CONCLUDING REMARKS

This paper detailed a method to capture workflow process definition and workflow audit data in a Decision Support System to enable business performance monitoring. The key contribution of this paper is an amended WfMC reference model that incorporates business performance monitoring needs. A case study was included to provide an example of how to implement this approach.

9 REFERENCES

Alter S.L., 1980, Decision Support Systems: Current Practices and Continuing Challenges, Addison-Wesley, Reading, MA.

Anthony, R.N., 1965, Planning and Control Systems: A Framework for Analysis, Harvard University Graduate School of Business Administration, Boston.

Brookes, C.H.P., 1984, "A Framework for DSS Development", Information Systems Forum Report, 84/1.

Gorry G.A., Scott Morton M.S., 1971, "A Framework for Management Information Systems", Sloan Management Review 13, Fall, pp55-70.

Kaplan R.S., Norton D.P., 1992, "The Balanced Scorecard—Measures That Drive Performance", Harvard Business Review, Jan-Feb pp 71-79.

Kaplan R.S., Norton D.P., 1996, "Using the Balanced Scorecard as a Strategic Management System", Harvard Business Review, Jan-Feb pp 75-85.

Keen, P., Scott Morton, M,S., 1978, Decision Support Systems: An Organization al Perspective, Addison-Wesley, Inc., Reading, MA

Leymann, F., Altenhuber, W., 1994. "Managing Business Processes as an Information Resource", IBM Systems Journal Vol 33, No. 2, 1994

McGregor, C., 2000, "Intelligent Workflow Monitoring Systems", proceedings of the Doctorial Consortium of The 11th Australasian Conference on Information Systems (ACIS2000), Brisbane, Australia.

McLeod, R. Jr, 1995, Management Information Systems, Chapter 14, 6th Edition, Prentice Hall International, Eaglewood Cliffs, NJ.

Mallach, E.G., 1994, Understanding Decision Support Systems and Expert Systems, Irwin Publishers, Burr Ridge, IL.

Martinsons, M., Davison, R, Tse, D, 1999, "The Balanced Scorecard: a Foundation for Strategic Management of Information Systems", Decision Support Systems 25, pp71-88.

Mintzberg, H., Raisingham, D., Theoret, A., 1976, "The Structure of Unstructured Decision Processing", Administration Science Quarterly, 21, June 1976.

Simon, H.A., 1960, The New Science of Management Decisions, Harper and Row, NY.

Sprague R.H.Jr, Watson H.J., 1980, Decision Support Systems—Putting Theory into Practice 2nd Edition, Prentice Hall, Eaglewood Cliffs, NJ

Turban, E., 1995, Decision Support and Expert Systems: Management Support Systems, 4th Edition, Macmillan Publishing Company, NY.

Workflow Management Coalition, 1994, The Workflow Reference Model Issue 1.1, Document Number WFMC-TC-1003, November, http://www.wfmc.org.

Workflow Management Coalition, 1998, Audit Data Specification Version 1.1, Document Number WFMC-TC-1015, September, http://www.wfmc.org.

zur Muehlen, M., Rosemann, M., 2000, "Workflow-based Process Monitoring and Controlling—Technical Organizational Issues", in Proceedings of the 33rd Hawaii International Conference on System Sciences (HICSS-33), Maui Hawaii, January.

zur Muehlen, 2001, "Workflow-based Process Controlling—Or: What you can measure You Can Control", Workflow Handbook 2001, Future Strategies Inc, FL, pp 61-77.

Workflow as a Web Application —the Grand Unification

Heinz Lienhard, ivyTeam, Switzerland

We propose the direct way from process (be it a business, government or technical one) to the web application in two steps: first a design, modeling and prototyping step followed by test, validation and automatic upload on a suitably prepared Web server.

The program logic of a Web application is most naturally defined and implemented by a graphical *process model*; i.e. the process model eventually controls the application's behavior. If the process is modeled by an appropriate modeling and simulation tool, its simulator can be transformed during upload to the application controlling engine—actually the workflow engine.

With this approach solutions that traditionally require different means and quite different software packages can now be implemented in a single coherent approach. Examples are workflow solutions and interactive Web sites (e.g. enterprise portals), which now become a single comprehensive application. Thus, a complex Internet or Intranet solution combining a Web front end like an e-commerce shop together with workflow—e.g. for the back office or supply chain processes—becomes now feasible to design and implement within the same framework. Or a DMS (Document Management System) solution may be obtained by integrating an electronic archive into such an application. Or your ERP (Enterprise Resource Planning), CRM (Customer Relationship Management) system—or any other IT solution for that matter—may be enhanced decisively in scope and functionality.

The so-called content management that may be required for the application, i.e. the means necessary to efficiently update the information on the dialog pages, can also be supported by appropriate content management processes that are designed and implemented in the same way as the application processes. Hence, the application itself (and the means to maintain or manage it) can both be implemented using the same approach.

All the underlying processes can at anytime be easily adjusted to new needs via process and/or content management, i.e. without programming; hence transparent and flexible applications are efficiently obtained.

ivyTeam has implemented such an approach with its ivyGrid software, containing a process module, local Web server, data bases etc. First pilot applications have been carried out with very convincing results, actually demonstrating a viable solution to what has been eloquently described in WfMC's Workflow Handbook 2001 by Mike Marin.

INTRODUCTION

It is a trivial observation that the ubiquitous Internet gradually turns computer users, be they consumers or employees, into Web clients—or, simply put, into Web surfers.

But the consequences are far less trivial. The way people work and network with one another will be influenced decisively by Internet related technologies.

One technical consequence will be that a single suite of protocols for interaction and communication remains relevant: the one that suits the Internet; all proprietary ones will be doomed. And the interface used on the computer (from PC to PDA) will be a browser—and not only to surf the Internet. It will be the interface people want to use. And the applications they invoke will mostly be Web applications, whether they run on Web servers, on the user's own PC—or on the PC of another user accessible via peer-to-peer network.

Looking at the latest furor about Web services, distributed applications of the future will likely be Web applications with machines as surfers that are searching for appropriate Web services to complete their task.

Here we want to go one step further: applications in the future will be Web applications. And that means all of them—almost all. These applications will be based on processes, processes that run on a PC or on a particular server or on a whole network.

And with these applications there will always come some sort of well-integrated content management (CM) making it very simple to choose a language in which one wants to interact with the application, or more general, with what sorts of forms (including their style) one likes to work with. Thus, the application may be customized according to the needs and taste of the user. Sooner or later users will not want to miss these possibilities, whether the application is actually a Web application or not.

IT applications are, in general—whether one realizes it or not—based on some process or set of processes; i.e. the application is driven by some sort of workflow. Although in today's implementations these processes are often not made explicit (one prefers to talk about program logic), they are there. Or, the processes were well understood but could not easily be realized in the final implementation.

These might be some of the reasons, why so many large and ambitious IT applications need such tremendous software development efforts, and more often than not end in a quagmire of cost and delay overruns. Recently some instructive cases have been heard of from major Swiss banks to the tune of hundreds of millions of dollars lost. In one example one hundred and fifty million was spent alone on consulting fees—probably resulting in huge piles of documents nobody ever read. And hundreds of millions went into computer code hardly anybody fully understood.

Therefore, we believe that successful IT applications of the future will be clearly based on explicit, well-tested and documented processes, allowing adaptations to process changes without resorting to computer programming. And these applications will also include an easy to use content management system. Thus, the absolutely crucial "separation of concerns" to master complex applications will be obtained as well as the necessary transparency and flexibility to maintain them.

We will see further on how this "separation of concerns" significantly influences the application architecture. Software supporting the whole chain from customer front end to supplier (or the Enterprise Portal, to use a fashionable term) should obviously be process-based, as has been remarked before. But this is just one example: since people will interact more and more with Web applications via browsers, and machines will interact increasingly with other machines via Web service calls (to other Web applications), one may start to wonder about the future position of today's bulky operating systems and traditional applications based on them. Will eventually an OS kernel suffice and all the rest will be just a myriad of transparent and flexible Web applications driven by workflow? Is this not at least a chance for a Grand Unification in the software world that so far has eluded the realm of theoretical physics?

Well—we made some hefty claims about the future. In the following chapters we try to substantiate those claims by giving an example of how things could be done differently via a concrete embodiment[1].

PROCESS MODELING

To properly implement a Web application—or any IT application for that matter—we must understand the processes behind it. As experience has shown us, such understanding is greatly helped by an executable process model; i.e. one that can be simulated and analyzed. Here again the separation of concerns is important: on one hand one likes to have a powerful yet easy-to-use set or palette of process building blocks (we call them standard elements) that can be changed or adapted to suit new needs. On the other hand a stable simulation engine and graphical editor is required that is not influenced by such changes. The trick is to build the standard elements from more primitive units and to base the simulator (later the control) engine on them. This becomes even more important when

---

[1] Patent pending, first products are in use.

moving from process simulation to actual implementation (see below).

The quark model. Yes, we borrowed the term from the physicists.
Our quarks represent the above-mentioned fundamental units of
which the standard process modeling elements are built. The
quarks do not concern the process modeler. The simulator or quark
machine (later even the control or workflow engine) operates on
them. Hence, the engine remains the same, whatever process elements are used. (Fig. 1 shows the abstraction layers in the quark
model.)

Actually, three quarks suffice to define the dynamics of quite diverg-
ing palettes of standard elements. As an example, Fig. 2 exhibits the
definition of the "Step" or "Workflow Step" element with the quarks
storeQ, synchQ, mapQ. We might also think of the standard elements as sort of micro processes that we want to hide from the
user[2].

Process/Process Component
Standard Elements
Quarks
Quark Machine (Simulator)

Fig. 1 Abstraction levels

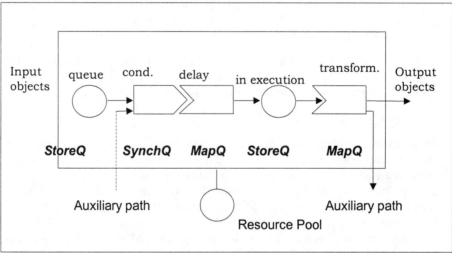

Fig. 2 Standard element "Step" as an example

All other process elements, including the ones we later need for realization (e.g. a data base element or e-mail element etc.), will be
defined in their dynamic behavior using the three quarks. We just

---

[2] These processes are micro Petri nets, so to speak

want to give a rough idea what these units are doing in the Step example:

- *storeQ:* it basically reflects a queue, e.g. the input queue. The capacity, i.e. the number of objects (events, orders, etc.) that can be stored determines the allowed length of the queue; while a delay parameter either gives a waiting time at the input or an execution time within the step.
- *synchQ:* it is used to synchronize objects entering an element, e.g. a data object to be processed within the step with the resource objects required to activate the step.
- *MapQ:* this quark maps attribute values of the entering objects to the attributes of the ones that exit the step. It may also have a duration parameter with it. If resources have been used they are released at the second mapQ in Fig. 2.

Each standard element has its associated *mask* to input parameter values and other data to specify in detail what the element has to do, e.g. what numerical transformation on the attributes it has to carry out.

Component/Sub-processes. Simple processes are built by interconnecting elements chosen from the standard element palette. Complex processes are usually composed of components taken from a catalog. Or, part of a process may be coarsened and in this way turned into a component for reuse. This way a bottom-up and top-down approach to structuring is supported.

In the future one may expect interesting process components—even component applications based on them—to become available via Web services. The possibility to simulate such components will be crucial to determine rapidly whether a component is useful for a given purpose or how it may be adapted. And those Web services themselves will likely be process-based applications.

FROM PROCESS MODEL TO APPLICATION PROTOTYPE

Merely for modeling a process one normally requires not more than a handful of standard elements: certainly a starting or generating element to generate events according to some statistics (or recorded real-life data) to get the process going in a desired way.

Control elements (e.g. a decision or alternative) serve to control the flow of the data objects. With a split and join element parallel processes may be spun and later merged. And of course, one needs an activity or general workflow step. What really intrigued us was the fact that by adding new process elements (and modifying some existing ones) a smooth transition became possible in going from process modeling to application building; i.e. to arrive at process-based applications at minimal effort and costs.

But let's do it together: now we want the process to really interact with the real world via Internet (or Intranet). Thus, the process simulation engine has to be coupled with a Web server package (e.g. Apache, IIS...) and the former process Start element becomes a *Start Request* element; i.e. the process is no longer started by some statistical regime, but by a request at the Web server.

Hence, the Start Request element responds to requests from Web clients via browsers or directly from other machines or sensory equipment etc. Thereby certain requests may trigger certain processes; and we may want to specify who or what is allowed to launch a particular process. And of course we now need standard elements that interact in a predefined way with the environment, e.g. *transaction elements* like a data base step (DB element with included DB assistant) to access pre-configured databases in an easily specified way, or *communication* elements like an e-mail step, to automatically send an e-mail, e.g. to confirm a customer order in an e-commerce application.

Because Web applications interact with users via browsers, *dialog* elements are needed that present a dialog page in the user's browser when activated in the process. Such dialog pages may simply give information to the user or they may represent forms through which the user is asked to enter certain information—or to simply click on some link to proceed. In their attributes, the data objects flowing through the process will carry information to be shown to the user (via dialog page), or information entered by the user to be used by other elements in the process, e.g. for transactions (storing in a data base) or numerical processing or transmission over the Internet to another site etc.

The palette of elements to implement these Web applications is likely to grow over time to accommodate new requirements and possibilities. With the *quark model* described above the behavior of such new process elements can be efficiently implemented. Those elements that have to interact directly with the real world (like the DB element) have an appropriate Java Bean embedded in them. Hence, combining the concepts explained before with Java Bean technology leads to a very powerful, open approach to realizing process-based Internet or Intranet solutions. Fig. 3 sums up the principal architecture of the process elements used for modeling and implementation.

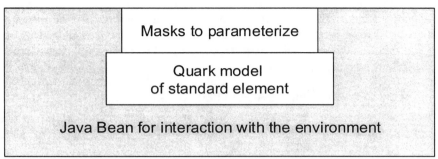

Fig. 3 Architecture of the standard elements

Below is an incomplete list of standard elements we presently use:

- *Control Elements*: with these elements the flow of the data objects in the process is controlled. In particular, the *Start-Request* element reacts on the request of a client via the Web server and thus starts the process it is connected to. Whereas the *Alternative* element selects different paths in the process, e.g. depending on certain attribute values of the data object entering this element, the *Split* element starts parallel paths which may later be merged by the *Join* element. The *End* element terminates a process (path) and may also generate a dialog in the user's browser to say good bye and to thank him or her for the visit.

- *Transaction Elements*: the simplest is the usual workflow *Step*, enabling transformations on the attribute values of the data object that enters the step. With the *DB* element databases can be easily accessed. By means of this element's inscribe menu an assistant may be started, allowing e.g. queries to be set up by just a few clicks. The *Task Assignment* element is used to assign one or several tasks to predefined roles.

- *Communication Elements*: with the *E-mail* element e-mails are automatically sent, e.g. for order confirmation in an e-Commerce application. Another example in this group will be the *SMS* element to automatically transmit short messages over the mobile phone. The so-called *Trigger* element will start another process, e.g. a back office or supply chain process.

In addition, there will be special elements for integration of other systems like a general *PI* (Program Interface) and a *SOAP* element (see below).

Each process element has its associated *mask* to input parameter values and other data necessary to specify in detail what the element has to do: e.g. attribute values, transformation formulas, database paths, selection criteria etc. These masks can be opened by the context menu "Inscribe" or by double clicking on the element.

As mentioned before, certain elements have an assistant or wizard associated with them, e.g. to support the design of dialog pages without having to resort to HTML or to set up database access in an elegant way without SQL (the necessary SQL code is automatically generated).

FROM PROTOTYPE TO RUNTIME APPLICATION

Now we come to the crux of the matter: going from prototype to the running application. This can be done without effort once the Web server that will host the application has been properly prepared. All that is needed is to upload the validated prototype by activating the Webapp Upload/Download assistant to obtain the runtime application specified by the prototype (see Fig. 4).

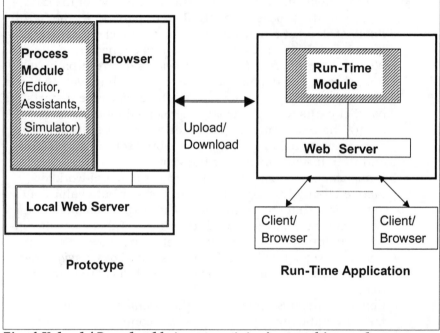

Fig. 4 Upload / Download between prototyping machine and server

Because the content, e.g. all the dialog pages managed by the built-in Content Management System, may be changed online, one can obtain a correct current and complete documentation by downloading from the server to the prototyping machine. If process modifications are necessary they can be readily carried out on the prototype, and with a new upload the modified runtime application is obtained.

As mentioned above, the server hosting the Web application needs to be set up accordingly. Basically, the runtime version of the process module has to be installed and coupled via servlet to a Web server program (Apache, IIS...). Fig. 5 exhibits a rough overview of the properly prepared Web server.

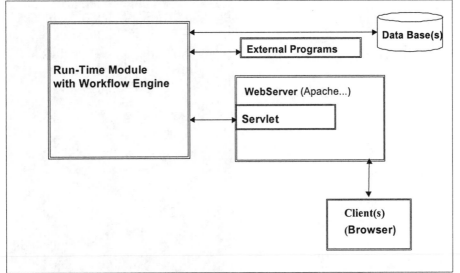

Fig. 5 Server installation: a usual Web server package (e.g. Apache) is connected via a servlet to the runtime module.

Using the servlet technique the runtime module is linked with a common Web server package. Through this link services of the Web server become accessible by the application. The runtime module contains the simulating engine used for prototyping that has become the controlling engine of the application. It now suffices to upload the process model, the database configuration (and possibly DB content) data and all content information of the content management system from which the dialog pages are generated.

A SIMPLE EXAMPLE

Let us now look at a simple workflow as a Web application to get a better feel of the approach.

In Fig. 6 below we exhibit the example in the prototyping mode: Assume R&D people (developers) want to have their projects released. For this an ok is necessary from both the technical manager (CTO) and the marketing head (CMO). Via a starting page at the appropriate URL the process is started. In the next step, the client is asked to input data concerning his project. The following task assignment element assigns the respective tasks to the roles "CTO" and "CMO".

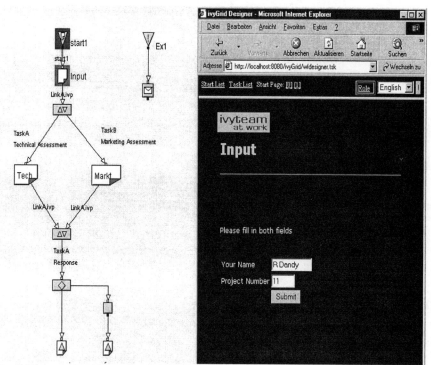

Fig. 6 *The process (on the left) has stopped at the Dialog Step "Input" which automatically produces the form on the right within the user's browser. After hitting the button "Submit" in the browser the process will proceed to the following Task Assignment element. (In the prototyping mode we observe simultaneously what is happening in the process on the server and what the client sees in his browser.)*

We now assume that the prototype has been uploaded, users have been registered and roles have been assigned to them.

After login onto the server the CTO will see in his work-list the projects waiting for his technical opinion; the marketing head will see the list of projects to be judged by him. Clicking on an entry will bring the process to the next dialog step "Tech" or "Markt" respectively. In these dialogs the opinion can now be directly entered e.g. by clicking on the corresponding check box.

The developer also has to login in order to see for which projects the evaluation has been completed. By clicking on "Response" he will get the answer of the evaluation.

In the following modified solution we separate a sub-process controlling the interaction with any Web client who wants his project evaluated (Web front end) from the actual workflow part for the assessment. Another process will be used to query the outcome of the assessment. In this solution the project is first registered in a database (Project DB), unless the particular project has already been entered (see Fig. 7).

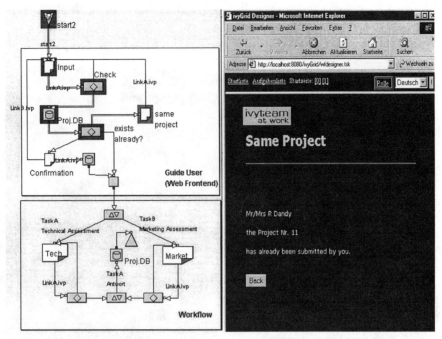

Fig. 7 Modified example with front-end sub-process and separate project database.

Once project registration is ok, the workflow sub-process will take over. The assessment results are stored in the corresponding fields of the project database. With the process as shown in Fig. 8, which again constitutes a Web front end process, anybody who knows the URL of the starting page may now obtain the assessment results directly from the project data base as soon as they are ready.

In this solution only the people involved in the workflow part, i.e. the CTO and CMO, have to login to the server to access their worklists. The actual workflow process will likely be accessed via an Intranet, whereas the front-end processes communicate with the Internet.

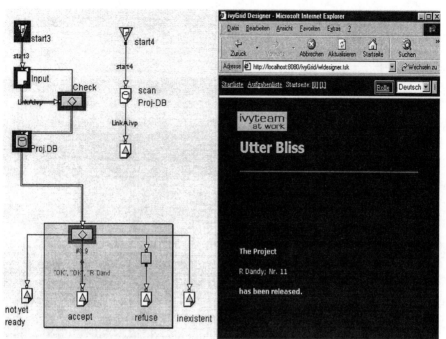

Fig. 8 Web front end process to query the project DB: we see the data object (the red dot) flowing through the process and just about to enter the end element "accept" carrying the attribute values which are partly visible. The client (on the right) shows the assessment dialog page associated with the element "accept."

The built-in content management system makes it easy to define alternate dialog pages in different languages that will appear according to the choice of the client.

THREE PHASE APPROACH

Our experience with projects has led us to propose the following steps (see Fig. 9) to obtain the final applications from the underlying processes:

1. Model, analyze, optimize and document the processes underlying the application.
2. Build the prototype starting from the modeled processes using the built-in wizards.
3. Integrate external applications using the special interface elements:

-   A *general PI* (for "Program Interface") element, within which the appropriate Java classes may be defined to connect in the most general way, possibly to proprietary interfaces.
-   A *SOAP* element with an assistant for connecting in a standard way via SOAP messages.
-   A *Web Service* element (based on SOAP RPC); i.e. the external application is treated as a Web service.

These three steps conclude the design/prototyping phase leading to a solution that can be simulated and thus validated together with the users. This prototype can now be uploaded to a web server with an installed *server* package—thus obtaining the final run time solution.

In this way fully *transparent*, *well-documented* and *flexible* solutions are obtained—and this is accomplished very rapidly and without requiring any software coding except possibly for some interfaces to other systems (PI elements).

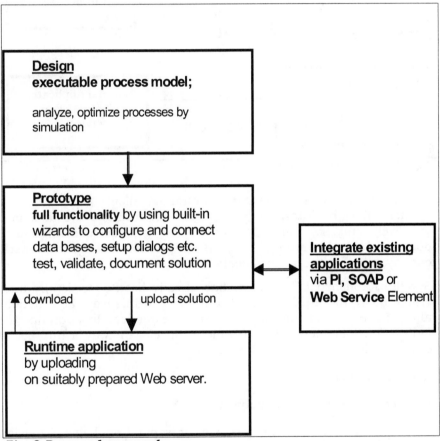

Fig. 9 Proposed approach

THREE LEVELS OF APPLICATION INTEGRATION (EAI)

It should be possible to integrate other applications via the above-mentioned basic *PI* element on different levels, depending on what protocols the application to be integrated offers.

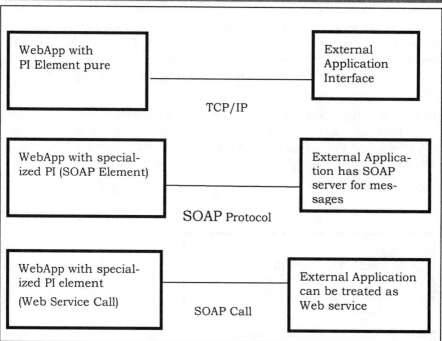

Fig. 10 Integration levels

Whereas the low level (Java programming) allows practically any application to be integrated, the higher levels make the task progressively simpler. In any given case it has to be decided whether to opt for a higher level at the expense of possibly having to properly encapsulate the external application.

A well-established ERP system has already been successfully integrated using the "medium level" approach. In this way the functionality of the system has been decisively extended. In addition, the foundation has been laid to couple in an elegant way a number of other applications to the ERP solution.

WHAT ARE THE BENEFITS?

The decisive benefit is productivity. Why?

In today's approaches one has a clear separation between design and implementation. Albeit some modeling tool may be used to support the design phase—the implementation is done using common tools of the trade like programming languages, application server pages (ASP), application servers etc. To go from design to running application is difficult and time-consuming. Often design and implementation are done by different groups and communication among them is not always perfect. Even worse: with time design and running application may drift apart and later modifications become very costly.

Here we go a different route: we provide a medium where the designer and customer of the application can meet and jointly validate the design. But most important: the design (prototype) becomes the running application if uploaded on the suitably prepared Web server (see Fig. 5), simply because the simulating engine of the design package becomes the runtime engine of the runtime application controlling the Web server (e.g. IIS[3] or Apache) via the process model.

Hence conception, specification, prototyping, testing, implementation and documentation of Web applications are all done in a unified way:

A first step in conception becomes a first step in implementation.

Solutions that traditionally have to be treated by different means using quite different software packages can now be realized by a single coherent approach. Examples are workflow solutions and interactive Web sites, which now become a single comprehensive application. Thus, a complex Internet or Intranet solution combining a Web front end like an e-commerce shop together with workflow, e.g. for the back office or supply chain processes, can be designed and implemented within the same framework. We obtain coherent unified solutions for all players involved (Fig. 11):

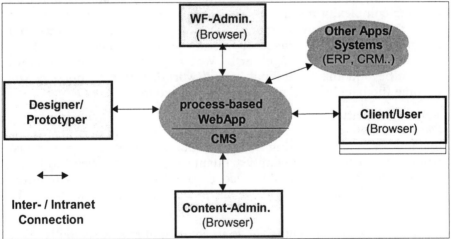

Fig. 11 The Web application players. Clients, workflow administrator and content manager (or administrator) only need a browser to interact with the system.

Web applications are designed in an almost playfully easy way:

- Draw the process model defining what the application does by inserting and connecting standard elements;

---

[3] Trademark of Microsoft.

- Use the dialog assistant with the dialog elements to define the data exchange between user and application within the process and define the database accesses with the DB element's assistant; input the required calculations and decisions into the masks of the appropriate transaction and control standard elements; where necessary parameterize the Program Interface elements;
- Animate and test the prototype;
- Upload the prototype onto the web server on which the server package has been installed for hosting the runtime application;
- Run it.

OUTLOOK

Sharp and McDermott write in their fascinating book[4] *Workflow Modeling* that EAI (enterprise application integration) should have been named, "enterprise *process* integration" to emphasize the importance of process-oriented approaches in this field. This is exactly what we have proposed above. In particular, integrating applications via Web services (Fig. 10) seems to become the solution of the future—and these Web services will likely be implemented in a process-oriented way.

In addition, today's standard solutions, which despite their ever growing complexity never provide all the functionality necessary in a dynamic business environment, may well give way to solutions that integrate smaller, manageable modules, well-focused on solving specific problems—tied together by Web application based workflow. Hence, beyond the traditional role of workflow this technology will become the backbone of next generation systems.

Turning our attention to the customer side, i.e. the Web front end, the focus has shifted from the traditional static home page to the dynamic Web site featuring many functions going from simple registration up to triggering complex business processes over the Internet. To do this successfully, also in this case, a process-oriented approach is called for. And we have demonstrated how it can be done.

Looking back at the claims made in the beginning, we hope to have shown a possible way to the "Grand Unification" with process-based Web applications.

---

[4] Alec Sharp, Patrick McDermott, Artech House 2001, p. 50

Peer-To-Peer Technologies and Collaborative Work Management: The Implications of "Napster" for Document Management

B. John Masters, Jr., Information Management Consultants, Inc.

Can over eighty-four million people be wrong? Bertelsmann (BMG) says that's how many users have registered for Napster. This pioneering Peer-to-Peer (P2P) file-sharing platform stood the world of Internet collaboration on its head in a big way. Even in bankruptcy, Bertelsmann was willing to pay nearly a billion dollars for the service.

Peer-to-Peer (P2P) computing is a parallel or distributed system with at least one of its sub-systems (e.g. control, data, processing or interface) distributed over more than one computing device, and with each one of them capable of communicating directly with any other.[1] Its main aim is to optimize resource sharing on the network. As this model eliminates the distinction between publishing resources and consuming them, it's "goodbye" to client/server, and "hello" to peers.

During 2000, file-sharing peer-to-peer networks such as Napster were in vogue. Napster allowed users to exploit the worldwide reach of the Internet to share music files. However, many well known P2P systems have been doing yeoman's duty for many years. These include Domain Name System (DNS) servers, Internet mail servers, distributed caching systems or even database servers. Although the Napster program initially gained notoriety because of its music-pirating ability, the real news was the impact of its very powerful distributed search and delivery platform search. The combination of changes and improvements in PCs (including the availability of newer Internet-aware technologies) and the wildly popular Napster phenomenon, has given credibility to an entirely new type of business model based on P2P computing.

The concept of peer-to-peer opens the way for some pretty extreme possibilities since the resources that can be shared between peers can be very diverse:

- Data sharing: Imagine the richness of a universal file system (video, documents, music...) that could be shared by all the peers connected to the network.
- CPU resource sharing: Think about the SETI@Home project, in which small bits of collected data are served out to

---

[1] N. Drakos, "Gartner Research Note COM-12-4960," February 23,2001.

thousands of computers for processing on the individual CPUs.

- Service sharing: Each peer can offer services to other peers, such as a simulation calculation service.[2]

In addition, P2P is not restricted to computers. It can apply to devices of all different types and sizes. Expect to see the convergence of digital and wireless technologies further increase the dissemination and distribution of information processing activities.

COLLABORATION

According to Suneeth Nayak, Chief Technology Officer of IMC, Inc., "The challenge is one of getting the right information to the right people at the right time... so effective decisions can allow organizations to succeed. Workflow, in its many forms, is part of the solution to this challenge, and P2P technologies can facilitate workflow in the new 'boundless' organizations and amongst the ad hoc project teams."

Workflow generally pushes filtered (and sometimes augmented) information to the next participant in a defined process.

According to IMC's Nayak, "A primary issue for any workflow management system is resource location. The whole concept of 'users and roles' exists to map people to the operations they are capable of performing to advance a business objective. Thus, workflow clients construct elaborate 'inboxes' that deliver work to a 'qualified' user."

In contrast to workflow, work management is where all participants have equal access capabilities and the desired resource is available to any person with the skills to service the request. "Information is free and ubiquitous. This is why Road Runner organizations capitalize on openness, for they know it's not the information and data that is crucial but what smart, creative people do with it."[3]

Work management systems can better and more timely support changes and exceptions to planned business processes. Disintermediation, demassification, and disaggregation have become the watchwords of cyberspace. New technologies are apparently breaking collectives down into individual units. It is predicted that any form of coherence and coordination beyond the individual will be the result of self-organizing systems.[4]

Collaborative work management systems enable the bi-directional exchange of "value" by two or more parties working together over

---

[2] Nicolas Farges and Habib Guergachi, "P2P and its Impact on the Enterprise," Intranet Journal, September 26, 2001.

[3] Chip R. Bell & Oren Harari, Beep! Beep! Competing In the Age Of The Road Runner, Warner Books, p.16.

[4] See, for example, George Gilder, Life After Television (New York, NY: W.W. Norton, 1994) for disintermediation; Alvin Toffler, The Third Wave (New York, NY: Morrow, 1980) for demassification; Nicholas Negroponte, Being Digital (New York, NY: Alfred A. Knopf, 1996) for disaggregation.

time. It usually transcends two or more organizations and accomplishes two primary goals: 1. facilitates agreement; and, 2. enacts the decision. Additionally, the systems must maintain a history of the process and facilitate post-agreement changes.

Peer-to-peer collaboration applications can be used for real-time meetings and communications and secure file sharing in ad hoc groups. Business groups can form and dissolve self-organized "webs" for collaboration on projects. Peer-to-peer collaboration can also be used to speed the development of new products and to decrease the cost and time involved in developing manufactured products by providing incremental increases in the speed of sharing information and ideas (collaboration), and organizing that collaboration into a rational and effective process.

ORGANIZATIONAL BENEFITS

There are few more dramatic impacts on today's businesses than the breakneck speed of technological change. Where decision cycles were measured in days or weeks, we now expect minutes, or even seconds; where people and businesses formed relationships for years or a lifetime, today the connections change constantly; where once we were content to make decisions based on the limited information available, technology's ability to process vast amounts of data have whetted our appetite for better and more information.

Today's world is not just about speed, it's also about anticipation, responsiveness, imagination, and most of all, agility. Speed is about pace; agility is about nimbleness.

In a world where linear speed is a commodity, any organization can use technologies that compress time. The key is this: What do you *do* with those technologies? What can you create that is different, unique, or special? In a world where speed is a commodity, being fast equals no more than surviving. The key to thriving is no longer just the ability to work fast, but *what* you are able to do fast.[5]

Unfortunately, all this collecting, indexing, and storing, has buried us under an avalanche of "data." In an average day, a typical worker must filter through 220 discrete messages. These may be e-mail, fax, voice mail, phone, letters, or even instant messages. Eighty percent more feature films are released today than 10 years ago. One estimate puts the number of publicly available Web pages at 2.1 billion, with 7.3 million new pages added every day, and we're expected to manage this information explosion in real time. According to the GartnerGroup, the average white collar professional spends 10 to 40 percent of every workday searching or waiting for information. The challenge that exists is to then discern what is valuable. Even our nomenclature recognizes this need. What was once a "data processing" (DP) department is more likely to be described today as an "Information Technology (IT) department" as new technologies

---

[5] Bell & Harari, P. 23.

are integrated into our organizations and lives. DP Managers begat IT Managers, who begat Chief Information Officers, and as we enter the 21st century, organizations have Chief Knowledge Officers and white collar workers are "knowledge workers."

Organizing knowledge across hybrid communities is the essential activity of organizational management. It is also difficult, though why is not often appreciated. Certainly, most managers will acknowledge that getting knowledge to move around organizations can be difficult. In general, however, discussions of such problems are reduced to issues of information flow. If, as the saying goes, organizations don't always know what they know, the problem lies with the organization: given the opportunity, information appears to flow readily. Hence the belief that technology, which can shift information efficiently, can render organizations, which shift it inefficiently, obsolete.[6]

The distribution of knowledge in an organization, or in society as a whole, reflects the social division of labor. As Adam Smith insightfully explained, such division of labor is a great source of dynamism and efficiency. The specialized tasks undertaken by communities of practice develop corresponding particular, local, and highly specialized knowledge within the community. [7]

In other words, loan-processing specialists know best how to process loans, while records management specialists know best how to manage records. Trying to move the knowledge without the practice involves moving the know-what without the know-how. Due to its social origins, knowledge moves differently within communities than it does between them. Within communities, knowledge is continuously embedded in practice and thus circulates easily. Members of a community implicitly share a sense of practice and standards for judgment, supporting the spread of knowledge. Without this shared sense of context, the community disintegrates.[8]

Business processes are made up of these embedded practices. Ideally, processes should allow groups, through negotiation, to align themselves with one another and with the organization as a whole to accomplish the business purposes of the organization. Business processes can enable productive cross-boundary relations by establishing a shared interpretation among different groups within an organization and across organizations. "In the right circumstances, the interlocking practices that result from such negotiations should cohere both with one another and with the overall strategy of the company. The processes provide some structure, the negotiations

---

[6] John Seely Brown and Paul Duguid, "Organizing Knowledge," University of California, 1998.

[7] Eric Von Hippel, "'Sticky Information' and the Locus of Problem Solving: Implications for Innovation," Management Science, 40 (1994): 429-439.

[8] John Seely Brown and Paul Duguid, "Organizing Knowledge," University of California, 1998.

provide room for improvisation and accommodation, and the two together can result in coordinated, loosely coupled, but systemic behavior."[9]

Traditional workflow systems have worked best in the organizational models of the recent past. The client/server model these organizations deployed lent itself to automated workflow based on precise business rules. Computing systems have largely reflected the strictly organized, rules-based hierarchical organizations that arose as a result of the need to perform decision-making in an environment with partially complete, partially correct and untimely information. This reflected the centralization of responsibility for risk management. An obvious extreme example was Soviet central economic planning. In this structure, all decision-making was done from a central committee with limited input from the "field" organizations that were impacted by the decisions. The controls were very rigid and discouraged entrepreneurial thinking from lower-level workers.

Today's organizations are more apt to flat and flexible in their organizational model. This has an impact on the types of information processing technologies that will be deployed. In their book, *Beep! Beep! Competing In The Age of The Road Runner*, Chip Bell and Oren Harari tell us:

Successful post-year 2000 organizations of two people or 200,000 are interlocked webs of alliances working anytime, anywhere to add new value. They are collaborative confederations of people with a common purpose: consolidating minds and energy to create something new. These alliances (often temporary) are confederations of equals, inside and outside—with permeability, and the ability to cross boundaries. A confederation means: 'being united in an alliance.' The connotation is: friend, companion, associate, accomplice, accessory, and ally.[10]

Knowledge-based repositories maintain information on three tiers. In going up each level from data to information to knowledge, facts and context are added to help understand the level below. Data forms the initial level in a digital archive, and includes the digital objects, which may themselves be very complex, plus the syntax of where records start and stop. The next level is information, which adds the tagged data, or metadata, to the data. Information includes

[9] For the notion of "loosely coupled" systems, see Karl B. Weick, "Organizational Culture as a Source of High Reliability," California Management Review, 29/2 (Winter 1987): 112-127; J. Douglas Orton and Karl E. Weick," Loosely Coupled Systems: A Reconceptualization," Academy of Management Review, 15/2 (April 1990): 203-223.

[10] Chip R. Bell & Oren Harari, Beep! Beep! Competing In The Age Of The Road Runner, Warner Books, P. 29.

the attributes or fields in the collection, plus an explanation of what they mean.[11]

Finally, the knowledge level includes relationships between metadata elements. This includes implied knowledge, which is information plus context and rules not necessarily contained or implicit in the data itself, which may come from sources external to the data.[12]

While a knowledge-based repository contextually linked to work management applications is not sufficient to deal with all exceptions, it can help facilitate re-use of best practices or identify the resources (e.g., colleague) that can help in a specific process situation.[13]

Without the rigid organizational structures and business rules of hierarchical workflows, advanced and flexible work allocation methods will use real-time data on the availability of resources to complete the process. A collaborative work management application could use P2P technologies to link to information dynamically and adapt work assignment decisions using context-sensitive allocation rules.

The dominant work allocation method in today's workflows is based on routing work items on predefined roles/groups instead of individuals, and workload balancing. This approach is not sufficient to address the requirement of a dynamic business environment where individuals play multiple roles. Ad hoc extension (or reduction) of tasks assigned to roles/groups, user-defined allocation rules, reservation or voting mechanisms for users/work items need to be added. Advanced work allocation methods will also be important as conflicting requirements on the usually scarce skilled resources surface in growing organizations.[14]

TECHNOLOGY IN THE P2P ENVIRONMENT

A number of new technologies enable P2P processes: Faster processors allow "clients" to acts as "servers;" the rollout of broadband allows for "always-on" connections and supports spontaneous messaging; cheaper storage allows for distributed caches; fungible naming provided by Virtual Name Spaces (AOL Instant Messaging, for example) allows an alias to be dynamically associated with an IP address.

---

[11] Regan Moore & Arcot Rajasekar, Persistent Digital Archives: A Knowledge Based Approach, NPACI & SDSC Online, Vol. 4, Issue 25, Dec. 2000.

[12] A. Gupta, B. Ludäscher, M. E. Martone, Knowledge-Based Integration of Neuroscience Data Sources , 12th Intl. Conference on Scientific and Statistical Database Management (SSDBM), Berlin, Germany, IEEE Computer Society, July, 2000.

[13] Regine Casonato, "Introducing Adaptive Work Management Systems," Gartner Research Note, February 25, 1999.

[14] Casonato.

Extensible Markup Language (XML) will become a key enabling technology of P2P-based work process management systems. Besides being a major search enabler, XML makes content portable. It can permit the encoding of "rights" into the content, and be used to "carry" the required process metadata. .As Kahlil Gibran wrote in *The Prophet*, "A little knowledge that acts is worth infinitely more than much knowledge that is idle."

Available technologies can:

- Optimize human involvement
- Automate recurrent tasks
- Minimize interaction related delays
- Optimize concurrency

All these capabilities act to compress time and increase agility.

Workflow has been an important part of many information management strategies for some years now. The workflow systems that have developed during this period have been reflective of the hierarchical, rules-based organizations and the technology infrastructures that support them.

Peer-to-peer tools can lessen the need for corporate IT to expand some of their services, such as Web servers, backup storage, and replacing outdated documents. Peer-to-peer computing also has the potential to allow a certain amount of network traffic to move from the corporate processing resources to less expensive infrastructure, such as switches, hubs, and routers.

Many organizations have stretched resources for the servers to the limits, while a network of underutilized client PCs sit idly by. Peer-to-peer computing can extend computing throughout the Internet, allowing every computer to serve as a server to those computers around it. This represents an enormous untapped resource. Large companies might be able to utilize their client layer in order to offer as much as 10 terabytes of spare storage (2,000 clients x 5GB/client) with trillions of operations per second of spare processing power available for intense calculations performed over the network without placing additional strain on the backbone.[15]

Cycle sharing allows workstations on the network to access the computing resources of underutilized machines. Design teams that require massive computing resources can leverage the machines from other groups who are not currently using their machines for heavy computations. This could reduce the time to market for the development and manufacturing of new products.

P2P technologies integrated into work management systems will provide knowledge-based repositories containing information on similar cases, participants, best practices, and representative user skill profiles for potential contributors.

---

[15] Serena Lambiase, "Peer-To-Peer Computing Technologies: An Introduction," GartnerGroup Research Note No. DPRO-97205April 5, 2001.

REQUIREMENTS

What is the required services infrastructure for peer-to-peer architectures?

A peer must *publish* a resource (allowing it to be located and accessed by other peers) with sufficient precision for the other peers to be able to broadcast their needs and receive meaningful responses.

Before a resource can be "used" it must located on the network. This can be difficult due to the ubiquity of resources and the unpredictability of their connectivity. Some real-time directory mechanism, such as Virtual Name Spaces, is essential.

Once located, the resource must be invoked. This will require some level of standardization since a peer is not necessarily familiar with the workings of the resource that it is invoking. One protocol that will aid this standardization is Simple Object Access Protocol (SOAP). SOAP lets one application invoke a remote procedure call (RPC) on another application or pass an object to a remote location using an XML message and the Internet.

SOAP satisfies the growing need for business partners to exchange structured data over the Web independently of each other's underlying application platform. It is designed to let organizations publish data and services over the Web as easily as they can publish HTML pages. As such, it functions as a wire protocol to connect multiple Web portals, each of which might use an information server, object broker, or other facilities to integrate and process the information.[16] Services such as security management (authentication, non-repudiation, confidentiality), transactional unity, availability (by failure recovery), or performance (by balancing loads across different peers) may be required. Like AOL and MSN Instant Messaging, many of these will be hosted or facilitated services.

These infrastructure services must operate on a network in which the connectivity of each peer is unpredictable. It is clear that these infrastructure services will need to be standardized in order to minimize problems of deployment for peers. GartnerGroup calls this the "crunchy edge" of peer-to-peer processing.

Several companies are currently developing P2P collaboration applications focused on the investment management industry. They claim their more simplified and automated workflow process will allow participants in the financial services community to connect directly with investment managers without a B2B exchange; such disintermediation could have significant impact on B2B exchanges.

Virtual Name Spaces allow almost any computing device to act as a server. This can enable more ad hoc workflows for project-specific activities. The Zaplet Appmail Suite is an enterprise technology plat-

---

[16] Deborah Hess, "SOAP, UDDI, and WSDL: An Introduction," GartnerGroup Research Note No. DPRO-92621, May 9, 2001.

form that claims to improve collaboration within corporations and among customers, partners, and suppliers.

The platform enables companies to create and host a kind of collaborative productivity application called "Zaplet Appmail." Zaplet Appmail brings together the people and information needed to contribute, make decisions, and take action on collaborative business processes or projects. Zaplet Appmail can be created by anyone within the enterprise—not only technical staff—and deployed as easily as sending an email. It can then be accessed via the inbox or Web browser.

RISKS

Peer-to-peer applications enable networked access to resources previously available to those with physical access; this can lead to security problems. Steve Gibson, a longtime high-level PC programmer and a former antivirus code programmer, has spent more time than most of us studying and worrying about computer security issues. Gibson says, "Today's typical user PC is not generally serving any data. Most users are just sitting on the Net, with no ports open, not accepting connections from random outside machines. But this changes in a big way with P2P! Now you're in a situation where your machine will accept any incoming TCP connection—and that changes a lot! There are going to be many ports open that weren't before, [so hackers] will get in."

Of course he's right. We all remember our alarm on seeing the intrusion attempts on our home computers after installing our first firewall software. The potential openness of P2P may make it even easier to slip a Trojan horse into our systems, or tools to launch a denial-of-service attack later—or just to run unauthorized commands on someone else's machine.

Intel has developed security software code that other companies can use when developing P2P applications. The Peer-to-Peer Trusted Library (PtPTL) includes full API documentation and provides support for digital certificates, peer authentication, secure storage, public key encryption, digital signatures, and symmetric key encryption. The library also provides simple support for networking and some operating system primitives. The API is freely available, and allows developers to add the element of "trust" to their peer-to-peer applications.

Sun Microsystems Inc. is developing a Web-based programming language called Juxtapose for use by companies looking to build distributed peer-to-peer computing applications. There are four mechanisms planned for JXTA: the ability to connect peers, logically group them together, monitor and control what they do, and add a security layer.

Since P2P computing is not centralized, managing P2P within a corporation can be problematic. While federated search (where each node reports local results and forwards the request to all known peers) is very powerful, the lack of centralization can pose a problem for search engines. Reliability is also a concern of many IT managers. What happens in a distributed computing application if certain PCs that are supposed to be cooperating (sharing storage or processing capacity) are unavailable?

Most enterprises do not have enough Internet bandwidth to sustain the flood of large file transfers that could result from use of P2P programs by their employees.

The still nascent peer-to-peer industry needs to develop common protocols and improve scalability, security, and management, and standards for interoperability. The lack of standards in P2P technology is not unusual for an embryonic process, but it does create concerns for IT managers. This is particularly true for companies that are decentralized. What happens if two different units invest in two different P2P platforms that are proprietary and not interoperable? What about a single division that uses several different P2P programs that require separate agents because they are not compatible?[17] Problems similar to those are already faced by corporate information management professionals, but with an added degree of complexity.

Finally, P2P implements processes "bottom-up," resulting in loss of managerial control. It creates a form of "functional anarchy." In today's business environment, this can be both frightening and enabling. Thomas Jefferson wrote, "I know of no safe repository of the ultimate powers of society but the people themselves; and if we think them not enlightened enough to exercise their control with a wholesome discretion, the remedy is not to take it from them, but to inform their discretion."

THE FUTURE OF P2P

New services being developed by several companies will allow users to synchronize messages from all their devices and retrieve them from a centralized Web application (e.g., http:// www.fusionone.com). This new way of delivering data utilizes the Internet itself as an "operating system," thereby transparently managing problems created by conflicting formats and allowing users to store data safely on the Internet and access it from any personal computer, cell phone, or Web appliance.

Microsoft is expected to aid the creation of such online applications through its .NET initiative, which they claim will enable every developer, business, and consumer to benefit from the new Internet devices and programmable Web services that characterize the Next Generation Internet.

---

[17] Stan Schatt, "Market Overview: Peer-to-Peer Technology Landscape Complex, but Some Winning Niches Emerging", Giga Information Group, September 20, 2001.

Peer-to-peer technology has evolved away from the centralized directory of Napster, but there is reason to believe that the B2B applications will return toward more centralized control, as seen in the approach taken by Groove Networks. The reason for this is to ensure a higher level of security and a higher level of control. There are serious issues right now that need to be resolved to achieve true peer-to-peer distributed computing.[18]

Groove Networks, Inc. software and services enable members of the enterprise to connect quickly with customers, partners, and suppliers in a secure interactive environment to share information and get things done. A unique peer computing platform, Groove erases technical and organizational boundaries, bringing together the people, information, and tools needed to speed decision-making, solve problems, and reduce time-to-market for new goods and services.

Groove runs on each user's computer and handles all communication functions. Most activity in Groove takes place in shared spaces—virtual interactive workspaces open only to invited members. Shared space members can work together, online and in real-time, or independently, offline, at times of their own choosing. All shared space content is automatically saved and synchronized on users' machines, making ongoing meetings and project management a breeze. According to Groove, any business process that requires dynamic communication and collaboration can be enhanced and extended.

In Groove, all data is automatically encrypted, both on-disk and as it moves over the network. Shared spaces—accessible only by authenticated members using pass-phrase protected accounts—are protected from rogue components by IT controls included in the platform.

Another type of peer-to-peer model is Web services. A Web service is a process published by an enterprise that may be connected to the firm's existing IT system. The notion of clients and servers disappears, since a consumer of a Web service may also be the publisher of another Web service. What makes Web services special is the fact that they are based on a triptych of standards that makes interoperability between diverse systems a possibility. As examples, the Web uses two protocols to exchange information: HTTP, a real-time TCP protocol used by browsers and servers, and SMTP, a store-and-forward protocol for e-mail. XML documents can pass through firewalls, are easily translated to internal formats, and allow applications and servers to process information without exposing their internal workings to the Web.

It is not uncommon during the early stages of each wave of technology adoption for architectural discipline to be abandoned in a rush

---

18 Stan Schatt and Colin Rankine, "Peer-to-Peer Networking: Lots of Turmoil, but Are There Practical Applications for Enterprise Clients?" Giga Information Group, February 2, 2001.

to implement. During two earlier shifts in particular—client/server and Internet applications—many "instant legacy" applications were created, i.e., applications without abstraction of business services, layering of user interface, business logic and data logic, integration with organization wide infrastructure for security and other services, or even, in some cases, Y2K compliance.

Such applications became maintenance headaches for the remainder of their useful lives. It will not be surprising to see the same phenomenon in the early adoption of Web Services, but the fact that some people are asking whether Web Services actually eliminate the need for enterprise architecture (at least, in the sense of centralized enterprise architecture) reflects how large a potential change Web Services represent. However, although Web Services may require enterprise architects to radically rethink their role within the organization, using Web Services as an excuse to abandon enterprise architecture altogether would significantly weaken an enterprise's ability to leverage and respond to future waves. Indeed, the lessons learned from those that have been most agile in leveraging past waves suggests a high correlation of this agility to those enterprises with the most effective architectural strategies.[19]

FUTURE PEER-TO-PEER WORKFLOWS

In future P2P workflow models, the work item and associated data will be packaged into a virtual envelope indicating the type of resource required. When a resource receives such an envelope, it can check its own profile for a skills match and/or forward the item to the next set of resources (perhaps based on the expected time to completion for the item; if the local resource can service it within some threshold, it will queue but not forward it; if the service time exceeds the threshold, it will queue and forward it; and if it lacks the appropriate skills, it will simply forward it).

In work management systems, "who does what" is not necessarily predefined, and may be more dynamic in collaborative environments. General George S. Patton once said, "Don't tell people how to do something... Tell them what to do, and let them surprise you with their results." Work management systems of the future will drastically improve the flexibility of work allocation methods, replacing the traditional client/server model with which we are familiar.

Design the workflow to readily allow for changes to the business process. Foresight and planning are needed. Maximizing the business rules (or flow control logic) in the work management system may be limited by the actual capabilities of the chosen work management (i.e., Is there a dedicated workflow engine?) or may negatively impact system performance. The importance of allowing the

---

[19] Carl Zetie and Mike Gilpin, "Web Services vs. Enterprise Architecture: Paradigms Shift, Agile Architecture Is Forever, "Giga Information Group, September 25, 2001.

user organization to change the workflow independently of the IS organization will be one of the primary drivers of this approach. Maximizing business logic in the application system can address performance issues, but will then require programming changes to modify the business process. An organization will have to determine the trade-offs appropriate to its own business priorities and operational environment.[20]

Think of your company as a fire department. It cannot predict where the next fire will take place, so it has to shape a flexible and efficient team that responds well to unanticipated events, no matter how extreme—Andy Grove, Former Chairman, Intel

By extending business processes through work management, collaboration and peer-to-peer technologies, organizations can better manage and automate critical business processes across an extended enterprise. This should lower the cost of delivery for more complex processes.

CONCLUSIONS

Eighty-four million can't be wrong. Peer to peer is definitely here, it has a future, and it does not encroach on traditional heavy or light client models. Although the idea of a generic peer-to-peer architecture might seem to be a theoretician's ideal that cannot be applied in the real world, it can in fact be entirely feasible for some types of applications. Success stories like Napster or Gnutella are proof of the viability of the peer-to-peer model for certain problems.[21]

The approach to adopt for peer-to-peer architectures should be utterly pragmatic; a good example of this is the Web services standard that will enable enterprise applications to be extended by letting them communicate using the P2P model.

The value of a virtual company does not come from its products or services, but from its knowledge, its web of alliances, and its capacity to transform know-how into results.[22]

In his book, *The Minding Organization*, UCLA Professor Moshe Rubinstein writes about the leadership required in this new chaotic age: "To create an adaptive, innovative, problem-solving organization requires a new form of leadership, the ability to provide guidance in the search for purpose and goals. Classical leadership— implementing stipulated goals—is committed to the status quo."[23]

Tomorrow's organizations will be loose confederations of people working anytime and anywhere. This will require supporting tech-

---

[20] Regina Casonato, "Six Steps To Deploying Work Management Successfully," GartnerGroup Research Note TU-IDOM-384, July 7, 1997

[21] Farges and Guergachi.

[22] Bell & Harari, P. 122.

[23] Moshe F. Rubinstein, PhD and Iris R. Firstenberg, PhD, The Minding Organization: Bring The Future To The Present and Turn Creative Ideas Into Business Solutions, 1999, John Wiley & Sons, Inc. P. 147.

nologies that are as flexible and agile as the organizations themselves. These will be technologies capable of working outside the traditional hierarchical organizational structure of centralized command and control.

While there are significant challenges to implementing workflow in a P2P environment, the results can have significant value to an organization. It will be necessary to once again rethink our business processes and how we manage them, and to accept the fact that they will always remain in a state of flux. Workflow systems that exploit the strengths of P2P technologies will do much to empower these new organizations and provide a competitive edge.

An XML based Architecture for Collaborative Process Management

David Hollingsworth, ICL/Fujitsu, UK

1 ABSTRACT AND BACKGROUND

The original ideas behind this paper go back to the presentation first given by the WfMC to the XML World conference at Boston in September 2000. At that time XML had arrived as an exciting new technology holding out the prospect of much improved integration between differing islands of IT automation. Since then considerable progress has been made in realisation of that potential both within the WfMC and the wider standards world.

This paper discusses the background to XML and provides a classification of the various diverse standards now defined within the XML framework. Their relevance to workflow architectures is discussed in general terms using the Workflow Reference Model and Web Services Architecture as background. An assessment is made of existing XML based standards with direct applicability to collaborative workflow along with potential areas for further standardization. The paper concludes with a view of a consolidated architecture for workflow applications based on the range of existing and potential XML standards.

The author gratefully acknowledges the contributions made to this subject by various colleagues within the WfMC, particularly Mike Marin, Marc-Thomas Schmidt and Michael zur Muehlen, who were co-developers of the original presentation, and Michael Rossi, who has coordinated work on the Wf-XML standard for several years.

2 CLASSIFYING XML STANDARDS

XML is essentially a standard for structuring and representing information. It is of course, supported by an amazing variety of software technologies to facilitate its practical use in many different application contexts. It was derived from the ISO Standardised General Mark-up Language (SGML) standard, which was (and still is) widely used within the publishing industry.

XML defines a generalized and extensible scheme for "marking-up" data in a way that enables a wide variety of different data structures to be derived from its basic data types. It includes a simple but powerful scheme for representing data structures by the use of Tag names and data delimiters.

In the context of the original ISO "7-layer" architecture XML sits at layer 6, defining standards for the presentation of data.

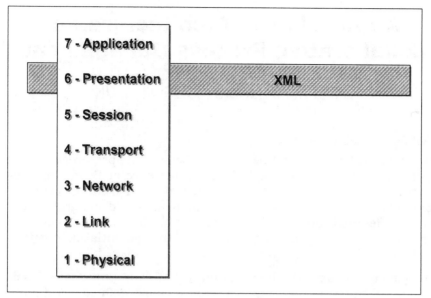

Figure 1—XML as a data presentation standard

Within the original ISO Reference Model the standards from the different layers were intended to integrate into an overall scheme of system interoperability with each layer providing a service to the layer above, whilst utilising the services of the layer below.

The result was a powerful but complex abstract model that was overtaken in practical usage by standards developed in industry and research groups such as the Internet Engineering Task Force (IETF).

In practice the ISO "7-layer" model has evolved into two areas of standardization:

I.   Those involved with the interconnection of information systems (layers 1-4), where the TCP/IP suite of protocols defined by the Internet Engineering Task Force (IETF) predominates

II. Those involved with the interworking of systems applications (layers 5-7) providing support for file transfer, email, remote procedure calls, support for distributed transactions and many other specialised services

The significance of XML is that it has overtaken much of this earlier architectural thinking and is now the essential language of standardization and systems integration. In retrospect this is completely logical—the representation and presentation of information is in many ways the key to achieving integration of diverse system components.

From the initial XML standard have sprung many related standards, which extend the use of XML into the interconnection domain as well as the application-interworking domain, yet all retaining XML at their core. There has been an explosion of XML related "standards" in recent years, with significant overlap in various areas and different rates of take up into the products of the software industry.

This workspace is being addressed by numerous organizations with different working approaches and motivations. Much of the standards making has moved from formal international bodies such as ISO (and its country constituent bodies such as ANSI, BSI, AFNOR and DIN) to specialised industry or trade based and groups. These vary greatly - from formal bodies enjoying wide industry support and product commitment to informal groups with a common interest but limited take up plans. In some cases individual vendors have defined a specific standard for use within their own products in the expectation that other organizations will also adopt it.

The overriding problem for the system designer, whether end-user or systems integrator, is to identify from this plethora of standards those which are genuinely significant to the task in hand and fit together in a cohesive way. Many current standards are relatively early into their lifecycle and may either change in subsequent versions, be overtaken by other competing standards, or fail to gain sufficient vendor support to fulfil their original purpose,

Two organizations are worthy of specific mention at this stage.

The Worldwide Web Consortium (W3C) has been generally successful in co-ordinating much of the overall development of XML-related standards. Most of the recommendations that pass through the W3C review and authorisation process to become full standards will achieve critical mass in the industry. The Internet Engineering Task Force (IETF), operating primarily in the interconnection and networking areas, also has a robust standards development process and has achieved generally good take-up of standards in these particular areas.

These two organizations in some ways form the lynch pin of current standardization activities around XML, supported by numerous other bodies operating in more specialised areas, including the WfMC.

When assessing the role of the various XML-related standards and how they fit together it is useful to have a classification scheme in which to place the individual standards. The diagram following offers one such classification scheme.

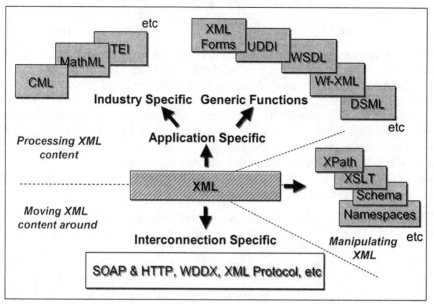

Figure 2—An XML standards classification scheme

From the original XML standard three broad areas of applicability can be identified:

I. Standards for moving XML content around
    These standards are not concerned with the general nature of the XML content but are defined to provide particular capabilities to carry XML content between different information systems. Initially HTTP and, subsequently, SOAP—which normally operates over it—dominated this area. Other initiatives have been made including Web Distributed Data Exchange protocol (WDDX) and, more recently, work within W3C on XML Protocol—an attempt to rationalise this area into a single protocol.

II. ***Standards for processing XML content***
    This is the principal area of interest from an application design perspective and covers numerous standards that are of significance to particular types of application. This area can be usefully split into two sub-classes.

    (a) Those which provide vertical industry specific information representations—there are numerous examples including those in the above diagram—CML (Chemical mark-up), MathML (Math Mark-up) and TEI (Text Encoding Initiative)

    (b) Standards applicable to horizontal areas of processing across all vertical industries—again there are numerous examples, some of which are a restatement of earlier standards but now in an XML format. They include work on web services architecture (WSDL, UDDI, etc) as well as on specific functional areas such as Wf-XML (distributed process execution), DSML (directory services) and XML Forms (form handling). From a process management perspective most of the standards discussed in the next section of this paper fall into this category

III. **Standards for manipulating XML**

These standards provide extensions in the way XML can be used and manipulated by applications. These include Xpath and Xpointer, plus DOM and SAX (related to the structures for processing XML), Namespaces and Schema (to extend the mark-up vocabulary for single XML documents to multiple sources and support validity checking) and XSLT (using style sheets to support the transformation of XML documents).

While not directly concerned with the application level meaning of the XML data, they add significant capability to the way in which an application can process XML and application level specifications increasingly need to reflect their use.

This is intended to provide the briefest overview of the types of XML related standards currently available. Readers will find a huge quantity of material available on the web, both from formal standards organizations (see particularly www.w3c.org) and many informed commentators. In the next sections of this paper I shall explore in more detail the requirements for process management standards and assess the currently available standards of direct relevance.

3 THE ARCHITECTURAL BUILDING BLOCKS

There are two key architectural models that provide the foundations for collaborative process management—the WFCM Reference Model and the industry web services architecture, constructed principally from W3C standards.

3.1 Workflow Reference Model

The original concepts of a workflow architecture remain valid when considering collaborative business processes, although the detailed emphasis will be somewhat different.

Firstly, process management is about the automated management of business processes through their lifecycle. This needs to cover support for the Analysis / Design / Operation / Audit / Improvement phases.

Secondly, process management concerns the management of resources. Within this lifecycle it needs to provide for the management of process resources—whether they are human, machine, information or physical consumables.

Thirdly, it needs to manage the business process flow through the application of procedural rules governing the sequence and relationship between business activities and associated resources.

The following diagram, taken from the Workflow Reference Model, provides a view of the required scope of process automation standards.

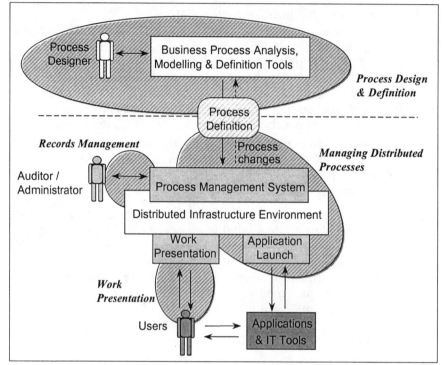

Figure 3—Workflow Reference Model Scope

The Process Definition

The business process is represented by the process definition whose significance can be seen from its position at the boundary between process design and process operation. It is the template from which the operational business process instances are created. (It is often described as Interface 1 from the Reference Model). Clearly an XML representation of the business process is one required aspect of the process management architecture.

Several specifications have been produced by different organisations, each with different strengths and weaknesses. None has yet established a strong presence in the market at product level, although it is still comparatively early days

The original work in this area was done by the WfMC, in the form of the WPDL specification, which was subsequently updated to XML format as XPDL. XPDL is comprehensive and is focussed particularly on describing workflow requirements for process flow, resource management and application tool support. It embodies some concepts of distributed process operation, but does not include a collaboration model as such. It does relate to runtime concepts such as state management, supported in associated execution standards such as Wf-XML

More recent work has been undertaken by the Business Process Management Initiative (BPMI) who have produced BPML—an XML based grammar for describing business processes. BPML is comprehensive and takes in a somewhat wider scope than XPDL, including for example the concept of synchronised data exchange. It has built quite significant industry participation and has a reasonable chance of establishing support particularly from CASE and BPR/BPM tool developers.

NIST has updated the originally PSL specifications using XML and this is also a comprehensive description language for business processes. It was particularly focussed on manufacturing applications and has some support in that context.

A recent specification of interest is WSFL (Web Services Flow Language). This has been produced by IBM, although there have been no announcements (at the time of writing) of planned support in products. This is focussed specifically on process flow through a series of process fragments expressed as web services. It includes the concept of internal and external (to the web service) views of the process and also encompasses "recursive process composition"— akin to the hierarchic sub-process model of the WfMC. It is not yet clear whether WSFL will attract the wider support to become a true industry standard.

Distributed Process Execution

The second main area of requirement is in the management of distributed process operation within and across distributed domains (this covers interfaces 3 and 4 from the Reference Model) The principal XML standard in this space is Wf-XML, defined by the WfMC. There have been no other really comparable standards defined in the industry and Wf-XML is a key runtime component of the architecture. It is not discussed in detail here as it is covered in other articles within the Handbook. The main process interactions that it supports are described later in this article (in Section 4).

Work Presentation

The third area is that of work presentation to the user (part of interface 2 from the Reference Model) and this is one area that has not yet been specifically addressed within existing XML standards. (It did form part of the original IETF SWAP work but was never progressed through to a final standard). Because this is part of the internal service interface to its participants it has assumed less importance when considering collaborative standards. Initiatives such as XForms and WSUI have some general relevance and given time, may well meet needs in this area.

Audit & Records Management

Finally comes the area of record management, capturing audit and compliancy information from the business process (Interface 5 from the Reference Model). This again has not had a data definition expressed in XML although is a candidate for such work. It is also considered further in Section 4.

3.2 Web Services Architecture

XML and web services fit very comfortably together and the increasing use of e-business interactions has lead to great interest in the deployment of web services carrying a wide variety of XML encoded business data as part of the service functionality.

The basic interaction model for web services is shown below.

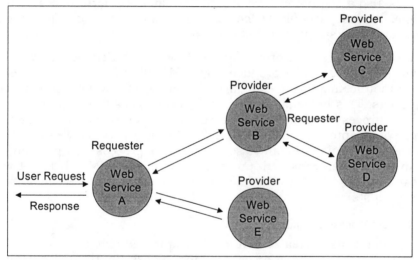

Figure 4—Web Service Interactions

Interactions between Web Services occur as a series of request—reply message sequences, in which various additional service elements may be added in a value chain. Interactions between Web Services occur as SOAP calls carrying XML data content and the service definitions of the web services may be expressed using WSDL as the common (XML-based) standard. The UDDI standard provides a means of discovering details of available web services from a web services directory for public or private Internet usage.

The basic model of interaction is the same as that incorporated in the WfMC Wf-XML standard, which defines the structure of service interactions between software components to support process management.

The paper *Process Management: A Fundamental Component of Successful Web Service Execution* published by Michael Rossi in this edition of the handbook provides a more detailed description of the subject. In particular it describes the key role of Wf-XML as the standard for the management of distributed process execution in a web services environment.

Clearly adoption of the core web services standards within the overall process management architecture is an important aspect within a collaborative workflow architecture. The key standards and their relationships are shown in the diagram below.

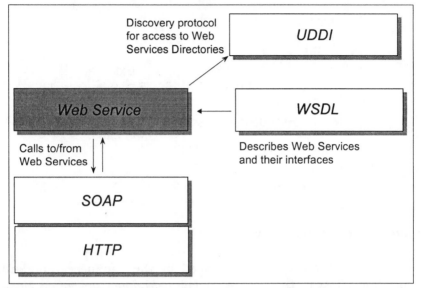

Figure 5—Web Service Standards

These are some of the core building blocks for the architecture. In the next section the additional components needed to support collaborative process management are considered.

4 COLLABORATIVE PROCESS MANAGEMENT

The major consideration for a collaborative process is the need to provide support in an e-Business environment, where the business process and its associated resources may be distributed across multiple organisations and trading partners.

This has particular significance in terms of the way a collaborative business process is defined.

Internal & External Behaviour

In a collaborative process environment, ownership of the process definition may be shared between several parties; all parties may agree on the overall stricture of the process at its highest level but individual organisations may then privately own and internally operate individual lower level elements of the process. Thus a collaborative business process may need to be defined at several levels with the expansion of lower level (non-shared) process fragments being handled internally by individual organisations and not made visible to other parties participating in the higher level process context.

Thus the traditional process definition, typically handled at a single level in a traditional workflow environment will normally require to be split into those aspects internal to a web service and those aspects visible at the web service interfaces.

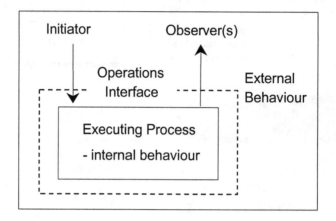

Figure 6—Process Externalization

This is a concept originally described by the Japanese Standards Association (JSA) in the document *Interworkflow Application Model: The Design of Cross-Organizational Workflow Processes and Distributed Operations Management.*

This envisages that a business process spanning two organizations is initially defined (jointly) in terms of the "Interworkflow Definition"—the data interactions between the parties. Each organization then expands the detail of the process within its own operational domain that deals with the processing of each of the data driven interactions.

The collaborative process management architecture builds on this concept using the assumption that a complete process definition for collaborative working should fully define all potential interactions that may occur between the parties. Such interactions include for example, all the message types defined within Wf-XML for runtime execution.[1]

---

[1] The architecture for collaborative process management may also require to support other interactions beyond Wf-XML. The paper by Michael Rossi in this publication discusses further possible options such as XAML and XLang. Such potential extensions are beyond the scope of this paper.

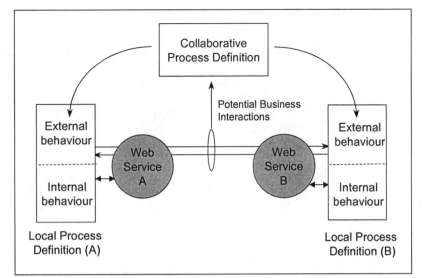

Figure 7—Interworkflow Principles

The principle of opaqueness applies at the boundaries of the executing process handling service. Work presented at a process service component is initiated by the external resource sending a message. The nature of the actual processing of the work within the process service component is opaque to the initiator. The service may process the work itself, or may pass some work on to one or more third party services or may satisfy the work request by some combination of local processing and some subcontracting to other parties.

Note that the collaborative process definition does not need to include any of the resource management elements associated with a normal process definition, such as participants, applications or locally significant process data. These are added locally by the participating organisations as part of the internal service definition.

State Information

However the collaborative process does include the concept of shared state—those states of the top-level process, which have business significance between the parties. (For example, this might include the point during its processing by the provider at which an order can no longer be changed by the initiator. It might also include the point in the process at which a service delivery is being initiated and this may need to be reported to the initiator/observer.)

These states are visible, or potentially visible, at the service interface. The initiator may be permitted to enquire of the status of the executing process within the provider service domain; he may even be permitted to change its state as part of the offered service definition. Similarly the provider may automatically report to the initiator changes of state occurring within the executing process.

Shared Process Relevant Data

The other shared information required at the service interface is a definition of the process relevant data that is to be exchanged during the various process interactions. The WfMC standards for process definition (XPDL/WPDL) includes a section describing such data The paper by Michael Rossi in this publication also provides an example in which the context data for such interactions within Wf-XML is defined within WSDL

Process Interactions

This results in the requirement for a specific set of work operations between parties within a collaborative process management context. The possible range of such supported operations, based on Wf-XML, is provided below, although not all business processes will necessarily require all operations to be supported

- Initiation of process work
- Notification of completion (or, more generally, of any change in state or events occurring during the execution) of a process work unit
- Instruction to change process state
- Transfer of process related data—either input data or result data

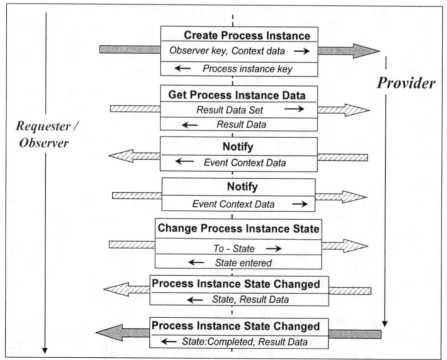

Figure 8—Wf-XML Interactions

Interactions designated with solid arrows constitute the minimum set (initiating and completing the process); interactions designated with hatched filling support exchange of information during process execution—state changes, events, context data etc.

The potential range of interactions that is supported must be defined within the collaborative process definition.[2]

Other considerations—Service Constraints

Although it is a fundamental concept that the detail of the actual resource processing to satisfy the request is not visible to the initiator, the initiator may wish to place constraints on the way in which the request is to be processed by the providing service. These might include prohibition of sub-contracting or various level of security handling etc. If such constraints cannot be met the request may not be actioned. Hence the definition of the collaborative process definition may usefully also include the general capability to include constraints.

Audit Data

A further category of information that may be considered at this point is the need for audit data specification. A key requirement in a collaborative workflow environment is that (at least parts of) such data should be shared between participants. One approach is for the service provider to have the option of describing what audit data is captured during process execution as part of the service definition.

The WfMC has published a comprehensive (non-XML) based standard for the content of audit data[3]. Much of this is concerned with capturing the internal status information associated with, and/or triggered by, changes of state within the executing process. Much of this information may be archived and only requires analysis if some form of audit investigation after the event is necessary for any reason. Several forms of usage are possible within a collaborative workflow context

(i)   The provider maintains audit data which is available for access by the initiator after the event, typically by some form of off-line retrieval

(ii)   Critical audit data is transferred to a third party (such as a compliance unit) and is available for resolution of enquiry or dispute

(iii) The provider returns key audit data to the initiator on process termination as part of the result data

---

[2] Note that in this simple model the requester is also the observer. It is possible to conceptually separate these roles, or to introduce multiple observers. In these cases a notification operation (event or state change) may be directed to an observer resource different to the requester.

[3] Document Number WFMC-TC-1015, Audit Data Specification

(iv)   No audit facilities are provided

Hence all that may be required at the service definition level is a description of the style of audit usage that is supported by the service provider. Where multiple options are supported the initiator would specify which option is to be adopted as part of the context data exchanged during process initiation.

5. COLLABORATIVE PROCESSES—EXPRESSING THE PROCESS DEFINITION

We have established that the collaborative process definition should include element definitions to support all of the following potential information relating to the service interfaces:

- Shared state related information
- Events of joint significance between the services
- Shared process data definitions, including audit data where relevant
- Any quality of service constraints which can be applied by the service provider (e,g, subcontracting prohibition or security levels)

Within the generic Web Services model the description of interfaces to the Web Services is defined using WSDL. Although the collaborative process definition could be defined in several specifications describing the process definition (e.g. XPDL, or BPML), since the use of a web services architecture is central to the collaborative process model a most natural (and convenient) way of describing the Web Service process aspects is within WSDL.

WSDL includes the following constructs that are made use of for the purposes of specifying the service and its external interfaces.

Services

A service groups a set of related ports together:

```
<wsdl:definitions...>
<wsdl:service name="nmtoken">
<wsdl:port.../>
</wsdl:service>
</wsdl:definitions>
```

The name attribute provides a unique name among all services defined within in the enclosing WSDL document.

Ports within a service have the following relationship:

- None of the ports communicate with each other (e.g. the output of one port is not the input of another).
- If a service has several ports that share a port type, but employ different bindings or addresses, the ports are alternatives.
- Each port provides semantically equivalent behaviour (within the transport and message format limitations imposed by each binding).

Ports

A port type is a named set of abstract operations and the abstract messages involved.

```
<wsdl:definitions...>
<wsdl:portType name="nmtoken">
<wsdl:operation name="nmtoken".../>
</wsdl:portType>
</wsdl:definitions>
```

The port type name attribute provides a unique name among all port types defined within the enclosing WSDL document.

Operations

An operation is named via the name attribute.

WSDL has four transmission primitives that an endpoint can support:

- One-way. The endpoint receives a message.
- Request-response. The endpoint receives a message, and sends a correlated message.
- Solicit-response. The endpoint sends a message, and receives a correlated message.
- Notification. The endpoint sends a message.

It may be observed that each of the WfMC interactions fits within this model. A service provider can describe his service interface endpoint using the following operation types.

WSDL Operation	Wf-XML Interaction
Request-Response	*Create Process Instance*[4]
	Get Process Instance Data
	Change Process Instance State
Notification	*Process Instance State Changed*
	Notify (outgoing events)
One Way	*Notify* (incoming events)
Solicit Response	Not used[5]

[4] For an example of the use of WSDL to define the Wf-XML "CreateProcessInstance" operation, including SOAP bindings, see the article by Michael Rossi in this publication

[5] There are no defined Wf-XML interactions which use this style of operation. However it could be used for describing event messages where the provider expects a returned correlated object

WSDL also includes definitions of how the various message types are bound to communication paths, including SOAP.

Bindings

A binding defines message format and protocol details for operations and messages defined by a particular portType. There may be any number of bindings for a given portType. WSDL defines a detailed and extensible grammar for describing bindings

The name attribute provides a unique name among all bindings defined within in the enclosing WSDL document.

In particular WSDL includes a binding for SOAP 1.1 endpoints, which supports the specification of the following protocol specific information:

- An indication that a binding is bound to the SOAP 1.1 protocol
- A way of specifying an address for a SOAP endpoint.
- The URI for the SOAPAction HTTP header for the HTTP binding of SOAP
- A list of definitions for Headers that are transmitted as part of the SOAP Envelope
- A way of specifying SOAP roots in XSD

This binding grammar it is not an exhaustive specification and recognises that the use of SOAP bindings is still evolving.

WSDL thus already includes all the necessary structures to describe Wf-XML interactions supported between web services.

However, the relationship between the participating web services (requester / observer and provider) also needs to support the concept of persistent process states that transcend the individual interactions. A provider that can accept certain forced changes of process state or that can report changes of process state needs a way, within the service description, of describing these state-related process characteristics that are of significance in terms of the service interface.

Extensions for Process State Information

WSDL was designed to be extensible and one potential extension is to incorporate this class of information. For the purposes of this article such extensions will be described as Web Service Process Description Language (WSPDL).

Sample WSPDL extensions to cover state related information are provided below. The important principle is that we have separated the internal and external views of a web based workflow (or process-based) application.

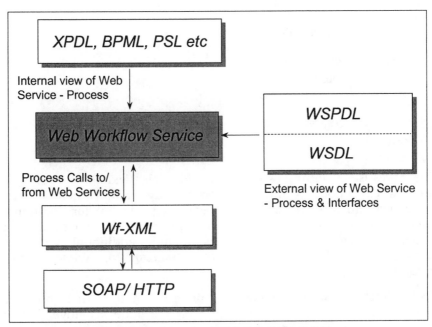

Figure 9—Web Workflow Standards and Relationships

The internal description of the web service is handled through one of the conventional process definition languages, but this is separated from the external definition, which is handled as part of WSDL with appropriate extensions.

The following example provides a view of the potential WSPDL structures that could be developed.

```
<StatesList>
<! This defines a list of valid states that have external visibility. The convention for state names is
a.b.c.d. etc where a is the root state with a substate b, c a sub-state of b, etc. A WfMC set of top
level states is predefined; further sub-states may be added by user specification >
        <Open>
                <Running>
                        <userdefined>

                        ....
                </Running>
                <NotRunning>
                        <Suspended>
                        <userdefined>

                        ....
                        </NotRunning>
        </Open>
        <Closed>
                <Completed>
                        <userdefined>

                        ....
                < AbnormalCompleted>
```

```
            <Terminated>
            <userdefined>
            ....
            </Terminated>
            <Aborted>
                    <userdefined>

                    ....
            </Aborted>
        </Closed>
</StatesList>
```

The StatesList structure provides considerable flexibility. In simple process executions a minimal states usage might include only open.running and closed.completed. However, a requirement for additional user defined substates within open.running is common. For example a supply management process might include additional open.running substates such as .ordervalidation, .stockallocation, .deliveryplanning, .orderdespatch, etc.

The StatesList structure is used within each of the other interface structures that describe operations that are state sensitive – state change commands and reports and event notification

```
<State_Change_Accepted_List>
<!list of state changes which are accepted by the executing process instance and hence may be
used as the argument to a ChangeProcessInstanceState command issued by the initiator resource
>
        <StatesList>

        ...
        </StatesList>
</State_Change_Accepted_List>
```

[Authors Note: this structure could be extended to specify valid state changes accepted according to the current state of the enacted process. For example an initiated process to fulfil a stock order may accept a change of state to amend or cancel the order whilst the process state is "validate order" but would not accept such a change once process state "stock allocated" has been reached. This would require the definition of a further data element associated with each changed state, listing the existing valid states in which the forced change can be accepted. This approach would provide more flexibility but at the expense of a more complex specification.]

```
<State_Change_Reported_list>
<!list of state changes which will be reported to an observer via a *ProcessInstanceStateChanged*
report>
        <StatesList>

        ...
        </StatesList>
```

```
</State_Change_Reported_list>

<Incoming_Notification_List>
<!list of notification events which may be sent to the process instance via an incoming Notify
message>
        <EventName>
                <AffectedObject>
                <ContextData>
                <StatesList>
                <!Optional list of states for which the incoming event is valid; if no list is provided
                the notify message is valid for receipt in all states >

                        ...
                </StatesList>
        </EventName>
</Incoming_Notification_List>

<Outgoing_Notification_List>
<!list of notification events which may be sent to an observer via an outgoing Notify message>
        <EventName>
                <AffectedObject>
                <ContextData>
                <States_List>
                <!Optional list of states from within which the outgoing message may be generated;
                observers may use this information in conjunction with a received
                ProcessInstanceStateChanged report to identify the currently valid set of
                messages which they may receive as observer>

                        ...
                </StatesList>
        </EventName>
</Outgoing_Notification_List>
```

The above XML structures (StatesList, State_Change_Accepted_List, State_Change_Reported_List, Incoming_Notification_List, Outgoing_Notification_List) provide a flexible and extensible approach to defining WSPDL—for process related characteristics of a web service.

Where shared, process-relevant, data is required to be specified as part of the WSPDL, two approaches are possible. The simple approach is to define the data structures inline within the existing WSDL or WSPDL grammar (this is the approach adopted within the above examples). Complex data structures that are used repeatedly, for example in many events or as arguments in multiple process initiation / completion operations may be separately specified within a process relevant data definition. This is already provided within XPDL standard or an alternative set of data definitions built up from XML could equally be used.

Both audit data requirements and other considerations such as security constraints need to be incorporated into the service definition at an appropriate time. By building on standard web services some security capabilities are introduced automatically. More work will need to be undertaken on process specific controls. A foundation for audit specifications already exists but requires rework to address the use of XML and the specific needs within a web services environment.

6. THE OVERALL ARCHITECTURAL MODEL

In developing an overall architecture for collaborative process management there are several important principles that should be met by our choice of standards.

1. The standards should fit together to provide a cohesive framework.
    Clearly selecting XML as a base technology helps in this; however the requirement goes further—the same XML structures should be applicable to different phases of the process lifecycle. The standards for process definition need to reflect the operations that are supported during process execution. The process audit data captured during execution should relate to that specified in the original process definition and will reflect the data exchanged between parties during process execution.

2. Business processes are persistent
    The process model must include state management; this is a fundamental part of a workflow architecture. The extensions described under WSPDL incorporate these concepts, allowing state and state transitions to be specified as part of the overall service

3. Support for distributed processes
    This is a fundamental concept of the e-business environment, needed for EAI, web integration, B2B, B2C, and Trading Frameworks / Hubs, etc. Wf-XML incorporates process execution standards for work transfer within & between organisations. A service distribution model based on web services is also fundamental, allowing the use of WSDL, SOAP and UDDI.

4. Processes must be defined and operate at two levels; those externally visible to the service, describing interactions between organisations, and those internal to the service, representing the internal process structure.

The core XML based standards that make up the architecture can now be seen to fit together in the following diagram.

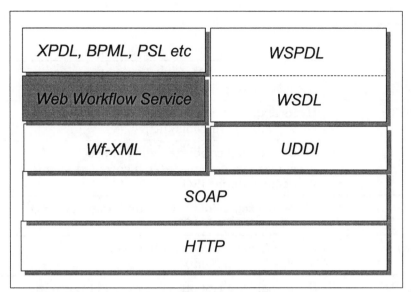

Figure 10—Collaborative Processes—Applicable Standards

The overall business process is distributed as a series of co-operating web workflow services, each service being defined with internal and external characteristic. The entire structure is XML-centric with the upper layers concerned with processing XML data and the lower layers with moving XML content between services.

Externally visible process characteristics are defined using standard web service terminology with extensions for defining process state and its relationship to the distributed process interactions. Process interactions use Wf-XML carried via SOAP / HTTP and are described within WSDL and WSPDL. The internal process definition can follow any of a number of process definition standards since compatibility across services is not a requirement of the architecture.

Overall the model brings together the industry standard web service architecture, the existing workflow architecture defined by the WFMC and the concepts embodied within the original JSA work on interworkflow.

REFERENCES (ALPHABETICAL):

BPML	Business Process Markup Language—see www,bpmi.org
HTTP	Hypertext Transfer Protocol—see www.w3.org/protocols/http
PSL	Process Specification Language—see www.mel.nist.gov/psl/—also accepted as a New Work Item under ISO 18629
SGML	Standardized General Markup Language, ISO standards 8879 & 10774
SOAP	Simple Object Access Protocol—see www.w3.org/tr/soap
UDDI	Universal Description, Discovery & Information (Ariba, IBM & Microsoft)—see www. uddi.org)
WDDX	Web Distributed Data Exchange (Allaire Corporation)see www.wddx.org
Wf-XML	Workflow Standard XML Interoperability Binding —see www. wfmc.org
WSDL	Web Services Definition Language (Copyright Ariba, IBM & Microsoft)—see www.w3.org/tr/wsdl
WSFL	Web Services Flow Language (IBM)—see www.106.ibm.com/developerworks/webservices/library/ws-ref7
XML	Extensible Markup Language—see www.w3.org
XML Protocol	see www.w3.org/protocols/
XPDL	XML Process Definition Language—see www. wfmc.org

Process Management: A Fundamental Component of Successful Web Service Execution

Michael Rossi, Computer Sciences Corporation, Supply Chain Solutions, USA

INTRODUCTION

This paper describes the role of process management in the Web Services environment. While there are several commonly known facets of a Web Service, such as discovery, description and collaboration protocol agreement, one equally important facet is the ability to control the execution of a desired service. Clearly, mechanisms exist today (such as XML/RPC and SOAP) to initiate and receive responses from Web Services. However, such mechanisms are inherently limited when dealing with potentially long-lived processes. They have served a key role in enabling first-generation Web Services, but more value must be added to the Web Services environment in order for it to reach its full potential. Web Services must evolve in their second generation to an environment in which interactions with people are as important as interactions among applications, and in which value-added processes are enabled in addition to simple procedures.

Examples of value-added services include processes such as document preparation, engineering analysis, data mining and report generation. But it is important to recognize that there is a basic distinction between the data-centric transactional services often described today and value-added services such as these that require other forms of interaction. When dealing with potentially long-lived services there must be a way not only to request that the service be initiated, but also to monitor its status, to suspend or terminate its execution on demand, to retrieve its in-process results and to be made aware of its completion. Such a mechanism should also be sufficiently standardized so as to be uniformly accessible by all service requesters. It must be a fundamental part of the Web Services infrastructure.

It is in this capacity that the Workflow Management Coalition's Wf-XML specification can play a vital role. Designed from the outset as a generic process interaction mechanism, this specification supports all the functionality required to enable next-generation Web Service execution. Furthermore, it fits in seamlessly with other essential layers of the Web Services architecture (such as UDDI, WSDL and SOAP) due to its XML based syntax and leverage of existing standards such as HTTP.

THE EVOLUTION OF VALUE-ADDED WEB SERVICES

Before we discuss some of the more detailed aspects of the Wf-XML specification and the Web Services environment, let's take a closer look at some of the ways this combination can enable new value-added functionality. The best way to do this is to first examine what the existing Web Services environment offers. Then we'll discuss some efforts to build on this foundation, and finally we'll describe the benefits of adding Wf-XML to this architecture.

First Generation Web Services

Today's Web Services allow system functionality previously hidden behind a corporate firewall or complex programming interface to be accessed much more easily over the Internet using standardized protocols and data formats, such as HTTP, SOAP and XML. However, these new interfaces are not designed to interact with humans in the way that we've grown accustomed to interacting with the Web via a browser. Instead, they are typically designed to allow systems or applications to interact with one another.

This capability in and of itself is of tremendous value when dealing with Business-to-Business (B2B) commerce and systems integration, since it simplifies and streamlines the process of integrating cross-organizational applications. But as is well known today, B2B interactions are only a piece of the overall commerce puzzle. Business-to-Consumer (B2C) interactions are an equally important component of any successful commercial endeavor. Furthermore, even B2B interfaces could be greatly enhanced if there were some provision for human interaction with (and within) a business process.

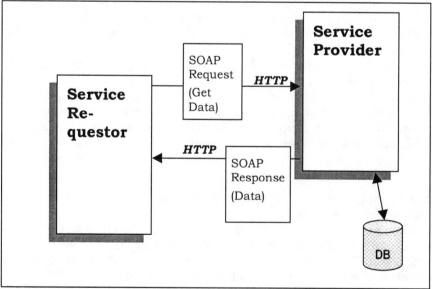

Figure 1: A Typical Web Service

Another characteristic typical of today's Web Services is the integration of simple, well-scoped functions. This is illustrated by the fact that most discussions of Web Services currently focus on examples of things such as stock quote retrieval, ID generation or various simple calculations. As illustrated by Figure 1, most of these services are one-step procedures involving information generation, retrieval or manipulation by a single well-scoped component. They generally don't address processes requiring multiple (possibly iterative and/or parallel) steps that often involve people on the back end as well as the front. They also don't account for activities where the requestor may wish to obtain the status of a process during its execution, or to suspend, terminate or update it during its execution.

Enhancements Underway

It is for these reasons that some organizations are beginning to recognize the need for enhancements to the Web Services environment as we know it. It is believed that one of these necessary enhancements is the addition of a (human) user interface component. This requirement is being seen most urgently by portal software vendors as they strive to bring access to Web Services to their users through the same browser-based interface already used for their other data and applications.

Now it's certainly very tempting to assume that the common unmodified Web browser can be used as this interface to Web Services, since it is an existing means of user interaction with the Web in general. But today's Web browsers aren't designed to interact with the types of applications supported by Web Services without some help. They can of course be made to do so, as demonstrated by the many e-Commerce applications currently available. But this generally requires extensive development by specialized programmers using any of a variety of somewhat proprietary languages, architectures or third-party applications. This approach doesn't fit easily or well into the Web Services environment, and so efforts are underway to provide a more uniform, standardized approach to developing a suitable user interface mechanism for these services.

An example of such an effort is the Web Services User Interface (WSUI) initiative (http://www.wsui.org). This effort aims to provide interactive access to Web Services using a standardized framework built on the same core technologies on which Web Services themselves are built: XML, XSLT, SOAP and HTTP, among others. Another specification offering great potential for building user interfaces to Web Services is the XForms recommendation (http://www.w3.org/MarkUp/Forms) from the World Wide Web Consortium (W3C). This specification will allow data-gathering interfaces to be built using the same core technologies. Still other XML based user interface development languages that may end up serving some type of Web Service duty include the eXtensible User-interface Language (XUL—http://www.mozilla.org) used in the

Mozilla/Netscape browser and the User Interface Markup Language (UIML—http://www.uiml.org). Some of these user interface efforts may in fact utilize existing Web browsers as their primary user agents. But they will allow these agents to be extended to interact with Web Services using a fairly simple, common, interoperable approach.

Still, even with the addition of a user interface to address consumer interaction, the Web Services environment will be inadequate for long lived, value-added services without further enhancement because it will still lack a means of controlling requested processes. In a B2C environment this control can provide the consumer with a much more robust interface, and in a B2B environment it can provide your company and trading partners with much greater flexibility.

Take for example the process of providing editorial services such as proofreading, fact checking or style guidance to an author or publishing company. It could be of great benefit to an independent author, start-up or specialty publishing shop to outsource these services if there were some efficient means of doing so available. However a traditional manual process could never be efficient enough to warrant this type of service. And the complexity of such a task doesn't fit well into the single operation style of Web Services currently available. This is because the publisher would need to do the following things (at a minimum):

- Initiate the request once the content has been authored, which includes transferring the content to the editorial service
- Monitor the editorial progress for overall status and schedule conformance
- Be notified of events in the process that may require synchronization or further input from the publisher
- Suspend or terminate the editorial process if changes occur during execution
- Be notified when the process has been completed, which includes transferring the finalized content (and any annotations, supplements, etc.) back from the editorial service.

While the addition of a user interface to first generation Web Services would allow the initiator of this process to perform some of these steps (probably just the first and last), the level of process management required here could not be easily accommodated. Certainly, these steps could not be accomplished in any open, standard fashion. Furthermore, in a more realistic scenario additional tracking, auditing and analysis requirements may need to be supported to facilitate the process optimization features of a full-featured BPMS.

The Next Step

Most, if not all of these requirements can be met by an implementation of the Wf-XML specification today. And adapting that implementation to the Web Services environment is simply a matter of describing and exposing it according to Web Service standards such as WSDL and UDDI.

We'll see in more detail a bit later how Wf-XML enabled processes can be described as Web Services. But first let us consider more closely some of the capabilities required by these types of processes. One of the more important functions described above is the ability to monitor the progress of a remote process. Unlike the simpler services common in today's environment, value-added Web Services will need to be enacted by long duration multi-step processes. Often, it will be necessary to monitor these processes during their execution, possibly retrieving in-progress results for interim inspections.

As an example, let's consider a large scale manufacturing enterprise. As part of such a company's normal operations, detailed engineering analyses are frequently required to determine the suitability of various components to a given purpose, as they must meet certain tolerances, dimensions and other specifications. The development of this analysis requires (minimally):

- Accessing the product data for the specified component, possibly resident in a legacy application or commercial PDM system
- Verification of all relevant specifications
- Gathering of actual product metrics/measurements
- Generation of the appropriate engineering reports
- Review of all final data by QA and other team members

In many cases, these analyses must be provided to a third party regulatory agency as well. Given that these tasks require specialized knowledge that may be difficult to attain in-house, the manufacturer wishes to outsource the engineering analysis to a specialty service provider.

In the current Web Services environment the manufacturer could easily initiate this service with a pre-selected provider, but it would have no visibility into the execution of the process. Not to mention that the provider would have to make special arrangements for delivery of the resultant analyses, since the simple procedure calls available in the current environment would be insufficient for such an asynchronous process. However, a Wf-XML based interaction with such a provider would allow the service requestor to query the provider for status and in-progress data as necessary during the analysis period. This information can also be passed on to a third party oversight organization if necessary, allowing full visibility into all stages of the manufacturing process by all involved parties in real time.

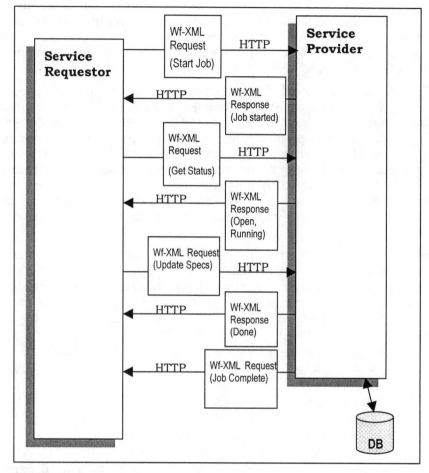

Figure 2: A Sample Wf-XML Enabled Web Service

In addition to this monitoring capability, a Wf-XML based service would allow the process to be synchronized with ongoing events when necessary, as shown in Figure 2. To continue with the current example, if a specified tolerance or capacity requirement had been changed while the component was under analysis, the manufacturer would be able to update the engineering provider with the current specifications via the Wf-XML based Web Service interface. Finally, the resultant analyses could be delivered to the manufacturer along with the process completion notification via the same Wf-XML based interface.

As you can see, these capabilities are especially valuable when dealing with multi-step human interactive processes. However, they can be of equal importance in a non-interactive environment such as that typically found in the area of systems integration. There has for some time now been a trend toward utilizing process management techniques to integrate systems and build composite applications due to the realization that such systems can derive great benefits from a process-oriented approach.

For example, it becomes much easier to respond to requirement changes in an integrated system when each component is treated as an individual task in a process. In addition, process management techniques add value to the system by allowing for greater monitoring and analysis capabilities than those typically achievable with more traditional distributed object systems. They also help to separate the business logic of an application from the component tasks, providing a more service-oriented architecture.

Wf-XML enabled Web Services allow these techniques to be implemented over the Internet via XML messaging. Again, systems can be chained together using first generation Web Services built on SOAP or other RPC mechanisms. But adding Wf-XML to the underlying Web services architecture adds a measure of process control to the integrated application, allowing it to be monitored, controlled, audited and analyzed as a functional whole. This capability adds value to the Web Services messaging layer by standardizing a process control layer above it.

A Natural Fit

Now that we've discussed some of the potential benefits of using Wf-XML with Web Services, let's take a look at how this can be done in practice. When one surveys the landscape of XML-based standards and specifications available today, the sheer breadth of their scope can cause doubt regarding their possible effectiveness. And while it is true that there can be some overlap among these specifications, there are many cases in which they can be brought together quite effectively to meet various goals. Such is the case with Wf-XML and a variety of specifications that currently exist in the Web Services world and various vertical industries.

The primary specifications that currently form the foundation for Web Services are:

- XML—the base format (syntax) for all data interchange
- SOAP—the fundamental messaging syntax for communication among applications
- WSDL—the format for describing the purpose of, and means of interacting with, a given Web Service
- UDDI—the registry/repository for Web Services, allowing applications to be found and interactions to be initiated

Since Web Services are built on XML based specifications such as these, there are numerous other specifications that can be used to implement them, such as XSLT, XLink, XPath/XPointer, DOM/SAX, etc. However, these specifications are generally even further "behind the scenes" then the primary technologies mentioned above, as they are used to process data rather than represent it. So they don't actually add any complexity to the standards picture, rather they improve it for developers.

Wf-XML fits quite easily into this core Web Services specification stack between SOAP and WSDL. Given that it is itself an XML based specification it is interoperable with all current XML processing methods and mechanisms. Furthermore, beginning with version 2.0 it utilizes SOAP as its messaging foundation. That is to say that the "envelope" used for routing and other basic communication semantics among applications is defined by the SOAP protocol. This foundation provides the benefit of easing integration with Web Services, but it also allows related mechanisms to be used in support of requirements such as security and file transfer.

For example, a service with strong security requirements may wish to ensure that all requests are properly authorized and all data is signed and encrypted during transfer. Since a Wf-XML enabled Web Service is based on XML, SOAP and common transfer protocols such as HTTP, available mechanisms such as XML Digital Signature (DSIG), Secure Sockets Layer (SSL) and PKI can be used to make it more secure. Also, if multiple file attachments need to be transferred along with the message, the SOAP with Attachments provisions can be used to accommodate this situation.

As noted above, in addition to these capabilities Wf-XML adds a layer of process control semantics to the SOAP envelope structure. Once this new Wf-XML enabled service is created it can be described by a WSDL document in the same way as any other traditional Web Service. Finally, the Web Service can be discovered using the UDDI registry, at which point one of the available bindings from the WSDL description can be used to initiate an interaction.

This is still only a partial implementation however, since Wf-XML does not (and can not) standardize the representation of the particular data required for any given process. This is known as context-specific data in Wf-XML and although its representation is not standardized, it can be accommodated by a Wf-XML message. This context-specific data may be marked up as appropriate for the application that is to process it.

For example, it may be necessary to develop a custom format for the data or there may be a suitable vertical industry specification available to represent it, such as CXML, xCBL, fpML, cl-xml, etc. Whatever the markup vocabulary, this context-specific data would be carried as the ultimate payload of a Wf-XML message in a placeholder designed for that purpose. In this way, a Wf-XML message can be combined with both Web Services protocols and vertical industry specifications to allow domain specific data to be exchanged between Web Services in a process managed environment compatible with all existing XML processing technologies.

IMPLEMENTATION DETAILS

Seeing the apparent complexity of the multitude of data format specifications involved in this scenario, it's natural to think that it would be very difficult to develop such an application or integrated system. In reality though, there are other factors that diminish this complexity. To begin, composite applications or integrated systems built using Wf-XML enabled Web Services are fundamentally service-oriented architectures and rely on the same principles of component based development with which many application architects are already familiar. Furthermore, there are already tool sets and development kits commonly available that support the development of SOAP and XML based applications as Web Services. These Integrated Development Environments (IDEs) shield developers from some of the more arcane aspects of working with this type of data, allowing them to focus on the business logic of the application. Finally, once appropriate Wf-XML enabled components have been built, GUI-based business process modeling tools can be used to define the distributed process, tying the various components together to form a higher-level service.

But to illustrate the relative simplicity of the service interface definitions themselves, let's examine some of the details of the data formats involved. The foundation of our new services will be the same as that found in first generation Web Services, namely SOAP. Therefore the same envelope, header and body structure prescribed by the SOAP specification will form the basis of Wf-XML enabled Web Services. This structure appears as illustrated by example 1.

Example 1:

```
<?xml version="1.0"?>
<SOAP-ENV:Envelope xmlns:SOAP-
ENV="http://schemas.xmlsoap.org/soap/envelope">
    <SOAP-ENV:Header>
    </SOAP-ENV:Header>
    <SOAP-ENV:Body>
    </SOAP-ENV:Body>
</SOAP-ENV:Envelope>
```

Within this SOAP enveloping structure lie the Wf-XML protocol elements. The Wf-XML specification defines operations that may be performed by a resource, with each operation being represented by an element type in a Wf-XML message. The children (sub-elements) of these operation elements represent various parameters that are input to or output from the operation. Wf-XML currently only specifies a handful of basic operations (four to be specific) required for interoperability: CreateProcessInstance, GetProcessInstanceData, ChangeProcessInstanceState and ProcessInstanceStateChanged. Some other convenience operations are specified, but may not be necessary in many cases. Example 2 illustrates a Wf-XML operation embedded in a SOAP envelope (assuming HTTP as the transfer protocol).

Example 2:

```
POST /SOAP-Processor HTTP/1.1
Host: www.exampleco.com
Content-Type: text/xml; charset="utf-8"
Content-Length: nnn
SOAPAction: "http://www.exampleco.com/Wf-XML"
<?xml version="1.0"?>
<SOAP-ENV:Envelope
 SOAP-ENV:encodingStyle="http://www.wfmc.org/standards/docs/Wf-XML"
 xmlns:SOAP-ENV="http://schemas.xmlsoap.org/soap/envelope"
 xmlns:wf="http://www.wfmc.org/standards/docs/Wf-XML">
     <SOAP-ENV:Header>
         <wf:Request wf:ResponseRequired="Yes" SOAP-ENV:mustUnderstand="1"/>
         <wf:Key SOAP-ENV:mustUnderstand="1">
             http://www.exampleco.com/processes/86947325
         </wf:Key>
     </SOAP-ENV:Header>
     <SOAP-ENV:Body>
         <wf:WfMessage xmlns="http://www.wfmc.org/standards/docs/Wf-XML">
             <CreateProcessInstance.Request>
             <ObserverKey>http://www.myco.com/purchasing/orders</ObserverKey>
                 <ContextData/>
             </CreateProcessInstance.Request>
         </wf:WfMessage>
     </SOAP-ENV:Body>
</SOAP-ENV:Envelope>
```

Note that the "SOAP-ENV:encodingStyle" attribute has been set on the root element to indicate that the SOAP header entries and the SOAP body (payload) are encoded according to the rules of the Wf-XML specification. Intermingling these protocols in this fashion allows standard SOAP and Web Service development toolkits to be leveraged in the creation of Wf-XML enabled Web Services and provides a familiar approach for those already accustomed to building these services. The SOAP processor will route the appropriate process management data onto the Wf-XML application specified by the "SOAPAction" HTTP header field. Responses to operations requested in this manner will be similarly encoded per the SOAP and Wf-XML specifications.

Now that the messaging interface has been defined, the Web Service can be made accessible to other applications via a WSDL description and a UDDI registration. A partial sample of such a WSDL description appears in example 3.

Example 3:

```xml
<?xml version="1.0"?>
<definitions name="Wf-XML"
targetNamespace ="http://www.exampleco.com/Wf-XML-Desc"
  xmlns:tns="http://www.exampleco.com/Wf-XML-Desc"
  xmls:wf="http://www.wfmc.org/standards/docs/Wf-XML"
  xmlns:soap="http://schemas.xmlsoap.org/wsdl/soap/"
  xmlns="http://schemas.xmlsoap.org/wsdl/">
    <import namespace="http://www.wfmc.org/standards/docs/Wf-XML"
              location="http://www.wfmc.org/standards/docs/Wf-XML/Wf-XML-20.xsd">
    <message name="CreateProcessInstanceInput">
        <part name="main" element="wf:CreateProcessInstance.Request"/>
        <part name="Observer" element="wf:ObserverKey"/>
        <part name="InputData" element="wf:ContextData"/>
    </message>
    <message name="CreateProcessInstanceOutput">
        <part name="main" element="wf:CreateProcessInstance.Response"/>
        <part name="InstanceID" element="wf:ProcessInstanceKey"/>
    </message>
    <portType name="Wf-XMLPortType">
        <operation name="CreateProcessInstance">
            <input message="tns:CreateProcessInstanceInput"/>
            <output message="tns:CreateProcessInstanceOutput"/>
        </operation>
    </portType>
    <binding name="Wf-XMLSoapBinding" type="Wf-XMLPortType">
        <soap:binding style="document"
            transport="http://schemas.xmlsoap.org/soap/http"/>
        <operation name="CreateProcessInstance">
            <soap:operation soapAction="http://www.exampleco.com/Wf-XML"/>
            <input>
                <soap:body use="literal"/>
            </input>
            <output>
                <soap:body use="literal"/>
            </output>
        </operation>
    </binding>
    <service name="ExampleCoEngAnalysis">
        <documentation>This service provides engineering analyses based on the se-
lected process and the input data provided.</documentation>
        <port name="Wf-XMLPort" binding="Wf-XMLSoapBinding">
            <soap:address location="http://www.exampleco.com/Wf-XML"/>
        </port>
    </service>
</definitions>
```

Although these descriptions may seem somewhat verbose they are easily created with a suitable toolkit. Once a complete service description is available your Wf-XML enabled Web Service is ready to be registered in a UDDI repository and found by those wishing to utilize it.

ENABLING INNOVATION

As we've now seen, Wf-XML enabled Web Services are a natural evolutionary step in the advancement of this critical technology. And yet, the scenarios depicted here are a somewhat modest leap of technological innovation. If we begin to think "outside the box", it starts to become readily apparent that there are numerous applications of this technology beyond the more traditional types of services with which we commonly associate it. In fact, just as the advent of Web Services has made us re-evaluate the way we approach these traditional services, perhaps this evolution of the Web Services environment should provoke us to rethink our approach to other types of processes.

This leads to many potential alternatives for implementing processes and solutions for which the current implementation mechanisms are taken for granted as being adequate, or even optimal. As a sampling of ideas, let's consider a few examples of current technology such as distributed/federated processing, supply-chain management and multi-threading.

Distributed Computing

One of the hotter technologies in wide use today is distributed computing. In large-scale enterprise systems this technology is often manifested in the form of distributed, or alternatively federated, database management systems. In other environments such as the Internet, distributed computing is often used to segregate large computing-intensive tasks among users' home PCs. However, in both of these environments the state of distributed computing is essentially the same as that of the first generation Web Services environment. It is highly effective for invoking single operation tasks, but lacks any process management capability.

One can certainly imagine the benefits of adding process management capabilities to these environments, using a distributed process management platform such as Wf-XML enabled Web Services. For example, let's consider some popular distributed projects such as those that search for alien life, try to find a cure for cancer or crack encryption algorithms. These efforts currently rely on an individual resource to perform all the required processing of a particular data set, encapsulating all the processing logic in some piece of client code resident on the resource. This model demonstrates some limitations when the processing logic needs to be changed, as the client code needs to be updated. There are also limitations associated with the interaction between the client and server. Using the capabilities described above, each resource participating in the effort could be assigned specific tasks or sub-processes dynamically based on the current workload. Work could also be assigned to the most suitable resources based on the resources' predetermined capabilities. Finally, it would be possible to enable more dynamic interactions between the client and server.

Supply Chain Management

Similar, while possibly more subtle advancements, can be achieved in areas such as supply-chain management and other trading partner scenarios. In these cases, there may or may not already be some level of process management employed. However, the ease with which these solutions can be developed, and the level of openness and interoperability that they can achieve would certainly be enhanced by the next generation of Web Services as well.

In many of today's online marketplaces and "value-chain" environments some form of systems integration and process management is required to provide useful connectivity between participants. But this integration is commonly accomplished using either proprietary data formats and protocols or complex EDI specifications requiring highly specialized skills. In some more advanced environments first generation Web Services may be employed to support more open standardized protocols, while simplifying the implementation. However, a value chain based on first generation Web Services doesn't support the full range of interactions possible with Wf-XML enabled Web Services. As discussed earlier, the business process control and monitoring capabilities provided by Wf-XML add even more value to the value-chain.

Multi-Threading

To elaborate on our final example we need to consider our interpretation of the term "process." So far we've mostly been considering processes in the sense of workflow—a series of steps usually enacted at least in part by humans. But a process is more generically considered just an ordered set of steps required to accomplish a goal. This is why the applications that run on our computers are internally represented as "processes." And Wf-XML was in fact designed as a means of interaction among processes in this more generic sense.

However, just as the limits of individual processes were reached in traditional computing, requiring new techniques to enable greater scalability, those limits will inevitably be reached in the Web Services environment as well. For this reason it will inevitably make sense to apply process management techniques similar to those used in traditional computing environments to the Web Services environment. One example of such a technique is multi-threading. Applying this concept to Web Services may result in a "distributed multi-threaded" environment in which related components resident on multiple heterogeneous systems work in concert not only to execute a single task, but to perform various roles in an application. In this way the full power of a distributed process can be realized.

A process management capable, distributed platform such as Wf-XML enabled Web Services can provide the necessary framework in which these new techniques can be developed. To a limited extent there already exists some support for these more advanced capabilities, given that Wf-XML currently supports the ability to synchronize the execution of multiple simultaneous tasks based on the dynamic occurrence of events. Of course some realignment of these techniques may be required to properly adapt them for use on the Web. But as the scalability requirements of the Web begin to have an impact on the Web Services environment, the robustness and flexibility facilitated by such techniques will become evident.

USE AS PRESCRIBED

So far we've discussed the many potential benefits of combining the process management capabilities of Wf-XML with Web Services, shown how easily these technologies can work together to achieve these benefits and thought about new ways of applying the technology. So it would only seem practical to put these capabilities into perspective. Used properly and for the right purpose, the specifications we've discussed can be a great asset. But there are certainly applications where they are not well suited, or are insufficient in and of themselves. Fortunately, in many cases complementary technologies can be used in conjunction with Wf-XML enabled Web Services to meet more stringent requirements.

A case in point is the implementation of Web Services in more transaction-oriented applications. Transactional environments such as Financial Management and Data Warehousing typically require more robust control over process execution in order to perform operations such as two-phase commits and compensating actions. While a well-designed process can certainly accommodate this functionality to some extent, there are dedicated efforts focused on meeting these specific requirements more explicitly. In keeping with the theme of Web Services and XML-based specifications, two examples of such efforts are notable: XAML and XLang. These specifications have been developed by teams familiar with transactional requirements to provide support specifically for these capabilities. So in cases where this type of support is a strong requirement, Wf-XML enabled Web Services alone may be insufficient and it would be more practical to use them in conjunction with other specifications such as these to meet all of an application's requirements.

In similar ways Wf-XML enabled Web Services can be used in conjunction with various other horizontal specifications tailored to a particular field. For example, the RosettaNet specifications for Partner Interface Processes (PIPs) can be enacted in a distributed Web environment via Wf-XML enabled Web Services. In the case of ebXML, Message Handlers can be used to interchange Wf-XML messages carrying payloads specific to the business process being executed. Many of these types of specifications add value to Web Services in addition to that provided by Wf-XML, helping to meet the requirements of all but the most unique environments.

SUMMARY

In conclusion, it is clear that the capabilities provided by the current Web Services environment are a vast improvement over previous approaches to web-enabling applications. If not for the new capabilities they can provide, then at least for the level of openness, standardization and ease of implementation that they offer. However, there are clear limitations in this environment that can be overcome by an additional layer of process management. Wf-XML adds the value of process management to the Web Services environment, and does so in an easily approachable way that can easily coexist with currently available tools and software development kits.

This new type of Web Service can be combined with other value-added horizontal specifications to accommodate specific application requirements, and can carry vertical industry specification payloads to support specific business processes. There are numerous ways this technology can be applied to create innovative new applications, and burgeoning efforts underway to create user interfaces to these services can only enhance those possibilities. Wf-XML certainly doesn't meet all the requirements for every application (its no panacea), but it does meet some very important requirements for enabling the next generation of Web Services.

Business Process Technology: From EAI and Workflow to BPM

Mike Marin, FileNET Corporation, USA

INTRODUCTION

Business process technology goes from simple component assembly to very complex workflow technology. The challenge for an organization is to classify the technology, and apply it to the right problem space. In today's business environments, problems often require the integration of several process technologies to address different areas of the complex problems faced by the organization. This chapter describes and classifies the different types of business process technology, and defines business process management (BPM).

The term business process technology encompasses workflow, BPM, and similar technologies. On the surface, these technologies seem to be the same. Reading their definitions does not help, because they try to solve the same problem. Their differentiation lies deep in their architecture and applicability.

In the past few years there had been attempts, by some vendors, to differentiate between BPM and workflow technology. Workflow vendors and practitioners insist that BPM is another acronym for workflow, but some vendors insist that BPM is new technology very different from workflow, and some analysts agree. In fact, there are three different views on this topic coming from workflow practitioners, BPM vendors, and analysts. In order to reconcile the different views, we first need to understand the evolution of enterprise application integration (EAI) that forced EAI vendors into process technology.

Enterprise Application Integration

Traditionally EAI technology does not include process technology, but the evolution of EAI technology coupled with competitive pressures and the Internet has forced EAI vendors to provide process technology. This has yielded a peculiar type of technology that has been called BPM by EAI vendors. However, as we will present latter, BPM requires much more than just EAI process technology.

Traditional EAI has used a hub-and-spoke architecture to solve the integration problem. Hub-and-spoke architectures are common, because coupled with adaptors (for each third party or legacy application) that can be plugged into the architecture, they reduce the integration problem from a point-to-point integration requiring $(n*(n-1))/2$ connections (shown in figure 1), to a centralized integration requiring n connections (shown in figure 2).

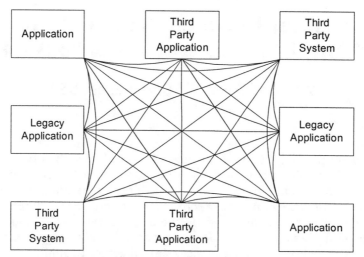

Figure 1—point-to-point integration

The EAI hub-and-spoke technology has been very successful in solving the integration problems of large organizations. EAI allow users to map fields and structures from one application into another application using simple and visual tools. The EAI engine located in an integration server then executes the mapping every time it is required. The mapping is normally triggered by an event from the originating application or system.

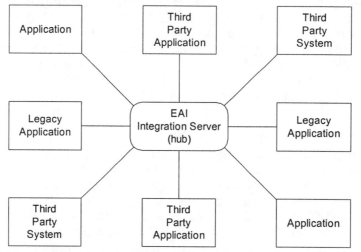

Figure 2—hub-and-spoke integration

An example of a traditional integration project includes inserting, updating, or deleting customer information in various legacy and third party applications. Under this scenario, every time you update a customer record, all the affected systems and applications in your organization will be updated. There is no process involved, it is mainly event driven; something happens in an application and it should be propagated to other applications and systems. Complexity arises because each application requires different fields and uses different codes and data types. EAI products hide that complexity, simplify the integration task, and allow for very complex integrations.

The next level of functionality for EAI tools is the ability to tie together sets of integrations into sequences, or flows of integrations. The flows of integrations then require conditional and parallel execution. This evolves into process technology that coordinates the low level integrations. The end result can be called EAI Process technology.

The Internet and the evolution of Business-to-Business (B2B) applications did bring new integration challenges that were solved by most EAI vendors by adding some kind of trading partner module. This extended the EAI's hub-and-spoke architecture in a natural way, by adding a specialized adapter with very sophisticated B2B functionality.

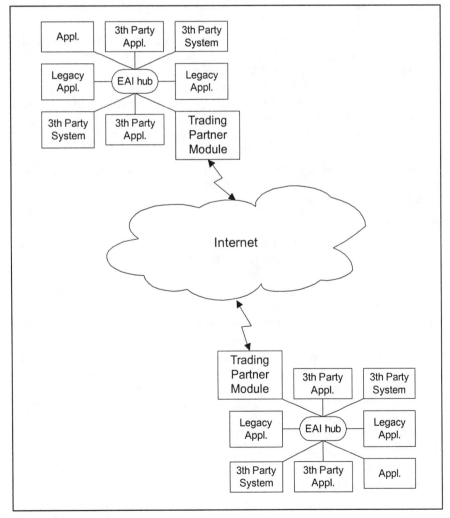

Figure 3—EAI B2B solution

Using this approach, B2B integrations are reduced to the EAI framework by correctly configuring the trading partner module, and treating it as another application. However, B2B semantics are in general much more complex, and so this simple mapping may not be sufficient to handle them. For example, the number of exceptions and invalid values is greater in B2B systems than with internal systems and applications. The extra complexity introduced by the B2B environments, and the need to handle a potentially large number of exceptions, can be handled by the EAI process technology.

The ability of process technology to handle exceptions is not limited to the B2B environment; it is also useful in traditional EAI projects where, of course, exceptions also occur. But process technology does not need to be confined to processing exceptions or sequences of integrations. Process technology nicely complements EAI technology, by providing the ability of taking independent integrations and combining them into higher-level processes.

The process technology resulting of this evolution differs from the process technology implemented by traditional workflow vendors, because it is based on the EAI infrastructure. EAI process technology is applicable for very short-lived processes, in which the process engine pushes the data from application to application, and in most cases there is no human intervention. Typical EAI process lifespan is measured in seconds or minutes, versus typical workflow process that are measured in days, or months.

An EAI vendor will equate BPM with EAI process technology, and may add B2B to complete the concept. However, BPM requires more than just EAI technology.

Workflow

Workflow technology has been process technology from its inception. The Workflow Management Coalition's glossary defines workflow as "*The automation of a business process, in whole or part, during which documents, information or tasks are passed from one participant to another for action, according to a set of procedural rules.*" From a workflow perspective, a participant can be a human, an application, a machine, or another process or workflow engine.

Workflow has evolved from a departmental tool used to solve small business process within a single department, into an enterprise technology. The technology has also evolved to address the Internet and B2B requirements. The end result is very sophisticated products able to define and manage process within the enterprise and into the more dynamic web and B2B environments.

Today, mature workflow products are able to solve very complex business processes, within the enterprise and between enterprises. In general, workflow products provide good tools and applications for humans to participate in the process, and interfaces to integrate applications and external systems into the process. For most products, EAI processes provided better application integration into the process than workflow products, and workflow products provide better interaction of human participants than EAI processes.

A workflow practitioner will equate BPM with workflow, and will argue that workflow has been evolving for years into a mature industry that have solved all the BPM requirements.

Analysts Perspective on BPM

Some analysts, today, make a distinction between BPM and workflow. However, their distinction is not based on the EAI versus workflow evolution or architecture. Their distinction is based on the management aspect of Business Process Management (BPM). They place more emphasis on management and business than on process. This emphasizes the business applicability of BPM, instead of the technological solution.

They are trying to avoid the perceived problems associated with business process reengineering (BPR), in which processes are analyzed, improved, re-implemented, and then forgotten. Although today's BPR tools allow for continue process monitoring, in the past, most BPR projects were focused on a one-time reengineering of a process.

Customers, say the analysts, should favor process technology that makes it easy to manage the process from a business perspective. Every process product provides either a process languages or visual process modeling tools that makes it easy to define the process. However, as analyst point out, more time is expended managing the process than defining it. Defining the process is the easy part, managing it is the key part of BPM and tools that does not support the business management aspect should not be considered BPM tools.

Process management goes all the way from the ability to version and document the process to the ability to analyze, control, and modify all parts of the running processes. Process management should not be confused with system administration. Good process technology should provide both system administration and process management tools. System administration tools allow users to fine-tune their process engine. These are tools for system administrators to monitor system resources, and to help with load balancing.

Business process management tools, on the other hand, are more than just process management or system administration tools, they adds business context. These are tools for the business user to understand, analyze, monitor, and improve the processes from a business perspective. These tools are not for the IT developer. The ability to correlate the process information with other business data, like cost, becomes extremely important. The business user should be able to monitor process bottlenecks, ROI, and other business related measurements. They require analytical tools that allow them to manipulate and study the data being collected from running processes, as well as historical data.

Process management is not confined to a single instance of a process, but to be able to manage all the process of a certain type, for example, claim processes. The business user should be able to study the claim process from historical or current data; he should be able to produce cost, or other business measurement, reports and graphs. He would like to "slice and dice" the information and measurements to produce business charts or reports. He should be able to analyze and compare the data or business measurements based on the different types of claims.

The ability to manipulate process definitions as documents that can be versioned and stored in a process repository allows the management of the process definitions as assets of the organization. If the process definitions documents are XML documents based on a process definition standard like XPDL, then third party tools can manipulate them. If in addition the process repository is XML-aware, then it can allow for extremely powerful queries and manipulation of the process definitions.

Simulation and forecasting are also important management tools, but may not be required for a product to be considered BPM. At a minimum, BPM products should provide analytical tools for the business user. Therefore, some analysts will say, if a product does not provide the ability to manage the processes from a business perspective, it should not be categorized as a BPM product. Under this definition some workflow products and EAI process products cannot be considered BPM tools.

CLASSIFYING PROCESS TECHNOLOGY

Over the years, there had been several attempts to classify workflow products based on the role the implemented processes plays in the organization. Most analysts have classified workflow products into production, administrative, collaborative, and ad-hoc. Today with processes spanning organizations and playing in a B2B environment, this classification is inadequate.

In order to delimit the BPM space, at least three different views of the process space are required. First, processes can be classified based on the process duration, which determines the infrastructure required to host the process. Second, processes can be classified based on organizational boundaries. Third, process management functionality should be considered.

Classification by Process Duration

Figure 4 classifies process technologies based on their typical process lifespan. It turns out that the average process lifespan determines the type of architecture required to implement the process engine. Very short-lived processes, that must last seconds, imposes different constraints to the process engine from those imposed for long-lived process in which persistency is important.

It can be argued that both extremes, component assembly and life-cycle, are outside of the process technology scope. However, they share some process functionality and are helpful in delimiting the technology.

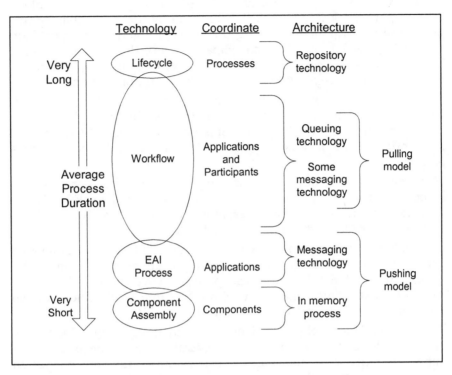

Figure 4—Process technology

Component assembly is a technology that allows the coordination and invocation of components from a centralized engine. Components are low level objects (COM, Java objects, CORBA objects, etc.). Process activities on this technology correspond to instantiation or method invocation in a particular object. It uses a pushing model to advance the process, which is normally very short-lived.

EAI process technology takes advantage of the EAI infrastructure to implement a process engine. This allows for the definition and execution of processes in which the activities are the invocation of application or system APIs. Processes are normally short-lived and the process engine uses a pushing model to advance the process.

EAI technology is normally based on a messaging architecture, and so, the process engine takes advantage of that infrastructure. The addition of a trading partner module to the EAI architecture allows the process engine to execute a B2B process.

The EAI expertise is integration, and this is reflected in the process engine. These engines are very effective when process activities are implemented by calling third party applications, systems, or legacy system. They are not very good at integrating people into the processes, because the engine is designed to handle short-lived processes in which data persistency is pushed into the applications that are invoked during the process. Therefore, the engine does not provide the infrastructure required to support slow human processing.

Workflow technology is normally based in a queuing technology used to park work items until they are pull by the participant or application in charge of completing the activity. For the most part this is a pulling model, in which participants query the engine for work. However, workflow engines, under certain circumstances, may use a pushing model, for example when launching an application.

In workflow terminology a participant is not limited to humans. A participant can be an application, another workflow engine, a machine, or a human. Workflow systems do provide out-of-the-box applications for the process engine to interact with human participants.

Workflow products may use messaging technology, but normally not in combination with adaptors or connectors, as does EAI. Those workflow products that use messaging technology simplify the integration with EAI tools and process technology.

Lifecycle technology allows users to define very long-lived processes that are centered around a document or an object. In fact, the document or object becomes the process. Lifecycle can be represented by a state machine, because it refers to a single object and so there is no parallelism associated with it.

For example, a loan object or document may have a defined lifecycle. The lifecycle for the loan may have several states: in negotiation, in approval, active, and then paid. In this example, the loan may be in the active stage for 30 years or more, and then it may be in the paid stage for another five to ten years, before it is disposed.

Lifecycle normally controls which processes can be applied to the object or document. For example, a delinquent process cannot be executed in a negotiation state, but it may be used when the load is in the active state.

Classification by Organizational Boundaries

In a B2B environment, a simple way to classify processes is based on the relationship with the hosting organization. This type of classification has been implicitly used by standard organizations to delimit their process technology standardization. Figure 5 shows that classification schema.

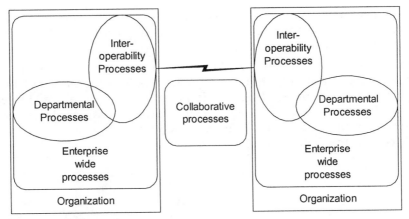

Figure 5—Types of processes

Departmental processes were the first type of processes implemented by workflow systems. They are confined to a particular department within the organization. All workflow products will handle this type of processes.

Enterprise wide processes are those expanding several departments and in some cases require the use of EAI technology. Depending on the complexity of the process, they can be addressed by EAI process technology, workflow technology, or more likely a combination of both.

Interoperability processes are those processes that expose internal processes outside the organization or department. Sometimes they require a B2B infrastructure. Both workflow and EAI process technologies can be used for interoperability. The decision will depend on which product provides better B2B support or integration.

Collaborative processes are definitions of how concurrent interoperability processes interact. This type of specification is not necessarily executable per se, but it defines a contract between two or more interoperability processes on the order in which their communications should take place. The term process choreography is sometime used instead of collaborative process.

Collaborative process should not be confused with the old term of collaborative workflow. Collaborative workflow was used to describe a workflow product that provides tools and facilities for human participants to collaborate on the solution to a particular problem.

Process Management Functionality

There are two aspects of process management, process definition management, and process execution management. Process definition management has to do with the storage and management of the different versions of a process definition. Process execution management is the ability to monitor and modify executing processes.

Processes are at the heart of any organization, the efforts spent analyzing, implementing, and optimizing those process produces valuable knowledge about the organization. The resulting process definition and corresponding documentation are valuable assets that describe how the organization operates. It is important for the organization to manage those assets.

Process management functionality is not a continuum, because it is composed of many different features and tools, which are not built one in top of the other. Figure 6 is an attempt to organize the features of process definition management and process analysis management, into a scale. Basic features went into the center with advanced features going into the extremes.

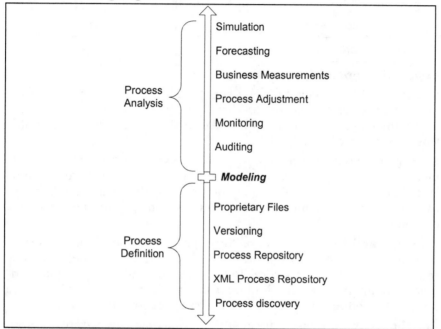

Figure 6—Process Management Space

Most process products provide the ability to define the processes in an authoring or modeling environment. Some very basic products do process definition via a scripting language. As described before, the resulting process definition should be considered an asset of the organization. Therefore, it is important for the organization to be able to manage those process definitions. Some of the capabilities provided by products to manage process definitions are the following:

- **Files**. Most products have a way to dump the product definition into a file. In some basic products that may be the only facility they provide to manage the process definitions. For most products the files are proprietary, although some products will generate files based on some standard, like XPDL. At this level of functionality, all the management of the process definitions files is left to the user.

- **Versioning**. It is the next level of process definition management, in which the product provides some basic source control capabilities. Versioning capabilities maybe simple, like sequential versioning, or sophisticated including version branching and merging. On either case, it allows users to maintain the history of the process definition.

- **Process repository**. A process repository is provided by more advanced products. The repository should behave like a document management repository supporting versioning, querying, backups, and other file management facilities. It may be part of a document management repository, or it may be a stand-alone repository. A process repository should not be confused with the storage of the process definitions in a database.

- **XML Process repository**. It is an evolution of the process repository, in which the repository understands XML. This assumes that process definitions are stored in XML, preferably using a process definition standard, like XPDL. It not only allows the repository to classify and query process definitions based on XML tags, but also allow third party XML tools to manipulate the process definitions for all kind of different purposes, like printing and documentation.

- **Process discovery.** It is the ability of the process repository to publish the process definitions in ways that other tools become aware of their existence, and provide information on how those processes can be used. The repository should support integration with a directory, like UDDI (Universal Description, Discovery, and Integration). This simplifies the integration of process engines, and the exposure that processes have in the organization.

The management of enacted processes is also very important from a process management perspective because it allows the organization to monitor and adjust the process to achieve their business objectives. Basic products provide system administration tools to fine-tune the process engine, with advanced products providing tools for the business user to monitor and measure the processes from a business perspective. Some of these levels of sophistications are:

- **Auditing**. The basic capability of writing an audit trail is provide by most products.

- **Monitoring**. The ability to see the current status and history of a running process is called monitoring. There are at least two levels of monitoring, going from the ability to monitor a single process instance, to the ability to monitor all the instances of a particular process.

- **Process adjustment**. More sophisticated products allow users to adjust or modify running processes on the fly by changing the process definition for one or more instances of a running process.

- **Business measurements**. The facilities to monitor processes from a business perspective, by allowing the definition and calculation of business measurements, are extremely important from a BPM perspective. Business measurements and reports allow business users to understand the process and evaluate it on business terms.

- **Forecasting**. The ability to forecast resource requirements and allocation based on current and historical process load can have a major impact on the operation of the organization by providing the tools to optimize resource allocation.

- **Simulation**. The simulation of processes is a valuable tool, specially if business measurements and forecasting can be applied to the simulation, because it provides business users the ability to test process ideas without committing the organization resources, and without disturbing current processes. Comparing simulated data with current process data allows managers to prove, or disprove, potential process improvement assumptions.

BUSINESS PROCESS MANAGEMENT

BPM is process technology enhanced with process management capabilities, implemented in a way that is appealing to business users. BPM is for the business user, not for the IT developer.

All of the process products allow users to define some type of processes and are able to enact those processes. However, BPM is more than process technology; products have to provide process management features to be considered a BPM product. The ability, from a business perspective, to analyze and change running processes is an important BPM feature, as is the ability to manage and version processes.

BPM does not need to involve the Internet, B2B processes, or collaboration processes, although it is difficult to imagine a BPM product that will not provide at least some features in those areas. BPM technology should be applicable to all kind of processes, including departmental, enterprise, interoperability, and collaborative processes.

Figure 7 positions BPM with respect to the other process technologies. It shows how BPM technology covers the same space as EAI process and workflow, but its focus is the business user, and provides more sophisticated management and analysis capabilities. The figure fails to describe the applicability of BPM for departmental, enterprise, interoperability, and collaborative processes. However, it does cover all the other aspects important to BPM technology.

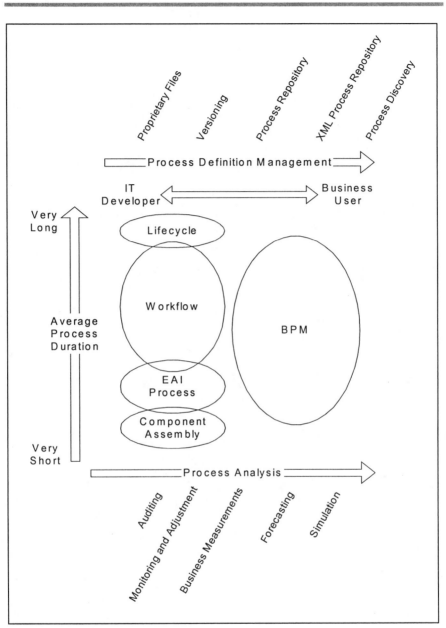

Figure 7—BPM Space

CONCLUSION

BPM is a convergence of different technologies integrated to help the business user to solve and manage his or her business processes. It is difficult for a single product to implement the entire spectrum covered by BPM, and there are no products in the market today that implements a full BPM feature set; however some vendors are providing product suites with multiple process technologies, integrated into a coherent framework.

Section 2

Workflow Standards

The Value of Standards

Betsy Fanning, AIIM International, USA

INTRODUCTION

When trying to understand the value of standards, you must gain an understanding of standards and the process by which a standard is developed. Standards, while valuable for those who use and implement them, are also in a state of conflict. Even though conflicts, in general, are not good, the conflict found within standards development assists in the definition of the value of the standards. This conflict exists between traditional standards developers, whose process is rigidly defined and slow, and the consortia or coalitions that make use of flexible development processes that result in the standards being made available much faster.

On first glance and from a traditional perspective, you might say that the standards development organizations are the good guys and that consortia are the bad guys. When you look at it from the perspective of the industry or from the user who needs to be able to implement a system that satisfies numerous needs in a complex information technology architecture, you might say that the consortia are the good guys and the standards development organizations are the bad guys.

This chapter will explore the area of standards development by first establishing some common ground for what standards are, some of the benefits they have for manufacturers, producers and users and then will look at the basic process by which standards are developed regardless of whether by traditional developers or consortia. It will conclude with some challenges that will be faced by either type of organization as they move into the future. This will leave the ultimate determination of which standards developer is best to you.

WHAT ARE STANDARDS?

So, what exactly is a *standard*? Webster's dictionary defines a standard as something established for use as a rule or basis of comparison in measuring or judging capacity, quantity, content, extent, value, quality, etc. It further states that a standard applies to some measure, principle, model, etc. with which things of the same class are compared in order to determine their quantity, value, quality, etc.

The Oxford Dictionary of Current English defines a standard as an object, quality, or measure serving as a basis, example, or principle by which others are judged. The International Organization for Standardization (ISO) defines standards as documented agreements containing technical specifications or other precise criteria to be used consistently as rules, guidelines, or definitions of characteristics, to ensure that materials, products, processes and services are fit for their purpose.

Similarly, a specification according to Webster's dictionary is a detailed description of the parts of a whole or a statement or enumeration of particulars, as to actual or required size, quality, performance, terms, etc. According to the Oxford Dictionary of Current English, a specification is detail of the design and materials etc. of work done or to be done. Regardless of which definition is used, a standard or specification defines something and all parties involved have agreed to what it defines.

The four basic types of standards include design criteria, dimensional standards, specifications, and test or quality methods. If you were to review a listing of all available standards, you would find that the majority of the standards titles could be classified into one of these four categories.

You can also look at the available standards as formal or de jure standards, industry standards, de facto or market driven or organizational standards. The de jure standards are developed by accredited standards organizations where the standards are developed using rigid procedures. A coalition or consortia of industry leaders who have identified a need in the industry that must be addressed develop industry standards and specifications.

Standards that are considered de facto or market driven are those that have received wide acceptance by the industry. For example, PDF, Portable Document Format, and TIFF, Tagged Image File Format, introduced by Adobe and Aldus, respectively, have become the accepted standard for transmitting documents in non-editable, non-revisable format. This happened not because one organization decided to start sending documents in PDF or TIFF format but because numerous organizations began to use it for this purpose.

While the de jure, industry standards and de facto standards have a far-reaching impact on industry, organizational standards are much more confined to the organization that has identified them for use in their enterprise. An example of an organizational standard might be the standard that your company has for how your logo is to be used, a style guide for formatting letters or drafting business reports or a policy mandating the use of XML schemas. Regardless of the type of standard, standards reflect where the industry is going not where it has been. Therefore it is important that organizations participate in developing standards to stay on the forefront of technology both from a product development standpoint and that of a technology user.

Whether standards are developed using a formal process or not, most all standards development is based on the very important concepts of openness and consensus. Traditional standards development adds due process to this. Openness means that anyone who is interested and may be directly or materially affected by the potential standard must be allowed to participate in the development process. By being open, standards involvement protects the interests of a manufacturer or producer while protecting the user's investment.

This also means that there should not be any constraints such as fees or organizational membership requirements for participation. An additional facet of openness is providing timely and adequate notification of actions to be taken with regard to the standard being developed or maintained as well as notification of meetings so that participants can attend and be well prepared for the discussions. Due process means that any person or organization with a direct and material interest has a right to participate in the development of standards and express their point of view. This allows for equity and fair play in the process. Consensus means that the representatives of the directly and materially affected interest categories have reached substantial agreement. This signifies the concurrence of more than a simple majority, but not necessarily unanimity. Consensus requires that all views and objections be considered, and that an effort be made toward their resolution.

Consortia, to some degree, embrace the concepts of openness and consensus that are key concepts of the traditional process while remaining market driven. However, they may not make use of due process or maintain a balance between interest categories that ensure industry acceptance of the standard.

Within the United States, there is an additional quality for standards development, that of being voluntary. This means that individuals and companies that participate in the development of standards do so on a voluntary basis. In other words, there is no governmental mandate that a company or individual must help develop a given standard. Likewise, there is no such mandate that a company or individual must use the standards that are developed. Unfortunately, this voluntary nature may not be so in other countries and can potentially impede the implementation of standards.

In the last few years, the conflict between the importance of traditional standards and the work produced by consortia has heightened. Nowhere is this more apparent than in the technology area. New technology is constantly being developed and more rapidly than ever before. Enhancements to existing technology are being introduced daily. Many believe the importance of formal standards is waning because it takes so long to produce a standard and that frequently the standard is made available just as interest in the technology is declining. Software can be developed and available for purchase in less than eighteen months while the development cycle for traditional standards may be measured in years. This is due largely to the fact that traditional standards attempt to take into consideration the views and opinions of all the parties who might be affected by the standard once it is published.

Consortia standards development efforts were initiated to address the market needs especially that of timeliness of standards developed. Here groups of interested, highly concerned people assemble based on an identified problem. Through their discussions, a standard or specification is developed that addresses the problem. They either continue on a related problem or disband.

Standards, regardless of who develops them or how, must guide the emergence of new technology. They must reflect the technology to come not the technology that is already in place.

PARTICIPATION IN STANDARDS EFFORTS

In order to participate in standards development efforts, you do not have to be a scientist or professor. However, the more knowledge-able of technology and business processes, as well as, the business and strategy of the company or organization being represented, the more value you bring to the effort. Much of the development process is communications based. Therefore, possessing excellent oral and written communication skills is a requirement. In this way you will be able to express a concept orally and write the detailed specifics for the standard.

Writing skills are very important in standards work. Not everyone can be in attendance at all meetings where the standard being im-plemented is discussed. Members of the team drafting the standard have the benefit of having participated in the discussions so they have an added understanding that, if not conveyed in written text, can be a problem to those implementing the standard. To be of value, the standard must be exactly worded, very detailed and spe-cific.

The ability to influence and negotiate, to ensure a particular issue is addressed or a concept is accepted, is also important. Not everyone on the team will share in a specific point of view. However, they can and must come to a common ground of understanding in order to develop the standard, which is where the skills of influence and ne-gotiation come into play.

Standards work can be used as an opportunity to build or use lead-ership skills through taking on a specific role in the committee. The basic committee roles are chair, editor and representative / partici-pant. Each role is equally important to the outcome of the commit-tee but each has differing responsibilities and/or requirements that must be fulfilled. Depending on the organization, these roles may have different titles but the basic concept is the same.

STANDARDS ORGANIZATIONS

There are several types of organizations that develop standards. Two basic types of standards development organizations exist, accredited standards development organizations or coalitions and consortia. Industry groups are another type of standards organization. These organizations are important to developers because they educate the industry and promote the use of standards, but do not actually de-velop standards.

An accredited standards organization develops standards according to a rigid set of established procedures. These procedures ensure that the principles of openness and due process have been followed in the approval procedure and that consensus of those directly or materially affected by the standards has been achieved. In the United States, the American National Standards Institute (ANSI) is the central body responsible for the identification of a single, consistent set of voluntary standards.

Similar organizations exist in other countries, for example, British Standards Institute (BSI) for the United Kingdom, Deutsches Institut für Normung (DIN) for Germany, Japanese Industrial Standards Committee (JISC) for Japan and others.

Virtually every country has a standards organization that protects national interests at the international level. Each of these organizations accredits other standards development organizations to develop standards on their behalf such as the American Petroleum Institute (API), AIIM International (AIIM), or Society of Automotive Engineers (SAE).

Traditional international standards are developed by ISO, International Organization for Standardization. ISO is a non-governmental organization established to promote the development of standardization and related activities in the world with a view to facilitating the international exchange of goods and services, and to developing cooperation in the spheres of intellectual, scientific, technological and economic activity. ISO's work results in international agreements, which are published as International Standards. Each of the national standards organizations listed above, as well as many others, are members of ISO.

In the mid-1990s, consortia and coalitions began to address technology's increasing need to produce standards in a timely manner. Groups like the Workflow Management Coalition (WfMC), the Object Management Group (OMG), DMA (Document Management Alliance), ODMA (Open Document Management API), and the W3C (World Wide Web Consortium) came into being. These organizations were assembled to develop standards to satisfy a very specific need in the industry. Their efforts were international rather than nationally focused with participants from many countries.

The following are some of the coalitions and consortia, which while formed to address other issues, are working in the workflow or business process arena.

- **Workflow Management Coalition** (WfMC)
  The Workflow Management Coalition (www.wfmc.org) is an international organization of workflow vendors, users, analysts and university/research groups. The coalition's mission is to promote and develop the use of workflow through the establishment of standards for software terminology, interoperability and connectivity between workflow products.
- **World Wide Web Consortium** (W3C)
  Developing common protocols that promote the evolution and ensure the interoperability of the World Wide Web is what the W3C

(www.w3c.org) was created to do. In the area of standardization, the W3C produces specifications that they call "Recommendations" that describe the building blocks of the Web.

- **Object Management Group** (OMG)
  The OMG (www.omg.org) was formed to create a component-based software marketplace by hastening the introduction of standardized object software. The organization's charter includes the establishment of industry guidelines and detailed object management specifications to provide a common framework for application development. Conformance to these specifications makes it possible to develop a heterogeneous computing environment across all major hardware platforms and operating systems.

- **Organization for the Advancement of Structured Information Standards** (OASIS)
  OASIS (www.oasis-open.org) is an international consortium that creates interoperable industry specifications based on public standards such as XML and SGML, as well as others that are related to structured information processing.

- **Internet Engineering Task Force** (IETF)
  The IETF (www.ietf.org) is a large, open, international community of network designers, operators, vendors, and researchers concerned with the evolution of the Internet architecture and the smooth operation of the Internet.

- **RosettaNet**
  RosettaNet (www.rosettanet.org) is a consortium of leading information technology, electronic commerce, semiconductor manufacturers and solution provider companies working to create, implement and provide open e-business process standards.

- **Business Process Management Initiative** (BPMI.org)
  BPMI (www.bpmi.org) is an organization that empowers business processes that span multiple applications and business partners, behind the firewall and over the Internet. Its initiative was established to promote and develop the use of business process management through the establishment of standards for process design, deployment, execution, maintenance, and optimization. This organization develops open specifications, assists IT vendors for marketing their implementations and supports businesses for using business process management technologies.

In addition to these organizations that develop standards, there are the industry groups that exist solely to promote standards and educate the industry on the technology and standards. Two of these types of organizations that promote and support the standards development efforts are WARIA and the Business Internet Consortium.

- **Workflow And Reengineering International Association** (WARIA)
  The charter of the Workflow and Reengineering International Association (www.waria.com) is to identify and clarify issues that are common to users of workflow, electronic commerce and those who are in the process of reengineering their organizations. The

association facilitates opportunities to discuss and share experiences freely while promoting the standards efforts of related organizations such as WfMC and BPMI.

- **Business Internet Consortium**
  (www.businessinternetconsortium.org)
  The Business Internet Consortium is an open industry group comprising leading e-business technology providers and end users. The mission of the Consortium is to accelerate the transition to e-business. To achieve this mission, the Consortium serves as an open forum for the exchange of ideas, provide architectural direction and recommend standards and best practices.

While most of these groups continue to be in existence today, some, like DMA and ODMA, have determined that the goals they set out to accomplish when they were created were met and have disbanded. When a consortium disbands, it provides new challenges to the industry. Specifically, these challenges deal with the availability and maintenance of the standards work created by the disbanded organization. In some cases, these challenges can be overcome through the use of Open Source where the standards work is placed into public domain. Some disbanded organizations have placed their specifications into open source with the hope that the standards will continue to live and evolve while making them very accessible to those who need them the most, the product developers.

PROCESS

When looking at the various standards organizations, whether they are de jure or coalition or consortium standards organizations, there are many similarities that can be found in the process by which they develop the standards. Standards efforts usually begin with a project proposal that identifies the scope of the work, potential participants in the effort and an assessment of the market relevance of the work. The market relevance is important in determining whether work on the project should take place. If the proposed standard cannot be viewed as being of value once completed, there is no need to expend resources to create it. Additionally, the degree of market relevance will dictate the speed that the standard is developed.

The standards and specifications produced by any standards organization will contain two types of information, normative text or the 'shall' and 'should' or requirements of the document and informative text. Technical committees are formed typically to oversee the development effort while assisting in the specification of the requirements for the standard. Working groups primarily develop the standard based on the requirements specified.

Differences in the process can be found with regard to the review process specifically, the length of time to allow for the voting process. In most de jure processes, a minimum of 30 days to six weeks is specified in the organization's procedures for the voting period to approve standards. Whereas in coalitions and consortia, most voting is done at meetings as the items are being identified to be included in the standard or specification. If the vote is not taken at the meeting, then a minimum number of days are designated to conduct an e-mail ballot.

In both cases, a meeting attendance requirement has been established for a member to be allowed to vote. Even among the coalitions and consortia, the number of meetings that are mandatory prior to being able to vote varies from two to three meetings whereas with traditional standards it is one meeting. Once you are a voting member of a committee, in either de jure, coalition or consortia standards development, you *must* stay active. This is only natural, because joining a committee but not attending meetings, not voting on documents and not contributing to the documents or discussions will not help your group establish a solid, stable standard.

The traditional standards process is benefiting from consortias' efforts specifically in placing emphasis on market relevance and shortened development cycle times for standards efforts. There is greater emphasis being placed on the statement of market relevance when a new standard initiative is started. In fact, many existing standards are being reviewed and maintained or withdrawn on the basis of market relevance. The traditional standards developers are exploring implementing new techniques and processes that shorten the time to develop a standard without sacrificing the quality and the basic objectives of openness, due process and consensus.

Through the use of the latest technology, additional timesavings have been realized in the development and approval process. More standards committees are holding Internet-based meetings or using chat room capabilities to continue their work between face-to-face meetings. Discussion boards are becoming a more valuable tool to promote the exchange of ideas. Collaborative authoring tools and templates are removing some of the formatting challenges when it comes to drafting a standard. Electronic balloting systems are becoming more widely used in the review and approval of standards resulting in a significantly shorter approval cycle.

Just as we have observed traditional standards development programs changing, we have also seen a tightening of consortia processes with more consortia producing procedures that they use to develop standards and specifications. Another element common to both traditional standards organizations and consortia is accountability where audits of the process are conducted to ensure the standards are being developed in accordance with established procedures.

While standards development in the United States is considered voluntary and is not under the specific control of the United States Government, that is not the case in some other countries. The American National Standards Institute (ANSI) is unique among national standards organizations in that the Federal government does not fund it. The United States has published OMB Circular A-119, Federal Participation in the Development and Use of Voluntary Consensus Standards and in Conformity Assessment Activities from the

Office of Management and Budget (OMB) that establishes policies on Federal use and development of voluntary consensus standard and on conformity assessment activities.

This directive authorizes the National Institute of Standards and Technology (NIST) to coordinate the conformity assessment activities of the Federal government agencies and establishes reporting requirements for participating in standards activities. OMB Circular A-119 directs United States agencies to use voluntary standards in lieu of government-developed standards except where they may be inconsistent with the law or it may be impractical to implement the standards. Through the implementation of this policy the US Government is eliminating the cost of developing its own standards, decreasing the cost of goods procured and the burden of complying with agency regulations as well as promoting and providing opportunities for standards to be established to serve national needs.

FUTURE

As we look to the future in standards development efforts, industry need will continue to drive standards, not only what standards to develop but also how quickly they get developed. The standards process will continue to increase the use of available technologies such as collaborative authoring tools, Internet-based meetings, chat rooms, discussion boards, and others.

In order to remain a viable standards developer, all of these technologies and more will need to be deployed. Gone are the days of using surface mail to distribute documents to meeting participants. In some respects, e-mail and listservs have served their usefulness and may not any longer fit. Real-time collaboration is the only way to satisfy the need. Technology used for electronic balloting and reviewing drafts for approval and drafting and editing tools such as electronic templates will become more readily available to streamline the development process.

In keeping with the theme of reducing cycle times, we will see standards efforts run more like businesses. We will begin to see more strategic planning occurring. Standards projects will be managed strictly by project plans, milestones and due dates to ensure they are brought to market in a timely manner. We will also see more organizations use standards as a strategic management tool to meet their objectives.

XML will become more widely used in standards development. Not only will standards be XML-enabled, meaning that they will contain XML coding as part of the specification, but they will be published using XML. The very nature of XML lends itself to standards documents with its capability to allow various views of the document to be defined. This will allow standards developers to provide all versions of the final approved standard to the industry making it easier for software or hardware developers to maintain products developed using an older version of a standard.

The issue of conformance has been one that standards developers have been addressing but possibly not very vigorously. In the future this will change, with greater emphasis being placed on conforming to standards. In the United States, OMB Circular A-119, discussed above, deals with the issue of conformity and will help to lead the industry into ensuring that their products conform to the standards.

Coordination of standardization efforts will be more important so that history does not have to repeat itself. The Electronic Industries Alliance united companies/manufacturers to support the time division multiple access (TDMA) standard. However, there were some dissident companies that decided to support an informal consortia standard called code division multiple access (CDMA) instead. To further complicate the issue, the Europeans took to the global system for mobile (GSM) communication that resulted in incompatible mobile phone digital formats. This means that your mobile phone will not work in Europe if it works in the United States or vice versa. We need to see standards being accepted and adopted without divergent efforts being initiated.

One of the keys to acceptance and adoption of standards is education. The industry needs to fully understand not only the standard but also the technology. Standards organizations must and will need to adopt the role of educator. They must realize that they are the ones directing the industry. They must also promote their standards work to governments to achieve the adoption and penetration levels to be successful.

CONCLUSION

Standards are needed to allow for interoperability, interchange; global marketing; and compatibility. They promote the rapid development of technology and allow the technology to be upgraded easily and economically.

The future is hard to predict just as it is difficult to determine whether a standard developed by a traditional standards developer or a consortium is better than the other. Given that both the traditional standards developers and consortia bring unique qualities and benefits to the standardization table, they can and will continue to co-exist for some time to come.

We need both consortia and traditionally developed standards to exist and further the development of the technology and push for a higher quality of standards. However, both will need to be flexible to meet the needs of the industry. Both the traditional and consortia standards organizations need you to help them to not only develop the standards but to use them.

Standards are and will remain to be important and to have value to product developers and users alike. They will continue to be a vital part of business and technology as we move forward further into an e-business world. Who and how they are developed is inconsequential; that they *are* developed is all that matters.

Wf-XML Challenge—Interoperability Demo by SAP and Staffware

Justin Brunt, Staffware Plc., United Kingdom
and Rainer Weber, SAP, Germany

SETTING UP THE PROJECT

In the fall of 2000, the WfMC issued a challenge to its members to demonstrate their support for the latest XML based version of the interoperability standard—Wf-XML 1.0.

In a nutshell, Wf-XML is an interoperability standard for workflow systems (see [HaPe00] for an introduction and [WfMC00] for the published standard). Its main function is to send a control message via the Internet from one workflow system (or more generally: some Wf-XML-capable service) to another in order to start a process in that system and to be informed when that process completes, which may be in the order of minutes up to weeks depending on the business processes.

The control messages are encoded in the XML-based standard Wf-XML that specifies exactly all the parameter names of the control messages, whilst the transmission of the data is achieved via HTTP. The language Wf-XML is transport-protocol independent; however, up to now only one transport binding has been specified.

SAP and Staffware shared common aims: SAP software drives the ERP, CRM and B2B components in most blue chip companies and Staffware is the leading independent Workflow/Business Process Management solution provider.

Both have major clients with a strong interest in business collaborative scenarios, as well as wanting to protect the investment that they have made in workflow technology. Often, as a result of takeovers and mergers, major companies have amassed several different workflow technologies, and getting these to integrate with each other is a major step forward, as is the ability to tighten up shared processes with partners over the Internet.

It is no surprise that both SAP and Staffware accepted the challenge and declared that they would cooperate to test their implementations against each other. Other WfMC members were interested in joining but to get the project going as quickly as possible it was decided to restrict the first test to two participants (first-come first-served).

Staffware had already participated in previous interoperability challenges using the MIME binding. These challenges had involved a number of workflow vendors demonstrating their implementations interoperating with each other's in a life like business scenario that had been devised specifically for the demonstration. These interoperability challenges took place at WfMC related public events.

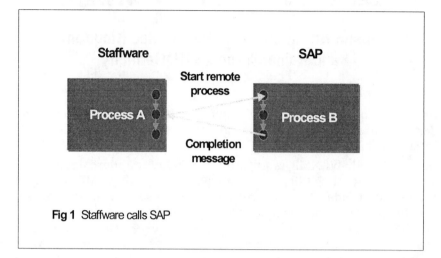

Fig 1 Staffware calls SAP

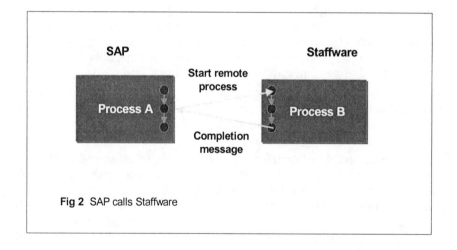

Fig 2 SAP calls Staffware

Staffware's MIME implementation has been turned into a product and is available as a standard Staffware product component.

SAP has been heavily involved in the specification of Wf-XML, and even before the publication of Wf-XML as a standard, SAP had already integrated the Beta version of the standard into their WebFlow engine.

This implementation was useful in checking whether the standard was really implementable and also how easily it could be done. Experience and many tests (alas, only between SAP systems) have shown that this was possible. At the time the Wf-XML challenge was issued, SAP was the only workflow vendor to have implemented Wf-XML, but it had only been tested against its own implementation.

However, in order to really gain confidence in a standard's implementation, tests between different systems are required, since it is possible that an implementation makes assumptions that are not covered by the standard.

The main interoperability scenarios that were tested are described below.

Staffware put together a project team in October 2000 to implement Wf-XML and test against SAP's implementation.

The Staffware project team consisted of:

- Justin Brunt Staffware's VP of Research and representative on the WfMC technical committee, acted as project manager.
- Martin Dean a Senior Consultant, who had been the lead developer in the 1999 Interoperability Challenge, as designer and developer.
- Naveed Shiekh a Consultant who has significant Web and XML expertise, as the second developer.

The project team on the SAP side consisted of:

- Alan Rickayzen: SAP's workflow product manager.
- Rainer Weber: Developer, SAP's representative in the WfMC, participating in the specification of Wf-XML
- Natalie Kratz: A consultant for workflow and related areas

The respective teams agreed that the testing would take place over the Internet rather than personal meetings at either of the organization's locations. This goal is in keeping with the type of collaborative scenarios for which Wf-XML is designed. However, if the first test attempt proved too difficult to perform remotely alternative plans would be made to test in the same location. This testing strategy therefore meant that both organizations needed to make a server available to each other to host the Wf-XML applications.

PROJECT WORK AT STAFFWARE

The Staffware team undertook a brief period of investigation of the technologies that would be needed for the implementation and produced a design specification of the propose solution.

From conference calls and emails exchanged it was clear that the SAP team were enthusiastic about the project. Not only were they keen to use their experiences of implementing Wf-XML to help Staffware but also they would have a different implementation against which to prove their own.

Once the design had been reviewed and validated Staffware's development commenced. The main components of the solution included:

- An ASP based POSTing acceptor to receive, process and respond to incoming messages from another workflow engine.

- A broker to Post messages to another workflow engine and process the responses received.
- Staffware process definitions (Procedures) to be used for testing the workflow instructions covered by the Interoperability specification. Both parent and child procedures were developed to enable testing both initiator and responder roles in the interoperability.

Staffware's Internal Systems department were commissioned to provide the website that would host access to the Wf-XML application whilst complying with the security policies. This turned out to be one of the most difficult and time-consuming aspects of the project.

As the development progressed, a number of decisions needed to be jointly made about some aspects of the implementation. One of the decisions that needed to be made concerned which 'ContextData' model would be mutually suitable. The released Wf-XML 1.0 standard includes suggestions for ContextData structures but leaves it to the interoperating parties involved to decide upon a model.

Using the same example data shown in the Wf-XML Binding document, the following construct of 'non-structured' tagged data was agreed as acceptable to both SAP and Staffware:

<ContextData>

      <VehicleType>Car</VehicleType>

      <Manufacturer>Buick</Manufacturer>

      <Model>Senator Cadillac</Model>

      <Customer>John Doe</Customer>

</ContextData>

During module testing XML documents supplied by SAP were made use of. At first this caused a big disappointment on both sides because the interface did not appear to work. However it was quickly realized that these were created by SAP's beta implementation. The Wf-XML 1.0 standard included significant changes from the beta version so it was no surprise that the documents could not be parsed properly. Once the mistake had been recognized, the 1.0 messages proved valuable and helped iron out potential problems before testing against SAP's implementation for real.

One of the issues that arose from using these example XML documents was SAP's use of embedded characters such as '&' and '!' and the way they are distorted when viewed in a Web Browser. Since this occurred during module testing rather than live testing the issue was quickly resolved through dialogue with SAP.

The Staffware team wanted to establish as early as possible that their method of POSTing XML documents to another workflow engine would succeed prior to the complications of attempting this across the internet and through firewalls at the remote end. Therefore, a simple Visual Basic application was written that incorporated the same HTTP controls to be used by Staffware's eventual solution. This application was sent to the SAP team for them to try on their intranet. The SAP team tried the test program out and were able to report that the it had successfully POSTed the required XML document to their implementation which had responded and the test program had successfully parsed the SAP response XML document.

Although the software to implement Wf-XML had been developed, Staffware had no applications yet developed that would make use of Wf-XML. Therefore, this was the next step in the project to be addressed. Business processes plus their supporting applications were developed and tested in-house on a LAN between two Staffware installations.

In parallel with this development work both SAP and Staffware were setting up their demonstration server systems. As mentioned earlier, establishing the correct Firewall access with security levels that complied with each organization's security policies proved to be time consuming and complicated challenges for both organizations. Eventually Staffware were able to prove a Staffware-to-Staffware test using a dedicated server in a DMZ via the Internet so confidence was high that the real thing would work. Completion of this test coincided with SAP also having achieved their server set up for operational testing.

SAP's ROLE

SAP's Wf-XML implementation already existed as a product. No development effort was required other than in the event of bugs being detected and they were prepared to supply bug fixes for the implementation. As it happened, this was only rarely necessary.

An outline sketch of the architecture of SAP's Wf-XML implementation follows. SAP's Wf-XML implementation is part of SAP WebFlow /Business Workflow. It uses SAP underlying technology for communicating with the Internet via HTTP (at that time the Internet Transaction Server was used for that purpose; later on the HTTP functionality is supplied directly by SAP's Web Application Server).

For handling XML, a set of methods from the Document Object Model, also a part of the SAP core product, was used to parse and construct Wf-XML messages.

The person modeling the workflow is shielded from the XML rendering, parsing and messaging. For the modeler, it just looks like calling a sub-process, the only difference being that he or she has to add a URL that determines where the process should be called. The XML handling takes place in the background and the conversion of the workflow data to the Wf-XML context data is automatic. For this purpose, a Web-activity construct has been integrated as a workflow modeling construct. It shields the modeler from the intricacies of the Wf-XML standard. The implementation includes tools for browsing incoming and outgoing XML messages, which helps trouble-shooting, which would otherwise be very cumbersome.

INTEROPERABILITY TESTING AND RESULTS

The aim was to perform the project via the Internet backed up by some telephone calls, E-mail for interpersonal communication and sending samples, and HTTP for doing the real testing. Before testing server-to-server, testing between a test program and server was often employed, with the test program producing a variety predefined sample messages.

A test plan had been agreed between SAP and Staffware that consisted of:

- Defining the order in which the Wf-XML commands would be tested
- Testing with and without Context Data
- Agreeing which Data Fields, including type and size, would be recognized by each party
- Exchanging the Universal Resource Identifier (URI) for each product's POSTing acceptor application for initiating a Child process instance i.e. the 'Key' to which 'CreateProcessInstance' request documents should be posted
- Agreeing the time delays between subsequent interoperation steps to be built into the Process definitions e.g. how long it would take a Child process instance to complete and consequently POST back a 'completed' message to the Parent process

Unexpectedly, the lion's share of the time was spent persuading internal IT to set up a system in the DMZ.

On the whole testing was successful but as one would anticipate there were a number of failures in the early days of testing. The types of failures could be categorized as:

- Software bugs in each of the implementations
- Different interpretations of the Wf-XML specification
- Ambiguities in the Wf-XML specification
- Differences in implementation decisions causing incompatibilities
- Operational problems

Some of the failures that occurred were:

- Having agreed to only exchange well-formed 'valid' messages, unintentionally some invalid / 'empty' messages were actually posted
- When testing without data, Staffware messages omitted the 'ContextData' tag / end-tag from the document. However the SAP implementation was expecting the tag to be present with an empty body i.e. mandatory use of the ContextData tag

- There are two mutually incompatible examples of how to represent the 'State' value in the Wf-XML specification which resulted in different implementations by SAP and Staffware
- Embedded '&' value in the SAP ProcessInstanceKey and ObserverKey values not being properly parsed and stored by the Staffware implementation
- The timing of subsequent interoperability messages which were generated automatically by the Workflow processes were not always mutually convenient. Sometimes the delays were too long, making the tester wait to receive an expected outcome. Sometimes too short, not giving the tester enough time to post another message to the same instance before it terminated.
- Following modifications to correct the errors already detected, the new versions of Workflow Processes were made 'live' without the correct authorization restrictions resulting in subsequent valid messages being rejected as 'not authorized'
- Not all of the theoretical 'State' transitions are relevant to every Workflow Engine and consequently not all of them are implemented in the Staffware solution. SAP inadvertently sent State changed messages which required a State transition which was not implemented in Staffware

Both Staffware and SAP committed dedicated effort to the testing phase. Consequently, any problems that were found were rapidly investigated, explained and resolved. Within a week of the commencement of testing both Staffware and SAP had successfully started instances of each other's 'Child' processes on their respective remote workflow engines. Both parties were justifiably pleased with their successes.

Within a further three weeks the testing was almost complete with both parties having successfully tested all four Wf-XML instructions both with and without Context Data in both directions. At the end of this phase only one known issue remained related to the SAP implementation of handling a GetProcessInstanceData POSTing from Staffware.

Since the formal testing was completed, both SAP and Staffware have kept their respective servers up and running to facilitate interoperability demonstrations being performed at will.

Based on their experiences of implementing Wf-XML 1.0 both SAP and Staffware provided feedback to the WfMC Interoperability working group to assist in making the forthcoming Wf-XML 1.1 specification as robust as possible.

Staffware has supplied the WfMC, via the University of Münster, its implementation for possible use as a reference implementation. In addition the Wf-XML implementation has joined the existing MIME binding implementation as a product component in its Staffware Process Suite.

In summary, the project was successful; both SAP and Staffware have working implementations of Wf-XML 1.0 that have been tested against 'alien' workflow engines. Both parties were able to draw on their previous experiences of WfMC Interoperability implementation.

Although SAP and Staffware are strictly competitors in the workflow arena, both teams cooperated with enthusiasm in the spirit in which the WfMC was founded, representing both vendors' and customers' interests, to successfully complete the challenge.

End-to-end the project took about three elapsed months, which is good considering that both parties continued to honor existing responsibilities within their organization. The Christmas break was mid-way through the project and setting the servers up, especially getting permission from internal IT, was a lengthy process. Once testing began, the problems discovered were minor and quickly resolved.

Indeed, it turned out that plugging the systems together was so straightforward that the teams never needed to meet face-to-face (although a trip to Germany would have been welcome- and vice versa!).

REFERENCES

1. [HaPe00] *Hayes, J.G., Peyrovian, E., Sarin, S., Schmidt, M.-T., Swenson, K.D., Weber, R:* Workflow Interoperability Standards for the Internet. IEEE Internet Computing, May/June 2000, pp. 37-45.
   Also in: L. Fischer: Workflow Handbook 2001, Lighthouse Point, Florida (Future Strategies Inc., Book Division), 2000, pp. 253-269

2. [WfMC00] *Workflow Management Coalition:* Workflow Standard-Interoperability Wf-XML Binding, WfMC-TC-1023, Version 1.0, May 2000; online available at http://www.wfmc.org/standards/docs/Wf-XML-1.0.pdf Called: 01-01-26

ACKNOWLEDGEMENTS

Special thanks are due to Connie Moore (Giga Information Group) and Martin Ader (Workflow & Groupware Strategies) for their encouragement for getting the project going.

Workflow Standard—Interoperability Wf-XML Binding Version 1.1

Document Number WFMC-TC-1023

Edited and coordinated on behalf of the WfMC by Program Manager, Joint Computer-aided Acquisition and Logistic Support (JCALS) with technical support from Michael Rossi, Computer Sciences Corporation (CSC), Rainer Weber, SAP and Mike Marin, FileNET

1 CHANGE HISTORY (NON-NORMATIVE)

A brief summary of changes made in this version follows:

- Enhanced support for asynchronous processing—A new message type (Acknowledgement) was added, as was specification of structures in the Transport section useful for correlation of messages.
- Support for batch processing added—This change allows multiple requests/responses to be delivered within a single message. Modifications to the content model of the root element (WfMessage) were required to effect this change.
- Enhanced support for Parallel-Synchronized processing—A new operation called Notify was added in the Observer group to allow for notification of arbitrary events.
- Context-specific data structures—A new recommended content model for context-specific data is specified that enhances interoperability through standardization.
- Errata corrections—Various changes to fix errors discovered in the 1.0 version of this specification.
- Miscellaneous—Editorial changes and minor technical clarifications throughout.

This list is a summary provided for convenience only and is by no means intended to be a comprehensive reference. The normative sections of this specification should be consulted for exact details of the changes made in this version.

2 INTRODUCTION (NORMATIVE)

This document represents a specification for a language based on the eXtensible Markup Language (XML) [1], designed to model the data transfer requirements set forth in the Workflow Management Coalition (WfMC)'s Interoperability Abstract specification [1]. This language will be used as the basis for concrete implementations of the functionality described in the Interoperability Abstract supporting the WfMC's Interface 4, as defined by the Workflow Reference Model [2].

2. 1 Version Compatibility

This version (1.1) of the Wf-XML specification is fully backward compatible with its previous version (1.0). For the sake of clarity, the term "backward-compatible" is used here to mean that all changes made to the specification in this version have been additive, making it is a superset of version 1.0. For a more detailed explanation of conformance implications, see section 6 Conformance.

2.2 Purpose

At a high level, these are the goals of this specification:

- Support chained, nested and parallel-synchronized models of interoperability
- Provide for both synchronous and asynchronous interactions
- Support individual and batch operations
- Remain implementation independent
- Define a light, easy-to-implement protocol

In order to achieve these goals, this specification will utilize a loosely coupled, message-based approach to facilitate rapid implementation using existing technologies. It will describe the syntax of these messages in an open, standards-based fashion that allows for the definition of a structured, robust and customizable communications format. For these reasons, this specification will utilize the eXtensible Markup Language (XML) [6] to define the language with which workflow systems will interoperate.

The XML language described herein, Wf-XML, can be used to implement the three models of interoperability defined in the Interoperability Abstract specification. Specifically, chained workflows, nested workflows and parallel-synchronized workflows are supported. Wf-XML supports these three types of interchanges both synchronously and asynchronously, and allows messages to be exchanged individually or in batch operations. Furthermore, this specification describes a language that is independent of any particular implementation mechanism, such as programming language, data transport mechanism, OS/hardware platform, etc. However, because HTTP is expected to be the most prevalent data transport mechanism used for interchanging Wf-XML messages, this specification provides a description of how Wf-XML messages are to be interchanged using this protocol.

2.3 Scope

The scope of this specification is equivalent to that defined by the Interoperability Abstract specification.

2.4 Audience

This specification is intended for use by software vendors, system integrators, consultants and any other individual or organization concerned with interoperability among workflow systems. Furthermore, it will be of value to those concerned with the design and implementation of integrated and/or distributed systems, as a protocol for the interaction of generic (possibly remote) services.

2.5 Background

This specification is based on previous work completed by the Workflow Management Coalition (WfMC), the Object Management Group (OMG) and many vendor organizations in an effort to define the functionality required to achieve interoperability among workflow systems. Subsequently, the following documents comprise the basis of this specification:

- WfMC Interoperability Abstract (IF4) specification [1]
- OMG Workflow Management Facility (jointflow) specification [3]
- WfMC IF4 Internet E-mail MIME binding specification [4]
- Simple Workflow Access Protocol (SWAP) proposal [5]

Readers of this specification are encouraged to familiarize themselves with these documents in order to gain a more comprehensive understanding of the concepts that provide its foundation.

2.6 Document Status

This document is a publication of the Workflow Management Coalition (WfMC), representing version 1.1 of the Wf-XML specification. It may also be obtained from our website via the Internet from: http://www.wfmc.org/standards/docs/Wf-XML-11.pdf or by e-mailing a request to: wfmc@wfmc.org.

2.7 Documentation Conventions
- In several of the examples provided in this document, an ellipsis (...) is used as a placeholder for other data. In certain contexts, this notation may also imply the optional repetition of previously indicated elements or content. In either case, it should not be interpreted as a literal part of the character stream.
- In addition to the examples that appear throughout this document, extracts from the Document Type Definition (DTD) are provided in line with the descriptive text. These extracts are intended to highlight the particular markup constructs used throughout this specification. They will appear inside a box as in the following example:

```
<!ELEMENT foo (bar)>
<!ELEMENT xxx (baz)>
```

- Where a description of a generic construct is necessary, the generic construct will appear in *Italics*. For example, where operations are discussed in general without reference to any particular operation, the reference will appear as "*OperationName.*" This string will be replaced by the name of a specific operation later in the document.

3 TECHNICAL SPECIFICATION (NORMATIVE)

3.1 Logical Resource Model

It has been determined that the concepts of interoperability among workflow systems can be naturally extended to accomplish interaction among many other types of systems and services. These other systems are deemed "generic services," and can represent any identifiable resource with which an interaction can occur. A generic service may further be viewed as consisting of a number of different resources. These resources may be implemented in any fashion, so long as they are uniquely identifiable and can interact with other resources in a uniform fashion as specified in this document, receiving requests to enact services and sending appropriate responses to the requestors.

An individual interoperable function is termed an "operation". Each operation may be passed a set of request parameters and return a set of response parameters. Operations are divided into different groups to better identify their context. The primary groups of operations required for interoperability are named ProcessDefinition, ProcessInstance and Observer. An additional group named Control also exists to support certain optional functionality in this version of the specification. A resource implements a group of operations by supporting the operations defined to exist within that group. Furthermore, a resource may implement more than one group of operations, such as ProcessInstance and Observer. A more detailed discussion of conformance to this specification is discussed in section 6: Conformance.

The Control group of operations serves to support the protocol level functions required to maintain interoperability among generic services. Currently, this group is used to enable the monitoring and control of batch messages only. However, it may also prove useful in future versions of this specification to support more dynamic forms of interoperability.

The ProcessDefinition group is the most fundamental group of operations required for the interaction of generic services. It represents the description of a service's most basic functions, and is the resource from which instances of a service will be created. Since every service to be enacted must be uniquely identifiable by an interoperating service or service requestor, the process definition will provide a resource identifier. When a service is to be enacted, this resource identifier will be used to reference the desired process to be executed.

The ProcessInstance group represents the actual enactment of a given process definition and will have its own resource identifier separate from the definition's. When a service is to be enacted, a requestor will reference a process definition's resource identifier and create an instance of that definition. Since a new instance will be created for each enactment, the process definition may be invoked (or instantiated) any number of times simultaneously. However, each process instance will be unique and exist only once. Once created, a process instance may be started and will eventually be completed or terminated.

The Observer group provides a means by which a process instance may communicate information about events occurring during its execution, such as its completion or termination. In nested subprocesses, there must be a way for a requestor of a service enactment to determine or be informed when a subprocess completes. Furthermore, in parallel-synchronized processes (where each process may play the role of an observer) there must be a way for each process to be informed of events or changes in the other. Finally, third-party resources may have an interest in the status of a given process instance for various organizational reasons. The Observer group will provide this information by giving a process instance the resource identifier of the requestor, which will be the observer of that process instance. If other resources are to be notified of events occurring in the process instance, it is incumbent upon the observer to pass along information about events that it receives to those resources. Diagram 1 indicates the relationship between the primary groups of operations explained above:

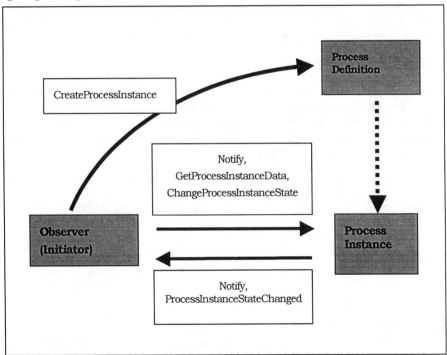

Diagram 1: Primary Operation Groups

3.2 Logical Interaction Model

In this specification, an "interaction" is considered to be the exchange between two generic services of protocol-related information. Wf-XML uses a "message" as the vehicle for providing interactions among generic services. Three types of interactions; called "Request," "Acknowledgement" and "Response," are used in messages exchanged between Wf-XML enabled services. A Request is used by a resource (A) to initiate an operation in a second resource (B), and/or to provide input to that resource.

An Acknowledgement is used in asynchronous implementations by a resource receiving a Wf-XML message to inform the sender that the message has been received. It should be noted that an Acknowledgement is used to acknowledge a message, as opposed to the interaction(s) contained in that message. In this case, the sender and receiver can be A or B depending on the message being acknowledged, which can contain an individual Request or Response, or a batch of interactions.

A Response is used by an enacting resource (B) to send the results of an operation to its requesting resource (A), providing output. Although the request and response interaction types are clearly complimentary, there is no requirement that they always be used in conjunction. That is to say that unlike the model used by HTTP (which also uses the names Request/Response), not every Wf-XML request requires a response.

3.2.1 Synchronous Messaging

In a synchronous exchange a resource (A) may wish to initiate a sub-process in a second resource (B) and suspend its normal processing until that sub-process completes, at that point becoming an observer of the sub-process. This lifecycle actually requires two separate synchronous exchanges.

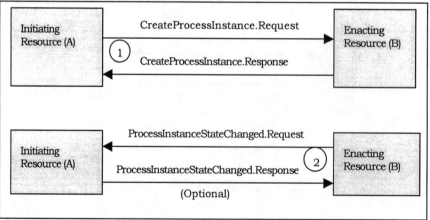

Diagram 2: Synchronous Message Exchange

As shown in Diagram 2, the initiating resource (A) sends a request to the enacting resource (B), which sends back a response (to A) indicating that the process has been initiated. When the enacting resource (B) completes the process, it sends a request message to the initiating resource (A) to inform it of the completion. This message may require no response, as it is merely informational, but is referred to as a "Request" message nonetheless.

3.2.2 Asynchronous Messaging

In an asynchronous exchange, as shown in Diagram 3, the initiating resource (A) sends a request to the enacting resource (B) to create a new process instance. The enacting resource (B) then sends an acknowledgement back to the initiator (A) informing it that the request has been received. This positive acknowledgement serves only to indicate that a message has been received and does not imply any additional semantics, such as the processing status of the operation. Exception or status information must be returned through subsequent protocol messages. Additional requirements for negative acknowledgements or other guaranteed messaging semantics should be handled at the application level.

At some later point in time, the enacting resource (B) sends a response to the initiating resource (A) indicating that the requested process instance has been created. The initiating resource (A) then sends an acknowledgement (to B) indicating that it received the response. Again, this acknowledgement serves only to indicate that the response message was received.

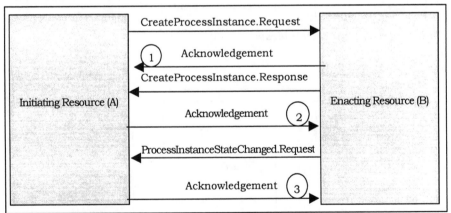

Diagram 3: Asynchronous Message Exchange

When the process being enacted by the enacting resource (B) subsequently completes, that resource (B) sends a request to the initiating resource (A) to inform it of the completion. The initiating resource (A) then sends an acknowledgement (to B) indicating that it received the request. In this case, the Request may require no response since it is only informational, and so the exchange ends here.

3.2.3 Batch Messaging

In addition to the individual exchange of interactions described above, it is also desirable in some circumstances to exchange multiple Wf-XML interactions in a single message. This type of "batch" processing can be useful in high-volume transactional situations, such as EDI-style transactions. This specification describes a data format suitable for managing both individual and batch processing.

When processing batch Wf-XML messages, the interaction types "Request" and "Response" defined above apply to individual operations within the batch message, whereas the type "Acknowledgement" always applies to a message as a whole. This is an important distinction in the batch processing model, as an implementation may choose to combine Requests and Responses in a single batch message as appropriate for a given purpose. However, only a single Acknowledgement is required for an entire batch message, regardless of how many operations the batch message contains.

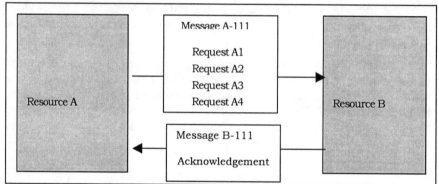

Diagram 4: Initial Batch Message

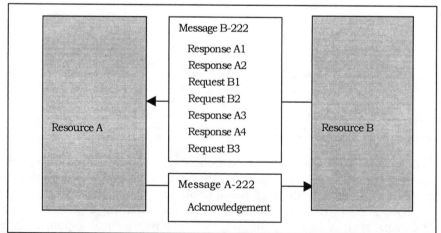

Diagram 5: Batch Message with Combined Interaction Types

When exchanging a batch of interactions, the batch may contain Requests only, a combination of Requests and Responses or Responses only, as appropriate to the situation. While this batching of interactions may be convenient, an implementation may also choose to send Individual Responses to operations requested via a Batch message. This approach can prove useful for incremental progress tracking or partial result processing. The following diagrams illustrate a hypothetical batch messaging interchange utilizing these techniques. This scenario also utilizes asynchronous processing in order to illustrate the combined usage of these processing models.

Note that in these scenarios neither resource is explicitly labeled as an initiating or enacting resource, since they each serve both roles at some point in the execution of their various business processes.

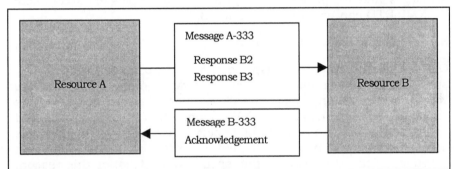

Diagram 6: Batch Message with Partial Result

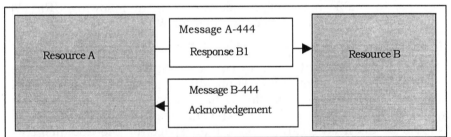

Diagram 7: Individual Response to Batch Requested Operation

While this scenario illustrates one possible message exchange using the processing models provided, there are clearly many other ways these messages and interaction types can be combined to accommodate different process management requirements.

3.3 Security

In general, security considerations are out of the scope of this document because they are largely dependent upon the transport mechanism used by an implementation. This applies to user identification and authorization, encryption, and data/functional access control. In many cases, while security mechanisms such as SSL,

PKI and LDAP may be sufficient for some applications, they may be viewed as insufficient or overkill by others. Therefore, the security mechanisms used between two or more interoperating services should be identified in the interoperability contract between them.

3.4 Wf-XML Language Definition

Every Wf-XML message is an XML document instance, conforming to the XML 1.0 specification. While not explicitly required by XML 1.0, each Wf-XML message will contain an XML declaration, for the sake of clarity and precision. The XML declaration will appear as follows: '<?xml version="1.0"?>'. This declaration contains no explicit encoding information, and therefore implies that the XML 1.0 supported character encodings of UTF-8 or UTF-16 will be used. This section will describe each element used within Wf-XML messages and its purpose, also providing examples. The complete Wf-XML DTD can be found in Section 8.

3.4.1 Wf-XML Namespace Definition

One of the most important aspects of an XML-based interoperability specification is its ability to interact with other XML markup vocabularies, mixing elements from each as necessary. This capability will be crucial to Wf-XML, as much of the data exchanged between workflow systems will be specific to those systems and the applications they invoke, and is likely to be marked up with languages defined outside of this specification. It is for this reason, that the "Namespaces in XML" specification [11] was created, and should be used in conjunction with this specification.

In order to enable usage of this mechanism, the following URI [14] will be used as the namespace identifier for Wf-XML:

"http://www.wfmc.org/standards/docs/Wf-XML"

It should be noted that this namespace definition does not imply the existence or location of any DTD or XML Schema, as the purpose of a namespace declaration is simply to provide a unique identifier for a set of XML elements. Within Wf-XML messages, this namespace should be declared as the default namespace for the document as follows:

<WfMessage xmlns="http://www.wfmc.org/standards/docs/Wf-XML">

Alternatively, this namespace may be explicitly declared on relevant elements within a message, as in the following:

<wf:WfMessage
xmlns:wf="http://www.wfmc.org/standards/docs/Wf-XML">.

Note however, that if explicit namespace prefixing is used on an element, all children of that element belonging to the Wf-XML namespace must also be prefixed. Although the namespace prefix "wf" used above is recommended, the Wf-XML namespace identifier may be bound to any prefix to avoid prefix collision with qualified element names outside the scope of this specification.

Using the above declarations, applications will be able to distinguish elements defined by this specification from those defined elsewhere, in order to achieve higher levels of interoperability without degrading conformance to this specification. It should be noted however, that due to the complexity involved in validating multiple-namespace documents against a DTD, no support is provided for this functionality in the Wf-XML DTD. Therefore, Wf-XML documents requiring multiple namespaces are only required to be well formed.

3.4.2 Data Types

Although DTD syntax does not support robust data typing, several required data types are provided for use with this specification. A future version of this specification will utilize the W3C's forthcoming XML Schema syntax, which will allow these types to be validated at the XML parser level. Where required, data fields may be of the following types:

- Boolean—value may be either "True" or "False"
- Integer—a numeric value containing no decimal precision component. Data fields of this type may be further constrained where used in this specification.
- String—value may contain a sequence of characters of arbitrary length
- Date—value may contain a date/time specification as described in section 3.4.2.1
- URI—value may contain a string conforming to the Universal Resource Identifier (URI) specification [14]. It should be noted that this is not required to be an absolute URI. In certain circumstances, it may only be necessary to provide a local identifier resolvable by the service processing a message. Furthermore, an implementation may wish to maintain base URIs internally, thereby only requiring a relative URI within the Wf-XML message. In these cases, semantics and mechanisms for processing these relative URIs should be agreed upon in the interoperability contract.
- UUID—value may contain a string conforming to UUID specification [15]

Where no specific data type is indicated for a value, the type will default to String. Within Wf-XML messages, context-specific data conforming to other specifications may be exchanged as described in section 3.4.7, "Representation of Process Context and Result Data". This data is not subject to the data type constraints of this specification and should be validated based on the specification to which it conforms.

3.4.2.1 Date and Time Values

A specific Date/Time format is provided for data of type "Date". All date and time values shall be represented as Greenwich Mean Time (GMT) based timestamps to ensure interoperability between resources that may not be in the same time zone. The Date/Time format shall be represented as:

YYYY-MM-DDThh:mm:ssZ

where:

**YYYY is the year in the Gregorian calendar
MM is the month of the year (range 01—12)
DD is the day of the month (range 01—31)
T is the separator between the date and time portions of this timestamp
hh is the hours of the day (range 00—24)
mm is the minutes of the hour (range 00—59)
ss is the seconds of the minute (range 00—59)
Z is the symbol that indicates Coordinated Universal Time (UTC) or GMT**

A time of midnight may be expressed as 00:00:00 or 24:00:00.

All dates and times should be represented to the users of the system in a way that meets their individual implementation requirements. This means if all date/times are to be represented as "user" local times, they can be because the UTC time variable allows the conversion to local time, regardless of location in the world.

If a particular resource requires dates/times to be represented locally (in the timezone of the resource) then it will need to perform the conversion from GMT to the local timezone.

3.4.3 Overall Message Structure

The following DTD segment defines the top-level (or "root") element of a Wf-XML message:

```
<!ELEMENT WfMessage ((WfTransport, (WfMessageHeader, WfMessage-
Body) *) | (WfMessageHeader, WfMessageBody))>
<!ATTLIST WfMessage Version CDATA #FIXED "1.1"
                    xml:space (default | preserve) #IMPLIED
                    xml:lang NMTOKEN #IMPLIED>
```

This root element is named "WfMessage," and it carries a required attribute named "Version," as well as the reserved XML attributes xml:space and xml:lang. These constructs have the following semantic constraints and meaning:

Version—The value of this attribute indicates the particular version of this specification with which this message conforms. It may be used by an implementation to determine whether this message can be processed. If the service receiving this message cannot support the version of the specification to which it conforms it must return a response containing appropriate exception information, as described in section 3.4.9.

xml:space—This attribute is used to indicate whether whitespace within this element is to be ignored or preserved, as specified by the XML 1.0 recommendation [6].

xml:lang—This attribute is used to indicate the natural language used within this element, as specified by the XML 1.0 recommendation [6].

Within the root WfMessage element, each Wf-XML message contains the following structure:

- An optional section for transport-specific information named "WfTransport". If necessary, this section will be used to convey information relevant to a particular implementation's transport protocol. For the purposes of asynchronous processing, this section will be used to convey acknowledgement information. For the purposes of batch processing, this section will be used to indicate that the special processing is required. Therefore, whenever asynchronous and/or batch processing is being performed this section of the message must be present.
- Zero or more message headers named "WfMessageHeader". The message header will contain information relevant to routing and preprocessing of the message. The message header must not be present in an acknowledgement message, in which all acknowledgement information will be conveyed in the transport section. A single message header must be present to perform an individual operation. Multiple message headers may be present if this message is to be processed as a batch. In this case, each message header must be accompanied by a message body.
- Zero or more message bodies named "WfMessageBody". The operation specific information is placed in the message body. The message body must not be present in an acknowledgement message, in which all acknowledgement information will be conveyed in the transport section. A single message body must be present to perform an individual operation. Multiple message bodies may be present if this message is to be processed as a batch. In this case, each message body must be accompanied by a message header.

Therefore, the skeleton of a Wf-XML message will appear as follows in an individual operation (with the optional transport section included):

Example 1:

```
<?xml version="1.0"?>
<WfMessage    xmlns="http://www.wfmc.org/standards/docs/Wf-XML"
Version="1.1">
    <WfTransport>
        ...
    </WfTransport>
    <WfMessageHeader>
        ...
    </WfMessageHeader>
    <WfMessageBody>
        ...
    </WfMessageBody>
</WfMessage>
```

and as follows in a batch operation:

Example 2:

```
<?xml version="1.0"?>
<WfMessage xmlns="http://www.wfmc.org/standards/docs/Wf-XML"
Version="1.1">
    <WfTransport>
        ...
    </WfTransport>
    <WfMessageHeader>
        ...
    </WfMessageHeader>
    <WfMessageBody>
        ...
    </WfMessageBody>
    <WfMessageHeader>
        ...
    </WfMessageHeader>
    <WfMessageBody>
        ...
    </WfMessageBody>
        ...
</WfMessage>
```

Lastly, the message skeleton would appear as follows in an acknowledgement message (used during asynchronous processing), with additional details of the acknowledgement information specified in section 3.4.4:

Example 3:

```
<?xml version="1.0"?>
<WfMessage xmlns="http://www.wfmc.org/standards/docs/Wf-XML"
Version="1.1">
    <WfTransport>
        ...
    </WfTransport>
</WfMessage>
```

3.4.4 Message Transport Mechanism

One of the goals of this specification is to provide an implementa-tion-independent protocol. An important aspect of this independ-ence is the ability to exchange Wf-XML messages over any transport mechanism. Therefore, this specification does not define any of the characteristics of supporting protocols and mechanisms used to exchange Wf-XML messages, such as details regarding message integrity, reliable messaging (retransmission, duplication detection), session management, etc. However, it will often be necessary to provide information to support these capabilities in a Wf-XML message. It is for this reason that the WfTransport section is provided. This section of a Wf-XML message is optional and contains markup constructs designed to facilitate the implementation of asynchronous and batch transport mechanisms. Details appearing in this section regarding the requirements of any particular transport should be specified by the binding protocol for that transport.

The following DTD extract illustrates the predefined structure of the WfTransport section:

```
<!ELEMENT WfTransport (Dialog?, CorrelationData?, Exception?)>
<!ELEMENT Dialog ((Acknowledgement, Key) | (ReplyToKey, Key?) | Key)?>
<!ATTLIST Dialog Type (synch | asynch) "synch"
                 Mode (individual | batch) "individual"
                 MessageID CDATA #IMPLIED>
<!ELEMENT Acknowledgement EMPTY>
<!ATTLIST Acknowledgement ReceivedAt CDATA #REQUIRED>
<!ELEMENT Key (#PCDATA)>
<!ELEMENT ReplyToKey (#PCDATA)>
<!ELEMENT CorrelationData (#PCDATA)>
```

These elements and attributes can be combined in a number of different ways to support a variety of messaging models (individual / synchronous, individual / asynchronous, batch / synchronous or batch / asynchronous), provided they adhere to the semantic constraints specified herein. Each of them, as well as the entire WfTransport element, is optional in order to allow specific transport bindings and implementations to use them as necessary. If the entire WfTransport element is omitted, the default messaging model is individual/synchronous. These structures have the following semantic constraints and meanings:

Dialog—This element contains information relevant to the kind of dialog being established between interoperating services, such as whether responses are to be handled synchronously or asynchronously and whether this message contains a single or multiple interactions. Specific characteristics of the processing required to support this message are described by the elements and attributes below. If this element is omitted the messaging model defaults to individual/synchronous. (optional)

Type—This attribute is used to indicate whether the message should be handled synchronously or asynchronously. If this attribute's value is "synch," this message must be handled synchronously. In this case, no further communication will occur until the requested processing is completed. Upon completion of the requested processing, a response must be returned to the requesting service immediately.

If this attribute's value is "asynch," this message must be handled asynchronously. In this case, the receiving service must return an acknowledgement to the initiating service upon receipt of a request. Upon completion of the requested processing, a response may be returned to the initiating service. If a response is returned, the initiating service must send an acknowledgement to the enacting service upon receipt of the response.

If this attribute is omitted, the message type defaults to "synch". (optional)

Mode –The value of this attribute indicates the kind of processing required for this message to the resource receiving it. If the value of this attribute is "individual," the message should be processed as a single interaction. If this attribute's value is "batch," additional information required for batch processing will be specified elsewhere in this message. If this attribute is omitted, the message's mode defaults to "individual". (optional)

MessageID –This attribute must be present when asynchronous or batch processing is being performed. It contains a unique identifier used to correlate an acknowledgement of a message, and/or to identify a batch message in control operations. In an acknowledgement, this attribute's value must correspond with the value of the same attribute in the message to which the acknowledgement relates. The value of this attribute must be of type UUID. (optional)

Acknowledgment—The presence of this element indicates that this is an acknowledgement, used in asynchronous processing. Therefore, this element must not be present if the value of the Type attribute on the Dialog element is set to "synch". If this element is present the message must not contain a message header or message body. Furthermore, an Acknowledgement must only acknowledge a single message and must be processed individually. Therefore, the Mode attribute on the Dialog element must be set to "individual" when this element is present, as an Acknowledgement message must not require batch processing information. Receipt of this message indicates that the corresponding message, identified by the value of the MessageID attribute described above, has been received. (optional)

ReceivedAt—The value of this attribute indicates the time at which the acknowledged message was received by the recipient. The value of this attribute must be of type Date.

Key—This element is used within the transport section of a message when batch and/or asynchronous processing is being performed. It supplements the Key element in the message header (described below) in two ways:

o   When batch processing is being performed the message contains multiple headers, making it impossible to use the Key element in the header to route the message. Therefore, this element provides the identifier of the resource to which a batch message is to be sent.

o   When asynchronous processing is being performed there is no way to include a Key in an Acknowledgement message, since it contains no header. Therefore, this element provides the identifier of the resource to which an Acknowledgement is to be sent.

The contents of this element must be of type URI. (optional)

ReplyToKey—This element must be present in messages containing Requests or Responses when asynchronous processing is being performed. It contains the identifier of the resource to which an acknowledgement or response to this message should be sent. This element should not be present in messages containing an Acknowledgement. The contents of this element must be of type URI. (optional)

CorrelationData—This element contains implementation-specific data and or structures necessary to correlate message traffic between interoperating resources. Since this data will be particular to the interaction between two interoperating resources, the specific details of its structure and format must be agreed upon in the interoperability contract. This element is maintained in this version of the specification for backward compatibility. (optional)

Exception—the Exception element that appears here is used to describe any errors that may have been encountered relative to the transport section. The content of this element is described in section 3.4.9 Error Handling. When this element is used in the transport section of a message, the exception code 800 "WF_OTHER" should be used and extended as necessary to convey the specifics of the error.

The following examples illustrate some of the possible ways the structures in the WfTransport section may be used to support various processing models. Example 4 illustrates the transport section for a synchronous exchange of an individual message.

Example 4:

```
<?xml version="1.0"?>
<WfMessage xmlns="http://www.wfmc.org/standards/docs/Wf-XML"
Version="1.1">
    <WfTransport>
        <Dialog Type="synch" Mode="individual"/>
    </WfTransport>
        ...
</WfMessage>
```

It should also be noted that given this processing model, any or all of the Type attribute, Mode attribute, Dialog element or WfTransport element could have been omitted without impacting the semantics of the message processing, as this is the default behavior. Example 5 illustrates the transport section for an asynchronous exchange of an individual request or response.

Example 5:

```
<?xml version="1.0"?>
<WfMessage xmlns="http://www.wfmc.org/standards/docs/Wf-XML"
Version="1.1">
    <WfTransport>
        <Dialog Type="asynch" Mode="individual" Mes-
        sageID="5a98d32e-7854-c751-5491-7d4a0c4e7102">
            <ReplyToKey>http://www.myco.com/purchasing/orders</
            ReplyToKey>
        </Dialog>
    </WfTransport>
        ...
</WfMessage>
```

Example 6 illustrates the transport section for an asynchronous exchange of a batch message.

Example 6:

```
<?xml version="1.0"?>
<WfMessage xmlns="http://www.wfmc.org/standards/docs/Wf-XML"
Version="1.1">
    <WfTransport>
        <Dialog Type="asynch" Mode="batch" Mes-
        sageID="5a98d32e-7854-c751-5491-8f55e8a210ba">
            <ReplyToKey>http://www.myco.com/purchasing/orders</
            ReplyToKey>
            <Key>http://www.exampleco.com/processes</Key>
        </Dialog>
    </WfTransport>
        ...
</WfMessage>
```

Example 7 illustrates an acknowledgement of the batch message in example 6. Note that the value of the Mode attribute on the Dialog element has been set to "individual" although this is an acknowledgement of a batch message. This is because the Mode attribute indicates the processing mode required to handle this message, not a message it might reference. Also, note that the message being acknowledged is correlated via the MessageID.

Example 7:

```
<?xml version="1.0"?>
<WfMessage xmlns="http://www.wfmc.org/standards/docs/Wf-XML"
Version="1.1">
    <WfTransport>
        <Dialog Type="asynch" Mode="individual"
        MessageID="5a98d32e-7854-c751-5491-8f55e8a210ba">
            <Acknowledgement ReceivedAt="2001-09-24T16:31:05Z">
            <Key>http://www.myco.com/purchasing/orders</Key>
        </Dialog>
    </WfTransport>
</WfMessage>
```

3.4.5 *Message Header Definition*

The message header contains information that is generically useful to all interactions, such as resource identifiers, operation names, etc. Separation of this information from the message body enables pre-processing of Wf-XML messages without having to parse the operation-specific information. The message header is defined as follows:

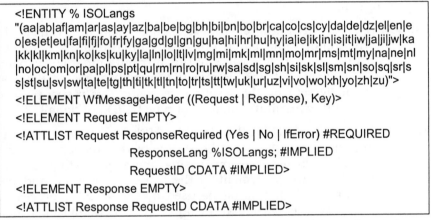

```
<!ENTITY % ISOLangs
"(aa|ab|af|am|ar|as|ay|az|ba|be|bg|bh|bi|bn|bo|br|ca|co|cs|cy|da|de|dz|el|en|e
o|es|et|eu|fa|fi|fj|fo|fr|fy|ga|gd|gl|gn|gu|ha|hi|hr|hu|hy|ia|ie|ik|in|is|it|iw|ja|ji|jw|ka
|kk|kl|km|kn|ko|ks|ku|ky|la|ln|lo|lt|lv|mg|mi|mk|ml|mn|mo|mr|ms|mt|my|na|ne|nl
|no|oc|om|or|pa|pl|ps|pt|qu|rm|rn|ro|ru|rw|sa|sd|sg|sh|si|sk|sl|sm|sn|so|sq|sr|s
s|st|su|sv|sw|ta|te|tg|th|ti|tk|tl|tn|to|tr|ts|tt|tw|uk|ur|uz|vi|vo|wo|xh|yo|zh|zu)">
<!ELEMENT WfMessageHeader ((Request | Response), Key)>
<!ELEMENT Request EMPTY>
<!ATTLIST Request ResponseRequired (Yes | No | IfError) #REQUIRED
                  ResponseLang %ISOLangs; #IMPLIED
                  RequestID CDATA #IMPLIED>
<!ELEMENT Response EMPTY>
<!ATTLIST Response RequestID CDATA #IMPLIED>
```

These structures have the following semantic constraints and meanings:

Request—The presence of this element indicates that this interaction is a request. If this element is used it must carry the ResponseRequired attribute described below. It may also optionally specify the ResponseLang attribute. (optional)

ResponseRequired—This attribute may contain the following values: Yes, No, or IfError. If the value specified is Yes, a response must be returned for this request in all cases, and it must be processed by the requesting resource. If the value specified is No, a response may, but need not be returned for this request, and if one is returned it may be ignored by the requesting resource. If the value specified is IfError, a response only needs to be returned for this request in the case where an error has occurred processing it, and the requesting resource must process the response.

ResponseLang—The value of this attribute indicates the spoken language to be used (English, German, Japanese, etc.) in language-specific data elements such as Subject or Description when that information is returned in the response to this request. The value of this attribute is chosen from a list of language identifiers defined in the ISO 639 standard [13] for language identifiers. If this element is not used, no assumption can be made about the language used in the response returned for this request. (optional)

RequestID—This attribute of the Request element is used in asynchronous and batch processing to uniquely identify a request (potentially within a batch of interactions) so that it can later be correlated with its response. The value of this attribute must be of type UUID. (optional)

Response—The presence of this element indicates that this interaction is a response. Receipt of this interaction indicates that processing of the corresponding request has been completed. (optional)

RequestID—This attribute of the Response element is used in asynchronous and batch processing to correlate a response with its request. The value of this attribute must correspond to the value of the RequestID attribute on a Request previously sent by the resource receiving this response. The value of this attribute must be of type UUID. (optional)

Key— This element contains the identifier of the resource that is the target of this request, or the source of this response. In the case of batch message processing, message routing is indicated by the Key element in the transport section, and the content of this Key must be used by the Wf-XML processor to identify the particular resource to which this operation applies. The content of this element must be of type URI.

For example, an asynchronous individual request message would appear as follows:

Example 8:

```
<?xml version="1.0"?>
<WfMessage xmlns="http://www.wfmc.org/standards/docs/Wf-XML"
Version="1.1">
    <WfTransport>
        <Dialog Type="asynch" MessageID="4308d23b-e78c-2390-
        6271-743891d60a52">
            <ReplyToKey>http://www.myco.com/purchasing/orders/4
            089259</ReplyToKey>
        </Dialog>
    </WfTransport>
    <WfMessageHeader>
        <Request ResponseRequired="Yes" RequestID="4308d23b-
        675d-3b47-0931-768c4a0528b3"/>
        <Key>http://www.exampleco.com/processes/86947325</Key>
    </WfMessageHeader>
    <WfMessageBody>
        ...
    </WfMessageBody>
</WfMessage>
```

An acknowledgement of this request would appear as in example 9.

Example 9:

```
<?xml version="1.0"?>
<WfMessage xmlns="http://www.wfmc.org/standards/docs/Wf-XML"
Version="1.1">
    <WfTransport>
        <Dialog Type="asynch" MessageID="4308d23b-e78c-2390-
        6271-743891d60a52">
            <Acknowledgement ReceivedAt="2001-09-
            24T16:48:30Z"/>
            <Key>http://www.myco.com/purchasing/orders/4089259<
            /Key>
        </Dialog>
    </WfTransport>
</WfMessage>
```

A response to this request would appear as in example 10.

Example 10:

```
<?xml version="1.0"?>
<WfMessage xmlns="http://www.wfmc.org/standards/docs/Wf-XML"
Version="1.1">
    <WfTransport>
        <Dialog Type="asynch" MessageID="4308d23b-430b-29e0-
        a867-32087b581afe">
            <ReplyToKey>http://www.exampleco.com/processes/8694
            7325</ReplyToKey>
        </Dialog>
    </WfTransport>
    <WfMessageHeader>
        <Response RequestID="4308d23b-675d-3b47-0931-
        768c4a0528b3"/>
        <Key>http://www.myco.com/purchasing/orders/4089259</Ke
        y>
    </WfMessageHeader>
    <WfMessageBody>
        ...
    </WfMessageBody>
</WfMessage>
```

Given that this example illustrates an asynchronous scenario, this response would be acknowledged as follows:

Example 11:

```
<?xml version="1.0"?>
<WfMessage xmlns="http://www.wfmc.org/standards/docs/Wf-XML"
Version="1.1">
    <WfTransport>
        <Dialog Type="asynch" MessageID="4308d23b-430b-29e0-
        a867-32087b581afe">
            <Acknowledgement ReceivedAt="2001-09-
            24T16:54:14Z"/>
            <Key>http://www.exampleco.com/processes/86947325</K
            ey>
        </Dialog>
    </WfTransport>
</WfMessage>
```

3.4.6 Message Body Definition

The message body provides operation specific data. For a request, it contains an *<OperationName.Request>* element, which further contains request parameters; for a response, it contains an *<Operation-Name.Response>* element, containing result parameters returned by the operation. This naming convention allows for the appropriate specification of the content of the operation elements based on their context (within a Request or Response). Therefore, the content of the WfMessageBody element is defined as follows:

```
<!ELEMENT WfMessageBody (%OperationRequest; |
%OperationResponse;)>
```

The entities referenced here contain element declarations for specific operations as described above, and so will be specified in the Operations section of this document.

This model would have the following structure for an asynchronous batch of request interactions. Note that multiple types of interactions (requests and responses) may be combined within a batch message. The examples shown here provide only one of the possible scenarios in order to illustrate the cycle of asynchronous processing.

Example 12:

```
<?xml version="1.0"?>
<WfMessage xmlns="http://www.wfmc.org/standards/docs/Wf-XML"
Version="1.1">
    <WfTransport>
        <Dialog Type="asynch" Mode="batch" Mes-
        sageID="e85327bc-dc9e-2878-4b52-947852107643">
            <ReplyToKey>http://www.myco.com/purchasing/orders</
            ReplyToKey>
            <Key>http://www.exampleco.com/processes</Key>
        </Dialog>
    </WfTransport>
    <WfMessageHeader>
        <Request ResponseRequired="Yes" RequestID="d4253789-
        ce42-9165-3bed-825731d8d941"/>
        <Key>http://www.exampleco.com/processes/86947325</Key>
    </WfMessageHeader>
    <WfMessageBody>
        <OperationName.Request>
                ...
        </OperationName.Request>
    </WfMessageBody>
    <WfMessageHeader>
        <Request ResponseRequired="Yes" RequestID="54879aac-
        ffe3-8d92-cd74-7983547bac21"/>
        <Key>http://www.exampleco.com/processes/79843209</Key>
    </WfMessageHeader>
    <WfMessageBody>
        <OperationName.Request>
                ...
        </OperationName.Request>
    </WfMessageBody>
    <WfMessageHeader>
        <Request ResponseRequired="Yes" RequestID="25b76322-
        8ac6-e509-baca-172483dabcf3"/>
        <Key>http://www.exampleco.com/processes/30817842</Key>
    </WfMessageHeader>
    <WfMessageBody>
        <OperationName.Request>
                ...
        </OperationName.Request>
    </WfMessageBody>
</WfMessage>
```

An acknowledgement of this message might appear as in example 13.

Example 13:

```
<?xml version="1.0"?>
<WfMessage xmlns="http://www.wfmc.org/standards/docs/Wf-XML"
Version="1.1">
    <WfTransport>
        <Dialog Type="asynch" Mode="individual" Mes-
        sageID="e85327bc-dc9e-2878-4b52-947852107643">
            <Acknowledgement ReceivedAt="2001-08-
            23T17:12:42Z"/>
            <Key>http://www.myco.com/purchasing/orders</Key>
        </Dialog>
    </WfTransport>
</WfMessage>
```

A response to this request might appear as follows:

Example 14:

```
<?xml version="1.0"?>
<WfMessage xmlns="http://www.wfmc.org/standards/docs/Wf-XML"
Version="1.1">
    <WfTransport>
        <Dialog Type="asynch" Mode="batch" Mes-
        sageID="832ba946-8754-4237-e8f0-924678a8e031">
            <ReplyToKey>http://www.exampleco.com/processes/orde
            r-handler.jsp</ReplyToKey>
            <Key>http://www.myco.com/purchasing/orders</Key>
        </Dialog>
    </WfTransport>
    <WfMessageHeader>
        <Response RequestID="d4253789-ce42-9165-3bed-
        825731d8d941"/>
        <Key>http://www.exampleco.com/processes/86947325</Key>
    </WfMessageHeader>
    <WfMessageBody>
        <OperationName.Response>
                ...
        </OperationName.Response>
    </WfMessageBody>
    <WfMessageHeader>
        <Response RequestID="54879aac-ffe3-8d92-cd74-
        7983547bac21"/>
        <Key>http://www.exampleco.com/processes/79843209</Key>
    </WfMessageHeader>
    <WfMessageBody>
        <OperationName.Response>
...
        </OperationName.Response>
    </WfMessageBody>
    <WfMessageHeader>
        <Response RequestID="25b76322-8ac6-e509-baca-
        172483dabcf3"/>
        <Key>http://www.exampleco.com/processes/30817842</Key>
    </WfMessageHeader>
    <WfMessageBody>
        <OperationName.Response>
                ...
        </OperationName.Response>
    </WfMessageBody>
</WfMessage>
```

Finally, an acknowledgement of this response might appear as follows:

Example 15:

```
<?xml version="1.0"?>
<WfMessage xmlns="http://www.wfmc.org/standards/docs/Wf-XML"
Version="1.1">
    <WfTransport>
        <Dialog Type="asynch" Mode="batch"
        MessageID="832ba946-8754-4237-e8f0-924678a8e031">
            <Acknowledgement ReceivedAt="2001-09-
            24T17:32:10Z"/>
            <Key>http://www.exampleco.com/processes/order-
            handler.jsp</Key>
        </Dialog>
        </WfTransport>
</WfMessage>
```

3.4.7 Representation of Process Context and Result Data

Typically, a process is associated with some number of data items specific to that process. These data items may represent the properties of the Process Instance (Workflow Control or Workflow Relevant data), and/or any application related data associated with invoked applications during process enactment (Application data). (These terms are defined within the WfMC Glossary [9].) This collection of data items is called the "context" of the process when the process is being instantiated, and the "result" of the process when the process has been completed/terminated. When the process is enacted, those data items must be specified and accessible. For this purpose, this specification provides a place to identify these data items in the form of elements named ContextData and ResultData. When a Process Definition is instantiated, the context of the resulting Process Instance is initialized with the contents of the ContextData element. When a Process Instance is completed, the resulting data is exchanged as the contents of the ResultData element.

The data within these elements may take many forms, depending on the type of data being exchanged and the particular requirements of an implementation. The structure of this data may also vary from process definition to process definition. Therefore, it is recommended that a detailed description of context and result data exchange requirements be agreed upon in an interoperability contract between interoperating services.

Because the nature and definition of this context data cannot be known (as it is particular to a given process definition), it can be difficult to define specific markup to identify it. Therefore, the content of the ContextData and ResultData elements must be specified on a case-by-case basis. As a placeholder for extensibility in this area, a default content model of "ANY" is defined for these elements. The reserved attributes xml:space and xml:lang are provided here, in addition to the root element, in order to allow these characteristics to be overridden for context-specific data. Appropriate specification of the content of these elements should be made in the interoperability contract between two enactment services, thereby extending this specification to meet their specific needs.

```
<!ELEMENT ContextData ANY>
<!ATTLIST ContextData xml:space (default | preserve) #IMPLIED
                      xml:lang NMTOKEN #IMPLIED>
<!ELEMENT ResultData ANY>
<!ATTLIST ResultData xml:space (default | preserve) #IMPLIED
                     xml:lang NMTOKEN #IMPLIED>
```

While the flexibility provided by this content model is essential, a more structured modeling of this data would allow for enhanced interoperability by providing a means by which a Wf-XML processor could distinguish the fields within a context-specific data section. These fields could then be dispatched for separate processing appropriately, as determined by the implementation. In order to foster greater levels of interoperability, this version of the Wf-XML specification provides the following markup to be used to specify parameters in the ContextData and ResultData elements.

```
<!ELEMENT Parameter (Name, Value+)>
<!ELEMENT Name (#PCDATA)>
<!ELEMENT Value (#PCDATA)>
```

These elements have the following semantic constraints and meanings:

Parameter—This element provides a bounding mechanism used to indicate that its contents constitute a single parameter to the process on which an operation is being performed. Two properties of this parameter, Name and Value, are provided as described below. However, further syntactic and semantic constraints of this parameter are to be determined by the agreements set forth in the interoperability contract. This element may appear zero or more times within the ContextData and/or ResultData elements.

Name—This element simply provides an identifier for the parameter. The syntactic and semantic constraints applicable to this element are to be determined by the agreements set forth in the interoperability contract, and any additional markup required here should be defined in that contract.

Value—The content of this element constitutes the value assigned to the parameter. Multiple values may be specified by including multiple "Value" elements within the parameter. The syntactic and semantic constraints applicable to this element are to be determined by the agreements set forth in the interoperability contract, and any additional markup required here should be defined in that contract.

The following example illustrates how this markup may be used to exchange context-specific data, assuming appropriate agreements have been made in the interoperability contract regarding the content of the Value element in the "VehDesc" parameter.

Example 16:

```
<?xml version="1.0"?>
<WfMessage xmlns="http://www.wfmc.org/standards/docs/Wf-XML"
Version="1.1">
    <WfMessageHeader>
        ...
    </WfMessageHeader>
    <WfMessageBody>
        ...
        <ContextData>
            <Parameter>
                <Name>POID</Name>
                <Value>3878547</Value>
            </Parameter>
            <Parameter>
                <Name>OrderConf</Name>
                <Value>http://www.exampleco.com/orders/3878547<
                /Value>
            </Parameter>
            <Parameter>
                <Name>VehDesc</Name>
                <Value>
                    <Vehicle>
                        <VehicleType>Car</VehicleType>
                        <Specification>
                            <Manufacturer>Audi</Manufacturer>
                            <Model>A4</Model>
                        </Specification>
                    </Vehicle>
                </Value>
            </Parameter>
        </ContextData>
        ...
    </WfMessageBody>
</WfMessage>
```

For compatibility reasons it cannot be mandated that this markup replaces the existing v1.0 content models. Therefore, although legacy (v1.0) content must be accepted by a version 1.1 compliant implementation, such an implementation should generate this Parameter markup as the content of the ContextData and ResultData elements in all cases, as this is the preferred way to achieve interoperability in this version of the specification. Using this markup allows an implementation to rely on receiving a parsable structure that can be delegated to an appropriate routine for further processing. For this reason, the ANY content model extensibility provisions from Wf-XML v1.0 are hereby deprecated.

3.4.8 Status

Another important aspect of a process is the state that the process is in at a given point in time. In general, a process may be active or inactive to some degree for a number of reasons. The WfMC has defined a standard set of valid process instance states. These states are organized into several levels of granularity. While the higher-level states defined here must be supported, an implementation may choose to omit the optional states or add additional states to those defined.

```
<!ENTITY % states "open.notrunning | open.notrunning.suspended |
open.running | closed.completed | closed.abnormalCompleted |
closed.abnormalCompleted.terminated |
closed.abnormalCompleted.aborted">
<!ELEMENT open.notrunning EMPTY>
<!ELEMENT open.notrunning.suspended EMPTY>
<!ELEMENT open.running EMPTY>
<!ELEMENT closed.completed EMPTY>
<!ELEMENT closed.abnormalCompleted EMPTY>
<!ELEMENT closed.abnormalCompleted.terminated EMPTY>
<!ELEMENT closed.abnormalCompleted.aborted EMPTY>
```

These structures have the following semantic constraints and meanings:

open.notrunning—A resource is in this state when it has been instantiated, but is not currently participating in the enactment of a work process.

open.notrunning.suspended—A resource is in this state when it has initiated its participation in the enactment of a work process, but has been suspended. At this point, no resources contained within it may be started. (optional)

open.running—A resource is in this state when it is performing its part in the normal execution of a work process.

closed.completed—A resource is in this state when it has finished its task in the overall work process. All resources contained within it are assumed complete at this point.

closed.abnormalCompleted—A resource is in this state when it has completed abnormally. At this point, the results for the completed tasks are returned.

closed.abnormalCompleted.terminated—A resource is in this state when it has been terminated by the requesting resource before it completed its work process. At this point, all resources contained within it are assumed to be completed or terminated. (optional)

closed.abnormalCompleted.aborted—A resource is in this state when the execution of its process has been abnormally ended before it completed its work process. At this point, no assumptions are made about the state of the resources contained within it. (optional)

These states are also used when performing batch message processing (by operations described in section 3.5.1 Control Operations) to indicate the overall status of a batch message. This status should not be confused with the status of processes initiated by these messages. Rather, it is the state of the message processing itself that is indicated. This state reflects the progress made on the processing of each individual operation that comprises the batch message, so that (for example) the batch is not considered complete until each individual operation is complete. Therefore, in the context of batch message processing, these structures have the following semantic constraints and meanings:

open.notrunning—A message is in this state when it has been received, but is not currently being processed. For example, the message may be in some type of internal queue awaiting processing.

open.notrunning.suspended—A message is in this state when it has been received and its processing has been initiated, but it is not currently being processed. This state may be the result of an explicit state change request or normal internal processing delays. (optional)

open.running—A message is in this state when it is currently being processed. Some of the operations in the batch may have been completed at this point, others may be in-progress and still others may not yet have been initiated.

closed.completed—A message is in this state when it has been completely processed. This means that all operations within the batch have been processed successfully. Responses to any requested operations in the batch will be (or have been) sent to the requestor.

closed.abnormalCompleted—A message is in this state when its processing has been completed abnormally. This means that one or more operations in the batch were not processed successfully, although some operations in the batch may have been completed successfully. Responses to any requested operations in the batch will be (or have been) sent to the requestor.

closed.abnormalCompleted.terminated—A message is in this state when its processing has been cancelled by the initiator. Some of the operations in the batch may have been completed at this point. Responses to any requested operations in the batch that have been completed will be (or have been) sent to the requestor. Operations that have not been completed when the message is terminated are ignored. (optional)

closed.abnormalCompleted.aborted—A message is in this state when its processing has been abnormally ended as the result of an internal processing error. Some of the operations in the batch may have been completed at this point. Responses to any requested operations in the batch that have been completed will be (or have been) sent to the requestor. Operations that have not been completed when the message is terminated are ignored. (optional)

3.4.9 Error Handling

Should any exception occur during the execution of a Wf-XML operation, information regarding that exception must be returned to the caller. Various types of exceptions can be anticipated, including temporary and fatal error types. Therefore, an element named "Exception" has been defined to carry this information.

```
<!ELEMENT Exception (MainCode, SubCode?, Type, Subject,
Description?)>
<!ELEMENT MainCode (#PCDATA)>
<!ELEMENT SubCode (#PCDATA)>
<!ELEMENT Type (#PCDATA)>
<!ELEMENT Subject (#PCDATA)>
<!ELEMENT Description (#PCDATA)>
```

This exception element will be returned as the contents of the *<OperationName*.Response> element, in lieu of the normal response data, from all operations in which an exception occurs. These structures have the following semantic constraints and meanings:

MainCode—This is a three digit positive integer defined in the operation specification. It is operation-specific and gives some indication of what went wrong. Programs can use this code to calculate what to do when this exception occurs. This specification defines main codes for all operations.

SubCode—This is also a three digit positive integer. It details the main code, e.g., when a main code says "Invalid Key," the SubCode could say more specifically that the format of the key is wrong. This is where a vendor would specify errors that are specific to their processing. This element may be omitted if the MainCode is deemed sufficient. (Optional)

Type—The type of the error that occurred. It can either be "F" for fatal error or "T" for temporary error.

Subject—This is a one-line text description of the exception.

Description—A several-line text description of the exception, which details the Subject. (Optional)

These elements are used to structure an exception in such a way as to enable interpretation of application-specific error codes and translation of error messages independent of any context-specific information. An example is shown below.

Example 17:

```
<?xml version="1.0"?>
<WfMessage xmlns="http://www.wfmc.org/standards/docs/Wf-XML"
Version="1.1">
    <WfMessageHeader>
        <Response/>
<Key>http://www.exampleco.com/processes/86947325</Key>
    </WfMessageHeader>
    <WfMessageBody>
        <CreateProcessInstance.Response>
            <Exception>
                <MainCode>502</MainCode>
                <Type>F</Type>
                <Subject>Invalid process definition</Subject>
<Description>Cannot create instance</Description>
            </Exception>
        </CreateProcessInstance.Response>
    </WfMessageBody>
</WfMessage>
```

3.4.9.1 Exception Codes

The following is a list of recommended MainCode three digit integer values, which can be used to report exceptions. Each MainCode category is listed below, with additional error information provided for that category. These exception codes are used in the operations' specifications.

WfMessageHeader   100 Series

These exceptions deal with missing or invalid parameters in the header.

WF_PARSING_ERROR	100
WF_ELEMENT_MISSING	101
WF_INVALID_VERSION	102
WF_INVALID_RESPONSE_REQUIRED_VALUE	103
WF_INVALID_KEY	104
WF_INVALID_OPERATION_SPECIFICATION	105
WF_INVALID_REQUEST_ID	106

Data   200 Series

These exceptions deal with incorrect context or result data

WF_INVALID_CONTEXT_DATA	201
WF_INVALID_RESULT_DATA	202
WF_INVALID_RESULT_DATA_SET	203

Authorization	300 Series

A user may not be authorized to carry out this operation on a particular resource, e.g., may not create a process instance for that process definition.

WF_NO_AUTHORIZATION	300

Internal	400 Series

The operation can not be accomplished because of some temporary internal error in the workflow engine. This error may occur even when the input data is syntactically correct and authorization is permitted.

WF_OPERATION_FAILED	400

Resource Access	500 Series

A valid Key has been used, however this operation cannot currently be invoked on the specified resource.

WF_NO_ACCESS_TO_RESOURCE	500
WF_INVALID_PROCESS_DEFINITION	502
WF_MISSING_PROCESS_INSTANCE_KEY	503
WF_INVALID_PROCESS_INSTANCE_KEY	504

Operation-specific	600 Series

These are the more operation specific exceptions. Typically, they are only used in a few operations, possibly a single one.

WF_INVALID_STATE_TRANSITION	600
WF_INVALID_OBSERVER_FOR_RESOURCE	601
WF_MISSING_NOTIFICATION_NAME	602
WF_INVALID_NOTIFICATION_NAME	603

Extensibility	800 Series

An additional exception main code is provided to allow implementations of the WF-XML specification to return additional exceptions.

WF_OTHER	800

The relevance of these exceptions to various operations is specified in the operation definitions given in section 3.5. Those definitions also reference "General" exceptions relating to all operations. The following codes are included in these general exceptions: 100 Series (100—106), 300, 400, 500, 800. All other exceptions are relevant to specific operations as defined in section 3.5.

3.5 Operation Definitions

The scope of this specification is limited to the operations shown in the following table. In brief, this section will discuss the collections of operations used for the Control, ProcessDefinition, ProcessInstance and Observer groups, as well as each of the operations in detail. In order to focus more clearly on the syntax of the operations, the examples in this section will assume synchronous individual processing. However, these operations can of course be processed asynchronously and/or in batch messages as described earlier.

	Control	Process Definition	Process Instance	Observer
GetBatchMessageState	X			
ChangeBatchMessageState	X			
CreateProcessInstance		X		
GetProcessInstanceData			X	
ChangeProcessInstanceState			X	
ProcessInstanceStateChanged				X
Notify				X

Table 1: Wf-XML Operations

For convenience, the list of valid operation elements is defined by two entities as shown below; one for Requests and one for Responses.

```
<!ENTITY % OperationRequest "(GetBatchMessageState.Request |
ChangeBatchMessageState.Request | CreateProcessInstance.Request |
GetProcessInstanceData.Request | ChangeProcessInstanceState.Request |
ProcessInstanceStateChanged.Request | Notify.Request)">

<!ENTITY % OperationResponse "(GetBatchMessageState.Response |
ChangeBatchMessageState.Response | CreateProcessInstance.Response |
GetProcessInstanceData.Response |
ChangeProcessInstanceState.Response |
ProcessInstanceStateChanged.Response | Notify.Response)">
```

3.5.1 Control Operations

This group of operations is used to affect administrative interactions among interoperating services. Such interactions are typically unrelated to specific processes. This group currently contains the operations GetBatchMessageState and ChangeBatchMessageState.

3.5.1.1 *GetBatchMessageState*

This operation is used to retrieve the status of a batch message previously sent to a given resource. The state of the batch is described using the status elements provided in section 3.4.8 Status.

```
<!ELEMENT GetBatchMessageState.Request (MessageID)>
<!ELEMENT MessageID (#PCDATA)>
<!ELEMENT GetBatchMessageState.Response (State | Exception)>
<!ELEMENT State (%states;)?>
```

These structures have the following semantic constraints and meanings:

Request Parameters:

MessageID—The unique identifier of the batch message whose status is to be retrieved. The data contained within this element must be of type UUID and must match the MessageID of a batch message previously sent to the resource receiving this request.

Example 18:

```
<?xml version="1.0"?>
<WfMessage xmlns="http://www.wfmc.org/standards/docs/Wf-XML"
Version="1.1">
    <WfMessageHeader>
        <Request ResponseRequired="Yes"/>
        <Key>http://www.exampleco.com/processes</Key>
    </WfMessageHeader>
    <WfMessageBody>
        <GetBatchMessageState.Request>
            <MessageID>e85327bc-dc9e-2878-4b52-
            947852107643</MessageID>
        </GetBatchMessageState.Request>
    </WfMessageBody>
</WfMessage>
```

Response Parameters:

State—The current state of the batch message, as described in section 3.4.8 Status.

Exceptions:

There are no exceptions specific to this operation. All general exceptions apply, as defined in section 3.4.9.1.

Example 19:

```
<?xml version="1.0"?>
<WfMessage xmlns="http://www.wfmc.org/standards/docs/Wf-XML"
Version="1.1">
    <WfMessageHeader>
        <Response/>
        <Key>http://www.exampleco.com/processes</Key>
    </WfMessageHeader>
    <WfMessageBody>
        <GetBatchMessageState.Response>
            <State>
                <open.running/>
            </State>
        </GetBatchMessageState.Response>
    </WfMessageBody>
</WfMessage>
```

3.5.1.2 ChangeBatchMessageState

This operation is used to change the status of a batch message previously sent to a given resource. The new state must be specified by one of the status elements provided in section 3.4.8 Status.

```
<!ELEMENT ChangeBatchMessageState.Request (MessageID, State)>
<!ELEMENT MessageID (#PCDATA)>
<!ELEMENT State (%states;)?>
<!ELEMENT ChangeBatchMessageState.Response (State | Exception)>
```

These structures have the following semantic constraints and meanings:

Request Parameters:

MessageID—The unique identifier of the batch message whose status is to be changed. The data contained within this element must be of type UUID and must match the MessageID of a batch message previously sent to the resource receiving this request.

State—The new state to which the identified batch message is to be changed.

Example 20:

```
<?xml version="1.0"?>
<WfMessage xmlns="http://www.wfmc.org/standards/docs/Wf-XML"
Version="1.1">
    <WfMessageHeader>
        <Request ResponseRequired="Yes"/>
        <Key>http://www.exampleco.com/processes</Key>
    </WfMessageHeader>
    <WfMessageBody>
        <ChangeBatchMessageState.Request>
            <MessageID>e85327bc-dc9e-2878-4b52-
            947852107643</MessageID>
            <State>
                <closed.abnormalCompleted.terminated/>
            </State>
        </ChangeBatchMessageState.Request>
    </WfMessageBody>
</WfMessage>
```

Response Parameters:

State—The new state to which the identified batch message has been changed. If the request was processed successfully, the contents of this element should match the state requested.

Exceptions:

In addition to all general exceptions defined in section 3.4.9.1, the following exceptions are specifically supported for this operation:

WF_INVALID_STATE_TRANSITION

Example 21:

```
<?xml version="1.0"?>
<WfMessage xmlns="http://www.wfmc.org/standards/docs/Wf-XML"
Version="1.1">
    <WfMessageHeader>
        <Response/>
        <Key>http://www.exampleco.com/processes</Key>
    </WfMessageHeader>
    <WfMessageBody>
        <ChangeBatchMessageState.Response>
            <State>
                <closed.abnormalCompleted.terminated/>
            </State>
        </ChangeBatchMessageState.Response>
    </WfMessageBody>
</WfMessage>
```

3.5.2 Process Definition Operations

This group of operations is used to perform actions on process definitions, such as creating process instances based on those definitions. The set of process definitions supported by a given enactment service must be predefined. Currently this group contains only the operation CreateProcessInstance.

3.5.2.1 CreateProcessInstance

CreateProcessInstance is used to instantiate a known process definition. The instance will be created with context-specific data set according to the input data, and automatically started.

```
<!ELEMENT CreateProcessInstance.Request (ObserverKey?, Name?,
Subject?, Description?, ContextData)>
<!ATTLIST CreateProcessInstance.Request StartImmediately (true | false)
#FIXED "true">
<!ELEMENT ObserverKey (#PCDATA)>
<!ELEMENT Name (#PCDATA)>
<!ELEMENT Subject (#PCDATA)>
<!ELEMENT Description (#PCDATA)>
<!ELEMENT ContextData ANY>
<!ELEMENT CreateProcessInstance.Response ((ProcessInstanceKey,
Name?) | Exception)>
<!ELEMENT ProcessInstanceKey (#PCDATA)>
```

These structures have the following semantic constraints and meanings:

Request Parameters:

StartImmediately—A Boolean value ("true" or "false"), indicating whether the newly created instance should be started immediately upon creation. The value of this parameter is currently always "true".

ObserverKey—URI of the resource that is to be the observer of the instance that is created by this operation. The resource specified must be the service requesting the operation. This observer resource (if it is specified) is to be notified of events impacting the execution of this process instance such as state changes, and most notably the completion of the instance. With the ObserverKey being set, the interoperability model of a nested or parallel-synchronized sub-process is implied, otherwise the model of a chained process is implied. (optional.)

Name—A human readable name requested to be assigned to the newly created instance. If this name is not unique, it may be modified to make it unique, or changed entirely. Therefore, the use of this name cannot be guaranteed. If the requested name is not used, the assigned name may be returned with the CreateProcessInstance.Response message to inform the initiator of the new name. (optional)

Subject—A short description of the purpose of the new process instance. (optional)

Description—A longer description of the purpose of the newly created process instance. (optional)

ContextData—Context-specific data required to create this process instance. This information will be encoded according to the data encoding formalism agreed upon in the interoperability contract (see section on Process Context and Result Data above).

Example 22:

```
<?xml version="1.0"?>
<WfMessage xmlns="http://www.wfmc.org/standards/docs/Wf-XML"
Version="1.1">
    <WfMessageHeader>
        <Request ResponseRequired="Yes"/>
        <Key>http://www.exampleco.com/processes/86947325</Key>
    </WfMessageHeader>
    <WfMessageBody>
        <CreateProcessInstance.Request
        StartImmediately="true">
            <ObserverKey>http://www.myco.com/purchasing/orders/40
            89259</ObserverKey>
            <ContextData>
                <Parameter>
                    <Name>VehDesc</Name>
                    <Value>
                        <Vehicle>
                            <VehicleType>Car</VehicleType>
                            <Specification>
                                <Manufac-
                                turer>Audi</Manufacturer>
                                <Model>A4</Model>
                            </Specification>
                        </Vehicle>
                    </Value>
                </Parameter>
                <Parameter>
                    <Name>Customer</Name>
                    <Value>John Doe</Value>
                </Parameter>
            </ContextData>
        </CreateProcessInstance.Request>
    </WfMessageBody>
</WfMessage>
```

Response Parameters:

ProcessInstanceKey—URI of the newly created process instance.

Name—The name actually assigned to the newly created process instance by the enacting resource. (optional)

Exceptions:

In addition to all general exceptions defined in section 3.4.9.1, the following exceptions are supported specifically for this operation:

WF_MISSING_PROCESS_INSTANCE_KEY

WF_INVALID_PROCESS_INSTANCE_KEY

WF_INVALID_PROCESS_DEFINITION

WF_INVALID_OBSERVER_FOR_RESOURCE

Example 23:

```
<?xml version="1.0"?>
<WfMessage xmlns="http://www.wfmc.org/standards/docs/Wf-XML"
Version="1.1">
    <WfMessageHeader>
        <Response/>
        <Key>http://www.exampleco.com/processes/86947325</Key>
    </WfMessageHeader>
    <WfMessageBody>
        <CreateProcessInstance.Response>
            <ProcessInstanceKey>http://www.exampleco.com/orders
            /86947325-32914 </ProcessInstanceKey>
        </CreateProcessInstance.Response>
    </WfMessageBody>
</WfMessage>
```

3.5.3 Process Instance Operations

This group of operations is used to communicate with a particular instance of a process definition (or enactment of a service), acquiring information about the instance and controlling it. Since a given instance may continue to execute for any amount of time, operations may be called on an instance while it is executing. These operations may obtain status information or obtain early results (although the results of a process instance are not final until the instance has been completed). This group contains the operations GetProcessInstanceData and ChangeProcessInstanceState.

3.5.3.1 GetProcessInstanceData

This operation is used to retrieve the values of properties defined for the given process instance.

```
<!ENTITY % ProcessInstanceData "Name | Subject | Description | State |
ValidStates | ObserverKey | ResultData | ProcessDefinitionKey | Priority |
LastModified">

<!ENTITY % states "open.notrunning | open.notrunning.suspended |
open.running | closed.completed | closed.abnormalCompleted.terminated |
closed.abnormalCompleted.aborted">

<!ELEMENT GetProcessInstanceData.Request (ResultDataSet?)>

<!ELEMENT ResultDataSet (%ProcessInstanceData;)+>

<!ELEMENT GetProcessInstanceData.Response
((%ProcessInstanceData;)+ | Exception)>

<!ELEMENT Name (#PCDATA)>

<!ELEMENT Subject (#PCDATA)>

<!ELEMENT Description (#PCDATA)>

<!ELEMENT State (%states;)?>

<!ELEMENT ValidStates (%states;)*>

<!ELEMENT ObserverKey (#PCDATA)>

<!ELEMENT ProcessDefinitionKey (#PCDATA)>

<!ELEMENT Priority (#PCDATA)>

<!ELEMENT LastModified (#PCDATA)>
```

These structures have the following semantic constraints and meanings:

Request Parameters:

ResultDataSet –This parameter contains a set of properties to be returned, where this set can be all of the properties or a subset of them. Note that the desired properties are specified by including their respective elements within this element. When included here, each property element should be empty. Any content of these contained elements should be ignored by the service receiving this message. If this element is not present, all process instance properties are returned. (optional)

The following example requests all properties of a particular ProcessInstance:

Example 24:

```
<?xml version="1.0"?>
<WfMessage xmlns="http://www.wfmc.org/standards/docs/Wf-XML"
Version="1.1" >
    <WfMessageHeader>
        <Request ResponseRequired="Yes"/>
        <Key>http://www.exampleco.com/orders/86947325-
        32914</Key>
    </WfMessageHeader>
    <WfMessageBody>
        <GetProcessInstanceData.Request/>
    </WfMessageBody>
</WfMessage>
```

The following example requests only the Name and Priority of a particular Process Instance:

Example 25:

```
<?xml version="1.0"?>
<WfMessage xmlns="http://www.wfmc.org/standards/docs/Wf-XML"
Version="1.1" >
    <WfMessageHeader>
        <Request ResponseRequired="Yes"/>
        <Key>http://www.exampleco.com/orders/86947325-
        32914</Key>
    </WfMessageHeader>
    <WfMessageBody>
        <GetProcessInstanceData.Request>
            <ResultDataSet>
                <Name/>
                <Priority/>
            </ResultDataSet>
        </GetProcessInstanceData.Request>
    </WfMessageBody>
</WfMessage>
```

Response Parameters:

Name—A human readable identifier of the resource. This name may be nothing more than a number. (optional)

Subject—A short description of this process instance. (optional)

Description—A longer description of this process instance resource. (optional)

State—The current status of this resource. (optional)

ValidStates—A list of state values allowed by this resource. This is the list of states to which the current instance can transition. (optional)

ProcessDefinitionKey—URI of the process definition resource from which this instance was created. (optional)

ObserverKey—URI of the registered observer of this process instance, if it exists. (optional)

ResultData—Context-specific data (as specified in the Interoperability Contract) that represents the current values resulting from process execution. This information will be encoded as described in the section Process Context and Result Data above. If result data are not available (yet), the ResultData element is returned empty. (optional)

Priority—An indication of the relative importance of this process instance. This value will be an integer ranging from 1 to 5, 1 being the highest priority. The default value is 3. (optional)

LastModified—The date of the last modification of this instance, if available. (optional)

Exceptions:

In addition to all general exceptions defined in section 3.4.9.1, the following exceptions are supported specifically for this operation:

WF_INVALID_RESULT_DATA

WF_INVALID_RESULT_DATA_SET

WF_INVALID_OBSERVER_FOR_RESOURCE

The following is an example of a response for a GetProcessInstanceData operation:

Example 26:

```
<?xml version="1.0"?>
<WfMessage xmlns="http://www.wfmc.org/standards/docs/Wf-XML"
Version="1.1">
    <WfMessageHeader>
        <Response/>
        <Key>http://www.exampleco.com/orders/86947325-
        32914</Key>
    </WfMessageHeader>
    <WfMessageBody>
        <GetProcessInstanceData.Response>
            <Name>Order32914</Name>
            <Priority>3</Priority>
        </GetProcessInstanceData.Response>
    </WfMessageBody>
</WfMessage>
```

3.5.3.2 *ChangeProcessInstanceState*

This operation is used to modify the process instance state; for example from open.running to open.notrunning.suspended.

```
<!ELEMENT ChangeProcessInstanceState.Request (State)>
<!ELEMENT ChangeProcessInstanceState.Response (State | Exception)>
<!ELEMENT State (%states;)?>
```

These structures have the following semantic constraints and meanings:

Request Parameters:

State—The new state to which the process instance should transition.

Example 27:

```
<?xml version="1.0"?>
<WfMessage xmlns="http://www.wfmc.org/standards/docs/Wf-XML"
Version="1.1">
    <WfMessageHeader>
        <Request ResponseRequired="Yes"/>
        <Key>http://www.exampleco.com/orders/86947325-
        32914</Key>
    </WfMessageHeader>
    <WfMessageBody>
        <ChangeProcessInstanceState.Request>
            <State>
                <open.notrunning.suspended/>
            </State>
        </ChangeProcessInstanceState.Request>
    </WfMessageBody>
</WfMessage>
```

Response Parameters:

State—The new state resulting from the operation.

Exceptions:

In addition to all general exceptions defined in section 3.4.9.1, the following exceptions are supported specifically for this operation:

WF_INVALID_STATE_TRANSITION

WF_INVALID_OBSERVER_FOR_RESOURCE

Example 28:

```
<?xml version="1.0"?>
<WfMessage xmlns="http://www.wfmc.org/standards/docs/Wf-XML"
Version="1.1">
    <WfMessageHeader>
        <Response/>
        <Key>http://www.exampleco.com/orders/86947325-
        32914</Key>
    </WfMessageHeader>
    <WfMessageBody>
        <ChangeProcessInstanceState.Response>
            <State>
                <open.notrunning.suspended/>
            </State>
        </ChangeProcessInstanceState.Response>
    </WfMessageBody>
</WfMessage>
```

3.5.4 Observer Operations

This group of operations allows the requester of work (the Observer of a process instance) to be notified of events and status changes impacting the execution of a process instance. This group contains the operations ProcessInstanceStateChanged and Notify.

3.5.4.2 ProcessInstanceStateChanged

This operation is used to support both closed.completed and closed.abnormalCompleted state changes. The ResponseRequired attribute will typically be set to false for this operation as it is normally only used as a notification to an observer that a state change event has occurred.

```
<!ELEMENT ProcessInstanceStateChanged.Request (ProcessInstanceKey,
State, ResultData?, LastModified?)>
<!ELEMENT ProcessInstanceKey (#PCDATA)>
<!ELEMENT State (%states;)?>
<!ELEMENT ResultData ANY>
<!ELEMENT LastModified (#PCDATA)>
<!ELEMENT ProcessInstanceStateChanged.Response (Exception?)>
```

These structures have the following semantic constraints and meanings:

Request Parameters:

ProcessInstanceKey—URI of the process instance resource that has changed.

State—The new status of this resource.

ResultData—Context-specific data that represents the current result values. This information will be encoded as described in the section on Process Context and Result Data above. If result data are not available (yet), the ResultData element is returned empty. (optional)

LastModified—The date of the last modification of this instance. (optional)

Example 29:

```
<?xml version="1.0"?>
<WfMessage xmlns="http://www.wfmc.org/standards/docs/Wf-XML"
Version="1.1">
    <WfMessageHeader>
        <Request ResponseRequired="No"/>
        <Key>http://www.myco.com/purchasing/orders/4089259</Ke
        y>
    </WfMessageHeader>
    <WfMessageBody>
        <ProcessInstanceStateChanged.Request>
            <ProcessInstanceKey>http://www.exampleco.com/orders
            /86947325-32914 </ProcessInstanceKey>
            <State>
                <closed.completed/>
            </State>
            <ResultData>
                <Parameter>
                    <Name>VehDesc</Name>
                    <Value>
                        <Vehicle>
                            <VehicleType>Car</VehicleType>
                            <Specification>
                                <Manufac-
                                turer>Audi</Manufacturer>
                                <Model>A4</Model>
                            </Specification>
                        </Vehicle>
                    </Value>
                </Parameter>
                <Parameter>
                    <Name>Customer</Name>
                    <Value>John Doe</Value>
                </Parameter>
            </ResultData>
        </ProcessInstanceStateChanged.Request>
    </WfMessageBody>
</WfMessage>
```

Response Parameters:

None

Exceptions:

In addition to all general exceptions defined in section 3.4.9.1, the following exceptions are supported specifically for this operation:

WF_INVALID_RESULT_DATA

WF_MISSING_PROCESS_INSTANCE_KEY

WF_INVALID_PROCESS_INSTANCE_KEY

WF_INVALID_STATE_TRANSITION

WF_INVALID_OBSERVER_FOR_RESOURCE

If the ResponseRequired attribute is set to "true" in the ProcessInstanceStateChanged request, a minimal response will be returned. This can be useful for trapping any errors that may occur during notification of the state change.

Example 30:

```
<?xml version="1.0"?>
<WfMessage xmlns="http://www.wfmc.org/standards/docs/Wf-XML"
Version="1.1">
    <WfMessageHeader>
        <Response/>
        <Key>http://www.myco.com/purchasing/orders/4089259</Ke
        y>
    </WfMessageHeader>
    <WfMessageBody>
        <ProcessInstanceStateChanged.Response/>
    </WfMessageBody>
</WfMessage>
```

3.5.4.2 *Notify*

This operation provides the means by which two process instances may communicate and synchronize while they are running. It is used to notify an observer (which is very likely another process instance) of the occurrence of an event in a process instance that is relevant to the further operation of the observer. This operation should not be used to inform a resource of state changes within a process instance, instead the ProcessInstanceStateChanged operation should be used for that purpose. This operation is to be used to notify a resource of application-specific events. The nature of these events and details regarding them must therefore be agreed upon in the interoperability contract in order to make use of this operation.

Typically, these notifications will deal with changes in application data that can impact the interoperation of the processes. Therefore, this operation may indicate (within ContextData) information regarding the affected data items in addition to information regarding the event itself. The Notify operation elements are structured as follows:

```
<!ELEMENT Notify.Request (ProcessInstanceKey, NotificationName,
ContextData)>
<!ELEMENT ProcessInstanceKey (#PCDATA)>
<!ELEMENT NotificationName (#PCDATA)>
<!ELEMENT ContextData ANY>
<!ELEMENT Notify.Response (Exception?)>
```

These structures have the following semantic constraints and meanings:

Request Parameters:

ProcessInstanceKey—Key of the process instance that invokes the operation.

NotificationName—Name of the message for notification. The contents of this element are subject to agreements made in the interoperability contract, as events are specific to particular application and/or process instance requirements.

ContextData—Context-specific data that represents application data to be delivered to the observer. This information will be encoded as described in the section on Process Context and Result Data.

Example 31:

```
<?xml version="1.0"?>
<WfMessage xmlns="http://www.wfmc.org/standards/docs/Wf-XML"
Version="1.1">
    <WfMessageHeader>
        <Request ResponseRequired="No"/>
        <Key>http://www.myco.com/purchasing/orders/4089259</Ke
        y>
    </WfMessageHeader>
    <WfMessageBody>
        <Notify.Request>
            <ProcessInstance-
            Key>http://www.exampleco.com/orders/86947325-32914
            </ProcessInstanceKey>
            <NotificationName>OrderChanged</NotificationName>
            <ContextData>
                <Parameter>
                    <Name>VehDesc</Name>
                    <Value>
                        <Vehicle>
                            <VehicleType>Car</VehicleType>
                            <Specification>
                                <Manufac-
                                turer>Audi</Manufacturer>
                                <Model>A4</Model>
                            </Specification>
                        </Vehicle>
                    </Value>
                </Parameter>
            </ContextData>
        </Notify.Request>
    </WfMessageBody>
</WfMessage>
```

Response Parameters:

None.

Exceptions:

In addition to all general exceptions defined in section 3.4.9.1, the following exceptions are supported specifically for this operation:

WF_INVALID_CONTEXT_DATA

WF_MISSING_PROCESS_INSTANCE_KEY

WF_INVALID_PROCESS_INSTANCE_KEY

WF_INVALID_OBSERVER_FOR_RESOURCE

WF_MISSING_ NOTIFICATION_NAME

WF_INVALID_ NOTIFICATION_NAME

Example 32:

```
<?xml version="1.0"?>
<WfMessage xmlns="http://www.wfmc.org/standards/docs/Wf-XML"
Version="1.1">
    <WfMessageHeader>
        <Response/>
        <Key>http://www.myco.com/purchasing/orders/4089259</Ke
        y>
    </WfMessageHeader>
    <WfMessageBody>
        <Notify.Response/>
    </WfMessageBody>
</WfMessage>
```

4 RELATIONSHIP TO OTHER STANDARDS

4.1 OMG Workflow Management Facility Standard (jointFlow)

The following discusses the mapping between the interfaces defined in the OMG Workflow Management Facility standard and the Wf-XML resources and operations. The Wf-XML standard uses the basic object model defined in the OMG Workflow Management Facility Standard specification. It supports a subset of the entities defined in this object model and it also combines operations that were separated in the OMG Workflow Management Facility interfaces into a single operation, thereby improving performance by not requiring such fine-grained operations.

The OMG Workflow Management Facility WfProcessMgr interface corresponds to the Wf-XML ProcessDefinition resource type. The Wf-XML CreateProcessInstance operation combines the OMG Workflow Management Facility create_process operation on WfProcessMgr, the start and the set_context operation on WfProcess.

The OMG Workflow Management Facility WfProcess interface corresponds to the Wf-XML ProcessInstance resource type; the OMG Workflow Management Facility operation change_state on WfProcess (inherited from the WfExecutionElement) corresponds to the Wf-XML operation ChangeProcessInstanceState. The WfProcess operation get_result in combination with the 'getter' functions for state variables on WfProcess correspond to the Wf-XML operation GetProcessInstanceData.

The OMG Workflow Management Facility WfRequester interface corresponds to the Wf-XML Observer resource type.

The OMG Workflow Management Facility specification defines some interfaces that are not represented by Wf-XML at this point in time: WfActivity, WfResource, WfAssignment.

5 IMPLEMENTATION ISSUES

5.1 Interoperability Contract

It is recognized that there may be additional requirements outside the scope of the specification that vendors may wish to fulfill in order to achieve basic interoperability. For this reason, it is recommended that an interoperability contract be established among vendors participating in interoperable workflows. This contract will clearly define each vendor's expectations and requirements in all areas that may impede interoperability. A list of topics to be included in the interoperability contract is provided here as an example, but this list should by no means be considered complete. Each interoperating vendor must ensure that all factors impacting their implementation are addressed completely.

Some of the topics that should be described in the interoperability contract are:

- Data Requirements—application-specific data required to be transferred in order to utilize basic or extended functionality. This data will appear in the ContextData and ResultData elements. Any specific data transfer requirements should also be addressed here.
- Data Constraints—application-specific data type requirements, field lengths, allowable characters, character set encoding, overall message size, etc.
- Error Handling—application-specific error handling requirements such as SubCodes, descriptions, required actions, etc.
- Transport Protocol Specifics—required protocol header data, timeout values, buffer sizes, asynchronous or batch processing requirements, etc.
- Security Considerations—encryption methods, user verification, firewall configuration requirements, etc.
- Key/ID Requirements—Details regarding management of (relative) keys, format of implementation-specific identifiers (of objects), etc.
- Process Synchronization—Specifics regarding events of which a process must be notified in order to synchronize

6 CONFORMANCE

For many product vendors and purchasers of workflow systems, it will be highly desirable to have a means of ascertaining a system's conformance to this specification. This section outlines several factors involved in doing so. In order to assist in determining conformance, this section also introduces several categories for features of the specification, and names for those features.

There are four high-level categories for specification features:

- Interoperability Models
- Message Processing Types
- Protocol Constructs
- Operations

The features within these categories are defined as follows. There are three Interoperability Models currently defined by the WfMC Workflow Reference Model: Chained, Nested and Parallel-Synchronized.

The Message Processing Types currently available as of this version are: Synchronous, Asynchronous, Individual and Batch.

The following Protocol Constructs are available as of this version: Header/Body, Transport/Header/Body, Transport Only and Transport & Multiple Header/Body.

The complete list of operations currently specified is: GetBatchMessageState, ChangeBatchMessageState, CreateProcessInstance, GetProcessInstanceData, ChangeProcessInstanceState, ProcessInstanceStateChanged and Notify.

These categories and features are organized into several conformance profiles, as described below. Products claiming conformance to this specification must provide a clear conformance statement indicating the following information:

1. The conformance profile(s) supported.
2. The transport mechanism(s) supported. For this version of the specification, HTTP is the only transport mechanism supported.

For example, a vendor can claim to implement this specification, and declare their implementation to be "conformant to the interoperability and asynchronous profiles over http."

6.1 Conformance Profiles

A vendor can claim conformance to one or more of the following profiles: Interoperability, Asynchronous, or Batch. Every conformant implementation must implement the Interoperability profile. The Asynchronous and Batch profiles are optional.

6.1.1 Interoperability (Mandatory)

Every implementation of this specification must implement the Interoperability profile, which inherently supports the Chained and Nested Interoperability Models. This profile includes support for the basic Message Processing Types: Synchronous and Individual. It also includes support for the basic Protocol Construct: Header/Body. The Protocol Construct Transport/Header/Body may also optionally be supported in this profile. Finally, in conforming to this profile an implementation must support the following Operations, as defined in this specification:

- CreateProcessInstance
- GetProcessInstanceData
- ChangeProcessInstanceState
- ProcessInstanceStateChanged

- Notify

6.1.2 Asynchronous (Optional)

An implementation of the optional asynchronous profile must support the Message Processing Type: Asynchronous. It must also support for the Protocol Constructs: Transport/Header/Body and Transport Only.

6.1.3 Batch (Optional)

An implementation of the optional batch profile must support the Message Processing Type: Batch. It must also support the Protocol Construct: Transport & Multiple Header/Body. Lastly, this profile includes support for the following operations, as defined in this specification:

- GetBatchMessageState
- ChangeBatchMessageState

6.2 Version Conformance

As stated in section 1.1 Version Compatibility, this version of the Wf-XML specification is backward compatible with version 1.0. In this section, we describe the conformance impact of changes made to this version of the specification.

This specification defines no requirement for a Wf-XML v1.0 processor to be upgraded to support version 1.1 messages. It also defines no requirement that a Wf-XML v1.1 processor support version 1.0 messages. However if a processor is to support both versions of this specification, it must ensure that any message it sends or receives is conformant with the version of the specification indicated by the value of the "Version" attribute on the message's WfMessage element.

The following table is provided to assist in determining which features are available in each version of the specification. This is not a conformance profile matrix, but is intended to segregate version 1.0 capabilities from those only available in version 1.1. As stated above, the asynchronous and batch processing features available in version 1.1 are not required to be supported in order for a processor to be conformant with this version of the specification.

	Version 1.0	Version 1.1
Interoperability Models		
Chained	X	X
Nested	X	X
Parallel-Synchronized		X*
Message Processing Types		
Synchronous	X	X

Asynchronous		X
Individual	X	X
Batch		X
Protocol Constructs		
Header/Body	X	X
Transport/Header/Body	X	X
Transport Only (Acknowledgement)		X
Transport & Multiple Header/Body (Batch)		X
Operations		
GetBatchMessageState		X
ChangeBatchMessageState		X
CreateProcessInstance	X	X
GetProcessInstanceData	X	X
ChangeProcessInstanceState	X	X
ProcessInstanceStateChanged	X	X
Notify		X

Table 2: Feature Availability

* *The Parallel-Synchronized Interoperability Model is partially supported in this version of the specification via the Notify operation. Complete support will be provided in future versions.*

6.3 Other Considerations

The critical factor in determining conformance lies in a vendor's ability to implement the functionality described by the specification according to the conformance profiles. However, other XML-related factors described here may also impact an implementation.

6.4 Validity vs. Well-Formedness

All XML document instances (in this case Wf-XML messages) may be in one of several states of "validity". They may be 'invalid' due to some syntactical error in their markup. They may be 'well-formed', meaning they are syntactically correct with regard to the XML specification. Finally, they may be 'valid', meaning they are not only syntactically correct (per spec), but are also fully compliant with a Document Type Definition (DTD) or XML Schema Description (XSD) file. The XML specification imposes no requirement on a document instance to be valid, only well-formed. In the case where well-formed data is to be processed, the burden of validating syntactic or semantic constraints over and above those specified by the XML specification lies entirely with the processing application.

For this reason, this specification does not mandate validity of all document instances, rather it only requires that all Wf-XML messages are well-formed and compliant with the semantic constraints imposed herein. It is therefore the responsibility of an application implementing this specification to ensure that these constraints are not violated.

However, there is an added measure of data integrity provided by validating a document instance via an XML parser. If an application should desire to do so, the DTD provided with this specification can be used for this purpose. Bear in mind though, that there will remain certain semantic constraints of this data that cannot currently be modeled in a DTD. These semantics will still have to be understood and handled by the implementing application.

6.5 Conformance vs. Extensibility

Another factor that can potentially impact conformance is extensibility. This topic has been addressed earlier in this document with regard to the provisions made within the constraints of the Wf-XML language. However, it is recognized that it may be desirable to extend an application's data exchange requirements beyond these limits. In cases where interoperating vendors have agreed upon functionality and message formats outside the definitions of this specification, or have simply utilized undefined markup that is to be ignored by their interoperating partners, they should be able to do so while maintaining conformance.

It is recommended that namespaces be used to facilitate the interchange of this application-specific data within Wf-XML messages. An implementation may utilize namespaces to differentiate process-related data from target application data, as well as from Wf-XML encoded protocol data. Proper namespace qualification of context-specific data will also shield it from changes to the Wf-XML protocol data as new versions are released.

This specification only requires well-formed data. Therefore, interoperating vendors may exchange any data they wish in the context-specific elements so long as that data meets the syntactic requirements of the XML specification. Although it would obviously be best from a functional perspective if the vendors were able to agree upon this data's markup, if they cannot the recipient of the unknown markup should simply ignore it and return it to the sender upon request. Conformance will not be degraded unless the vendor fails to comply with the markup declarations provided here.

7 TRANSPORT LAYER BINDINGS

Wf-XML messages for workflow interoperability can be communicated between interoperating workflow systems using many different transport mechanisms/protocols. As these protocols support a fundamental requirement of message-based inter-operability, their behavior and the actions they specify must not be compromised in their usage by this specification. Furthermore, the behaviors and actions specified by Wf-XML must be supported by these underlying protocols, while not having any dependencies on any particular protocol. Therefore, this section will define the relationships and interactions between Wf-XML and its underlying transport mechanism.

This section provides a specification for a Hypertext Transfer Protocol (HTTP) [12] binding. This is considered the most common transport mechanism utilized to communicate Wf-XML messages between interoperating enactment services. The support of this or any other particular transport layer binding is not required for an implementation to be compliant with this specification. However, one of the specified transport layer bindings must be used to realistically effect interoperability, and this is the only specified binding to date.

7.1 HTTP

For HTTP, the communicating enactment services are considered HTTP servers (services may communicate directly via HTTP, or they may be combined with another program to enable them to send and receive HTTP methods). Wf-XML messages for all the operations specified earlier are integrated as input data or output data with respect to HTTP interactions.

In more detail, an operation is encoded in the HTTP-method POST. POST is directed to some URI [14] and may have MIME (Multipurpose Internet Mail Extension) body parts for input and output. For Wf-XML, exactly one MIME body part is used for input and exactly one MIME body part is used for output.

The URI to which a POST method is directed is the key of the resource from the Wf-XML message. This key can be found in one of two places within the message. The primary location is the "Key" element within the WfMessageHeader element. However if the message is an Acknowledgement (used in asynchronous processing) or a Batch message (containing multiple headers), then the "Key" element within the Dialog element of the WfTransport section serves as the identifier of the resource to which a POST method is directed.

As an alternative to absolute addressing, an implementation may chose to maintain the base URI for a resource internally and combine this with a relative URI in the message header to formulate an absolute URI. If an implementation wishes to utilize relative URIs in this way, further details should be agreed upon in the interoperability contract. In either case, this data is vendor-specific and must either be known beforehand (e.g., in case of a process definition key) or obtained as the result of a response parameter returned by a prethe purposes of this binding, all final URIs will be resolvable via HTTP, i.e—they must be of the form "http://...".

In synchronous processing, the Wf-XML Request message is the one MIME body part for input and the Wf-XML Response message is the one MIME body part for output. Furthermore, these messages must be included with their respective HTTP requests/responses. That is to say, that a Wf-XML Request message must be sent with an HTTP request and a Wf-XML Response message must be sent with its HTTP response.

In asynchronous processing, the Wf-XML message (consisting of Requests and/or Responses) is the one MIME body part for input and the Wf-XML Acknowledgement message is the one MIME body part for output.

All Wf-XML MIME body parts must use the MIME content type "Content-type: text/xml" in the HTTP-method header, and the Content-length must be set according to the length of the Wf-XML Request or Response message respectively.

All Wf-XML message processing is subject to the successful execution of HTTP method processing. Therefore, all HTTP status codes must be interpreted independently of this specification, and all Wf-XML processing assumes successful completion of HTTP procedures prior to execution. For authentication, the usual HTTP mechanisms should be used. This includes usage of the respective HTTP header fields.

8 DOCUMENT TYPE DEFINITION (DTD)

This section provides the Wf-XML DTD for the purposes of implementation reference and optional data validation by an XML processor.

This DTD is designed with the intention of being simple and easy to implement, while supporting a robust and flexible structure.

```
<!-- ~~~~~~~~~~~~~~~~~~~~~~~~~~~~~~~~~~~~~~~~~~~~~~~~~~~~~~ -->
<!-- Wf-XML DTD, Revision 1.1 - 24 October, 2001            -->
<!--                                                        -->
<!-- If a DOCTYPE declaration is required to parse this set of declarations,
the following line should be     --> <!-- prepended to this file:     -->
<!--  '<!DOCTYPE WfMessage ['                                -->
<!-- and the following line appended:                        -->
<!--  ']>'                                                   -->
<!--                                                        -->
<!-- If a PUBLIC identifier is used to reference this DTD from a document
instance, the following     --> <!-- identifier should be used:        -->
<!--  'PUBLIC "-//WfMC//DTD Wf-XML 1.1//EN"                 -->
<!--             http://www.wfmc.org/standards/docs/Wf-XML-1.1.dtd  -->
<!-- ~~~~~~~~~~~~~~~~~~~~~~~~~~~~~~~~~~~~~~~~~~~~~~~~~~~~~~-->
```

```
<!-- ~~~~~~~~~~~~~~~~~ Entity Declarations ~~~~~~~~~~~~~~~~~~~ -->
<!-- The ISOLangs entity provides the choices for the ResponseLang
attribute of the Request element. These language codes are taken from the
ISO 639:1988 standard, which can be used for further clarification of the
names of each language and can be obtained from
http://www.iso.ch/cate/d4766.html. Additional information is also available at:
http://www.oasis-open.org/cover/iso639a.html. -->
<!ENTITY % ISOLangs
"(aa|ab|af|am|ar|as|ay|az|ba|be|bg|bh|bi|bn|bo|br|ca|co|cs|cy|da|de|dz|el|en|e
o|es|et|eu|fa|fi|fj|fo|fr|fy|ga|gd|gl|gn|gu|ha|hi|hr|hu|hy|ia|ie|ik|in|is|it|iw|ja|ji|jw|ka
|kk|kl|km|kn|ko|ks|ku|ky|la|ln|lo|lt|lv|mg|mi|mk|ml|mn|mo|mr|ms|mt|my|na|ne|nl
|no|oc|om|or|pa|pl|ps|pt|qu|rm|rn|ro|ru|rw|sa|sd|sg|sh|si|sk|sl|sm|sn|so|sq|sr|s
s|st|su|sv|sw|ta|te|tg|th|ti|tk|tl|tn|to|tr|ts|tt|tw|uk|ur|uz|vi|vo|wo|xh|yo|zh|zu)">

<!-- The xml:space attribute may be used to indicate that white space should
be preserved. -->
<!ENTITY % space "xml:space (default | preserve) #IMPLIED">
<!-- The xml:lang attribute may be used to indicate the natural language used
in an element. -->
<!ENTITY % lang "xml:lang NMTOKEN #IMPLIED">

<!-- The following entities are used to define the request and response ele-
ments for each operation. -->
<!ENTITY % OperationRequest "GetBatchMessageState.Request |
ChangeBatchMessageState.Request | CreateProcessInstance.Request |
GetProcessInstanceData.Request | ChangeProcessInstanceState.Request |
ProcessInstanceStateChanged.Request | Notify.Request">

<!ENTITY % OperationResponse "GetBatchMessageState.Response |
ChangeBatchMessageState.Response | CreateProcessInstance.Response |
GetProcessInstanceData.Response |
ChangeProcessInstanceState.Response |
ProcessInstanceStateChanged.Response | Notify.Response">

<!-- The ProcessInstanceData entity defines the properties of a process
instance that may be obtained using the GetProcessInstanceData operation.
-->
<!ENTITY % ProcessInstanceData "Name | Subject | Description | State |
ValidStates | ObserverKey | ResultData | ProcessDefinitionKey | Priority |
LastModified">

<!-- This is the list of valid states defined by the WfMC for version 1.1 of Wf-
XML. -->
<!ENTITY % states "open.notrunning | open.notrunning.suspended |
open.running | closed.completed | closed.abnormalCompleted |
closed.abnormalCompleted.terminated |
closed.abnormalCompleted.aborted">
```

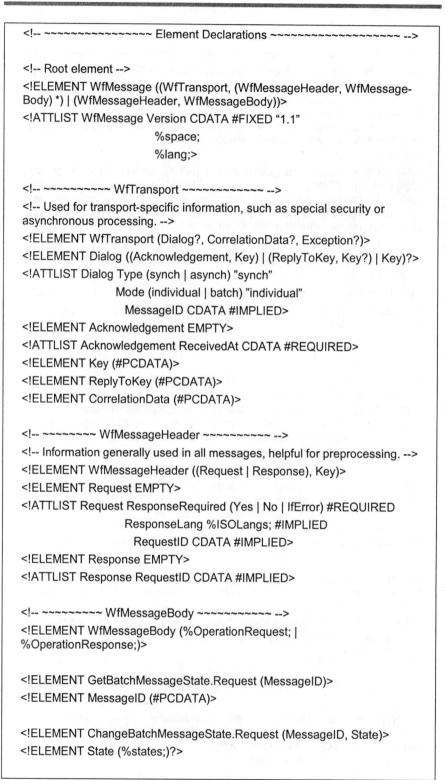

```
<!-- ~~~~~~~~~~~~~~~ Element Declarations ~~~~~~~~~~~~~~~~~~~~ -->

<!-- Root element -->
<!ELEMENT WfMessage ((WfTransport, (WfMessageHeader, WfMessage-
Body) *) | (WfMessageHeader, WfMessageBody))>
<!ATTLIST WfMessage Version CDATA #FIXED "1.1"
                        %space;
                        %lang;>


<!-- ~~~~~~~~~ WfTransport ~~~~~~~~~~~~ -->
<!-- Used for transport-specific information, such as special security or
asynchronous processing. -->
<!ELEMENT WfTransport (Dialog?, CorrelationData?, Exception?)>
<!ELEMENT Dialog ((Acknowledgement, Key) | (ReplyToKey, Key?) | Key)?>
<!ATTLIST Dialog Type (synch | asynch) "synch"
                Mode (individual | batch) "individual"
                MessageID CDATA #IMPLIED>
<!ELEMENT Acknowledgement EMPTY>
<!ATTLIST Acknowledgement ReceivedAt CDATA #REQUIRED>
<!ELEMENT Key (#PCDATA)>
<!ELEMENT ReplyToKey (#PCDATA)>
<!ELEMENT CorrelationData (#PCDATA)>


<!-- ~~~~~~~~ WfMessageHeader ~~~~~~~~~~ -->
<!-- Information generally used in all messages, helpful for preprocessing. -->
<!ELEMENT WfMessageHeader ((Request | Response), Key)>
<!ELEMENT Request EMPTY>
<!ATTLIST Request ResponseRequired (Yes | No | IfError) #REQUIRED
                    ResponseLang %ISOLangs; #IMPLIED
                    RequestID CDATA #IMPLIED>
<!ELEMENT Response EMPTY>
<!ATTLIST Response RequestID CDATA #IMPLIED>


<!-- ~~~~~~~~ WfMessageBody ~~~~~~~~~~~ -->
<!ELEMENT WfMessageBody (%OperationRequest; |
%OperationResponse;)>


<!ELEMENT GetBatchMessageState.Request (MessageID)>
<!ELEMENT MessageID (#PCDATA)>


<!ELEMENT ChangeBatchMessageState.Request (MessageID, State)>
<!ELEMENT State (%states;)?>
```

```
<!ELEMENT CreateProcessInstance.Request (ObserverKey?, Name?, Sub-
ject?, Description?, ContextData)>
<!ATTLIST CreateProcessInstance.Request StartImmediately (true | false)
#FIXED "true">


<!ELEMENT ObserverKey (#PCDATA)>
<!ELEMENT Name (#PCDATA)>
<!ELEMENT Subject (#PCDATA)>
<!ELEMENT Description (#PCDATA)>
<!ELEMENT ContextData ANY>
<!ATTLIST ContextData %space;
                      %lang;>


<!ELEMENT GetProcessInstanceData.Request (ResultDataSet?)>
<!ELEMENT ResultDataSet (%ProcessInstanceData;)+>


<!ELEMENT ValidStates (%states;)*>
<!ELEMENT open.notrunning EMPTY>
<!ELEMENT open.notrunning.suspended EMPTY>
<!ELEMENT open.running EMPTY>
<!ELEMENT closed.completed EMPTY>
<!ELEMENT closed.abnormalCompleted EMPTY>
<!ELEMENT closed.abnormalCompleted.terminated EMPTY>
<!ELEMENT closed.abnormalCompleted.aborted EMPTY>


<!ELEMENT ResultData ANY>
<!ATTLIST ResultData %space;
                     %lang;>
<!ELEMENT ProcessDefinitionKey (#PCDATA)>
<!ELEMENT Priority (#PCDATA)>
<!ELEMENT LastModified (#PCDATA)>


<!ELEMENT ChangeProcessInstanceState.Request (State)>


<!ELEMENT ProcessInstanceStateChanged.Request (ProcessInstanceKey,
State, ResultData?, LastModified?)>
<!ELEMENT ProcessInstanceKey (#PCDATA)>


<!ELEMENT Notify.Request (ProcessInstanceKey, NotificationName,
ContextData)>
<!ELEMENT NotificationName (#PCDATA)>


<!ELEMENT GetBatchMessageState.Response (State | Exception)>
```

```
<!ELEMENT ChangeBatchMessageState.Response (State | Exception)>

<!ELEMENT CreateProcessInstance.Response ((ProcessInstanceKey,
Name?) | Exception)>

<!ELEMENT GetProcessInstanceData.Response
((%ProcessInstanceData;)+ | Exception)>

<!ELEMENT ChangeProcessInstanceState.Response (State | Exception)>

<!ELEMENT ProcessInstanceStateChanged.Response (Exception?)>

<!ELEMENT Notify.Response (Exception?)>

<!ELEMENT Exception (MainCode, SubCode?, Type, Subject,
Description?)>
<!ELEMENT MainCode (#PCDATA)>
<!ELEMENT SubCode (#PCDATA)>
<!ELEMENT Type (#PCDATA)>
```

APPENDIX A—TERMINOLOGY

In large part, the terms used herein and their meanings are as stated in the Workflow Management Coalition Glossary [9]. However, throughout this document various terms, acronyms and abbreviations are used that may have ambiguous or conflicting definitions for individuals who have been exposed to similar terminology in other industries. These terms are specific to XML as used in this specification. In order to make certain that these terms are properly understood, several essential terms and definitions are provided here.

- DTD—Document Type Definition, a set of markup declarations that provide a grammar for a class of documents.
- Element—A component of an XML document consisting of markup and the text contained within that markup.
- Root Element—The outermost element of a document instance, such that the element does not appear in the content of any other element in the instance.
- Attribute— A component of an XML document used to associate named properties with an element.
- Entity—A unit of storage in which the contents of the storage unit are associated with a name.
- Document Instance—An instance of a document type (or class of documents).

APPENDIX B—FUTURE DIRECTIONS (NON-NORMATIVE)

This appendix describes several features of the Wf-XML specification for which enhancements are being considered in future versions. It is provided as a convenience for developers, as it may provide some insight into possible future directions for an implementation. None of the changes discussed here should be relied upon in any way, as they are merely preliminary suggestions and are highly subject to change.

B.1   Messaging Protocol

This specification can be considered to consist of two major components: a messaging protocol and core interoperability functions. The messaging protocol is essential in that it comprises the overall message structure, an exception handling mechanism, an identification and addressing mechanism, and transport layer bindings. The WfMC created the messaging protocol used by Wf-XML from scratch, as there was no known suitable protocol available at the time of its creation.

However, there has been much attention focused on this area by industry and standards bodies as the use of XML-based messaging became increasingly prevalent. Recently, this attention has resulted in the development of protocols such as XML-RPC, Blocks (BXXP), SOAP, XP and ebXML TR&P. The coalition is now considering some of these protocols as alternatives to the native Wf-XML protocol. This consideration may result in the replacement of the Wf-XML messaging protocol by one of these emerging standards, or independence from the messaging protocol layer if no single standard can be selected.

B.2   Specification Meta-Language

This specification currently uses the Document Type Definition (DTD) syntax to define the Wf-XML vocabulary and grammar. However, it is recognized that due to the diverse usage of XML there are now numerous alternative schema definition languages available. These include the W3C XML Schema Definition language (XSDL), Schematron, RELAX, TREX and others.

It is highly likely that the next version of this specification will leverage the W3C XML Schema Definition language's enhanced capabilities for enhanced semantic and data type validation. There is also some potential for updating the specification in a schema-neutral fashion, allowing for the creation of "schema language bindings" to accommodate multiple preferences. However, this flexibility will need to be balanced against the possible impact to interoperability.

B.3   Operations

The operations contained within this section are reserved for future use. High-level descriptions of these operations are provided here, although details of their functionality have yet to be determined. The following table summarizes the operations covered in this section.

	Control	Process Definition	Process Instance	Observer
WfQueryInterface	X			
ListInstances		X		
SetData			X	
Subscribe			X	
Unsubscribe			X	
GetHistory			X	

Table 3: Additional Operations

B.3.1   Control Operations

B.3.1.1 WfQueryInterface

This operation is used to query an implementation for various generic capabilities. In particular, it can be used to determine the capabilities of an implementation to support various security requirements, conformance to this specification or XML processing features.

B.3.2   Process Definition Operations

B.3.2.1 ListInstances

This operation is used to retrieve a list of instances of the given process definition. Each instance in the returned list is identified with its key, name and priority.

B.3.3   Process Instance Operations

B.3.3.1 SetData

This operation is used to set the values of any number of properties of the given process instance resource. This operation allows all of the settable properties of a resource as parameters, dependent on the interface in which it is invoked. At least one parameter must be provided in order for the operation to have any effect, but all parameters are optional. Current values of all the properties of the resource are returned.

B.3.3.2 Subscribe

This operation is used to register a resource with another resource, as a party interested in status changes and events that occur. If this particular resource does not support other observers, an exception will be returned to the caller.

B.3.3.3 Unsubscribe

This operation is used to remove a resource from the list of registered observers of a resource. The calling resource will no longer receive event notifications after executing this operation.

B.3.3.4 GetHistory

This operation is used to retrieve the list of events that have occurred on this resource. If the service implementing this resource has not kept a transaction log, there may not be any history available. However, if there is, it will be returned by this method.

B.4   Ancillary Supporting Mechanisms

This section describes developments being considered that may or may not be specified within this document. Nevertheless, these developments would lend to interoperability and/or assist developers in implementing this specification and validating their implementations.

B.4.1   Interoperability Contract

While certain recommendations are made within this specification pertaining to the interoperability contract between workflow enactment services, there is currently no well-defined syntax or structure for such a contract. As the creation and usage of web services continues to propagate throughout various industries, advances are being made in the area of dynamic interoperability. One such advance exists in the form of the trading partner agreement Markup Language (tpaML) specification, which is targeted for use by the ebXML initiative. This specification may prove useful as a basis for Wf-XML interoperability contracts.

B.4.2   Reference Framework Implementation

A very helpful tool for any implementers of a new specification is a reference implementation framework on which development can be based. The coalition would like to make such a reference framework available, pending availability of resources. There is also consideration being given to developing such a framework in an open source environment.

B.4.3   Conformance Testing Harness

Conformance testing of its specifications has long been a goal of the WfMC, and this is true in the case of the Wf-XML specification. Steps have been taken to facilitate this testing by the coalition both within and outside of this specification, and further work will be done in future versions of this document to enhance its testability. There is also some potential to develop a test harness or certification mechanism of some sort in conjunction with the framework development discussed above.

APPENDIX C REFERENCES

1. "Workflow Standard—Interoperability Abstract Specification," The Workflow Management Coalition, WfMC-TC-1012, 1.0, 20 Oct. 1996. http://www.wfmc.org/standards/docs/if4-a.pdf

2. "The Workflow Reference Model," The Workflow Management Coalition, WfMC-TC-1003, 1.1, 19 Jan 1995. http://www.wfmc.org/standards/docs/tc003v11-16.pdf

3. "Workflow Management Facility," Joint Submission, bom/98-06-07, revised submission, 4 July 1998. ftp://ftp.omg.org/pub/docs/bom/98-06-07.pdf

4. "Workflow Standard—Interoperability Internet e-mail MIME Binding," The Workflow Management Coalition, WfMC-TC-1018, 1.1, 25 Sep. 1998. http://www.wfmc.org/standards/docs/I4Mime1x.pdf

5. "Simple Workflow Access Protocol (SWAP)," Keith Swenson, Internet-Draft, 7 Aug. 1998. http://www.ics.uci.edu/~ietfswap

6. "Extensible Markup Language (XML)," W3C, REC-xml-19980210, 1.0, 10 Feb. 1998. http://www.w3.org/TR/1998/REC-xml-19980210

7. Open Database Connectivity (ODBC), Microsoft Corporation. http://www.microsoft.com/data/odbc

8. "Data elements and interchange formats -- Information interchange -- Representation of dates and times," International Standards Organization, ISO 8601:1988, 1, 4 March 1999. http://www.iso.ch/cate/d15903.html

9. "Terminology & Glossary," The Workflow Management Coalition, WfMC-TC-1011, 3.0, Feb. 1999 http://www.wfmc.org/standards/docs/glossy3.pdf

10. "Audit Data Specification," The Workflow Management Coalition, WfMC-TC-1015, 1.1, 22 Sep. 1998. http://www.wfmc.org/standards/docs/if5v11b.pdf

11. "Namespaces in XML," W3C, REC-xml-names-19990114, 1.0, 14 Jan. 1999. http://www.w3.org/TR/REC-xml-names

12. "Hypertext Transfer Protocol—HTTP/1.1," R. Fielding et al., Request for Comments 2616, June 1998. http://www.ietf.org/rfc/rfc2616.txt

13. "Code for the Representation of Names of Languages," International Standards Organization, ISO 639:1988, 1, 30 November 1992. http://www.iso.ch/cate/d4766.html

14. "Uniform Resource Identifiers (URI): Generic Syntax," T Berners-Lee, R. Fielding, L. Masinter, Request for Comments 2396, August 1998. http://www.ietf.org/rfc/rfc2396.txt

15. International Organization for Standardization, ISO/IEC 11578 (1996). "Information technology—Open Systems Interconnection—Remote Procedure Call (RPC)". See also: http://www.opengroup.org/onlinepubs/009629399/apdxa.htm#tagcjh_20

Section 3

Case Studies:
Global Excellence in Workflow Awards

Anova, Netherlands

Award Finalist, Europe, 2001

OVERVIEW

Dutch-based medical insurance firm Anova, part of the Agis Group, completely overhauled and updated its document management and workflow system with software and consultancy from Staffware, with dramatic long-term benefits to the organization and its competitiveness.

SYSTEM OVERVIEW

The solution at Anova had to accommodate the merger in 1998 between Anova and two other Dutch healthcare companies, Anoz and ZAO. Together, the three now form the Agis Group. The new IT infrastructure had to embrace the legacy systems of all three companies, and the solution had to be available to managers in all three organizations.

The implementation at Anova has two distinct elements: one, computerizing and automating the document management system from the original patient records, and two, automating its business processes by introducing a workflow system which embraces a revamped call centre solution. Another crucial aspect is the linking and integration of three separate back office environments at Anova, Anoz and ZAO, so that the resulting system and reporting facilities support the business goals of the Agis Group.

The back office system has to manage over 200,000 medical applications from prospective patients per year; 100,000 annual declarations from specialists, doctors and hospitals, which means 1.2 million records every month; 400,000 declarations of insurance every year; and 1,100,000 changes to existing documents every year.

There are almost 800 employees at Anova, and over 2,200 employees within the Agis Group. Anova is divided into three clear divisions, the backoffice, frontoffice and healthcare, as well as senior management and the board. The objective was to integrate and improve synergy between all employees and departments, and improve efficiency in dealing with all customers and contacts.

The new process of document management has the incoming documents being scanned by the Scan PCs at facilities management. The scanned documents are manually processed by using a separate program and sent to the Documentum server in batches on a regular basis. The Callcentre Workstations are able to store changes to the documents by taking changes received by telephone directly into the system. The Rend PC manages the conversion of Word and Notepad documents to the PDF format, and the COLD PC receives printfiles every night from the legacy mainframe which it coverts into separate documents for storage to laser disk. These are later exported to the corresponding file on the Documentum server.

The distributor servers continuously poll the Documentum server for new documents to process. Different barcodes on the documents make it possible to store each in the appropriate file on the Documentum server and depending on the document type, the server program can make automatic changes to the software in the Unisys mainframe through OMR (optical mark recognition) software and DDE (dynamic data exchange). The distributor servers also start a workflow case within a procedure and place this in a queue on the Staffware server. Thus the documents are processed and managed reliably, efficiently and rapidly and moved around the organization to those departments and managers who need them. At the backoffice, the users open and finish each case by using a Microsoft BackOffice enabled workstation.

When each case file is opened, the Documentum DIS-viewer displays the text and the Staffware software guides the user through the procedure by asking questions. The user can select from a menu of answers. The software can also use Microsoft Word to write a letter and incorporate data from an active or stored document, or use Microsoft Excel to create a spreadsheet and incorporate data from an active or stored file, or by integrating data from applications in the legacy Unisys mainframe. Thus complete automation and integration is achieved, and all insurance and business processes managed direct from all departments and desktops throughout the organization.

The decision to automate and computerize was originally taken in 1995 when it became clear that the existing business processes were no longer tenable and it was felt that the computer-based options were sufficiently developed and proven to be reliable enough to be considered. It was clear from an internal audit undertaken in 1995 that the company not only needed to automate its existing business operation but it also needed to reorganize and rethink the way it worked. It was decided that by combining its administrative operations as well as introducing process orientated thinking and new integrated IT solutions like workflow and document management, Anova could dramatically improve its long term efficiency and deliver and maintain superb customer service.

Anova reviewed all the options available on the market and selected Staffware on the basis that it offered a best-in-class product, the potential for integration with other applications now and in the future, and experienced consultancy advice from the vendor. Staffware could also offer a reference site of similar market sector and business size, which instilled additional confidence.

After an initial audit, appraisal and recommendation of a solution, Staffware introduced a pilot scheme that initially involved automating over 100,000 documents in Anova's insured parties operation. This involved an integrated solution comprising not only workflow but also DIS (document information system) which includes introducing a barcode system, an OMR (optical mark recognition) system and COLD (computer output to laser disk) system, as well as links to the existing legacy Unisys mainframe system. Thus the pilot was a complete miniature of the final organization-wide system.

The pilot demonstrated that it could improve operational efficiency by 50 percent, and the plan to automate all document storage and workflow processes throughout the Anova enterprise was approved.

The new system included all documents and paper being partially or fully scanned and input in the mailroom, which meant that major changes had to be introduced to the way that the Anova organization worked. Some simple activities became redundant and the system provides far higher levels of management control. This means that the staff members have to think in a more process-orientated manner. But the level of quality and data integrity has improved dramatically overall, so staff have welcomed the new system and can see its benefits.

KEY MOTIVATIONS

The healthcare insurance sector in Holland is increasingly tough and competitive, with aggressive market forces driving rapid change throughout the industry. Other insurance enterprises are becoming increasingly competitive, and in addition deregulation has allowed fresh competitors from non-traditional financial companies such as supermarkets and overseas organizations to enter the market. While these factors enable change within the industry and arguably provide extra choice for customers, they also make it tough for even the most hardened companies to survive.

To remain dominant it was necessary for Anova to maintain and evolve its techniques and processes so that applications and claims could be processed as fast and accurately as possible. Only by introducing full automation to the workflow and document management processes could Anova achieve the necessary competitive edge, and a radical overhaul of the business was essential.

In Holland where the Agis Group is one of the largest care insurers, Anova handles over 600,000 private and compulsorily insured customers, excluding 135,000 covered by the Police Medical Service. The company already generates an annual income in excess of 1.3 billion guilders. It has always been focused on maintaining a competitive edge through the best customer service, with an expansive and specialized range of products, but recognizes that these require support by the right IT strategy.

Anova also recognizes that with so much choice available and high public expectations, an existing or potential customer can easily be lost to the competition through inadequate telephone-based customer support. Even putting them on hold for a minute too long could be enough to lose a customer. Consequently the call centre became a critical core of the new strategy, to enable levels of support that cannot be surpassed by any other insurance provider.

The business is currently set to grow and expand, but already handles over 1,000,000 new applications and changes to existing policies each year. This creates a mountain of contractual and administrative paperwork, and automation was the only option if continued business innovation and data integrity was to be guaranteed. But the new IT system, combined with effective cost management and the right internal techniques, training, culture and processes, will enable Anova to undergo the necessary radical overhaul and achieve the necessary competitive edge to improve revenue, profit and reputation.

RESULTING BUSINESS INNOVATIONS AND BENEFITS

The first major impact of the new solution is that staff members are freed from labor-intensive data input and document management tasks to more important, valuable and stimulating work. Thus their individual job satisfaction levels improved and their interest in the overall business rose.

The guarantee of data integrity means that Anova can process and manage a greater number of claims and applications with more accuracy but with less staff assigned to that aspect of the business. Staff can be reassigned elsewhere, more profitably, while the levels of assured integrity of the data is raised.

Queries can be processed more effectively, changes to case notes made immediately and claims processed more rapidly. Because some fields in the forms are mandatory, the levels of data capture are improved, and consequently the levels of management reporting are better. The customer support procedures and customer relationship and sales development processes are improved, and the distribution of information and levels of access to information are far better from anywhere in the organization.

The reduction of claim and application process time is part of the overall service quality improvements. Consequently, Anova's reputation for competent and rapid claim processing is improved, with dramatic competitive business effect, which in turn improves profitability. The quality of service that Anova can now deliver to both its public and private sector customers is raised, and these improvements are noted by observers and analysts.

RESULTING TECHNICAL INNOVATIONS AND BENEFITS

Previously, Anova relied on an early mainframe and some desktop PCs, but mainly claims and applications were processed manually. Now, with document management and workflow including scanning and barcoding, the claims and applications can be processed more quickly. There are now PCs throughout the organization that are linked both to each other and to the historical systems. There has been no redundancy of existing investment, and all previous IT purchases have been included and made part of the new solution.

The new software ensures that all questions on a form are completed, while previously some paper forms were stored when still incomplete. The structured approach ensures better quality but still allows for intelligence and initiative in the documentation and management.

The new implementation includes the new document management and workflow software, scanning hardware and software and new document storage systems using laser disks. These mean that the capacity and efficiency of data and document storage and retrieval are dramatically improved.

The new Staffware system ensures that customer service is kept to an optimum, with numerous deadline facilities in the software set to inform Anova's operatives when a customer call-back is due or a letter has to be sent. This level of automation also provides an essential audit trail of actions, which ensures that high levels of customer service are achieved.

USERS' EXPERIENCE

The renovation project has made a dramatic difference to the way that all Anova's staff works. Previously the system and processes were labor and paper intensive, but now technology and IT systems take care of all the laborious aspects, leaving them clear to supervise, make strategic decisions and ensure that the highest levels of customer relationship are maintained.

The project was driven primarily by the users' requirements and their view of the best way to automate the processes, not by the IT. Consequently they like and approve of the new systems. There was good change management before and throughout implementation, so that users knew at all times what was being planned and why, and were able to make their own suggestions. Therefore they felt involved and part of the new system, and were keen for it to be optimized to the best possible efficiency and effect.

Users are now able to access all applications and claims at any part of the process, and senior staff are able to generate reports and statistics which give them a far better overview of the business and how it is managing documents and customers.

Some staff were naturally concerned before implementation that they would not have a job to do after automation, but good consultancy, change management and training has ensured that any fears or doubts were quickly allayed and now all staff view the new system very positively. All can see the benefits of reduction of labor intensive mundane work and the ability to have greater automated control and document access.

Staffware ensured that all skills were transferred so that the internal Anova employees are now able to access the system, generate reports, and manipulate images and documents whenever they want without having to involve or wait for Staffware's help.

From the users' point of view, the biggest improvement is the fact that wherever they are in the company, each individual can access all documents to their level of authorization, create and generate personalized reports and make immediate changes. This means that users are considerably more empowered than before, with considerable improvement in job satisfaction as a result.

HURDLES OVERCOME

When an organization uses one system for many years staff can become reliant on it and be reluctant to change. Despite the commercial, technical and practical reasons for upgrading and changing, there was still resistance among some managers who felt that their jobs would be at risk. There were also fears that when the processes were automated and controlled by rules and procedures, there would be no room for individual discretion, which many managers felt was part of their job.

However a thorough consultancy, educational and retraining program ensured that even before the new system was implemented, all managers were informed about the benefits and the improvements to their jobs. Consequently the implementation was greeted with enthusiasm and since implementation the staff have adapted easily and well.

Some of the existing processes had to be changed, which meant that departments and their interactions had to be reorganized and restructured. Again, there was some initial resistance through fear of the unknown, but this was swiftly resolved through an open approach and a good educational program.

System Configuration

Anova has implemented over 60 callcentre workstations, each using a Pentium II chip and 64 Megabytes of RAM, with Windows NT 4.0 as the operating system and running Microsoft Office 97 and a callcentre application developed in Visual Basic 6. This is a Staffware workflow application which registers changes in any documents and processes them to the backoffice.

A bespoke Documentum document management application also built in Visual basic 6.0 handles all document image processing. Each workstation also acts as a terminal emulator for the legacy backoffice system which is an ancient mainframe.

Documents are scanned into dedicated PCs, each using a Pentium III chip and running Windows NT 4.0, and ramped up for scanning with a Kofax KF-9275 internal board and Scansoftware, bespoke using Visual Basic 6.0 using Kofax Image Controls. The scanner is a Bell and Howell 8080D.

A PC is dedicated to rendering the images. This also uses a Pentium III chip running Windows NT 4.0, and Autorender for Windows NT software, which renders Word and Notepad documents to PDF format.

There is a Hewlett Packard HPUX.11 (N-series) server dedicated to handling the Documentum document management software and processing the document images. This uses six processors and an HP 1200ex MO jukebox with ten MO drives each with 5.2 Gigabytes and 238 platters. The Documentum software is version 3.1.7.2a running on Oracle 7.3.4.

A COLD PC (computer output through laser disk) manages the storage of the document images, using a Pentium II chip with 128 megabytes of RAM running Windows NT 4.0 and Microsoft Office 97. The Acrobat Distiller software runs with the COLD application, developed in Visual Basic 6.0.

There are five distributor servers, each running a Pentium II chip and 64 megabyte of RAM, running Windows NT 4.0 and Microsoft Office 97. The Infoconnect terminal emulator ensures interoperability with the legacy mainframe, and an OMR (optical mark recognition) application developed in Visual Basic 6.0 and using Image Basic handles the image processing. Staffware 97 client version software, version 7.2. E3 and Documentum client software version 3.2.6 together handle the workflow and document processing.

Anova has over 200 workflow workstations, each running a Pentium II chip and 64 megabytes of RAM using Windows NT 4.0 operating system and Microsoft Office 97, with the Nxview terminal emulator to ensure interoperability with the legacy mainframe. Staffware 97 client version software, version 7.2. E3 and Documentum client software version 3.2.6 together handle the workflow and document processing.

Anova's legacy mainframe is a Unisys NX4800—DMSII, still running three registration systems. These are the IKAZ system for common health insurance, the APART system for private health insurance and the ARIS system for special treatments insurance. The Nxview software ensures complete operability between this mainframe and the workstations and servers in the system.

There is also a dedicated Staffware server, a Sequent Dynix ptx 4.2, hosting the Staffware 97 software, version 7.1. E2-O for Oracle (version 7.3). The new system is a full integration of Staffware, Uniface Services, Tuxedo, Documentum, CRM, and IKAZ, and so delivers complete integration but with transparency achieved through a simple user interface tailored for each user.

COST SAVINGS, REVENUE AND PRODUCTIVITY IMPROVEMENTS

Since implementation, Anova has seen the number of outstanding work-in-progress jobs decrease from 60,000 to 4,000, an improvement of 93 percent. The number of calls to the callcentre was 18,000 per week, and this has reduced to 10,000 a week, an improvement of 44 percent. The nature of calls has also changed from mainly problem solving to mainly information dissemination. The average time it takes to process an application or claim has decreased from 16 to 2 days, and 75 percent of Anova's jobs are now processed within a single day, giving it distinct and massive advantage over its competitors.

Anova has also seen an improvement in the quality and level of management information, which is now available to individual managers online. The standardization of forms and processes has led to overall quality improvements, which are favorably reported and commented on, by operatives and customers. There is less negotiation and discussion required, less management involvement in each claim and claim processing is far smoother.

Anova can now rightly claim to be the biggest and most efficient provider of special treatment insurance in Holland. This is supported by the fact that the contract for the Dutch Government's Social Health Security system has been awarded to Anova, based on surveys and reports by Government officials, which included comparisons with other providers. Is an indication of the size, reliability and efficiency of the Anova operation, and the level and quality of assured customer service.

COMPETITIVE ADVANTAGES

Since Anova implemented the Staffware solution the overall targets for the insurance sector, customer expectations and Anova's standards for application and claim management have been improved dramatically. Now, customers can expect to telephone any Anova operative and have them able to see their application or claim on screen within seconds.

The individual operatives are able to make decisions and input changes to documents while the caller is on the telephone, with complete audit and process control for the managers so that no changes are made without report and tracking. The managers within Anova are able to make better management decisions because they have instant access to crucial business and statistical information that affects their strategies. Strategies are more accurate, timely and effective. The result can be seen in the increase in business and bottom line profits.

THE FUTURE

Already Anova is integrating the Internet with its workflow and document management systems, and eventually the enterprise will be completely e-enabled. This will mean that customers will have easier and faster access to the company and operatives will have easier access to files.

A key development currently under development and implementation is the 'Poseidon Project', a four-layered structure for the entire Agis Group, which has a pilot currently being run at Anova. This involves the IKAZ system moving from a mainframe to an object-orientated system.

Staffware will be responsible for the process layer of this new implementation and the result will be a back office which can cope with all 1.2 million records a month. The system will only send 'exceptions' to the users for manual checking and amendment where necessary. As a result, the Staffware software and the new system will handle most declarations of fitness automatically.

The system already offers connectivity between all authorized internal managers, but another development in the pipeline will be complete chain integration between Anova and its customers, the doctors, Medical Institutions and other parties in the health sector.

In time, quotations and decisions will be WAP-enabled, so that customers can access the company through mobile phones as well as laptops and other remote devices. Ultimately, voice technology will be integrated so that customers and operatives will be able to have still easier interface with the system, with continual backup and auditing of all changes and decisions.

A continuous program of upgrading and improvement will mean that the Anova organization will remain at the forefront of the insurance sector, without apparently dramatic upheavals. There is a continuous ongoing process to incorporate new innovative technologies, as they are developed to sustain Anova's competitive edge.

City of Salzburg, Austria
Jungle of Signs

Silver Award, Europe, 2001

System Overview

Salzburg is not only Mozart's birthplace but also the home of 145,000 inhabitants and about 8,000 companies. As the central administrative body of the city of Salzburg, the municipal authority deals with a huge amount of administrative processes, databases and paper forms.

Under the 1997 elected government and in the scope of "file 2000," the municipal authority set itself the challenging tasks of putting customer-oriented administration at the top of its priorities and re-emerge as a strong business center in the future. From the start, private economy standards were put forward as a scale to compete with.

The only way to achieve these objectives was to implement an overall system across the Municipal Authority. A challenge to optimize the processes by implementing workflow and document management with the name: **FILE 2000**

The following time-table shows the composition of the frame-project FILE 2000.

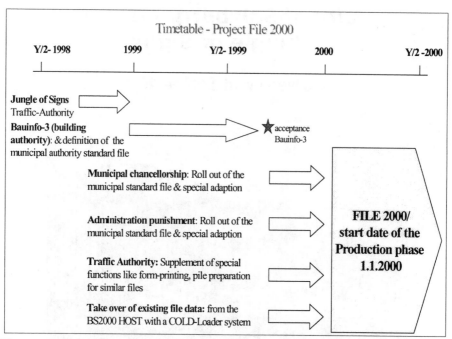

The overall goal of FILE 2000 was creating optimized citizen-oriented procedures and making the city an attractive business center for the future.

The project started mid 1998 and went in production on January 1st 2000, exactly on schedule.

Before starting with the core project of FILE 2000, "BauInfo-3" (Building Authority and creation of a standard file), the Municipal started with a short warm-up project, the "Jungle of Sings" (Traffic Authority).

The "Jungle of Signs" optimizes and automates the creation and approval of traffic signs.

The workflow and document management solution, built with FABASOFT components, is integrated with the existing Geographical Information System (Geomedia) and the oracle database containing the traffic sign information (GIS). It enables the authority to process the creation and approval of traffic signs completely electronically and in one go.

In "BauInfo-3" the creation and approval of building applications within the area of the City of Salzburg are optimized and automated.

The legal situation requires that eight or nine expert officers, scattered over six different buildings, be consulted for the approval of a building application. Each office needs to consult a variety of databases to complete the approval. It was a procedure that took 150 days and often had to deal with "misplaced" documents.

A standard file for the Municipal Authority was defined, in the same FABASOFT environment as the traffic sign solution. The electronic file contains all required documents for the approval and is "steered" around by means of workflow. The application is also integrated with Geomedia and the other databases and applications that need to be consulted. Due to the solution, the processing time is reduced from 150 to 50 days. The status of a building application became transparent and can be consulted at any time.

The standard file, which was created in BauInfo-3, had also to be implemented in the Municipal chancellorship and the Administration punishment before January 1st 2000. After January 2000, the City of Salzburg started planning the roll out over the rest of the Municipals.

THE KEY MOTIVATIONS

As other public offices, the City of Salzburg was dealing a huge amount of administrative processes, databases and paper forms. Most of the processes were still processed manually, existing applications were stand-alone applications and the documents were all kept in filing cabinets.

The in 1997 elected government decided to change this situation and roll out FILE 2000, an overall electronic system across the Municipal Authority of the City of Salzburg

The Municipal decided to start with a warm-up project (cf. general overview—time frame), which was called **"Jungle of Signs."** It had two specific goals.

Regulating the traffic-sign creation and re-approval process

All information about Salzburg's 20,000 road signs was kept on paper, which caused different hurdles. Access of information required a search through the filing cabinets, which was a time consumable activity and caused misplaced documents.

The existing Powerbuilder application 'Shilderwald,' that was used for graphic positioning of traffic signage, was a stand-alone application. It enabled users to access data related to streets, traffic sign description and legal principles but did not allow processing a demand for ordering or removing traffic signage.

The demand for ordering or removing a traffic sign was done manually and required accessing the filing cabinets and GeoMedia, again a time consuming, inefficient and unsurveyable activity. The lack of overview brought redundant and conflicting roadsings about. But the real nightmare was the legally obliged two-yearly approval of all 20,000 roadsigns. With the existing manual procedures and the available number of staff, this was an almost impossible task.

The objective of an integrated, automated solution was to facilitate the creation of new signs, rule out conflicting signs and regulate the two-yearly approval of the roadsigns, without increasing the existing staff.

Confirming the successful integration between the Fabasoft solution and GeoMedia

In order to prove that Unisys and Fabasoft were the ideal partners to roll out FILE 2000, the municipal started with this short and well defined project. The "Jungle of Signs" started mid 1998 was built and implemented in only two months.

It had less contact points in terms of workflow but included all relevant components at the Municipal, like the integration of a Geographical Information System (Geomedia) and the automatic generation of documents.

The successful integration with the legacy systems, successful document management and workflow implied the start of the core project: BauInfo—3.

With **"BauInfo–3"** which is the optimization and automation of the administrative processes for approving building legislation, the municipal authority aimed to:

Create customer-oriented and faster administrative procedures

In the municipal authority, the legal situation requires that eight or nine expert offices are consulted in order for an application for building permission to be inspected and reported on. In addition, these eight or nine offices are scattered among six separate buildings. Before implementing the workflow solution, the applications were processed manually on paper forms. Different stand-alone applications and paper files needed to be consulted and the paper application file needed to circulate through the eight or nine different offices.

The whole procedure took an average of 150 days for processing an application. Furthermore, citizen could not get information about the status of the application while it was being processed It could happen also that parts of a file got misplaced while being processed, which slowed the procedure even more down.

With the workflow solution, the municipal authority wanted to create transparent procedures that permitted fingertip accurate information at any moment (for applicants, employees and management), one-point of contact for the citizen (one phone number) and moreover, a faster legal approval for building permissions.

Promote the City of Salzburg as an important economic location

An economic goal was to re-emerge the City of Salzburg as a strong business center in the future. A prerequisite to make the city attractive as a business location, were easy-going business-to-government relations.

Faster and transparent procedures, one single contact point, and standard files that could be easily rolled out over all authority-departments were necessary for the City of Salzburg to strive after a strong economical position.

THE OVERALL BUSINESS INNOVATION, SHOWING IMPACT TO MANAGEMENT

The implementation of FILE 2000, made from the Municipals of the City of Salzburg an integrated, optimized, automated, controllable, citizen-oriented, user-friendly, competitive and modern forward-looking organization.

The "Jungle of Signs"

Due to the fact that the solution for the placement of traffic signs was built as an extension of the existing GeoMedia, the new system contains already all necessary information about roads, bridges, buildings, sewers, electricity and gas lines, registry etc.

The developed application permits users to manage positioning of traffic signs directly in GeoMedia and it supports the administrative creation process for legal approval of new signs. By creating a new sign in GeoMedia, a file is created and the legal procedures are started automatically. The right information about the traffic signs, which has to be added to the approval file, is obtained by creating a two-way-communication to a separate Oracle database; Powerbuilder application 'Shilderwald' . Templates of administrative documents use OLE links to insert variable information stored in an oracle database. (In a future version of the solution, these OLE links will be replaced by a high sophisticated textmodule-management system.)

A separate authorization design ensures that only authorized persons and divisions have access to records and procedures of the traffic department. Supported via workflow, the file is processed.

The solution enables the users to issue administrative orders in one go and within half an hour into an inquiry and therefore enables the ministry to complete the obliged traffic orders check-up every two years without increasing existing staff. The automation of the process creates a considerable time saving.

Looking up documents takes no longer than a few second and misplaced or lost documents are no longer a plague at the department.

At any time, any managment can access every traffic sign creation file, which contains the history of the creation.

Due to the visible overview in GeoMedia it's practically impossible to create contradicting traffic signs. This brings about a striking change in the streets: contradicting traffic signs have become ruled out!

"BauInfo—3"

To optimize the exhausting building application approval procedure and create an automated solution, a document management solution was designed that integrated the different existing applications and databases by means of a workflow system. The Solution consisted of a standard file that was created to be rolled out in the whole of the Municipals. (Municipal chancelorship and the Administration Punishment already completed)

To geographically locate sites and buildings in question in accordance with the cadastral plan, the building departments' processes were integrated with Geomedia. Data from the databases for population and address administration was migrated to another host system and information that was only available in paper form, was incorporated by means of a bar-code-based standardization.

Incorporation of external public bodies into the processes by means of the workflow (state government, environmental authorities, etc.) is enabled by state-of-the art communication technology.

A new application file is created in BauInfo-3 when a citizen posts a building application request. The paper application is scanned and added to the electronic file. In a standard situation, the workflow pushes the file automatically to the different departments that need to deliver feedback. In special situations, the workflow can be altered manually in a graphic editor.

Where in the past, the paper file had to physically circulate one by one to the different departments before the tasks could be completed, the electronic solution allows parallel flows.

The legally obliged presence of paper documents while processing the electronic variant is solved by means of a bar-code-based standardization between the paper and the electronic workflow.

Users have at any time access to all necessary information. The solution has links to GeoMedia and other legacy databases that need to be consulted and the file itself contains the information related to the building application request (what, location, when, legal situation, signature, access control list, versioning, relationship to other files, former files, objects, notepad, the workflow).

When all feedback is collected, the law obliges to carry out administrative procedures on site with a commission. By using laptops, employees can use Bauinfo-3 during this negotiation process. Protocols or supplements to negotiation documents for example, can be loaded on the laptop and can be altered.

Standardization of the data added on-site takes place automatically when a mobile client is next logged in at the municipal authority.

After this, the committee decides upon the permission and the answer is send back to the applicant.

The impact is considerable. BauInfo-3 generates significant optimization of the business processes. Routine activities are automated and different tasks are done in parallel. Activities on site are done directly on the system. All this has lead to a significant reduction of processing time from 150 to 50 days.

The chance to make mistakes is smaller due to the standard workflow and automation of routine activities.

Lost or misplaced documents are completely ruled out. Almost all documents have a electronic variant and bar-code standardization gives information about the location of the paper file.

The knowledge base of the workflow tool contains explications for special administrative handling, which reduces education time for new staff.

Automatic history of the file-workflow ensures up-to-date and accurate information about every handling executed at the file in the past. This electronic availability of the file-history ensures at any time, information about the building application to the end-users and management.

THE OVERALL TECHNOLOGICAL INNOVATION

Due to the fact that the sub-projects from FILE 2000 are all developed in the same Fabasoft platform, we will discuss the technological innovation without distinction between the "Jungle of Signs" and "BauInfo-3"

The Fabasoft platform provides the users with one single application which allows then to process all tasks from the same desktop. The workflow and document management system gives homogenous access to all necessary information and all tasks can be processed without leaving the PC or the application. Depending on the task that needs to be fulfilled at that step of the workflow, the required view of the application can be chosen.

In the screenshots below, some of these different solutions-views are shown.

A self-definable register card (screenshot 1) is created for each object class and added to the file, whereafter it is steered throughout the workflow. The content of the register cards varies depending on the object class.. They contain documents and case related information.

- the location,
- what it is about,

- when it is started,
- it describes the legal situation,
- has links to the signature database,
- provides a access control list,
- gives information about versioning,
- describes the relationship to other files and also to former files,
- it includes all related objects, and foreign information.
- has access to the notepad
- and it gives a graphical overview of the workflow that can be altered. Color differences show the status of the workflow.

The register card of the standard file, is being rolled out further over the rest of the City of Salzburg.

Screenshot 2 and 6 show how GeoMedia (an application from the company Intergraph) is integrated and can be accessed from the application (respectively from the traffic sign and building site administration). It enables users to consult the necessary information about roads, bridges, sewers, electricity, gas lines etc.. which gives them a complete and up-to-date overview about the environmental situation without leaving their PC or the application.

In screenshot 2 can be seen how street-signs are created directly in GeoMedia. This visual overview of their positioning and the field with the additional text of the sign minimizes the number of contradicting and redundant signs.

- Integration is also make to a separate GIS-Oracle database with contains traffic sign information like the legal status, additional texts etc... Via a bi-directional communication between the GIS-Oracle database and the Fabasoft application, all information can be consulted.
- The HOST-Interface, allowing access to central data (like person and company data) is as well integrated into the application.
- Other public process are also integrated in the workflow (for example: building permission process, demolition permits, building declaration...)
- In screenshot 3, the hierarchical file structure is shown. All files and all incoming and outgoing documents can be find and accessed via this structure.
- Older files were migrated from the Host via COLD.
- Documents that were initially only available on paper can be accessed by means of a viewer and are stored directly in the environment of the applications. (screenshot 4)
- The synchronization of the paper-form and electronic-form based workflow, that is legally obliged, is done by the means of bar-code-based standardization.

- A highly sophisticated text management module automatically generates documents. It consists mainly of legal regulation documents and the layout is very flexible. At the moment, the template database contains approximately 100 MB documents. (screenshot 3)

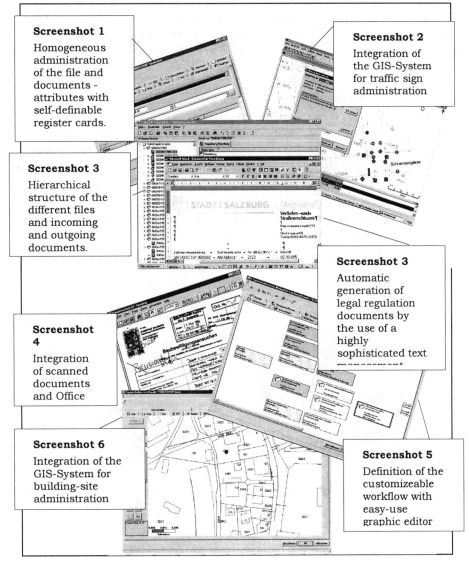

Screenshot 1

Homogeneous administration of the file and documents - attributes with self-definable register cards.

Screenshot 2

Integration of the GIS-System for traffic sign administration

Screenshot 3

Hierarchical structure of the different files and incoming and outgoing documents.

Screenshot 3

Automatic generation of legal regulation documents by the use of a highly sophisticated text management

Screenshot 4

Integration of scanned documents and Office

Screenshot 6

Integration of the GIS-System for building-site administration

Screenshot 5

Definition of the customizeable workflow with easy-use graphic editor

- When a task is completed and the next step in the workflow needs to be taken, users can chose to follow the predefined workflow or in special cases, chose to customize the workflow via an easy-use graphic editor. (screenshot 5)
- The workflow allows parallel work via networked business processes, which speeds up the approval

procedure considerably. There are 6 workflows that each consist of 20 to 30 activities.

A special requirement was the capability to work on site. The developed mobile clients allow users to use the same application environment during the negotiating process on site.

Before going on site, all required information is loaded on the mobile client. It can be consulted and altered on site. Data added on site will be automatically synchronized with the online file, when the mobile client is next logged in at the municipal authority.

THE SYSTEM USERS AND WHAT THEIR JOB NOW ENTAIL

The procedures at the Municipal Authority were very unstructured and everything had to be done manually. There were different host systems and documents (for instance legal regulations) were stored in separate file systems or in filing cabinets.

The system users were confronted with different applications and a high access time to special information. There was lots of paper and often there were various versions of files. Often, paper files or separate documents were misplaced and couldn't be found

The graph below shows the different application, files and archives that had to be consulted.

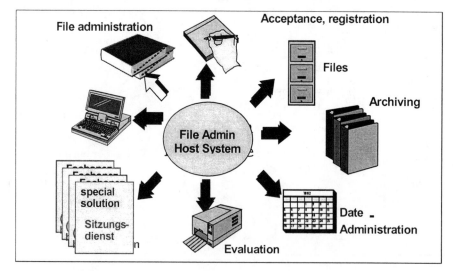

The "Jungle of Signs"

Pre-installation

The system users had no visual overview about the positioning of the existing roadsings. They needed to consult GeoMedia to get information about the environment situation (cf. Question 3) and access the existing Powerbuilder application 'Shilderwald' for graphic positioning and the right information about the signs.

With the "Jungle of Signs"

The new integrated environment allows the creation directly in GeoMedia. When a new traffic sign is created, the legal procedure is automatically started and steered by the workflow.

"BauInfo—3"

Pre-Installation

Processing a building application was done manually and with a paper file. There were different Host systems, but they were only used for attribute administration. Documents (for instance legal regulations) were stored in separate file systems or in filing cabinets. The system users were confronted with different applications and high access time to special information (cf. Graph above).

The paper situation brought about that the file had to be in sequences sent from one department to the next (eight or nine departments, scattered over six different locations). Below is a graph showing the building permission process and all the involved authorities that the file needed to circulate in.

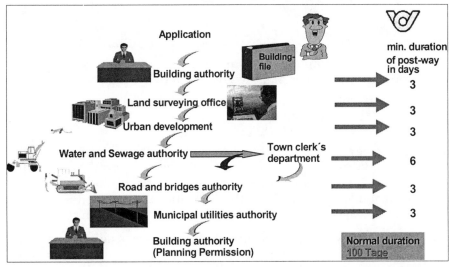

A normal duration of this process was approximately 100 days, the average processing time however was 150 days due to the fact that documents often got lost or misplaced.

With "BauInfo-3"

With the new solution, the user creates a file in the document management system when a building application comes in. All relevant information is added to the register cards and the user sends it into the predefined workflow. The electronic technology allows parallel working. If necessary, the workflow process can be altered in the graphical view.

The process is structured in a way that minimizes the risk of mistakes.

A screenshot of this workflow is shown below.

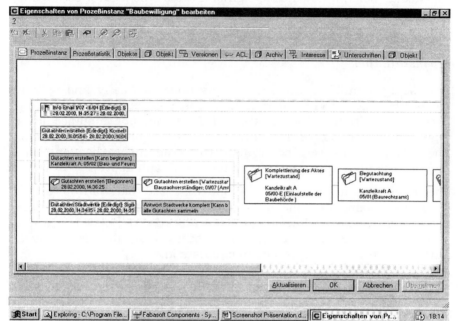

The boxes in the graphic editor are a synonym for an activity and the color stand for a special status of this activity.

- Green: Activity is fulfilled
- Yellow: Waiting position
- Grey: Can be started

This technology allows also synchronizing the paper workflow with the electronic workflow, which allows users always to allocate documents. The graph above shows how the paper-flow is marked with the small folder-icon. The other activities are involved in a pure electronic workflow. Again the color indicates the status of the file.

This is necessary because some documents are available only in paper format. (for instance large format plans DIN A0 in the building authority). Making these documents electronically available requires special scanners, which would be too expensive at the moment. On top, the legal situation requires the paper presence of some documents when approving a building application. Both the paper and the electronic workflow are synchronized by the means of bar-code-based standardization.

At any time the users of the system can look at the workflow and see in which phase the building request is at that particular moment and by consulting the automatically created history the get accurate information about the actions done to it. This gives the building authority the possibility to provide the citizens at any time with the necessary information about the administrative procedure of e.g. the building permission. Unlike in the past, the citizen has only one point of contact. (Cf. Graph below)

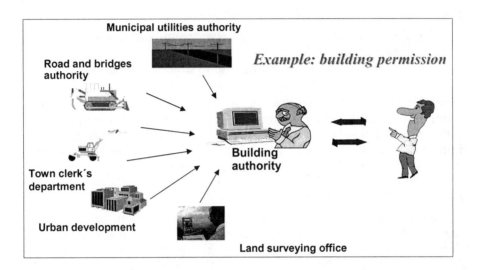

Example: building permission

Municipal utilities authority

Road and bridges authority

Building authority

Town clerk's department

Urban development

Land surveying office

THE BIGGEST HURDLES OVERCOME IN MANAGEMENT, BUSINESS AND TECHNOLOGY

The biggest technology challenge was creating the integration with the GIS-System (Legacy oracle database which contains the traffic sign information). In a first phase, the integration was done directly in the register cards. This caused however a unacceptable low performance.

To solve this problem, Unisys specialists developed a new integration with GIS by means of an active AGM graphic internet viewer. The new integration more than doubled the performance of the solution.

From a management point of view, it was very important that the standard electronic file could be rolled out in a second phase into the rest of the departments of the City of Salzburg. Therefore, while creating the standard file, Unisys needed to take these future requirements into account.

The Building authority was chosen to develop this file, due to the various departments related to the process in that department. The success of this critical creation phase was due to a very intensive cooperation between Unisys and the City of Salzburg.

The production date was very strictly. On the first day of January 2000, the new system needed to go in production. This was not due to Y2K problems but to the fact that the data-migration from the host system would take three weeks. At the turn of the year, these systems could be shut down. If the deadline was not made, they would have had to wait for another year before implementing the solution.

The data migration from the Host-system and the consistent-check within three weeks of:

All attributes of approximately 600.000 Files

- All attributes of approximately incoming and outgoing documents (1.500.000)
- 100.000 MS Word documents in different versions
- 2.000.000 Person and company data

This strict deadline implied that the whole staff needed to be trained within four months. Taken in account that a great deal of employees at the municipal where not at all acquainted with computers or applications, this was a challenging objective. 450 employees were trained from September 1999 till December 1999.

THE NEW SYSTEM CONFIGURATION

The developed solution for the department traffic signage runs on Microsoft NT and windows 2000, more specifically the applications Microsoft Office 2000 and backoffice. Data are stored in a Microsoft SQL Server and exchanged with an Oracle database, which is necessary for the GeoMedia (Geographical Information System) application. The workflow is supported by Fabasoft components

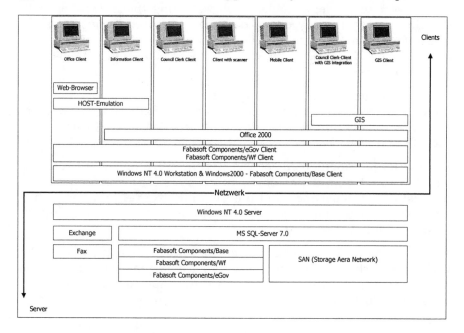

(Base, ELAK/KV, Wf) and is integrated with GeoMedia. This application is currently installed on approximately 800 workstations.

The application structure

The graph on the previous page shows a detailed overview about the application client/server structure.

The hardware structure

The next graphic gives a rough overview of the corresponding hardware.

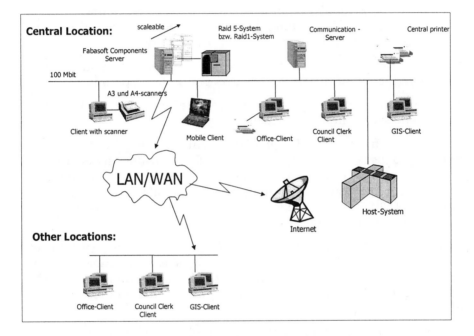

- **Clients:**
  There are 800 Clients (app. 1/10 are Laptops with Windows2000)
  - Workstations with the configuration: 600MHz, RAM 128 MB, 8 GB hard disc
  - Laptops with the configuration: 333MHz, RAM 128MB, 6GB hard disc
- **Server:**
  current situation is one Server: Dual Pentium III 500MHz, RAM 1,3 GB
- **Raid-System:**
  for the operating-system 2x18 GB RAID-1
  for the data 7x18 GB RAID-5

but they plan to implement an SAN (Storage Area Network), in the moment there is no optical archive.

- **Peripheral equipment:**
  15 scanners (1 DINA3 color , 2 DINA3 Xerox 220, 12 DINA4)
- approximately 400 printers for the whole municipal authority
- Two high speed printers Xerox 220
- **Network:**
  100Mbit

COST SAVINGS, INCREASED REVENUES, AND PRODUCTIVITY IMPROVEMENTS

The main productivity improvements is the reduction of the duration of the whole building permission process from 150 days to approximately 50 days.

Without any doubt, this productivity improvement results in a serious reduction of the emp.   e costs per building permission file.

The electronic workflow reduces the physical post traffic with 60 to 80 percent which implies big cost savings.

Concerning the Jungle of Signs, the legal situation in the City of Salzburg obliges that every two year all the traffic signs are re-regulated. With this new technology, the issuing of such a regulation takes now half an hour and so the administration of the amount of 20.000 signs can be managed with the existing staff without increasing them.

A further cost saving factor is that by this new system of approximately 6000 redundant traffic signs can be eliminated in 2001. The price of such sign is about 220 Euro. Because these 6000 traffic signs no longer need to replaced, it means a total cost saving of 1.320.000 Euro.

Compared with the total cost of the project, which was 250.000 Euro, this is an enormous cost saving.

In the past, the filing cabinets and archive rooms kept growing day after day. Desks were always filled with piles of paper files. Slowly, the first signs of paper reduction became apparent after implementation.

COMPETITIVE ADVANTAGES

It is impossible to address this topic because there is no competitive situation in the public sector.

IMMEDIATE AND LONG-TERM PLANS TO SUSTAIN COMPETITIVE ADVANTAGE

Immediate plans

At the moment City of Salzburg plans the rollout of the standard electronic file supported with workflow over the rest of the Municipals' departments. This rollout is foreseen to start in the autumn 2000 and is planned to be finished by the end of 2001.

Long term plans

In a special workshop between Unisys and the municipal authority a long-term plan was discussed.

The keyword for future steps is "e-Government."

To accomplish "e-government" and not only optimize the procedures even more but also anticipate future citizen oriented procedures making use of the internet, the following new technology-facts are discussed:

- Electronic Signature:
  - This electronic signature can be used for signing documents
  - It also can be used for a special LOGIN-mechanism
  - There are two kinds of such signatures (soft-certificate, qualified-certificate like chipcard-solution)
- Biometrics: (for instance fingerprint-scanning)
  - As approval mechanism (for instance in case of budget approval as a task in the workflow)

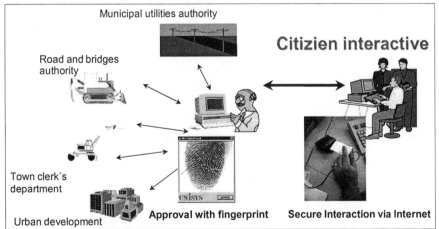

What is the advantage of such a high sophisticated technology?

- The citizen can submit an inquiry to the public sector in electronic form via internet.
  This inquiry can consist of the application form and scanned documents (for instance a building plan).

- The electronic signature would be necessary to submit inquiries. Via a special authentication procedure, access can be granted to a personalized homepage where the citizen is permitted to submit such an inquiry.
- The citizen can access the administration procedure at any time and inquire easily the information about the status from his building approval request without contacting an official in charge.
- Once the approval procedure is finished, the citizen can be informed via e-mail. The approved document could be afterwards downloaded via the internet.
- Procedures would be even more optimized since the documents would from the beginning be electronically available and the building authority would have to deal less with requests about the status of the application files.

The below graph shows a rough overview of the configuration how such an e-government solution could be implemented.

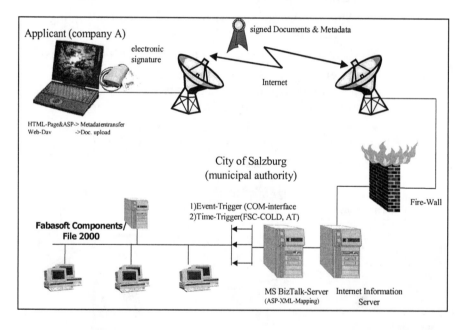

Dubai Police: United Arab Emirates General Department of Administration and Personnel

Silver Award, Africa and Middle East 2001

INTRODUCTION:

The General Administration Department of the Dubai Police is the center of all its paper work. Every document that enters the Dubai Police offices from the outside passes through the general administration department. Therefore, the archive and administrative departments faced the ever-challenging tasks of managing and filing the documents and correspondence in a systematic fashion.

There are numerous other departments such as personnel, inspection, archive, legal, etc., that also deal with masses of paper-based documents. These documents are routed for decision-making purposes to various officers in the administration hierarchy.

The solution designed and implemented to address the electronic imaging and workflow requirements of Dubai Police is based on eiStream WMS (formerly known as Eastman Software) imaging and workflow products.

OBJECTIVES:

Dubai Police authorities selected a computer-based imaging and workflow system to automate the flow of paper-based documents within the organization. The main objectives set were:

1. Replace the manual document handling with automated workflow electronic archiving.
2. Reduce the movement of paper documents between different users to achieve higher efficiency and reduce the time required to process documents.
3. Shorten the time required to locate and retrieve the documents.
4. System should produce audit trail to display the flow of the document.
5. Use the latest technology standards of communications and networking by enabling all the managers to administer their documents through workflow and daily work not only from the offices, but also from their homes and cars.

DEPLOYMENT:

Dubai Police started to use this system with 20 users on December 1997 and now they have over 60 users using the system achieving tremendous success. The results encouraged them to deploy the application not only in few departments already started but also transparently to all other departments. It is expected in few years to deploy Imaging and Workflow to all Dubai Police departments.

Over 700 cases and documents arrive daily each with an average of 30 pages. Routing these diverse documents to the different managers within the various departments now happens easily and quickly, enabling managers to achieve their workloads.

Eastman Software, with its high capabilities in the smooth operation of imaging and workflow, has assisted the Dubai Police attain its goals. It is the first site in 1997 to use software imaging and particularly workflow in the Middle East region, where the time Eastman Software was handling the marketing of this product.

Emirates Computers with Eastman software succeeded in implementing the paperless management solution to the Dubai Police. This is considered the first enterprise workflow solution with the most users in the whole region. It is a daily success where a new user or department is added to the system with permanent stability and optimal performance.

From time of first deployment to date the workflow and indeed, the whole system, has grown significantly as the organization extensively depends on it for their daily operations. At a regular pace, with stability the solution has been extended from one department to many more. The scalability of the solution has been major factor in achieving this objective.

ACHIEVEMENTS:

- Eliminate the paper work previously used in the Dubai Police and successfully deploy the paperless management system
- Speed up the search operation and eliminate the heaps of papers residing in the offices by archiving these documents with electronic media and route them electronically to the appropriate people.
- Wide deployment of the application in most of Dubai Police departments and strategically planning to deploy it in the remaining departments in the coming few years.
- Enable all managers to access the system from their offices, homes and cars, which dramatically helped in achieving faster and more accurate work.
- Cooperate with other departments, government sectors and private sectors requesting progress of their documents, cases or requests in the Dubai Police administration by providing them with online information to finish their projects.
- Permit access by fax, email or phone which reduced the human interference and the queues that used to exist.
- Prove success in implementing fast, successful electronic services as an example for other governmental departments and ministries.
- Facilitate document searches based on different criteria.

SYSTEM OVERVIEW:

1. The Open/Image and Open/Workflow Software runs on Microsoft Windows NT Server.

2. The system database information is stored in Microsoft SQL Server RDBMS, with a distributed, modular architecture.

3. Development tools are Borland Delphi, MS Visual Basic and Crystal reports.

4. The hardware infrastructure is state of art and very robust and stable in order to provide accurate performance.

Optical Disk Management Software:

The Optical Disk Management Software (ODMS) supplied with Open/Image supports a variety of optical jukeboxes and optical drives. Using this software, the documents that completed the processing cycle are moved from local server hard disk to high volume optical disks for permanent archiving. Keeping in tune with the latest technology the storage media now is RAID, with automated backup and safe storage carefully maintained.

Imaging and Workflow Client Software:

Document Management Workstation Software (DMWS) provides a general-purpose interface to access work item documents, folders and batches. This software is loaded on Windows 95 Client PCs. DMWS also supports batch scanning features to scan multi page documents using desktop, medium speed scanners from Fujitsu, Ricoh, Bell & Howell, etc.

For high-end transaction-oriented applications, the system supports high performance workstation software.

Using an optional Remote Access Module and an ISDN gateway, remote users over ISDN lines can run Open/Image and Open/Workflow applications.

Route Builder

Eastman Software provides a very strong and powerful routing utility that allows designing of complete workflow and as well as the ability to program it to operate based on the conditions and criteria.

The route associated with the engine is very closely integrated and follows the flow very intelligently. The route available at Dubai Police has been very well planned and designed with the involvement and support of the Project Head of Dubai Police and at regular intervals is updated and monitored for fine operation.

Application Programming Interface (API)

For applications requiring tight integration or customized interface, a complete set of APIs can be used to create custom workstations. DDE APIs and Client APIs allow seamless integration with user applications. These APIs are callable from a variety of programming languages such as Visual Basic, C, and C++ etc.

It has used MS visual basic with Client APIs techniques for calling the Eastman software imaging and workflow different functionality. Also, batch scanning was used due to the large amount of documents processed daily.

DTAS and DMFS Application Software

Since the Electronic Imaging and Workflow System for Dubai requires a tailor made, Arabic front end, the application was built using Arabic Enabled Windows 95, Open/Image and Open/Workflow DDE APIs, and Arabic-enabled Visual Basic programming language. The application related data is stored using the Microsoft SQL Server RDBMS on the Server.

The system was implemented in two phases. During the first phase of the project, DTAS (Document Transfer and Archiving System)

- Document capturing by scanning,
- Document Indexing and
- Document Archiving features are implemented.

The second phase of the project, DMFS (Document Management and Flow System) deals with:

- Document Workflow,
- Automatic Document Flow Tracking and
- Follow-up.

Security:

The application is using client server architecture and the network available at Dubai Police is a highly configured where all users with the specific rights can login and implement their works. All necessary security on the network and application is set properly and it did not lose control of any documents on the system. No event was registered regarding losses, corruption or access violation to the application, database, documents, file system and other storage media. Different sections of the application have level-based security so that features can be applied or rejected as needed.

In brief, the overall solution is very scalable and extensible, offering ease of use while keeping pace with technology.

Government of New Brunswick, Canada, Department of Supply and Services

Automated Management of Translation Requests

Silver Award, North America 2001

OVERVIEW

A bilingual province of Canada, New Brunswick generates a large volume of documents to be translated. These translation activities are in keeping with complex assignment, management, and budgetary charge processes all of which are regulated by extremely tight deadlines. The Department thus assigns these translations to a large number of in-house Translators and Freelancers.

GENER-X (a software division of Ordiplan Inc.) developed a solution enabling the user to submit, via the Internet, documents to be translated by including all essential parameters such as documents, translation requirements, deadlines, formats and other specifications. All operations and tasks required for complete process implementation are performed automatically. All functions are performed in real time and within a collaborative context on the Internet. This solution enables in-house Translators and Freelancers to not only improve the processing time, but reduce costs thanks to the retrieval of existing contents as well as follow project progress, improve quality using automated validation phases and evolve within a fully computerized environment.

SYSTEM OVERVIEW

Translation providers today seek solutions that enable their rapid adaptation to new recent global economic standards. They seek the ability to offer via the Internet, to their existing and potential customers, high quality services and a "Business to Business" management model. This has become an imperative to maintaining a competitive edge. The translation request management system (TRMS) transforms a company's language services from a manual business process into an automated application. Based on a document routing solution, the main feature of the system is that documents are sent to the languages service through the Internet using electronic forms. The solution distributes assignments between users (using the Web or e-mail), coordinates and tracks the work progress until completion, and determines the activities pending for each business process. All functions and tasks required for complete process implementation are performed automatically in the following manner:

- Capture, content search, and document management functions;
- Routing and schedule management functions;

- Budgetary, payment, and account transfer functions;
- Task assignment, quality control, and security functions;
- Project management functions.

All these functions are performed in real time and within a collaborative context on the Internet.

The solution enables users to submit, from the Web, documents to be translated by including all essential parameters such as documents, translation requirements, deadlines, formats and other specifications. The Government of New Brunswick now has a more streamlined and powerful management tool for its whole translation request process.

The TRMS process is Internet-based, reducing much of the paper flow load. The system ensures that work allocation is monitored more efficiently and that status information is readily available.

Electronic documents are managed entirely by the Document Workflow Solution (DWS) and the Electronic Document Vault (EDV). This allows for easy access and referral to online documents, and for consistent management of the EDV knowledge base.

The successive stages of the management process are:

- For each assignment applicable to the request, the router selects a Translator (in-house or external) and sets a deadline for translation.
- Then, the assignment process is carried out automatically.
- Next, the Translator receives the assignment(s), with the relevant documents, via the Internet.
- Finally, the translated documents are sent back to the requesting party by e-mail. (The translated document can be downloaded from an electronic form.)

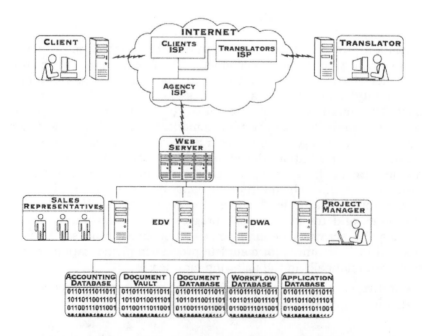

THE KEY MOTIVATION BEHIND INSTALLING THIS WORKFLOW SYSTEM

Today, organizations turn toward Internet-based solutions to render their business processes more efficient, more cost-effective and secure. As a platform, the Internet is asked evermore to support the automation of work and information flow-processes, which are becoming increasingly essential for in-house operations.

The Government of New Brunswick, like most organizations, wanted to improve the efficiency of its Department of Supply and Services with a solution that would streamline the department's translation request process.

In view of Canada's New Brunswick implementation in generating large volumes of documents for translation, these translation activities are in keeping with complex assignment, management, and budgetary charge processes, all of which are regulated by extremely tight deadlines. The province's Translation Bureau assigns these translations to a large number of in-house Translators and freelancers.

Processing translation requests has traditionally been a paper-based process, with all its attendant difficulties: sluggish, error-prone, and costly, etc. The Province of New Brunswick wanted improvements that would address the following problems:

- Unnecessary delays in administrative procedures
- Poorly integrated participants and tasks
- Irregular document processing
- Poor control of the paper circulation
- High paper-related costs (printing, stocks, delivery, obsolescence)
- Weak coordination (non-optimal productivity)
- Inadequate work distribution and follow-up
- Weak security and confidentiality

The Common Problem of a Traditional Translation Bureau

Process

With a traditional Translation Service Bureau (internal or external), the processing of translation requests is very slow. Also, the cost associated per request is very high, due to the significant amount of paper processing required.

Request Forms and Documents

Translation request forms and documents are submitted on paper media and must be dealt with physically. Also, translation tasks are assigned manually.

Operations

Managing the paper trail becomes an additional load on operations. The procedure calls for the duplication of records, which becomes extremely cumbersome to manage. Multiple entry points and request formats impose matching multiple data capture methods and data stores, which all need to be coordinated manually.

Retrieval of Key Information

The retrieval of vital management information is slow and untimely. When information needs to be retrieved quickly, normal activities are disrupted (because the information is not readily available from an integrated source).

THE OVERALL BUSINESS INNOVATION

The solution offers:

- Facilitated processing and management for its users
- Improved turnaround time and reduced error rates (related to the existing paper process)
- Easy access to the service from anywhere in the world
- Complete management of the entire translation request process, all in a paper-free environment

Developing that solution comprises:

- Creating an integral business solution out of several existing software packages
- Automating the routing process of documents through the Internet
- Automating the work assignment for every document submitted
- Automating the work distribution via the Internet
- Creating tools for real-time management of the assignment's progress status

TOTAL AUTOMATION EFFICIENCY

Workflow Application

The TRMS Document Workflow Application (DWA) provides the ability to support and track the flow of documents as well as manage an organization's translation requests. The TRMS powerful workflow tools are designed to automate business processes by coordinating the interaction of people, information, and computer application rules.

DWA benefits day-to-day operations by:

- Ensuring that documents move along at a prescribed pace, and that the appropriate person processes them in the correct order.
- Allowing Managers and System Administrators to optimize assigned work within an organization.
- Allowing clients and Project Managers to get the latest online progress information of a specific job.
- Allowing documents to be processed in parallel; allowing multiple people to work on the same document for multiple language requirements.

- Improving managerial efficiency by permitting the viewing of the entire work process.
- Allowing organizations to add translation tools to maximize organization efficiency.

Securing Client Asset

Documents represent the collective recorded knowledge of any organization. These documents are very important if not critical to an organization's capability in attaining its mission and goals. Advanced document management systems can manage document assortments of any size in support of critical business functions. TRMS's Electronic Document Vault (EDV) module manages documents through their life cycle, from inception through development, review, storage and dissemination all the way to their destruction.

EDV Benefits:

- Electronic Document Vault allows the management of all documents fast and efficiently
- All documents are available within seconds on a PC, and at a much lower cost level compared to a paper-based system
- With the EDV module, New Brunswick can manage millions of documents and reuse common information
- Allows for tight control of document access
- Manage document versioning, frequently implicated in the translation process
- Allows users throughout the organization to access corporate knowledge through one entry point.

E-business for E-success

TRMS is a Web-based solution with an easy access to the service from anywhere in the world. User access is boundless; the platform is flexible, which favors future developments.

At the heart of the administrative activities of an organization are its business forms, which amass vast amounts of data that require major investments in handling resources. An E-form (electronic form) is a computerized version of the paper form. Electronic forms can be viewed on a computer screen, filled in, printed, transferred via the Internet and stored on disk.

E-form benefits:

- Elimination of the cost of printing, storing, and distributing pre-printed forms,
- Elimination of obsolete forms.
- E-forms can be filled out faster because the programming associated with them can automatically format, calculate, look up, and validate information for the user.
- With digital signatures and routing via e-mail, approval cycle times can be significantly reduced.

- Submitting electronic forms can eliminate the cost of re-keying data with its associated errors.

Managing Translation Projects

Project Management includes the activities of planning, initiating, monitoring, controlling and closing out projects. The TRMS Project Management module is vital in handling all aspects of resource accessibility tasks management, costs assessment and time response. In order to make quality decisions a Project Manager needs reliable information and the ability to timely access that information. The TRMS Project Manager allows an organization maximum flexibility to keep up with the fast pace of the new global economy.

TRMS project management benefits:

- Automatic client to Project Manager selection for fast client response
- Instant access to Translator information and availability for rapid job assignment
- A feature-rich assignment section to plan all tasks for single or multiple document requests
- Project management allows each single job to be set into a rigid production or ad-hoc collaboration process
- Instant knowledge of every job in progress for every Project Manager
- Project management allows a tight control over each task deadline assignment
- Full control of all cost progressions for every job request.

THE OVERALL TECHNOLOGICAL INNOVATION

In light of its specific expertise in the field of business automation, Ordiplan was retained by the Province of New Brunswick as the main contractor for this development project. GENER-X, the software division of Ordiplan, carried the responsibility for the development of an automated system for the management of the province's translation requests.

The technologies applied to the development of this solution, offer wide control over information. They also enable information to be structured and distributed quickly, easily, and securely, with many ensuing benefits:

- Web-Based: User access is unbounded; the platform is flexible, which favors future developments.
- Graphical User Interface (GUI): The display of work lists is easy to grasp and navigate. The work lists can also be customized, as can be the preferences for the display of the work course, searches, reports, etc.
- Non-Electronic Documents: The system can manage non-electronic documents.
- Security: Both the Workflow engine and the Document Management System control appropriate access.

Several software technologies were tapped for the solution:

- COM/DCOM: Distributed object technology (Microsoft)
- InTempo and FormFlow: Workflow engine and e-forms software (JetForm Corp.)
- DOCS Open: Enterprise document management (Hummingbird)
- Internet Explorer: Internet browser (Microsoft)
- MS SQL, Windows NT and IIS: Database management system, operating system and Web server (Microsoft)
- VirusScan: virus detection application (Network Associates)

The Power of Technology Integration

By integrating workflow technology with other technologies as diverse as document management, e-business, the Internet, supply chain management and project management, TRMS represents a new automated solution in its own right, with improvements in process management. Also, brushing aside the unavoidable barriers between technologies, today's users demand a user-friendly environment capable of simplifying task execution, versatile tools and translation requests readily available:

- Improve productivity.
- Reduce operating and labor costs.
- Improve customer service.
- Reduce waste and duplication.
- Improve access to timely information.
- Minimal IT and job-specific training.
- Improve security and confidentiality by controlling access to critical information.

In the present instance, the integration of technologies also opens up extended functions:

- Extraction of metadata for automatic indexing of documents
- Automatic document comparisons to preclude repetitive translations
- Assessing tasks for duration and deadline
- Confirmation of participant's scheduled availability
- Real-time work allocation of multiple tasks among multiple participants
- Follow-up on projects for all participants
- Extended reporting and billing
- Complete integration of all processes

THE SYSTEM USERS, AND WHAT THEIR JOBS NOW ENTAIL COMPARED TO PRE-INSTALLATION.

By using the solution developed by GENER-X, the Translation Bureau of the Government of New Brunswick now processes translation requests through a single electronic form. More precisely, the main benefits of the process automation are the following:

- Reducing error rates by eliminating the paper process and its related problems. The processes are standardized.
- Improving productivity and reducing costs by significantly reducing, or even eliminating, the time spent searching for documents or recreating lost information.
- Saving time by providing quick access to the documents and facilitating document production. In general, workflow implementations lead to gains (in terms of response time) of 30 percent to 90 percent in total case processing time.
- Improving safety and confidentiality by controlling access to critical information. Each participant is granted access to a set of procedures and activities that is limited in accordance with their role.
- Improving decision-making by putting the information at the disposal of persons who need it, when required.
- Increasing user collaboration by putting forward an organization-wide solution.
- Determining precisely the progress of requests by instantly inspecting the state, assignments, and the participant responsible.
- Elimination of procedural irritants for the staff
- Improvements in morale and job enrichment
- Improvements in the ability to keep job data current
- Better opportunity and capability to deploy current resources into new areas
- Better opportunity to attract, train and promote ever more talented people to the translation services

THE BIGGEST HURDLES OVERCOME

Management

The project was initiated at the management level, the champion was the director of the Translation Bureau, and its vision was to render the Translation Bureau a profitable business unit within the Government. Two major hurdles were identified as:

- Overcoming the development process, due to the unavailability of a Web Interface
- Managing the over-budget resulting from the development modifications of the Web Interface.

Business

Implementation the workflow solution at the New Brunswick Translation Bureau created some problems for the external participants involved in the day-to-day operations. Clients were not accustomed to filling out electronic forms; they were in the habit of sending emails directly to the Translation Bureau.

The new electronic process required clients to spend more time filling out electronic forms and attaching the necessary documents. It took a period of three-month learning curve to instill this new procedure. Currently, clients are now using the application without problems.

In order to assist the external Translator, the Translation bureau prepared a document to introduce the new system. Part of the package was a form that required filling out and returning with a check for the amount of $100. New Brunswick forced the external Translator to purchase a client license for the application if they desired to have translation assignments from the government. This process created some initial problems but users quickly adapted.

Technology

The total project time from the initial requirement gathering to the final deployment took over 2.5 years. This long process was mainly due to the technology available at the time, ideal platform product selections and resolving multi-computer environment conflicts.

At the initial phase of the project, Web workflow tools were not full commercial applications, and the initial project was a mail-based workflow solution. This process involved the installation of custom-developed application on each participant station. During the pilot implementation phase, we discovered that to offer the necessary support to the Translation Bureau, further workflow tools were required. The project was delayed until JetForm introduce its web interface module to its workflow tools.

After the Web development phase, the implementation process faced environment problems on the Client's side. The Web interface (Internet Explorer and the custom made Active-X control) was not functioning properly on all the workstations. The New Brunswick Translation bureau had to deal with additional service packs from Microsoft and Dell computers as well as Novell.

From the External Translator side, the deployment didn't create problems other than requiring on some installations new browser versions and service packs.

THE NEW SYSTEM CONFIGURATION

The New Brunswick implementation comprises the following components:

Equipment:

Equipment Type	Description	Number of Unit
Server	Web server, DWA server, EDV server, Database server, Document server	The architecture makes use of 3 servers to install the software. All units are Pentium III processors with 256 Megabytes of RAM and RAID disk

		technology.
Workstations	Clients, project managers, and translators	Clients 200, PM 9, Translators 100.

Software:

Software Type	Item	Description
Platform	Windows NT, IIS and MS SQL	The application is running under MS Windows NT using ASP pages
Service application	DWA Intempo from Jetform	The core application is the workflow structure tool from Jetform corporation
	EDV PcDocs from Hummingbird	The document management solution required to store client documents, versioning and audit trail
Custom application	Generic workflow route	The workflow route was developed to allow easy modification. Variables are called to the MS SQL database
	EDVAgent	A workflow service allowing communication with the document management system
	Virus Checking	A workflow service allowing for virus checking on all documents
Client side Active-X	Encryption and compression component	During file transfer all documents are encrypted and compressed for easy download
	File transfer component	HTTP file transfer
	Project assignment component	A complex project management component allowing flexible project planning, resource allocation and deadline management

COST SAVINGS, INCREASED REVENUES, AND PRODUCTIVITY IMPROVEMENTS

The Translation Request Management System enables in-house Translators and Freelancers to not only improve the processing time, but also reduce costs (thanks to the retrieval of existing contents as well as the tracking project progress), improve quality (using automated validation phases), and evolve within a fully comput-erized environment.

- Reduction in overall costs
- Reducing error rates by eliminating the paper process and its re-lated problems. Processes are standardized.
- Improving productivity and reducing costs by significantly reducing, or even eliminating, the time spent searching for documents or rec-reating lost information. In general, workflow implementation leads to gains (in productivity terms) of:
- Five percent to 10 percent savings related to the planning of tasks and to their assignment
- Five percent to 10 percent savings related to case status responses
- Ten percent to 30 percent savings related to immediate access to the case data and to the use of tools
- Compound gains of 20 percent to 50 percent can be achieved
- Saving time by providing quick access to documents and facilitating document production. In general, workflow implementations lead to gains (in terms of response time) of 30 percent to 90 percent in total case processing time
- Reduce operating and labor costs
- Reduction in paper handling, which results in reduced processing time for translation requests
- Increases in productivity at all levels (individual, workgroup, sec-tion, and organization)
- Reduction in printing costs, because information can be sent across the web
- Streamlining of the workflow process at all levels (individual, work-group, section, and organization), which results in increased pro-ductivity
- Improvements in the quality of products and services at all levels (internally and externally), which results in the continuous im-provement of customer satisfaction
- Greater ability to monitor and report on organization's impact on clients
- Greater ability to respond quickly and effectively to new regulations, requirements, or emerging business opportunities, which resulted in increased revenues.

COMPETITIVE ADVANTAGES GAINED AND HOW THE COMPETITIVE GOAL POSTS FOR THIS INDUSTRY WERE MOVED

Being a Government Translation Bureau, the business model does not imply a competitive gain vis a vis external organizations. The necessity to implement a workflow solution comes from the internal requirement that all services should be at maximal performance, and costs under control.

From a management perspective, the workflow implementation al-lows a tight management process always to be in the forefront of the needs of all government departments. By collecting valuable data for all the processing steps, the department director has access to strategic reports allowing for proactive decision-making.

IMMEDIATE AND LONG-TERM PLANS TO SUSTAIN COMPETITIVE ADVANTAGE

The Translation Bureau of New Brunswick offers two major types of service:

1. Document Translation service.

2. Interpretation service.

Interpretation services are very small by comparison to translation requests and are not part of the initial implementation. It is the goal of the Translation Bureau to add an Interpretation module to the current solution in order to make allowance for centralized management and reporting.

This new module will allow not only task assignment and resource allocation to be processed but will also manage the equipment requirement for an interpretation project. The equipment process will allow inventory management, equipment selection and equipment transfer.

A more robust project management is currently in development to allow a scheduling function, in order to monitor selection and availability of all Translators.

From a developer point of view (GENER-X), the application being developed for the New Brunswick department represents a new vertical business market. Because, at the present moment, no competitor is addressing document workflow processes over the Web with an Enterprise Resource Planning (ERP) approach, developments are being made to enhance the application with the goal of generating sales of the TRMS solution over a global clientele.

Embedding Business Process Management Technology: iJET Travel Intelligence, USA

Paula Negron and Ronald Alepin,
Fujitsu Software Corporation, USA

I. INTRODUCTION

Embeddable workflow technology began to emerge in the late 1990s to fulfill the growing need for software developers to provide workflow functionality as part of their product and service offerings. Packaged workflow applications were not flexible enough and lacked the integration capabilities developers sought. In addition, web-based applications changed the role of workflow technology in enterprise architectures. Products relying on local-area networks, fat client-side software and e-mail routing to manage processes were no longer sufficient. Integration APIs, adapters, open and modular architecture, thin client software and access to source code starter-kits were "must haves" for this new breed of e-business application developers.

Some e-business application developers built their own proprietary workflow engines and hard-coded the business logic. They believed (and, at the time, they were correct) that their workflow requirements were so rudimentary as to not require a full-fledged commercial product. Other e-business application developers required special features that none of the contemporary commercial products provided. Their only alternative was to build it themselves.

Many software vendors battling with process management requirements realized that building a business process management engine is not a trivial development task. They also understood that embedding a commercial business process management engine would enable them to launch their process-enabled products to the market quicker and on schedule. The marvel that is our market economy worked its magic. Companies emerged to fulfill this need, developing the next generation of process management software—embeddable, dynamic and keyed to the needs of the e-business application developer community.

Enterprises have also found embeddable business process management engines useful for integrating business processes that span many disparate systems and departments. Today's business process management engines coordinate the routing of data from application to application, prompting users to intervene when decisions need to be made about exceptional cases. Business process management engines can be tightly integrated into enterprise applications. There they enable enterprises to extract the business logic into reusable business process components instead of hard-coding the frequently changing logic into applications.

EAI vendors have been actively building, buying or acquiring business process management technology as they have come to realize the importance of automating business processes in application integration. To date, the process management capabilities of EAI vendors have been fairly limited in the area of human participation. Some EAI products still require developers to code steps where processes involve human interaction and decision-making. Timers, complex branching, and dynamic process editing may be missing or incomplete in EAI offerings.

The ability to change business processes dynamically while the processes are running is crucial in the world in which e-business application software operates. When making changes to business processes, many products require significant levels of technical product knowledge and programming skill in addition to detailed knowledge about the enterprise's business. This effectively eliminates any hope of dynamic process evolution. Have you ever noticed that you can't find a programmer when you really need one (like when you find a new way to cut your process cycle time)? This is problematic due to technical staff members' relatively limited understanding of the business process domain.

EAI vendors tend to have only minimal capabilities for supporting dynamic process change. Exceptions occur and routings must be changed while processes are in progress. Users are not willing to waste time with implementations that require them to start the process all over again in order to make simple changes. It does not fit the description of today's dynamic business environment where responsiveness to changes in the market may be key to a company's survival. Products are emerging today that can combine the best of EAI and business process management.

II. BUSINESS PROCESS MANAGEMENT ENGINES FOR ISVS AND ENTERPRISES

For many years now, it has been an established fact that use of workflow technology can lead to remarkable cost savings and increased efficiency and productivity. And workflow technology has evolved to business process management engines with rich integration and reporting features. Enterprises and software developers have come to understand that such an engine can be applied to increasingly complex problems. Automating business processes end to end, integrating applications to process steps, and opening up processes for collaboration with partners and customers represent just the beginning of what can be expected from process management engines. Application integration and B2B collaboration simply are not possible without such business process management technology. Processes are the DNA of businesses, and competitive advantage is embedded into business processes. Increasingly workflow-based process management solutions are the answers to more and more problems.

Today's new business environment requires business process management technology that can be integrated seamlessly inside e-business applications and molded easily to fit into changing architectures. Today's generation of embeddable business process management engines were designed to be flexible, leaving the door open for future technologies and standards. They fit naturally to the dynamic and evolving business environment.

Independent software vendors and solution providers have realized that embedding business process automation engines adds more than just bells and whistles to their product offerings. Workflow and process automation have become essential components, as the graphical process design tools enable them to visualize to the customer exactly how they plan to solve the business problem at hand. Business process management plays an ever more important role in their applications. Increasingly, ISVs and solution providers rely on an embedded process management engine to stitch together the different elements and functions of their applications. These developers have learned that homegrown, "quick and dirty" process management engines are dead-ends. They recognize the need for a flexible, full-featured solution, from a vendor whose core competence is process management.

III. CASE STUDY: EMBEDDING A BUSINESS PROCESS MANAGEMENT ENGINE IN THE IJET TRAVEL INTELLIGENCE SYSTEM

Overview of iJET

iJET Travel Intelligence focuses on delivering real-time intelligence and alerts to the travel industry. iJET's regional and category specialists staff an around-the-clock operations center where they continuously monitor over 5,000 sources worldwide. Their goal is to help international travelers avoid travel disruptions. iJET's specialists analyze and verify every piece of information before it is added to iJET's Global Travel Intelligence Database.

iJET's Business Process Management Requirements and Technology Selection

iJET recognized early on when designing their service that they would need some sort of process management capability. iJET considered solutions including document management, change management, content management systems and, of course, building their own.

Document Management

For iJET, document management systems lacked in comprehensive BPM features. Moreover, iJET's documents were small (a few lines about a hurricane forecast, for example). Document management software was overkill.

Content Management

Content management systems did not meet iJET's strict versioning requirements.

Change Management

iJET found that change management systems dealt mostly with statically stored information and were not suitable for viewing the content in the context of geographical and subject matter expertise.

Build Your Own

In the course of reviewing available solutions, iJET came to realize that a business process management engine would be at the core of their business. iJET also reached two other conclusions:

1. iJET realized that building the kind of engine they needed was beyond their current expertise, would require an enormous amount of time and money, and would delay their time to market; and

2. A commercially available embeddable business process management engine could meet their requirements. (iJET could not find a product with the versioning capabilities they required, and accordingly, iJET was forced to develop its own.)

iJET conducted a rigorous review of the features it would require of an embeddable BPM product. The development team identified component-based design and a comprehensive Java API as essential. iJET product management insisted on the ability of the business process management engine that can integrate within various IT environments, as they needed it to work with a wide variety of proprietary and off-the-shelf software applications. Since intelligence data changes very quickly the iJET business people required that any off the shelf product have the ability to change business processes easily. Finally, everyone at iJET identified vendor support as critical.

Embedding Business Process Management Technology at iJET

iJET embedded the business process management engine to create, streamline and automate its intelligence creation process, ensuring that all editorial and approval guidelines are followed and that the final Travel Intelligence™ product is in the hands of customers where it can help them avoid travel problems. Intelligence objects are routed through the process managed by the business process management engine. The intelligence objects consist of metadata mapped to itinerary information and personal profile data. Personal profile data includes items such as the traveler's contact information, age, gender, and medical conditions. This mapping enables iJET's software to determine where and when the intelligence might affect travelers.

iJET's goal is to deliver integrated, timely and high quality travel intelligence to its customers 24 hours a day, seven days a week and 365 days a year. A flexible and open business process management engine will allow iJET to meet their goal—from the beginning. The business process management engine iJET selected allowed iJET to implement the production system in just three months with only two developers dedicated to the process management aspects of the system. The combination of iJET's software and the BPM engine enables a continuous stream of updates that provide up-to-the-second travel intelligence gleaned from more than 5,000 sources worldwide, on topics ranging from health, security and transportation to entry/exit rules and communications.

Using the BPM engine, iJET quickly linked its application server, quality of assurance systems, automatic content acquisition agent and various analytical tools used for its Travel Intelligence business. iJET feeds data such as process start and stop times from the BPM engine into analytical tools. iJET is then able to control its costs and maintain the quality and timeliness of its information. iJET can ensure that the right amount of time is spent on various types of intelligence objects. iJET also incorporates the time management features from the BPM engine in its business processes. Timers ensure that activities progress according to the priority ranking of the individual processes. Task level timers are used for ensuring timely completion of individual tasks.

iJET has a library of between 40 and 50 modular process definitions, comprised of several sub-processes. The use of sub-processes maximizes the reusability of the process designs. iJET process definitions vary from simple designs with no more than 4 to 6 steps all the way to complex structures containing dozens of steps. iJET analysts provide input about business process requirements to developers who are in charge of creating process definitions and adding scripting rules to the processes where necessary.

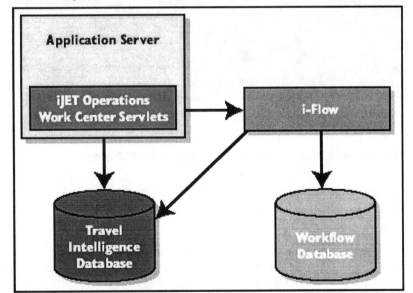

Figure 1—High-level architecture at iJETconsists of BEA's WebLogic application server, Oracle database and Fujitsu's i-Flow business process management engine.

Users' Views of Business Process Management Technology at iJET

About 45 experts from several countries and areas of expertise make up the iJET Operations Center workforce. Operations Center experts typically have 20-30 years of experience in intelligence analysis. These experts are enthusiastically outspoken about the tools iJET has provided, praising them as superior to any they have ever used. In fact, these advanced business process management tools have helped iJET attract and hire experienced intelligence experts from workplaces that do not provide comparable technology and tools. The intelligence experts are pleased with the easy-to-use BPM engine. According to user feedback, the iJET system is generations beyond the systems that the intelligence experts used in their previous positions.

Figure 2 Intelligence experts at work in the iJET Operations Center

iJET Processes Create Travel Intelligence and Alerts

iJET uses the business process management engine primarily for automating two essential aspects of its business:

1) Intelligence Creation Process, and

2) Watch Process.

iJET's Intelligence Creation Process ensures that the iJET Travel Intelligence system continuously provides useful and accurate information for the traveller prior to and during the trip. The Watch Process is used to determine what information should be sent to the traveller immediately in a form of a travel alert.

Intelligence Creation Process:
1. An Intelligence Manager gathers intelligence requirements.

2. That Intelligence Manager adds intelligence requests to the queue, which will form work lists for the users.
3. Source Specialists identify and rank most relevant sources based on the intelligence requirements. Information about the sources is attached to the business process.
4. A Collection Specialist determines where within the source the relevant intelligence is located, assesses the reliability of the source, and determines how often the source intelligence changes. Based on the frequency of the changes the source is queried at regular time intervals.
5. An Intelligence Manager assigns an analyst based on their regional and subject matter expertise.
6. The assigned analyst creates an Intelligence Object based on the source information.
7. Regional, legal and subject matter experts collaborate to review the Intelligence Object and verify the relevance of the sources.
8. Final editorial changes are made and the Intelligence Object is routed to the Intelligence Manager for sign-off.
9. After sign-off, the intelligence will be published to the system and travellers will be able to access it based on their trip and personal profiles.

The Watch Process:

The Watch process generates and manages travel alerts using the BPM engine. A critical travel alert is an important notice that the iJET system sends to travelers about events that would definitely have an affect on their trip, for example flight cancellation, accommodation cancellations and outbreaks of dangerous diseases. This business process ensures that the critical alerts are informative, accurate, and delivered in such a way that busy travelers on the go can get to the information quickly.

1.Information Analyst Identifies Potential Critical Alert

iJET Information Analysts constantly obtain up-to-the-minute travel information from proprietary sources. Typically they can obtain in-formation for their particular specialty area far in advance of the news agencies covering this same specialty area. When an iJET specialist receives information that is a potential alert for travelers, he or she identifies it as such, and routes it immediately to an Alert Watch Manager using the BPM engine.

2. Alert Watch Manager Assigns Alert Status

The Alert Watch Manager ascertains whether it is actually an alert and, if so, assigns it one of the following alert statuses:

- Informational: Probably will not affect someone's travel
- Warning: May affect someone's travel
- Critical: Will, in all probabilities, affect someone's travel

The alert status assigned by the Alert Watch Manager determines the set of business processes used to handle it. The following steps de-scribe the processes used in handling a critical alert.

3. Verifying the Information Source

The BPM engine automatically routes the potential critical alert to a Verification Expert. If the Verification Expert confirms it, the critical alert is routed to a Subject Matter Analyst to be written.

4. Writing the Critical Alert

The Subject Matter Analyst writes the Critical Alert, notifies that she has written it, then the business process management engine routes the newly written alert to an Editorial Analyst, Verification Expert, and Legal Analyst for review.

5. Reviewing the Critical Alert

The business process management engine manages the review process, routing the alert to the reviewers for comment, then back to the Subject Matter Analyst to make any necessary corrections. This back and forth routing continues until all the reviewers approve the critical alert for publication. The alert is then sent to the Alert Manager for final signoff and publication.

6. Signoff and Publication of Critical Alert

The Alert Manager makes a final review of the alert then publishes it. The critical alert is sent to all travelers for which it is relevant.

iJET makes heavy use of the business process management engine's parallel and conditional processing capabilities in the Watch process. Often a watch process can contain dozens of conditions based on the repository metadata describing the type of alert. For example, if an alert concerns a terrorism threat it has to be routed to both security experts and regional experts whereas medical alerts would be routed only to the medical experts for review. The business process management engine must evaluate the numerous decision parameters fast as the duration of the Watch process is typically only a few minutes.

With such an elaborate review process superimposed over information with potentially a very short shelf life and a high degree of immediacy, it is easy to understand why iJET would want to monitor the processes to ensure things are moving smoothly.

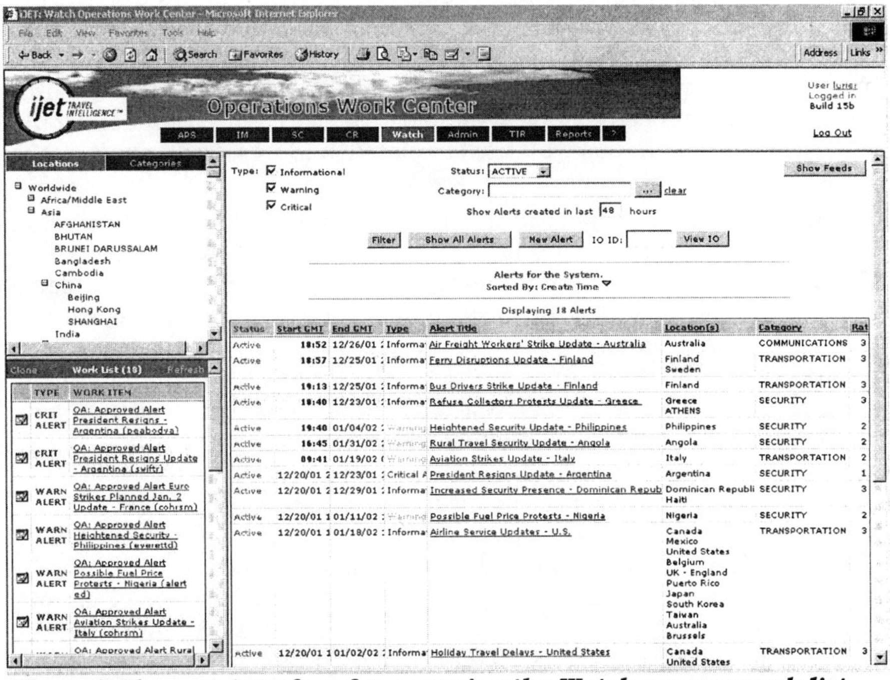

Figure 3 The user interface for accessing the Watch process work list.

Each Operations Work Center user has a web-browser based work list generated according to their role in the process (see Figure 3). After logging in to the system, the user selects a work item from the work list based on the priority of the alerts. Color-coding is used to identify the critical alerts on the work list. The business process management engine pulls up the module that contains data relevant to the task. A user can take ownership of a task by accepting it. Simultaneously, the work item will disappear from the work lists of all other users. There are various levels of task completion available, and a user can choose to keep the work item on his or her personal work list for further edits, release the task to other users, or mark the task as complete allowing the process to move to the next step.

Benefits of Business Process Management to iJET

By embedding the business process management engine into its internal Operations Work Center, iJET successfully manages complex, real-time intelligence creation processing. The business process management engine streamlines and automates its intelligence creation process and delivers the final Travel Intelligence information directly to iJET's customers.

Using BPM technology to automate the processes of information gathering, review and distribution has increased the reliability and efficiency of iJET's Travel Intelligence system. Process management improves the consistency of iJET's processes, and iJET rests assured that the procedures implemented will be executed in the same manner every time they are performed.

The BPM engine enables rapid publication of travel alerts to travelers using its service. Highly efficient and reliable editorial and approval procedures are vital to ensure that Travel Intelligence delivers the most accurate information to travelers in a matter of minutes. Without the proper processes and technology in place, the company would risk drowning in a flood of travel related updates from around the world.

Together, the BPM engine and iJET turn mountains of information into comprehensive, timely, accurate, precise, objective, and personalized Travel Intelligence that allows travelers to avoid travel problems worldwide. The business process management engine is the key for processing information quickly and enables iJET to continuously produce alerts faster than the major newswires and media channels, including breaking news television. The business process management engine helps drive iJET's business.

IV. REQUIREMENTS FOR EMBEDDABLE BUSINESS PROCESS MANAGEMENT ENGINES

In 2001 a rapidly growing number of ISVs and solution providers chose to develop or adapt their e-business applications to J2EE-compliant application server platforms such as Fujitsu's INTERSTAGE, IBM's WebSphere and BEA's WebLogic. Accordingly, they established J2EE compliance as a requirement for any embeddable business process management engine. Many of the leading process management engines were developed prior to the J2EE era, and consequently, these products have been undergoing architectural updates over the past several months. Some engine vendors are now shipping the EJB versions, optimized and tested to run on these leading application servers. At least one vendor has been able to provide the same programming and user interfaces for the EJB and non-EJB versions—offering customers a complete range of deployment platforms and preserving the customers' investment in the business process management engine.

Enterprises that deploy application servers from multiple vendors should be wary of business process management engines that are tightly coupled with only one application server product. They should rely on vendors that have tested and optimized their business process management engines to run on all the application servers deployed in their organization to avoid surprises.

Calling EJBs from the process definitions is an important part of the J2EE requirement and business process management engines vary in their support. In best implementations, users can configure EJB invocations via user-friendly graphical user interfaces. However it remains a job that requires assistance from developers familiar with Java.

As process management becomes an increasingly important component of the e-business application, ISVs and solution providers have come to recognize that they need to select a vendor who can deliver not just technology, but support, stability and vision. They appreciate the need for a vendor that understands the environment in which their applications will run—the enterprise; and what it takes to measure up in that environment.

Initially, embedded workflow found its strongest support in the development community where integration interfaces matter more than user interfaces. As a result, some process automation engine vendors must catch up in the area of supplied user interfaces and reporting tools. Reporting tools must be designed with business professionals in mind. It should be possible to compile reports graphically without having to master a set of reporting APIs. Business process reporting can provide valuable information about process bottlenecks and areas of improvement. Business managers should be provided with visual tools for monitoring and analyzing business processes. The same tools should allow them to fine-tune and optimize processes and business rules based on real-time process metrics.

Through the end of 2002, business process management engine vendors will transform their product architectures to support web services. Business process management engines will coordinate web services offered by different partners and systems forming adaptable end-to-end business processes. Numerous initiatives have formed since the inception of web services specifying standards for defining and executing business processes in the context of web services. However none of these standards as yet have been broadly adopted and implemented. Only time will tell which standards the market will accept. Until then, business process management engine vendors need to ensure that their products are open, so they can support any standard.

V. CONCLUSION

Dynamic and agile businesses are automating processes that span applications, platforms, workgroups, companies and continents. Technology for managing business processes must be adaptive to support changes to these processes anytime. Modifications to business processes cannot be made quickly if the business processes are hard-coded into applications. Off-the-shelf workflow products can be used to extract the business logic from application logic but their architectures are not flexible enough to interact with the multitude of applications enterprises have accrued over the years. Embeddable business process management engines have open architectures that allow integration with legacy as well as future technologies. They enable human participation in business processes just as easily as straight-through processing. Some business process management engines can accommodate changes at both design time and runtime, whereas most EAI products lack the support for runtime changes. Embeddable business process management engines remain the best candidates for enterprise-wide business process automation.

Extensible, full-featured process management is an essential component of enterprise-class e-business applications. Developers of such applications confront some very real decisions: Do we acquire the expertise necessary to develop a process management engine? Or do we acquire an embeddable process management engine from a supplier? The decision is not simply about resource allocation—spending money to become process management software design experts. Time and effort spent on such "infrastructure" is time away from solving the application problem and extending the application functionality. Furthermore, internal development of process management software raises a time-to-market issue. A "battle-tested" embeddable process management engine from a third party is ready now and for a known cost. There is enough risk in software development schedules without adding process management engine development.

In addition, internally developed solutions tend to be difficult to maintain and enhance. Only if the business process management requirements are very rudimentary or exceptionally unique, should an ISV consider building a business process management engine in-house. Even in the case of unique requirements a detailed review often reveals workarounds that prove embedded process management to be the most cost-effective alternative.

R.R. Donnelley & Sons Company
Graphics Management Division

Gold Award, North America, 2001

OVERVIEW

In 1998 the R.R. Donnelley & Sons Company, a leading North American printer, communications services, and logistics company, realized that one of their divisions was facing a growth challenge. R.R. Donnelley's educational book publishing customers were requesting the Graphics Management division to produce custom educational projects with greater complexity than projects produced in previous years. These requests for custom work were causing the division to experience a challenge in managing their expanded workload.

As a result of this change in the market, the Graphics Management division conducted a time-based study to assess their current business practices. They reviewed the process by which they were designing and producing educational and marketing kits, as well as their services that included research and analysis, structural design of kits and packages, prototype development; manufacturing, procurement; project quality and supply chain management.

The analysis showed that increasingly complex projects were creating significant amounts of non-value-added work for key personnel—limiting both present and future capacity for Graphics Management. As a result, R.R. Donnelley decided to invest in developing PRISM, a web-based project management system to support the Graphics Management team.

Graphics Management's Challenge

Graphics Management's business with its customers was becoming increasingly complex. The division needed to produce custom projects that were complicated to develop and that included multiple components. The K-12 (kindergarten through 12th grade) educational curriculum content had moved from simple book offerings to content packages that included multiple forms of media.

For example, the number of components per project for elementary and secondary education curriculums has increased from primarily textbooks to multiple media projects, including CDs and Internet technology, and interactive learning tools like games and puppets. Five years ago, components per project averaged to two to five pieces, and recently projects contain up to 24 components.

During the production process of a project, Graphics Management work together with customers and suppliers, After Graphics Management receives a project from a customer, the division bids out components of the project to suppliers. From the beginning of the bidding process to the completion of a project, Graphics Management continually needs to collaborate and negotiate with suppliers, while meeting the commitments that revolve around deadlines, deliverables, prices and etc. With the advent of multiple component projects, this process was becoming complicated and harder for Graphics Management to manage.

One reason Graphics Management was having trouble managing the production process was that the major contributors to projects, the suppliers, were outside of R.R. Donnelley's control. Suppliers adhered to their own business processes that were different from Graphics Management's. Since the division had a commitment to their customers for producing the final project, the division was ultimately responsible for the suppliers to complete the components. Graphics Management was unable to easily collaborate and manage commitments made with suppliers, and this became even more critical, especially if unanticipated changes or problems occurred.

For instance, when a customer requested a modification of a book cover's design, Graphics Management needed to renegotiate with a supplier. The current system was time-consuming, paper intensive and cumbersome for the project management team and prevented responding to this type of change order effectively and easily. The increase in complex, multiple component projects magnified the pain of unanticipated changes.

It became clear that R.R. Donnelley needed a way to stay flexible with its suppliers, and at the same time manage and track changes in deliverables. The division's goal was to synchronize business processes with customers and suppliers that were outside of R.R. Donnelley corporate boundaries, and outside of its direct control.

Graphics Management Solution

In order to meet the new demands of customized multiple component projects, it became crucial for R.R. Donnelley to adopt an innovative business process system that would enable internal staff to collaborate and track commitments and changes, as well as negotiate with customers and suppliers. PRISM was R.R. Donnelley's solution.

Utilizing ActionWorks® Metro, PRISM provides R.R. Donnelley the power to involve suppliers and customers in collaborative commerce.[1] As defined in this case study and utilized by R.R. Donnelley, collaborative commerce occurs when customers, suppliers and partners create a unified business process or project that enables participants from across corporate boundaries to design, develop and deliver new products or services uniquely tailored to customer

---

[1] ActionWorks® is a registered trademark of Action Technologies, Inc.

needs. Collaborative commerce embraces the web's capacity for rich interaction, allowing participants to collaborate, negotiate, and manage commitments. In addition, PRISM is web-based; participants can exchange information and provide updates online. ActionWorks Metro provides the solution for Graphics Management to manage complex projects and successfully meet their commitments to customers.

KEY MOTIVATORS BEHIND INSTALLING PRISM

Internal Factors that Necessitated a Solution

When launching a packaging or kit project, an Account Management Specialist (AMS) at Graphics Management works with the customer to define the scope of the project and the manufacturing specifications for each of the project's components. The AMS is a project manager and serves as the coordinator for both the customer and the supplier.

Upon customer approval of a project's scope and specifications, the AMS begins a bidding process to obtain quotes from a selection of suppliers for each of the project's components. Throughout this bidding process the AMS receives bid information for project components from multiple suppliers and, based upon those bids, quotes a price for the entire project to the customer.

Upon approval of the quotes, the AMS manages the manufacturing and fulfillment processes to create the complete kit. These processes have become much more complex as the number of components for each project has grown. In addition, Graphics Management is ISO certified.[2] The certification requires Graphics Management to obtain bids from at least three suppliers for each component quote. Obtaining three quotes per component added yet another layer of complexity to the entire process.

As customers approached Graphics Management to produce these multi-component kits, it became more time consuming for the AMS team to present customers with timely and complete pricing information because that information was dependent on getting bids from suppliers quickly and accurately. The greater complexity of each job also increased the AMS team's need to coordinate with a larger pool of suppliers for the fulfillment of each job. As a result, the AMS staff was spending a lot of non-value-added time manually assembling job quotes for their customers and tracking their communications with suppliers. Fast becoming buried in administrative

---

[2] ISO, (The International Organization for Standardization), is a non-governmental organization established in 1947. The mission of ISO is to promote the development of standardization and related activities in the world with a view to facilitating the international exchange of goods and services, and to developing cooperation in the spheres of intellectual, scientific, technological and economic activity, http://www.iso.ch/infoe/intro.htm#What is ISO.

tasks, revenue per AMS was a critical issue, and could possibility impact plans for business growth.

The time-based study detailed how this complexity was impacting the AMS staff's day-to-day activities and what could be done to assist them. The study revealed that the staff was spending increasing amounts of time on limited value-added administrative tasks such as phoning and faxing project information to suppliers and customers. At that time Graphics Management had clearly outgrown its existing Windows-based quoting system. To obtain better leverage of their AMS staff, it was clear that they needed a more comprehensive and efficient way to coordinate work.

With a new system Graphics Management hoped to improve:

- Managing the bidding process with suppliers
- Collaborating with suppliers
- Supplying customers accurate quotes
- Meeting commitments
- Efficiency of administrative tasks
- Accuracy and accessibility of historical information

BUSINESS INNOVATION

Jim Schultz, Graphics Management's Division Director, recognized that the increase in administrative time was a hindrance to the division's growth. He decided that the division needed to develop an infrastructure that would automate processes, to increase productivity and drive business growth.

Schultz believed the challenge for R.R. Donnelley was to automate the collaborative business process between customers, Graphics Management and suppliers. Equally important was the need to accurately capture information in a data repository, making it available to the entire workgroup and supply chain. Additionally, they needed a system to track the status of work, such as the commitments made by each supplier. Such a system would provide better leverage of their AMS team, improving productivity, and allowing the current AMS team to handle additional clients within the existing structure.

The infrastructure Graphics Management conceived resulted in the development of PRISM, an application that would provide Graphics Management with a web-enabled process system. The ultimate objectives of PRISM were to create e-business relationships with customers and suppliers, so as to improve the business process of the entire supply chain: the publisher, Graphics Management AMS teams and the certified supplier base. In addition, the data repository would allow project-by-project review and feedback to all the participants.

The Role of the ActionWorks Business Interaction Model

PRISM provides users the ability to track and complete their projects in order to fulfill associated commitments. In PRISM, making and managing commitments requires a structure to ensure "customer/performer" agreement and the flexibility to negotiate and change agreements. This customer/performer agreement simply states that the person making a request takes on the role of customer while the person(s) doing the work takes the role of performer. It is only the customer role that decides and accepts work as being complete. Satisfaction with the work done is evaluated against explicit conditions.

As stated, this feature allows Graphics Management to effectively respond to unanticipated changes. PRISM utilizes ActionWorks Metro's ability to ensure a closed-loop business interaction—where commitments are met and chaos is transformed into a smooth running business process.[3] PRISM utilizes Metro's flexible structures that are necessary to negotiate and modify complex agreements.

The means for achieving the closed-loop interaction is derived from ActionWorks Business Interaction Model. The Model has a theoretical basis described in the book, *Understanding Computers and Cognition*, written by Terry Winograd and Fernando Flores.[4] Based on this work, Action Technologies has received seven patents for Human Communication and Business Process Management. The basic concepts of the Model, (as depicted in Figure 1), are the following:

1. A strong definition of roles. Every agreement clearly defines who is the customer and who is the performer.

2. The Business Interaction Model maintains the context of all business interactions necessary to achieve the satisfaction of customer requests. This defines what actions come next and who does them.

3. Conditions of satisfaction are explicitly specified so that interactions are focused on completely satisfying the customer.

---

[3] The term "closed-loop" in this case study is defined by the **customer** starting a loop of business interactions that become closed when the **customer** declares satisfaction.

[4] Terry Winograd and Fernando Flores, *Understanding Computers and Cognition: A New Foundation for Design*, Ninth printing, Addison-Wesley Publishing Company, 1994.

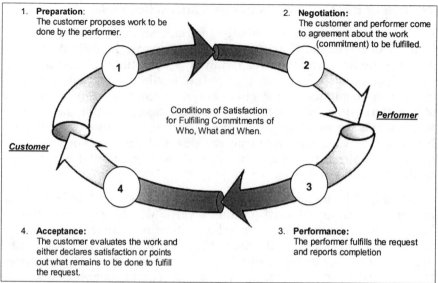

1. **Preparation:**
   The customer proposes work to be done by the performer.

2. **Negotiation:**
   The customer and performer come to agreement about the work (commitment) to be fulfilled.

Conditions of Satisfaction for Fulfilling Commitments of Who, What and When.

Performer

Customer

4. **Acceptance:**
   The customer evaluates the work and either declares satisfaction or points out what remains to be done to fulfill the request.

3. **Performance:**
   The performer fulfills the request and reports completion

Figure 1 Source: Action Technologies

Utilizing Metro, PRISM manages the collaborative interactions required for Graphic Management to facilitate internal and external business processes. For example, after an AMS accepts a bid from a supplier to produce a component, a commitment is negotiated between the AMS (the *customer*) and the supplier (*performer*) for the supplier to provide the component (the *what*) by an agreed due date (the *when*). PRISM is able to support modifications from the supplier, such as changing the due dates and design modifications, and having kit additions and alterations, etc.

TECHNOLOGICAL INNOVATION

David Oberst, Graphics Management's IT Manager, served as the key project leader and was the principle IT advocate for PRISM. He formed a cross-functional IT team with internal representation from Operations, Finance, Sales, Quality, and Design. His team chose to work with The Revere Group, an e-business consulting firm, to manage the technical project.

The initial vision for PRISM was to create an application sitting on a data repository that would allow suppliers and Graphics Management's employees to view, among other things, project information, reports and order status.

Development of PRISM

During the prototyping stage of PRISM, Oberst's team realized that they needed to integrate three traditionally separate technologies: a project information database, a business process database and R.R. Donnelley's financial system. This integration was accomplished by completing a thorough operation process map. Using ActionWorks

Metro Process Builder Developer Edition, the team mapped out Graphics Management's procedures from selling a project to the point when purchase orders are issued to suppliers.

The development team used the detailed process map to identify key areas of potential productivity gain. Next, they identified the appropriate technology for each process step that would help attain the desired productivity benefit. Third, they completed a 3-month RAD design. The database was designed first. Then, the storyboard or general business process flow was designed in collaborative sessions with the business users. Finally, the business logic was designed.

During the development process it became apparent that keeping the data (such as reporting, work order, purchase order forms) updated and making it accessible online was integral to making the application not only accurate, but a vital reporting mechanism as well. The database needed to be linked directly to Graphics Management's operational processes. The development team understood that the repository would only be as good as the ability to automatically update it.

This was an important factor in the development team's decision to use Metro. One of Metro's features is the software's ability to link data to the organization's business processes. The fact that PRISM would collect business process data and information data would be essential for R.R. Donnelley's business growth. To automate the collaboration between customers, Graphics Management and suppliers, the development team therefore created dynamic and personalized interfaces for each person's role on the team. This was accomplished by combining the collaboration-driven business process management of ActionWorks Metro with customized web interfaces.

Metro enabled R.R. Donnelley to create a flexible, web-based system that automated many functions previously requiring paper, phone or fax. And, because the application captures relevant data at each interaction point in a process, dynamic reporting allows them to analyze and improve their processes. Metro also enabled users to manage commitments, collaborate and negotiate over the Internet.

To capture information correctly, and make it available to the entire workgroup and supply chain in a productive manner, Graphics Management created more than 40 standardized information capture templates, (e.g. Books, CDs, tabs, corrugate, etc.) The AMS team uses the templates to build a Bill of Materials based project structure and specifications. As a result Graphics Management has experienced benefits such as better quoting capability and reduction in errors.

The developers used ActionWorks Metro Process Builder to create the templates. Two examples of forms are below.

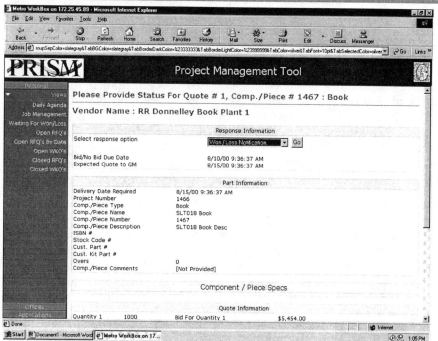

Image 1: Main Customer Reply Form

The Customer Reply Form is an example of a user-friendly form.

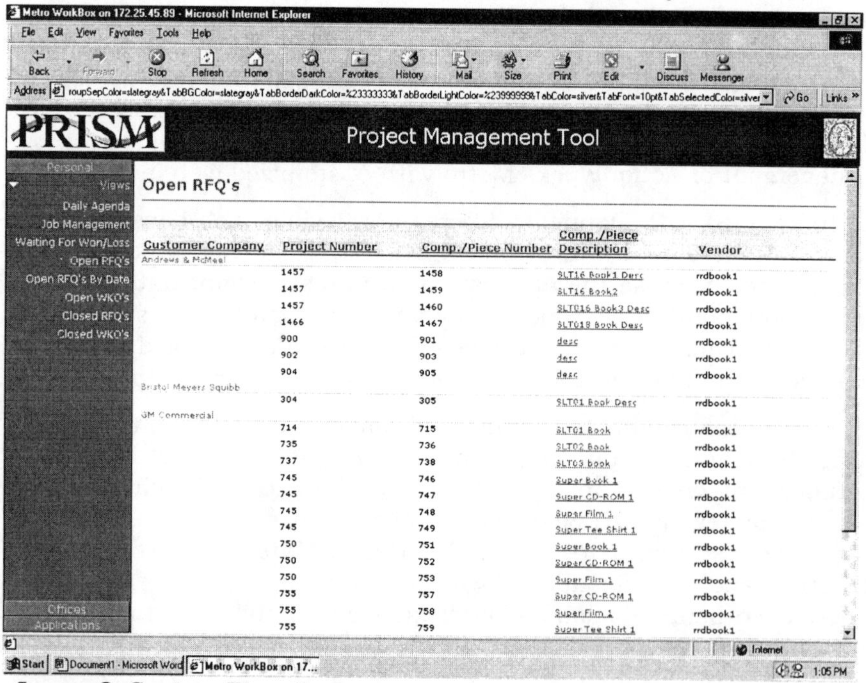

Image 2: Custom View Form

The Custom View Form allows users to customize views. In the form below, the user has chosen to view Open RFQ's. Users can sort views based on projects. They can choose to view a particular project by clicking on the project name. When clicking on a project's name, a work order page opens. The user can see the stage of all processes in a project.

For the developer, ActionWorks Metro also simplifies future changes and enhancements of PRISM, as it did for initial application design. ActionWorks Metro is engineered to maintain the business process integrity of an application by the use of intelligent versioning. Developers do not have to manually review tedious lines of code looking for potential breakdowns when planning a change. Instead, when a change is implemented the ActionWorks Metro software remembers what version any current work was started under and will intelligently complete the open work using the appropriate application version.

Mike Mudry, the lead Graphics Management PRISM Developer, commented on the ease of use of Metro, "You do not have to be a hard-core programmer to work in ActionWorks Metro Process Builder to create the forms & the functionality that is required. You just need a little bit of programming knowledge to make your application work. With this knowledge you can personalize and customize forms and make them user-friendlier. The ActionWorks Metro forms are out-of-the-box and are very straightforward. All of these features save me time."

Technical Benefits to Organization

One of Graphics Management's goals was to build an application that would support internal and external users. Therefore, PRISM supports customers and suppliers plus multiple internal departments including design, account project management, finance, sales and quality management. The application's online tracking of all interactions regarding the publisher's production—from kit design and specs, to request for quotes, to inventory of components, to production status—delivers optimal inventory management, online access to ISO certified suppliers, and reduced administrative time and cost.

The application is 100 percent Internet-based, and allows for efficient managing of data and rich interactions between parties. Users access PRISM through a secure website, which requires a User ID and password for access. Internal and external users are actively managed and can interact together in a singular system. Users are not able to add themselves to the system without approval. Graphics Management's Supply Chain Manager must certify suppliers before they are added to the PRISM system. The user interacts with the system via a web browser and the Internet or R.R. Donnelley's Intranet.

Instead of a cumbersome stand-alone system, dependent on manual input, Graphics Management now has a web-based quoting, tracking, and production status Project Management system.

Given R.R. Donnelley's business and technical requirements, the company benefited from choosing ActionWorks Metro because it offers:

- Web-based interface allows access by multiple value chain companies
- An attractive ROI (return on investment)
- Management of uncertainty in the production process
- Complete Microsoft platform
- Quick Implementation
- Scaling capability to handle current as well as future needs
- Easy maintenance of the process components by the development team

System Users And What Their Jobs Now Entail

The AMS as a User

The AMS staff is now empowered to successfully manage relationships with customers and suppliers via the Internet. These service professionals communicate and negotiate with both parties, often frequently and throughout the day. They no longer have to rely on mental Rolodexes, (paper files and perfect memories). AMS teams have information at their fingertips and can quickly search the online data needed to build accurate quotes, enabling them to make agreements and meet commitments with customers. All AMS members are equally equipped to access PRISM's database and find the information that is required to supply quotes to customers.

PRISM allows AMS staff to take advantage of many features of Metro. One such component of the software is the ability to monitor the status of projects. Through status monitoring, an AMS has the means to immediately know when a component is delayed.

Because all work is now web-based, AMS team members can work at remote locations including the customers' offices, suppliers' offices and at home. Thus PRISM has allowed Graphics Management to create a collaborative commerce application that: (a) improves the efficiency of getting bids from suppliers, (b) creates quotes for customers, and (c) enables interaction among AMS geographically distributed team members.

The Supplier as a User

The ease of using the online template empowers suppliers to proactively bid for Graphics Management jobs. One instrumental feature Metro provides is the ability for suppliers to view a 3D image of structural components. Since suppliers have Internet access of the image, they are able to provide a more accurate quote and submit their bid more quickly.

Another feature of Metro is the ability to perform live calculations. While suppliers are entering the bids online, PRISM will check their quotes against the form for accuracy. This results in greater accuracy in the bid to Graphics Management, and subsequently Graphic Management's quotes to customers are more accurate.

With each bid a supplier submits, the AMS team lets the supplier know if they won or lost the bid. The suppliers that were not selected are given feedback about why they were not chosen. The feedback helps the suppliers adjust future bids to try to win business from R.R. Donnelley. The feedback loop has resulted in bids that are more accurate for R.R. Donnelley. While at the same time, suppliers have recognized additional benefits. Suppliers are already reporting that they too are experiencing noticeable productivity gains within their organizations and improved accuracy of initial quotes as well. The intention of R.R. Donnelley is to have PRISM enable a 15 to 20 percent productivity improvement across the supply chain by reducing administrative tasks.

The Customer as a User

Customers also use the system to keep updated. Customers have the ability to go online and see where their product is in the production process. PRISM also allows customers check inventory. As the suppliers post inventory to Graphics Management, Graphics Management verifies and consolidates the information and posts it to the customer.

Process Steps for All Three Users

PRISM has changed the way in which projects are managed at Graphics Management. Below is an outline of the process steps that are now taken to complete a client project:

1. Project Orientation: An AMS enters a project into PRISM. At this point there is an option to search for past project information. Throughout the entire life of a project an AMS only has to enter data once. When a user chooses to generate a form, the data is automatically inserted into the form—saving the user time.

2. Bill of Material: Next, the AMS conducts work according to a Bill of Material—an internal work-order form that includes specifications for each component of a project. Previously, a Bill of Material was paper-based, and kept by the AMS working on a particular project. It was difficult for the AMS to keep track of the specs of each component. In addition, it was time consuming to look through historical Bills of Material to help provide a quote. Now, a Bill of Material is electronic. If an AMS wants to work on a component such as a hardcover book project, the component and supporting data can be easily accessed online.

Accessing a Bill of Material online allows the AMS team to be proactive in production planning. If a supplier has to modify a commitment, the negotiation seamlessly takes place online with the AMS team. Eliminating uncertainty and resetting expectations and commitments is a key benefit of the Metro system.

3. Supplier RFQ: In PRISM, the AMS now searches online for the appropriate suppliers for each project. The AMS accesses an online supplier list and searches for suppliers that specialize in the area required, such as fast turnaround capability when printing large quantities of a 200 page hardback book. When the AMS selects a supplier, ActionWorks Metro automatically sends that supplier an RFQ (request for quote.) The supplier receives an email notification of the RFQ from the system that includes a link to the secure PRISM website. Providing their password, the supplier is then able to access the RFQ. As the supplier enters a bid, a live calculation of the quote appears that enables quick and accurate completion of the form.

4. Bid Grid: PRISM also allows the AMS to view a user-friendly presentation of the bids. When an AMS selects a project component an on-screen Bid Grid for that particular component pops up. With this view, the AMS can quickly choose the supplier that provides the best quote.

5. View/Generate Quote: Selecting a quote on the bid grid allows the AMS to view all of the relevant information for that quote. When a quote is selected, the AMS can add information to it, such as additional supplier data (e.g. percentage amount), and generate the approval quote.

6. Receive Approval: Next the AMS must get approval for the selected quote from the sales manager and enter that approval into PRISM.

7. Send Quote to Customer: Once the approval is entered in PRISM, the system automatically generates a quote document that is sent to the customer via the Graphics Management Sales Representative. The document is stored in PRISM's relational database.

8. Customer Approval: When the AMS receives customer approval of the quote and enters that approval information into PRISM, the system then automatically interfaces with the R.R. Donnelley financial system to create purchase orders to suppliers.

9. Generate Work Order: PRISM automatically generates a work order and notifies suppliers if their bids were accepted or rejected. This feedback step utilizes Metro's closed-loop Business Interaction Model. As the supplier reports completion of a component, the AMS uses Metro's closed-loop model to accept or reject completed work based on the agreements the two parties negotiated within Metro.

10. Status: Throughout the assembly and fulfillment process the suppliers send status reports to PRISM. Customers and Graphics Management' s employees can check online to see where a particular project component is in the fulfillment process. Customers use this capability to track inventory, receiving and shipping information, and production status. Graphics Management has found that making key information available to customers, in a timely manner, has improved project and inventory management and also customer satisfaction. This, in turn, has also resulted in increased customer trust.

11. Final Delivery: Product is delivered to customer.

12. Integrate with R.R. Donnelley Financial System: The AMS staff creates a daily transfer file for uploading to R.R. Donnelley's financial system.

13. Supplier Quality Review Form: Upon project completion, the AMS team reviews the suppliers' performance and posts scores in PRISM. Internal staff and suppliers can access the information. The scoring of suppliers includes the timely delivery of product, quality of work and competitive pricing. This helps build a knowledge database regarding suppliers' capabilities. AMS members can assess the capabilities of each supplier and capture that data for future projects. The suppliers also have access to their scoring information. Suppliers value this data; it helps them win future bids and improves their business relationship with R.R. Donnelley.
Having access to this data about each supplier, gives R.R. Donnelley a powerful strategic advantage when negotiating future bids with suppliers. For instance, an AMS can quickly pull up the price of a past project and compare the price with a future bid.

14. Customer Feedback: Over time, using PRISM will also help customers forecast costs and response times. Tracking a number of projects for each customer and gathering information about those projects will provide historical trend data to the clients. Analysis of this information will enable the client companies to better forecast time and costs for various project types. Metro's audit trail of all interactions makes this possible.

Interactions Utilizing PRISM

PRISM has widened the communication pipeline between R.R. Donnelley's internal staff and both sides of the supply chain. The diagram following displays examples of interactions utilizing PRISM.

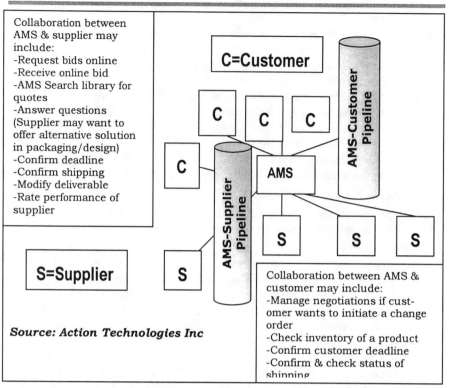

Collaboration between AMS & supplier may include:
-Request bids online
-Receive online bid
-AMS Search library for quotes
-Answer questions (Supplier may want to offer alternative solution in packaging/design)
-Confirm deadline
-Confirm shipping
-Modify deliverable
-Rate performance of supplier

C=Customer

S=Supplier

Source: Action Technologies Inc

Collaboration between AMS & customer may include:
-Manage negotiations if customer wants to initiate a change order
-Check inventory of a product
-Confirm customer deadline
-Confirm & check status of shipping

BIGGEST HURDLES OVERCOME

R. R. Donnelley's Graphics Management division wanted to move its business processes from the desktop to the World Wide Web, and connect its AMS teams with its supply chain and its customers.

Before PRISM, it was a challenge for the AMS staff to communicate with its suppliers. The AMS staff had to rely on suppliers returning their phone voicemails, memos and faxes. There was inefficient collaboration between suppliers and Graphics Management. Without supplier communication, the AMS teams had to manually verify where projects were in the production cycle. PRISM brings Graphics Management's suppliers into direct online collaboration with the project management process.

PRISM tracks and provides project status checking in real-time, via the web. AMS staff can reach suppliers, regardless of the time of day or the location of the supplier. This has proved to be a significant benefit; now the AMS teams have the ability to track the status of their projects anytime, anywhere. Graphics Management overcame the challenge of getting non-technical users proficiently using PRISM by making certain the Intranet pages were user-friendly and consistent with one another. Metro provided tools to help achieve success with this challenge. The software easily lets the developer to create user-friendly pages. For example, in Metro, a developer can choose a button or an icon and create titles on pages to help guide users.

Scott Leonard, Senior Web Developer, led the web development team in building PRISM. All applications that his team develops for the web are customized. Scott noted, "It would have been a challenge for my team to integrate legacy, new, and custom systems. Because Metro contains all of the necessary web-based business process front-ends, the software integration was straightforward and saved us time."

NEW SYSTEM CONFIGURATION

To build a fully functional application, the development team constructed PRISM with a 3-tier architecture—User Interface, Business Logic, and Data. The team developed each tier in parallel. Milestones were created for interim integration and testing. The milestones methodology allowed Graphics Management to closely monitor the implementation for each stage. PRISM works with standard Microsoft technology. All users must be connected to the web to use PRISM. Users can use Netscape 4.5 or greater or Internet Explorer 4.01 or greater.

The developers used the following system configuration:

- ActionWorks Metro Process Builder to build the application, Process Builder Developer Edition is the development and mapping tool used to define business processes
- Microsoft Visual Studios
- Microsoft SQL Server for the relational database that recorded information
- Microsoft NT 4
- Microsoft IIS4
- Internet Information Server
- Microsoft Transaction Server
- Microsoft SourceSafe
- Microsoft Visual Basic
- Visual InterDev
- Open messaging to deliver complete solutions

COST SAVINGS, INCREASED REVENUES, AND PRODUCTIVITY IMPROVEMENTS

The business objectives of R.R. Donnelley for the PRISM project were to create durable e-business relationships with both customers and suppliers and to improve productivity to help build profitable business growth. Originally, the team estimated PRISM would enable a 12 percent gain in productivity. Since April 2000, post-project completion review proved that the productivity gain was in the 14 to 16 percent range—well surpassing Graphics Management's original estimates. R.R. Donnelley has experienced lower transaction costs and has benefited from a reduction in errors, and rework costs. The increase in productivity will enable R.R. Donnelley to significantly grow its business. Graphics Management can now manage much larger projects (in the million-dollar range) and AMS team members can accept a larger number of complex projects per year. Prior to PRISM, AMS members could handle approximately 6 to 10 complex components; now, AMS members work in teams and can work with more than 24 different components, and manage more projects at once. Achieving much greater leverage of their AMS staff lays the foundation for Graphics Management to grow.

COMPETITIVE ADVANTAGES GAINED

PRISM has elevated R. R. Donnelley's Graphics Management division into a leadership position with its customers and suppliers.

Mel Hennrich, Graphics Management's Process Manager, noted, "PRISM is Graphics Management's link to customers as the provider of print procurement and project management services. The application has built barriers to customers exiting and publishers feel connected to the production process. PRISM has strengthened communication with customers, improved productivity through standardizations which is helping to build increased customer loyalty."

Graphics Management now has more control over the supply chain management process. AMS teams access a supplier's cost and work history and are able to choose a supplier based on past performance. The speed of the Internet for checking the status of projects in real-time allow AMS teams to quickly solve unexpected problems. PRISM has streamlined the management process, and the application has helped Graphics Management get closer to the ideal of zero inventory. By working with customers and suppliers to reduce inventory, Graphics Management now has increased control over both internal and external business processes.

IMMEDIATE AND LONG-TERM PLANS TO SUSTAIN COMPTETITIVE ADVANTAGE

PRISM has heightened the awareness of Graphics Management within the company's target market. Other business units of R.R. Donnelley are making inquires about how the PRISM business model could help streamline their e-business processes. Discussions are already under way about the implementation. This in turn might help control and share capacity and capability between plants thus strengthening scheduling and equipment utilization rates.

David Oberst states, "PRISM has allowed R.R. Donnelley to gain a significant competitive edge over competitors in the areas of managing complex multi-component projects. PRISM has allowed Graphics Management to integrate its Supply Chain Management, Customer Inventories, Structural Design and ISO-based Project Management/Quality systems. PRISM improved customer demand and will help R.R. Donnelley build a framework for the future."

R.R. Donnelley has experienced such a high degree of success with ActionWorks Metro that it plans to expand PRISM's application. The company's strategy would allow the publishers even more direct access to PRISM, thus hoping to build even stronger corporate relationships and even higher barriers to overcome.

Taylor Nelson Sofres, France

Nathalie Génieux, W4, France

EXECUTIVE SUMMARY

Taylor Nelson Sofres is the French market leader for ad hoc research, market surveys, polls and consultancy. The company provides a full range of qualitative and quantitative services across the spectrum of consumer, social and industrial research spanning all business sectors. It is well known for pioneering opinion polls in France in the 60s and has been a major player in this activity ever since.

Taylor Nelson Sofres' strategy is to develop more and more its survey activities in order to face stronger competition in its own territory. In that context, it is expected that the competition will evolve not only on the field of services and geographical coverage, but also on the productivity and quality of services offered. Taylor Nelson Sofres voluntarily chose to resist the competitive pressures by increasing the quality of its services and improving the treatment of survey production.

Survey processing requires tight cooperation between various departments and involves a great number of users to work better together, and compiles a great amount of information. Additionally, the survey production processing represents an important part of the workload for Taylor Nelson Sofres. It represents 80 percent of its turnover. These requirements lead the technology choice to a workflow based solution as to enhance the quality of services in spite of a specialized distributed work organization.

Therefore, they recently led a complete reform of their work methods. Having invested in the renewal of their production tools (CATI and CAPI), Taylor Nelson Sofres had in view the processes automation and optimization of their survey production.

The project aimed to use the Intranet of Taylor Nelson Sofres created in July 1999 but left on the back burner since. In fact, Taylor Nelson Sofres had an information system made of a certain number of isolated management applications. These applications didn't form any consistent information system. In-house, Taylor Nelson Sofres had no computer network. It clearly appeared that the workflow application would be the keystone of the new network increasingly directing collaborative work applications.

After a preliminary analysis of workflow technical capabilities, including a first round consultation of potential vendors, the head office finally decided to concentrate their efforts on a workflow project dedicated to the process of manufacturing quantitative surveys on Intranet.

A workflow system was chosen to be the pillar of this new information system, as a frame of reference for the procedures of surveys production, as well as a frame of reference for the data and documents related to a survey and a linking factor between the applications of surveys production.

Taylor Nelson Sofres nominated a driving committee consisting of 10 persons, survey managers and members of each Production management unit. The prototyping phase was conducted directly with users. This collaborative design phase, supported by prototyping of the application accessible on the Intranet, was essential to the whole project success. Members' participation was active and intensive.

The workflow application was prototyped, developed and deployed in nine months time. Today, the workflow is deployed with over 300 participants in 15 departments, making daily use of this application.

The workflow application is the first production application implemented on the resources of the Intranet. In a single year, the workflow application implemented three hundred users and upheld its promises. Workflow was identified as a way to enhance productivity and quality of services, and a project started on a process mastering the critical core process of the Sofres' survey production. The selected workflow tool, making a graphic design operational, has enabled to describe and enhance the business complexity and functional richness of Taylor Nelson Sofres.

In fact, this application has demonstrated the high complexity of the Sofres' core business. It contains one main procedure and three sub-procedures, more than 200 steps, and over 1 000 variables for each work case. This complexity is inherent to Taylor Nelson Sofres' core business itself and not to the workflow.

Migration of users to the new Intranet/Workflow environment and acceptability of the workflow paradigm was higher than expected. The users appreciated both the power delivered and the interface flexibility that has allowed the users extremely ease of use of the application. They have really mastered the application and decided at the same time to make the workflow available through an enterprise portal to place a test application on line for training themselves on the workflow process.

Workflow suppresses physical transfer between all services, reduces capture operations, develops the Information System as a cross application and increases communication between the different enterprise applications. Thus, it allowed Taylor Nelson Sofres to provide productivity gains, and the expected increase in quality of service was achieved. Information circulates seamlessly, workgroups gained in efficiency, and time to market has been dramatically reduced.

With a good acceptability of the technology by Taylor Nelson Sofres employees, the project has demonstrated La Sofres' capability with the selected technology to develop rapidly and economically deploy the workflow application as to empower processes over a large number of participants. By combining in-depth market knowledge with the latest research techniques and sophisticated use of state-of-the-art-technology in Workflow, Taylor Nelson Sofres provides its clients with immediate and informed market analysis and innovative business solutions.

Thanks to the workflow technology, Taylor Nelson Sofres was able to drive the project in the best possible conditions. The workflow application has become the core structure and an essential pillar of the corporate information system.

OVERVIEW

Taylor Nelson Sofres had an information system comprising a certain number of isolated management applications. These applications didn't form any consistent information system. In-house, Taylor Nelson Sofres had no computer network.

The Information System Unit in charge of the project, under the control of Arnold Haine, the Production Information Systems Manager, realized that workflow was the solution. "It clearly seems that the workflow application is going to be the keystone of the new network increasingly directing collaborative work applications. The Workflow processing was identified as a major potential source of progress for both productivity and quality of services."

The need is to have a workflow that could progressively merge with the Taylor Nelson Sofres global groupware Intranet architecture.

Taylor Nelson Sofres required a workflow system:

1. To be the pillar of the information system and the cement between isolated management applications,
2. To improve the collaboration and consistency between the various department of the specialized distributed work organization,
3. To reduce enormous volume of paper,
4. To remain independent from the e-mail system,
5. To enhance the quality of the services offered.

Such a critical project, impacting its very core business, is of extreme importance at Taylor Nelson Sofres. No mistakes are allowed.

The workflow application was prototyped, developed and deployed over a period of nine months. In September 2000, the application was developed according to the spiral methodology, in close collaboration with the employees involved, and deployed step by step within the company.

This application is very complex, it contains one main procedure and three sub-procedures, more than 200 steps, and over 1,000 variables for each work case.

This complexity is inherent to the Taylor Nelson Sofres' core business itself and not to the workflow. Only a workflow tool, making a graphic design operational, enables users to describe and master the business complexity and functional richness.

In fact, the key characteristics of the workflow project were based upon:

1. A project management including active users participation,
2. As simple as possible user interfaces tailored to users' working conditions,
3. Maximize users' efficiency, and
4. Keep it as simple as possible in order to train users in a short time.

Those characteristics were essential in the acceptability of the solution by users, as well as the productivity and quality gains observed.

Today, 300 people make daily use of this application, and would not consider going back to the old methods. Two and a half hours training was given to users, who were then able to use all the basics and thus master the application.

The combined effects of tangible productivity gains and quality efficiency together with low development and deployment costs resulted in a positive return on investment and a dramatic reduction on time to market.

The project has demonstrated La Sofres' capability to develop and deploy workflow-enabled processes rapidly and economically for a large number of participants. The acceptability of the technology by Taylor Nelson Sofres employees was demonstrated successfully. This will form a solid foundation for further extensions of workflow applications.

KEY MOTIVATIONS

Five crucial objectives motivated Taylor Nelson Sofres ' choice in implementing the workflow:

5. Qualitative objectives
6. A strong need for collaboration and consistency
7. Organize and optimize the treatment of the information associated to a survey
8. Remain independent from the e-mail system
9. Become the pillar of the information system

Qualitative objectives

Methodology: Taylor Nelson Sofres reappraised its whole organization. With a volume of more than 1,000 surveys produced a year, representing roughly one million questionnaires, the main object of this "reform" was above all qualitative, reliability and normalization of the processes.

Acceptability of the Technology: 300 employees daily use this application, more than two hundreds tasks were modeled. Head Office considered this project as strategic for the company. All these reasons lead the project leader to focus on the acceptability of this new technology. A first assessment shows that Taylor Nelson Sofres employees get a better control and follow-up of their business processes. New employees' training is made faster and easier.

Communication and Control: Taylor Nelson Sofres has optimized the collaboration among users scattered geographically and control on information, with an accurate records follow-up. The workflow application has allowed a better communication between all actors involved in the survey production. The workflow system dispatches the tasks at the right time to the right persons, and guides the user all through the process. Information circulates in a seamless way and workgroup has gained in efficiency.

Company archives: This new workflow application is a key for the company's overall memory. All the current or past surveys are stored in a central database and can be quickly accessed by every employee concerned.

A need for collaboration and consistency

Need intranet to collaborate: In order to address the problems related to the number and geographical repartition of the different units and market researchers (60 specialists in 15 centers), Taylor Nelson Sofres deployed a quality control and groupware infrastructure through Intranet.

Need Workflow to cooperate: With the Taylor Nelson Sofres organization, survey activities are operated in various specialized centers. The process requires close cooperation between the Production department and the various market researchers, dispatched in teams of over 60 specialists in 15 centers. This was a strong motivation to launch a workflow project, with the goal to enhance the quality of services despite a distributed work organization.

The Product management unit, which previously had a strong "black box" image, wanted to be more transparent for all, and especially for the survey managers. All the participants should be able to follow any survey process in real time.

Need Workflow to control: After implementing a set of quality processes and deploying the Intranet infrastructure and the groupware tools, they needed a workflow solution allowing their employees to control the consistency of a highly critical, complex process driving their core business: survey production. The workflow covers the whole production processing of the quantitative surveys, from the negotiation of the contract to the distribution of results.

Need Workflow to organize: The number of surveys to be treated is over 1000 a year with 300 persons involved. The process includes hundreds of activities. It is mandatory that the workflow be centered on the market researcher's needs and the Launch cell of the Production Department. These two "actors" should be able to know at any time the status of any survey, notably during the field inquiries. An electronic document should be attached to the flow. Also, the notification of a document should be assured. The modifications, for instance: changes, additions, withdrawal, etc., should be in an easily identifiable form.

Organize and optimize the treatment of the information associated with a survey

Reduce the volume of paper: The primary target of the system is to reduce the enormous volume of paper, which accompanies every stage of the survey production. This reduction is obligatory to have an indispensable flexibility in the evolution of each process (dynamic modifications).

Optimize access to the information: By suppressing physical transfer between all services, reducing capture operations, developing the Information System as a cross application, increasing communication between the different Enterprise applications, the workflow has allowed Taylor Nelson Sofres to obtain productivity gains with an expected increase in quality of service.

Remain independent from the e-mail system

At the architecture level, the software is installed on a dedicated NT Server and has its own database (Oracle) with its own users' directory. The application must not communicate with the e-mail system. This independence is rather a good thing for questions of solidity and availability. The workflow engine has to execute the modeled processes in the database (task implementation in real time to the right performers).

All these goals were achieved with this application, which also brought several unexpected benefits: a better mutual understanding between the participants, the establishment of a common thesaurus between several market research managers, the general management of the information system (particularly the management of the researchers) concerning the workflow, and a very strong impact on the working habits.

The workflow application as the pillar of the information system

Building up an information system: In 1997, like many other French mid-size companies, Taylor Nelson Sofres had an information system made of a certain number of isolated management applications. These applications didn't form any consistent information system. In-house, Taylor Nelson Sofres had no computer network. In order to communicate, a postal shuttle was used to transport documents and floppy disks to the various participants of a market survey. Each person who intervened in a market survey, and particularly the market research manager, who is commercially in charge of the surveys, had only a fragmented view of the surveys, their production and their progress.

Consequently, the managers created a real information system about the company's core business; the production of market surveys. The aim was to enable the market research managers to follow a survey entirely, from its beginning to the result delivery.

The information system objectives: The workers who intervened in a survey's production knew their jobs, but had no knowledge of the actions performed before and after their intervention, and there were no descriptions to make all the survey production process consistent.

- The workflow's first goal was to update all the procedures.
- The second expected goal was to suppress reentering data; workflow being the link between the existing applications.
- The third expected goal was the entire tracking of the surveys, while they were being produced and once they were achieved, providing a progress follow-up as well as a knowledge base.

The Workflow as the pillar of the information system: The features of the existing information system associated to the objectives of the new system leads the managers to choose the W4 workflow system as the pillar of this new information system. The workflow is the frame of reference for the procedures of survey production, as well as the frame of reference for the data and documents related to a survey and is the linking factor between the applications of surveys production.

THE WORKFLOW PROCESS OVERVIEW

Requirements

Essential needs that the application should satisfy:

- The modelling costs must be reduced, and, above all, the adaptation costs must be reduced, since this is SOFRES' core business. The application must be easy to modify in order to reflect the process changes,
- Major importance given to process monitoring and deadline monitoring,
- Keep the main organizational work in place unchanged, except for obvious adjustments,
- Enforce regulatory aspects of the process but without attempting to redesign them; and
- Give priority in the application design to ease of use and ease of learning.

The training and appropriation costs must be reduced, mostly because of this business' high turnover.

Human organization

With more than 500 permanent employees and 300 market researchers dispatched over several specialized expertise centers (corporate, semiometrie, Sofres inter@ctive, IT/telecoms, Internet, consumer, politics, Healthcare, Retails, surveys, medi@, automotive, marketing services, financial communication etc.), Taylor Nelson Sofres produces surveys covering the country business activity.

Each center deals in a specific activity. The overall consistency is ensured by cross management units focusing on the critical phases of collecting and processing information. The Information system management unit provides the technological infrastructure, and the Production Unit, driving Sofres core business, supplies the tools needed by the survey departments to drive the many missions and their follow-up.

These several units, (dispatched geographically) grouping over 300 market researchers, are in charge of the survey production. Their missions cover four main activities:

1. Initializing the process by transmitting a demand to the Launch Cell.

2. Definition of the target to be interrogated, the quota to be respected, the methodology to be followed.

3. Transmission of the orders for capture (total capture if paper—partial if CAPI-CATI).

4. Validation of data and coherence with the expected results and transmission to the final client.

A complex workflow process

The workflow is centered on the market researcher's needs and the Launch cell of the Production Department. These two "actors" should be able to know at any time the status of any survey, notably during the work field.

- The workflow is initiated after the customer's agreement when the market research manager forwards a launch request to the production managers and the arrival point is the delivery of the survey's results to the manager.
- The Launch cell of the Production Department validates the launch request and coordinates the numerous manufacturing processes (sampling, reprography, sending, collection, work field, telephone or face-to-face, entering data, handling, computer operating, CD-ROMs digitization).
- The sampling department prepares the survey's samples and, if needed, prepares the sample bases.
- The Reprography Department manages the creation and/or the duplication of all the necessary documents.
- The Sending Department sends the paper supports and the CD-ROMs to the researchers.

- The CD-ROMs Digitization cell converts multimedia supports and duplicates CD-ROMs, which are then sent by the Sending Department.
- The Collection cell programs the questionnaire for the surveys made with CAPI (face-to-face) or with CATI (by phone). Once programmed, the questionnaire is tested by the market research manager. Within the framework of a CATI survey, the Collection cell gives the survey to the field.
- The Computer Operating Department provides the CAPI surveys and ensures that the data collected by the researchers are communicated.
- The telephone (CATI) or face-to-face (CAPI or pencil) fields ensure that information is collected by the researchers' network. The fields inform the managers and the Launch cell of how the survey progresses.
- The Data Entering workshop enters the open-ended questions resulting from the CATI/CAPI surveys and the paper questionnaires resulting from the fields.
- The Data Processing Department goes through the collected data and analyzes them, and gives the results to the market research manager.

Each manufacturing cell as well as its production process is taken into account in the workflow, so that every actor can clearly know the state of each survey, whether the survey is still planned, running, stopped or achieved.

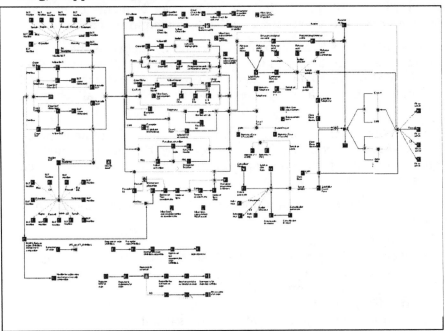

Figure 1: One of the application processes

The very complex application demonstrates the main features required for La Sofres' events processing. The process definition includes one main procedure and three sub-procedures, more than 200 steps, and over 1,000 variables for each work case.

This complexity is inherent to the Taylor Nelson Sofres' core business itself and not to the workflow.

It incorporates comprehensive business rules evaluating activity participant decisions and critical activities.

A survey includes numerous parameters that have to be finalized and validated by several people. The process must also manage the various changes, which can occur before launching or even during the survey. The possible changes can influence the rhythm, and therefore the budget allocated to the survey.

This involves processes that must follow very precisely the defined procedures and internal regulations. With traditional paper-based technologies, this involved relatively long processing delays, due to the numerous transmissions between actors in the processes.

This was a source of dissatisfaction. It was not always easy to respond to these claims, due to the lack of adequate tools to follow up each case in its various stages. These processes were obvious candidates for electronic assistance through workflow technology.

To illustrate this complexity, we shall briefly describe the role of the Launch Cell and the Sampling. The field handling, the collection of data and the result processing are some other elements of this application's complexity, but shall not be described in this document.

There is permanently an information exchange between the market researcher and the Launch manager. For each modification, the request is redistributed to various receivers. The modifications and their dates are indicated in the headers. Records of all changes must be kept.

All the information is strengthened in a main document called Launch request. Exhibits, usually added by the market research manager (e.g.: a table containing a quota definition, ...) are attached to this document.

There may be several types of modifications concerning the Launch request:

- Planning modification
- Modification of the collection type (paper vs. CAPI)
- Modification of the sending type
- Briefing (added or suppressed)
- Intermediate Return
- Modification of the quantity of interviews (goal)
- Target modification
- Quotas modification
- Modified or additional Information for the Sampling (file)

10. Quotation (drawn up afterwards or modified).

The team in charge of the Sampling receives the launch request. It does not intervene at this time on the application, but it must nevertheless indicate any change related to its activity field (e.g: quotas definition, files). These are basic elements, since they enable to check the consistency between the market research manager's request and the quotation (or a former study, which serves as a reference).

Example concerning the Sampling, which may be changed:
- Sphere of survey
- Interviewed person
- Inquiry method
- Variables and practical details
- Use of inquiry bases and various problems linked to their use
- Realization dates (sending date for the face-to-face survey and field date for the telephone survey).

When it is necessary to purchase survey bases in order to perform the surveys, one ought to check that these costs are included in the quotation. If available, the person responsible for the quotation, or else, the Launch team, is asked to carry out this verification. If need be, the market research manager is informed of the price differential and his agreement is requested.

In the case of complex face-to-face surveys, the method can even be corrected on the Samplings, Field or the Launch teams' initiative.

The Sampling team established the following information:
- The survey's realization goals are sent to the survey's research manager, to the Field team (telephone or face-to-face, according to the method of survey), and to the Collection team
- Geographic matrix objectives
- The quota list is sent to the Launch team, to the research manager, and to the face-to-face Field team
- Exhibits are sent to the Field team
- The survey bases are sent to the Collection team
- The record drawing(s) are sent to the Collection team
- The adjustment goals are sent to the research manager.

Binary management Interface

The intranet interface of the workflow project consists, in broad outline, in two accessible boxes via a unique login identification (one of the requirements in order to slow down the codes access to the applications). A first box manages all the tasks to be executed for an interlocutor into the survey production process, whereas the second box contains the thesaurus of all works in which it is possible to find the complete electronic file of the survey (together with collected data and forms). There is no indexation process strictly speaking; research can be made through the number of the file or the customer's name at any time.

User Interface

The application interface was designed and refined together with the user, with the following goals:

- Keep it as simple as possible,
- Tailor it to users working conditions,
- Maximize users' efficiency, and
- Automate controls as far as possible.

The resulting implementation combines in a single application features that more complex workflow applications do not always provide together like:

- Mix of query-based and work list-based interface to deal with frequent unexpected events that modify the expected flow for a study.
- A work list handler interface tuned to users roles for usability,
- Next activity automatic delivery for efficiency,
- Selective activity and collections of activities execution for efficient "batching" of actions,
- Many tailored controls on fields values data entry in forms for quality of data,
- A query-based follow-up interface accessible to users for self control, and
- A non-intrusive notification based on the use of colors.

These characteristics were essential for acceptability by users, as well as the productivity gains observed. We present them shortly in the following section as an example of the level of adaptation to users requirement that Taylor Nelson Sofres was able to provide with the selected Internet based workflow engine.

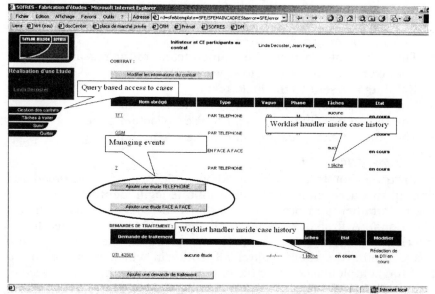

Figure 2. Mix of query-based and work list-based interface to deal with frequent unexpected events

Unexpected process modifications must often be performed during the surveys. This is an interface's native functionality, and most actions meant to modify a survey's progress are triggered from the record windows.

These actions trigger sub-processes, independent branches or exceptions of the main process. This is a simple and ergonomic implementation of a "factual" workflow, which is completely under the users' control, as opposed to a "procedural" workflow, which requires an operative mode for each work list.

Work list handler interface tuned to users roles

The user interface was designed to be as simple as possible through tailoring to each user's working environment and roles played. It separates the browser window into a left and a right pane.

On the left pane are presented:

- The connected user's identification and unit, and
- A menu of options representing process creation command, process follow-up command or work lists display commands.

On the right pane are presented:

- A tabulated and sorted list of activities, or
- The form representing an activity interface, or
- The result of a search command.
- The next figure shows an example of the work list.

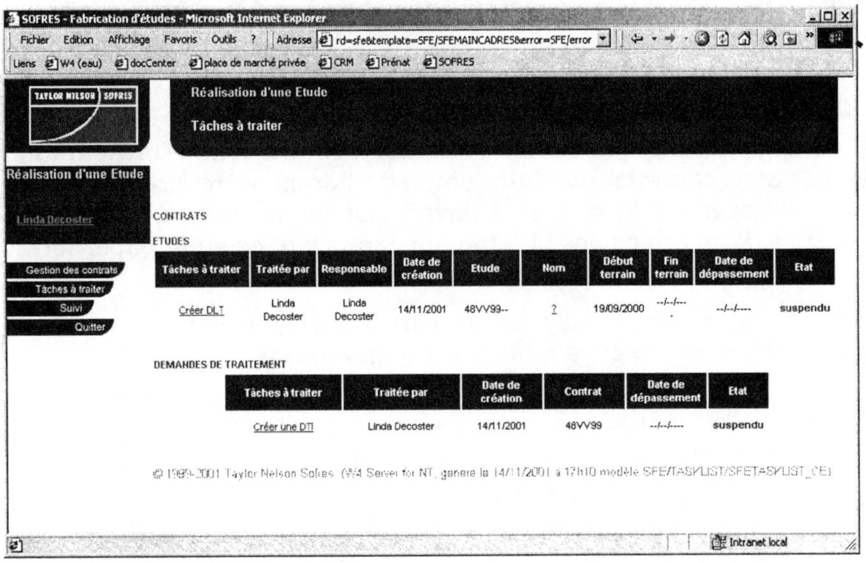

Figure 3: example of work list handler for the market researcher

Dealing with complex forms, capability to suspend activities

A survey's full description contains hundreds of pieces of information. Each form can be filled-in in any order. You can suspend this operation at any time, and save without publishing the information you entered.

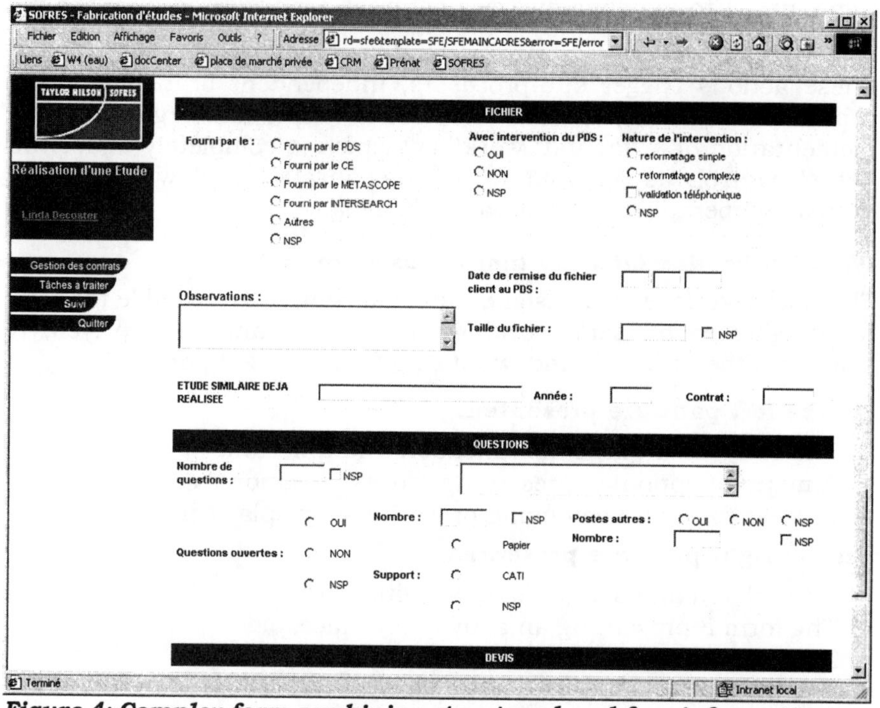

Figure 4: Complex form combining structured and free information mode

Electronic forms, and printed output

Special attention was given to forms definition and presentation with strict controls on data entered. Forms were created using Dreamweaver for layout, and JavaScript for fields and forms level controls. Whenever possible, the appearance of existing paper forms was kept in order to minimize adaptation time.

Generating automatically all a survey's representative states in Word allows you to get a quality print on request.

PROJECT MANAGEMENT

The project management represented 3 steps:

- Establishing the Specifications
- Prototyping
- Realization

Specifications

From the beginning, this project was seen as a very important one (Sofres' biggest computer investment during the last few years) and a very structuring one.

A full specifications document was created, assisted by Martin Ader, of W&GS, a worldwide domain expert (www.wngs.com)

Martin Ader's assistance was to define the processes, express the needs, establish the specifications and choose the tools, and to increase the senior management's awareness.

Prototyping: User-Centric Project Management

The W4 product was chosen at the beginning of the prototyping phase, which was conducted with a total cooperation with a piloting comity made up of 10 persons (research managers and production representatives).

The iterative method recommended by W4, which enables to iterate successive prototypes, was implemented, and allowed to focus the needs expressed by the piloting comity, as well as the developments, towards the W4 tool.

The prototyping phase was conducted directly with users. An HTML-based interface was tuned to users' work context and user training was based essentially on the process characteristics rather than the technology itself.

The prototype goal was to validate a more general approach to work-flow-enabling processing on a significant basis. It was conducted in that spirit under severe constraints and has concluded positively both in terms of provided benefits and in terms of quality increase.

Besides verifying the above capacities, the prototype had to answer to some critical concerns before any further generalization towards exceptional events management:

- Ease of people migration from a traditional paper-based and host transaction-based working environment to an Intranet-based workflow application,
- Acceptability by Taylor Nelson Sofres employees of a workflow paradigm,
- Positive impact on quality of service and productivity; and
- Taylor Nelson Sofres' capability to master the assembled technologies with a reasonable cost of operation, deployment, and administration.
- Within two months, the process and the interfaces had been validated and developed, and the users had appropriated the application, mostly because they were totally involved as a proposition force.

The prototype was validated at the end of December 1999, and Taylor Nelson Sofres General Manager agreed to start the development process, completed in April 2000.

Realization and deployment

The workflow application was prototyped in two months time, from September 1999 to December 2000, and developed and qualified in three additional months, from March 2000 to May 2000. It has then been deployed within 6 weeks to 400 participants.

Since September 2000, 1200 surveys have been handled through the workflow solution, which is now the backbone of SOFRES' information system.

The prototyping phase involved a group of 10 representatives of the users, coming from the surveys and the production management units. For a few weeks, meetings were devoted to the analysis of the process, supported by possible on-screen examples.

Between meetings, the prototype was updated and installed on Taylor Nelson Sofres ' Intranet. This gave each participant the potential to experiment the proposed application, thus increasing its evaluation and evolution.

This collaborative design phase, supported by prototyping of the application accessible on the Intranet, has been essential to the whole project success. Members' participation was active and intensive.

They appreciated both the power delivered and the interface flexibility. The workflow is available through an enterprise portal. They log in and find all the relevant information for their activity. Using this personalized portal, they have a direct access to their own entry point, customized according to their profile. Through highly customized menus, they are able to find all relevant information in a FAQ database, a glossary, flash demonstrations, etc., all items related to their own business. Additionally, on the enterprise portal dedicated to the workflow, a test application is on line where users can train themselves on the workflow process.

OVERALL BUSINESS INNOVATION

The main innovations concern:

- The managed process' complexity, and
- The use of a workflow solution as the backbone of an information system.

The Process Complexity

More than 200 steps, more than 1,000 variables, a huge need for flexibility since it is possible to re-define at any time the survey's contents and progress, and a very high human added value that must be preserved: this application is probably one of the most complex ever developed by a workflow product.

W4 not only proved its ability to support such a complex process, it also allowed Sofres organizational employees to master it and make it evolve.

Using the workflow as the backbone of an information system

Sofres' ambition was to build a consistent information system on all the existing management and production applications.

Using a workflow solution to federate applications, to help integrate applications, and to urbanize the information system, was a very innovating approach. This goal was more than achieved, since the workflow product also gives a structuring dimension, and modifies the working habits.

BUSINESS BENEFITS

This image, used to welcome users, became the symbol of workflow for Sofres. It sums up all the benefits workflow brought to Sofres.

The expected increase of quality of service was achieved. In addition, the workflow application resulted into fewer errors at the operation definition level, and suppression of errors in orientation to the right service for further processing.

By suppressing all physical transfer between services, and reducing operation entry errors and orientation errors, the application provides productivity gains representing an average of four minutes of working time per process. The combined effects of tangible productivity gains, and low development and deployment costs, result in a positive time to market: top quality, tracking, state-of-the-art, users' satisfaction and total acceptance.

Cost savings

Time saved per process come from several sources:

- Savings in document handling (in between paper folders transfer, distributing documents to participants);

- Savings in time required to fill in documents through assisted data entry;
- Reducing codification and orientation errors, and consequently additional activities;
- Easy answer to customer inquiries through process follow-up tools.

COMPETITIVE ADVANTAGES GAINED AND FUTURE PLANS

Workflow-based exception events processing has been clearly identified as one of the potential sources of progresses of both productivity and quality of services, as well as a perfect tool to maintain service efficiency in a geographically distributed organization.

The workflow application has demonstrated the capability to develop and deploy rapidly and economically workflow enabled processes over a large number of participants. The acceptability of the technology by Taylor Nelson Sofres employees was demonstrated successfully.

This will form the basis of further extensions of workflow applications. Resources applied to those strategic projects will then become available to fully exploit the know-how acquired through a successful real size project and deployment of even most complex procedures.

Triumph International, Japan

Dinesh Kumar, TIJ, Japan

1-1. SYSTEM OVERVIEW:

After achieving considerable success with Workflow implementation, culminating in the 2000 Pacific Rim Gold Global Excellence in Workflow Award, Triumph International Japan has continued to develop novel workflows with our ActiveFlow workflow system. This has resulted in a very measurable efficiency improvement. In this paper we review some of the recent developments at Triumph.

Our review includes complete e-commerce integration, from order right through to the print out of shipping documents. A similar system for our mail order catalog sales, orders being accepted via—phone, fax, postcard and even I-mode mobile phones. An integrated Cash Advance and Settlement System that interfaces to an expert fare look-up tool for Travel Expenses. Web Enabled POS integration for our Fashion Boutiques, Software Development Life Cycle (SDLC) to manage both "in-house" and "out-sourced" projects. Lastly we look at the ordering of Japanese name cards—"Meishi" with an interesting card preview.

EXPANDED OVERVIEW:

We are continuing to document our processes using the ActiveModeler process definition tool. Wherever possible we are trying to automate these defined processes using the ActiveFlow web based workflow engine. Considerable benefits have been attained in the following areas:

E-Commerce Integration:

- Integration of orders from our two online shopping sites—www.triumphjapan.com and www.amosstyle.com to the UNIX backend systems.
- Orders arrive as E-mail and this triggers a workflow that is processed by a Checker. The order is automatically raised to the UNIX system given that stock is available and payment type is COD.
- If payment type is Credit then a Card Handler processes the payment using an interface to an online billing company. This step is for our official site because the customer does this online. An order can only be raised if we have confirmation of successful payment.
- We also have a Customer Support function that handles stock not-available situations.

- Shipping documents are automatically printed from a customer information file generated that is generated when an order is successfully raised.

Mail Order Integration:

- Catalogues are placed at our Fashion Boutiques and can also be requested for over the phone or be sending a fax or postcard. More recently by accessing our I-mode shopping site www.amosstyle.com/tsuhan.
- The workflow form has been designed in such a way that orders can be entered while talking to the customer over the phone.
- The stock availability is checked online and credit payments are handled using and interface to an online billing company.
- The order entry job has now been outsourced to a third party and they can access our workflow over the Internet. This has been achieved by utilizing the Microsoft ISA tool.
- I-mode orders are fully integrated and require no manual intervention. The customer is provided with stock status as well as the interface to an online credit billing company.

Cash Advance & Settlement Integration:

- We started off with a travel expense workflow interfacing to an expert fare lookup third-party application and now we have increased its scope to include the settlement of other expenses as well.
- Also a new workflow to apply for a Cash Advance has been added. This has been integrated to the Expense Settlement workflow.
- Now whenever a user starts a Settlement workflow, the system automatically identifies any outstanding Cash Advances for the current user and they can be settled in this manner.

Web enabled POS Integration:

- The POS cash registers in our Fashion boutiques have been web enabled and they can now participate in the Head office workflows.
- Not only workflow but also all circulars regarding shop layout etc. that were sent to these outlets are now available on the intranet in an electronic format.

SDLC—Project Management:

- This workflow allows timely tracking of a system related request right from the point that the request is raised all the way through to the implementation of a project.
- It is now also possible to group all related requests and to deal with them in a way that requires the least amount of development.

"Meishi" Ordering:

- In Japan it is a custom to exchange business cards with all the persons that you meet on a daily basis. Also the periodic rotation of staff members within departments is not uncommon.
- Our "Meishi" ordering workflow has automated not only the approval process but also the sending of e-mail order to the Printing agent. An attached file contains the card information in the format required by the printer.
- In this way it is possible for even the printer to automate his side of the process and this has resulted in next day delivery in most cases.

2. KEY MOTIVATIONS:

The following have been the key motivations behind the development and enhancement of the Integrated Workflow System.

E-Commerce Integration:

- Eliminate printing of order mails.
- Reduce manual processing and data entry.
- Speed up the process to cater to increasing volumes.
- Ensure integration with Head office and Warehouse systems.
- Enable status checking to cater to customer queries.
- Ensure standard business procedures.
- Formalize the business process.

Mail Order Integration:

- Reduce paper work and manual data entry.
- Stream line the process and stock look up.
- Enable the outsourcing of the order handling.
- Access the growing I-mode user market.
- Develop a CRM database.

Cash Advance & Settlement Integration:

- Reduce paper flows and manual processing.
- Merger related paper flows into a single workflow.
- Ensure that Cash Advances are settled.
- Improve the accuracy of data entered into the accounting journals.
- Proper audit trail for the archiving of receipts.

Web enabled POS Integration:

- Enable Fashion Boutique staff to participate in all workflow.
- Reduce paper flows and postage costs of circulars.
- Receive online sales data form the stores.
- Enable the development of a Loyalty scheme.
- Develop an integrated CRM database across the various sales channels.

SDLC—Project Management:

- Reduce paper flows and improve tracking.
- Improve the analysis of the pending system development requests.
- Improve deadline adherence.

"Meishi" Ordering:

- Reduce paper flows and processing time.
- Give a visual preview of the layout of the final card.
- Reduce the lead-time for delivery. (1 week)

3. BUSINESS INNOVATION:

The impact to management as result of continued improvement of existing Workflow's and implementation of new Integrated Workflow's has been as follows.

E-Commerce Integration:

- Increased productivity.
- Reduced human errors.
- More efficient shipment of goods.
- Full integration to Head Office systems as well as warehouse systems.
- Integration to Business Partner for credit payment processing.

Mail Order Integration:

- Improved cost effectiveness through outsourcing of data entry.
- Increased productivity by integrating Telephone, Mail and Fax orders.
- I-mode orders require no manual data entry.
- More efficient shipment of goods.
- Full integration to Head Office systems as well as warehouse systems.
- Integration to Business Partner for credit payment processing.

Cash Advance & Settlement Integration:

- Integration of numerous paper flows into a single workflow.
- Ensuring that advances are settled and only adjusted payments are made.
- Full integration to Accounting systems.
- Correct and precise detailed entry into the Accounting ledgers.
- With reduced paperwork it is now possible to accomplish timely month end closing.

Web enabled POS Integration:

- Online sales analysis rather than previous day.
- Reduced postage and communication costs.
- Workflow participation from the Boutiques.
- Integrated Frequent Shopping Program across sales channels.

SDLC—Project Management:

- Improved tracking of work in progress.
- Unambiguous view of the status and number of requests pending.
- Ability to juggle the priority of the requests from various departments according to company policy.

"Meishi" Ordering:

- Improved efficiency.
- User-friendly graphic interface.
- The request passes through the proper channels before the order is placed.
- Integration to Business Partner systems.

4. TECHNOLOGICAL INNOVATIONS:

Various new technological innovations have been achieved through in-house adaptation and integration of numerous hardware and software products.

Catalog orders can be made using the I-mode Cellular Phones

E-Commerce Integration:

- Using the "virtual client" function of ActiveFlow it is possible to "parse" e-mail and then populate a workflow form with the required data.

- In this way the arrival of e-mail automatically triggers a Workflow.
- If certain conditions are met no human intervention is required right from the receipt of the e-mail to print out of the shipping documents at the warehouse.
- Integrated interface to a Business Partner for credit card handling, minimum data entry is required.

Mail Order Integration:

- A unified order entry interface for all orders.
- Form is designed in such a way to allow entry while speaking to customer on the Telephone.
- Interface to an interactive postcode to address lookup and vise versa.
- Online stock check greatly reduces unsuccessful orders.
- I-mode portal integration to workflow, once again the virtual client function of ActiveFlow is used to trigger the workflow.
- I-mode customers have online access to our systems and only successful orders are processed by workflow. 100 percent shipment rate.

Cash Advance and Settlement Integration:

- Interface to a 3rd party fare lookup system.
- Imported fares are displayed in a different color and do not require double checks.
- Complete integration to the Accounting system enabling automatic bank transfers on final approval.

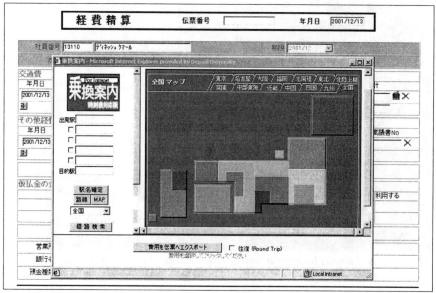

Screen shot showing the Fare look-up Interface.

Web enabled POS Integration:

- Central PLU (price lookup) database.

- Remote workflow access.
- Frequent shopping program that incorporates the Boutique, Web and Mail order customers.
- Credits attained are accumulated centrally and can be redeemed through any channel.

SDLC—Project Management:

- Full integration of the requesting process and the development process.
- Offshore developers have access and can update the status of projects.

"Meishi" Ordering:

- Unique graphic interface that shows a preview of the actual appearance of the card.
- Automatic e-mail with and attachment sent on final approval.
- Attached file format allows integration to Business Partner systems.

5. END USER JOB—NOW AND PRE-INSTALLATION:

The enhancement of existing workflows and the development of new novel workflows have affected the end users jobs to a great extent.

E-Commerce Integration:

- Review details of orders on screen compared to print out of e-mail and manual data entry.
- Online credit card billing compared to manual faxing and waiting for authorization.
- Prompt customer service compared to calling back after manual search.
- More focused on Sales planning rather than Sales handling.

Mail Order Integration:

- All data entry has been out sourced.
- Prompt customer service by using the comprehensive reporting functions of ActiveFlow.
- I-mode order integration has further reduced the time spent of order entry.
- More time dedicated to Sales planning rather than Sales handling.

Cash Advance & Settlement Integration:

- Paperwork has been greatly reduced.
- The process is now faster and it is even possible to track the status of ones application.
- On the accounting side also a lot of paperwork including fare checks and filing has been eliminated.

- Two persons who were dedicated to full time data entry in the accounting department have been diverted to other more productive duties.

Web enabled POS Integration:

- Less paperwork, the user can now participate in workflow—travel expenses, attendance, etc.
- Easily stay up-to-date with the required store layout etc.
- Use e-mail to communicate to the Head Office.

SDLC—Project Management:

- Less paperwork as the request form is now electronic.
- Automatically flows through the approval process.
- Easy status lookup using the reports function.

"Meishi" Ordering:

- Less paperwork.
- Fewer data entry mistakes.
- No need to keep a large stock.

6. HURDLES OVERCOME:

Hurdles have been overcome in all areas of improvement and new development.

E-Commerce Integration:

- Extracting the required data from the mail was a major hurdle because it is meant to be a confirmation for the customer and only a copy is sent to the merchant.
- Not only does the mail contain a lot of unnecessary information but also the format would change without notice.
- Interfacing to the card company was also a significant hurdle, as great care must be taken with the credit card details.
- Internal integration was smooth.

Mail Order Integration:

- The third part has access to our workflow over the Internet and this sometimes leads to connection problems.
- A major hurdle has been to keep comprehensive logs of to cater to any data lost en route.
- Once again the interface to the credit card company is also via the Internet.
- With the I-mode development the size of the screen was an impediment.
- There is also a limited amount of animation that can be used with this medium.
- Further the screen size and resolution varies with the handsets resulting in a layout that may not be optimum for all.

Cash Advance & Settlement Integration:

- No major hurdles, mainly integration to internal systems.

Name card order form with preview function.

Web enabled POS Integration:

- Integrating the credits for purchases made through different sales channels posed some difficulties.
- But overall a smooth implementation.

SDLC—Project Management:

- We have a continuous supply of requests from our demanding sales teams. Simply managing this volume has been a hurdle.

"Meishi" Ordering:

- Sending e-mail with an attachment is a standard function of ActiveFlow resulting in a smooth implementation.

7. SYSTEM CONFIGURATION:

The system configuration can be best displayed using the following diagram.

The Triumph International Japan computer configuration. (Shown below)

- Unix backend processors with Emc2 disk arrays.
- NT Servers.
- 600 Head Office PC's connected on the Intranet.
- Store SIS—1,300 CE devices connected to the Internet.
- Local offices connected via Frame Relay Network.
- 150 Boutique Web enabled POS registers connected to the Internet.

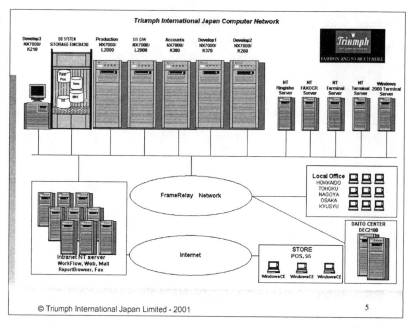

Computer Network at Triumph International Japan

8. RESULTS—COST SAVINGS, INCREASED REVENUES, PRODUCTIVITY IMPROVEMENTS ETC.:

The improvement and development of new novel workflows continues to considerably reduce the man hours required to perform many routine tasks resulting in cost savings, increased revenues, and increased productivity overall.

E-Commerce Integration:

- A cap of six persons regardless of the sales volume.
- Cost savings through decreased paperwork integration between systems.
- Productivity is greatly increased through the automation of routine tasks.
- Increased revenues through one on one sales as a result of the Frequent Shopper Program.
- Time saved spent on a better web design and selection of goods also resulting in increased sales.

Mail Order Integration:

- Significant cost savings as a result of outsourcing of the data entry process.
- Out of a total of six dedicated staff, three diverted to other tasks.
- Saved time spent on market research and improved catalog design.
- I-mode sales represent a whole new market and sales continue to grow.

- The cross channel Frequent Shopper Program is also contributing to increasing sales.

Cash Advance & Settlement Integration:

- Two data entry staff diverted to other duties.
- Eliminating paperwork has reduced processing time.
- It has even been possible to relax the weekly cut off date by one day.

Web enabled POS Integration:

- Greater productivity as resulting from participation in workflow.
- Costs related to distribution of paper materials have been eliminated.
- All information is now available online and market trends can be grasped immediately.
- Ability to share purchase credits across channels is contributing to sales.

SDLC—Project Management:

- One person-employed full time to manage the backlog of system requests is now able to devote his time more productively.
- Increased productivity as a result of less paperwork.
- Less time spent looking for paper sheets and deriving the status of requests.

"Meishi" Ordering:

- Next day delivery is possible in most cases.
- Proper authorization is required to place an order resulting in more conservative ordering.
- Graphic interface reduces mistakes and saves time.

9. COMPETITIVE ADVANTAGES:

Triumph International Japan has gained competitive advantages that have resulted from the continued improvement and introduction of new workflows.

E-Commerce Integration:

- Marketing through all available channels has increased brand recognition.
- As the Internet boom kicks off in Japan, we are targeting a whole new market.
- By automating our systems we are able to meet delivery requests thus increasing trust in the E-commerce sector.
- A cross channel Frequent Shopping Program gives the customer freedom to move between sales channels and still be recognized as a loyal customer.

Mail Order Integration:

- One on One sale eliminates the middleman and help to increase profits.

- The customer has a variety of ways to submit the order, Telephone, Fax, Mail or even using and I-mode cellular phone.
- With I-mode orders the system is completely automated and interactive so we need no human intervention regardless of volume.

Cash Advance & Settlement Integration:

- By reducing paperwork all persons can concentrate on productive tasks.
- All applications are thoroughly checked along approval process.
- Cost savings allow funds to be transferred to sales generating tasks.

Web enabled POS Integration:

- Full integration of the ERP system into the various Head office systems.
- Workflow participation achieved from the Boutiques.
- All communication to the stores are online and market trends can be grasped in a timely fashion.
- Circulars and shop layouts can be presented in color without raising costs.

SDLC—Project Management:

- Considerable cost benefits are achieved by In-house development.
- The means to manage projects in a consistent manner helps meet the sales requirements in a timely manner.
- By inviting system improvement/development requests from all members of the company we are constantly getting new ideas.

"Meishi" Ordering:

- By automating routine office tasks it is possible to give employees more time to spend on revenue-generation duties.

10. IMMEDIATE AND LONG-TERM PLANS:

We will continue to integrate more Head Office paper flows into the Intranet. We would also like to integrate our systems regionally with our offices in Asia. We have completed the first phase of this integration, namely the documenting of all the major business processes in the various countries in the Asia/Pacific region.

The Japanese workflow requirements are very demanding and we are sure that the systems that are developed here will be adaptable to other countries in this region as well as internationally.

Year 2000 Decennial Census, USA

Award Finalist, North America 2001

SYSTEM OVERVIEW

The Lockheed Martin Mission Systems Data Capture System 2000 (DCS 2000) utilized barcode, digital imaging, optical recognition and Staffware workflow technologies to check-in and extract the data from 151.4 million forms. This is the equivalent of 1.5 billion 8.5" x 11" pages processed for the United States 2000 decennial census. Seventy percent of the data was extracted automatically with an accuracy of over 99 percent. This feat was accomplished at four data capture centers starting March 6, 2000 and ending August 3, 2000. All of the US Bureau of Census' intermediate processing milestones were met ahead of schedule. However, the sheer size and daily production of more than 1.2 million forms make this the largest workflow and automated data capture system in the world. The system has provided a model for other similar systems in other countries for a faster and more accurate census.

The requirement for a census was specified in the United States Constitution adopted in 1787 to deal with the problem of apportioning representatives and, at that time, for assessing taxes. The decennial census has become the nation's most comprehensive and expensive statistical data-gathering program. Census results are used during the ensuing decade to address countless public and private data needs. Most importantly, census results are used to reapportion seats in the House of Representatives and redraw congressional, state, and municipal legislative district boundaries. Thus, a key ingredient of an accurate census is not just counting everyone—a formidable challenge in itself—but counting persons in their proper locations. As a result of the 1990 census, eight states gained and 13 states lost at least one congressional seat.

Public decision-makers also use census data to help meet numerous program policy needs. For example, census results are used to help guide the distribution of billions of dollars in Federal aid. After the 1990 census over 100 Federal programs providing grants at the state and local levels use data from or based on the census in formulas that ultimately obligated an estimated $116 billion in fiscal 1991.

Businesses make extensive use of census data for various marketing purposes, including selecting business sites, forecasting demand, allocating advertising and managing sales forces. Census data provide the foundation for volumes of academic and policy research and also assist individuals doing historic research by providing, for example, time-series data and genealogical information.

Since 1970, the Bureau of the Census (BOC) has used essentially the same census methodology—the Bureau develops an address list of the nation's housing units, mails census forms to the vast majority of households, and asks them to mail back the completed forms. Temporary census-takers, known as enumerators, are then hired by the hundreds of thousands to gather the requested information from each non-responding household. The data entered on the forms is then converted to computer process-enabled data for compiling the census reports.

The 1990 decennial census low mail back response rate contributed to making it one of the most controversial censuses in the nation's history. In 1990, 63 percent response was achieved as compared to a predicted 70 percent (1980 was 75 percent). The undercount of millions of persons, 2.1 percent of the enumerated population of 248.7 million, or approximately 5.3 million persons was another contributing factor. Of the many major thrusts identified to correct the 1990 deficiencies, the Bureau resolved to provide a user friendly form to improve response rates and capture the data from returned forms more quickly to better inform the field operations to improve their enumeration efforts.

Since the 1960s, a specially developed Film Optical Sensing Device for Input to Computers (FOSDIC) has been used to convert the census form from paper to microfilm and to display the form to a computer operator for computer input. In 1990, this technology was enhanced to sense marks on the microfilm image and eliminate the manual input process for marks. However, the form required the use of computer registration marks and the form was compacted to reduce the number of paper pages to be processed. If the form could be simplified, the time needed to understand and complete the form could be reduced leading to higher response rates. This led the Bureau to seek a form data capture solution that utilized digital imaging, optical recognition and workflow technologies that did not require a specialized form and could capture the data submitted on the form quicker.

In March 1997 the Bureau awarded to Lockheed Martin Mission Systems the Data Capture System 2000 (DCS 2000) contract to develop, integrate, deploy, maintain, administer and decommission the system to capture and provide to the BOC the data from 130 million census forms in 150 days, an increase of 30 million forms from 1990. The major objectives of the system were:

- Check-in of mail returns within 48 hours of receipt, where mail receipts may be as high as 12 million per day, by recording the barcode viewable through the form envelope's window. This data was forwarded to the Bureau for their purposes of determining non-responding households.
- Capture 85 percent of the surname data from 7.5 million specific forms, or the equivalent of 85 million 8.5" x 11" pages, in a 22

day period ending on April 11, 2000. This data was forwarded to the Bureau to aid in field operations.

- Use digital imaging and recognition technologies to reliably extract the constrained hand-printed and marked contents of census forms and record those contents as ASCII data with 98 percent accuracy.
- Provide capability to manually review and correct data that cannot be recognized with confidence.
- Audit and control quality of the data capture.

The system processes a short form and a long form. The short form consists of a single sheet of paper measuring 11" x 25.5" that is tri-folded with data entry possible on both sheet sides. The long form consists of 10 sheets measuring 11" x 17" that is folded and bound with two staples to form a booklet with data entry possible on both sheet sides of all sheets. The long form requests considerably more information; however, it was only requested of approximately one in six households.

The system implementation was verified through three demonstrations and a census dress rehearsal in a fifteen-month period. The demonstrations were scheduled about four months apart and each was characterized by increasing system functionality and integration, i.e., from technology proof of concepts and these technologies integrated into subsystems to a working system. The demonstrations led to a census dress rehearsal where a live census was performed for Columbia SC, Sacramento CA and the Menomonee Indian Reservation.

Following the implementation the system was to have been "locked down" and the system deployed. However, after the dress rehearsal, many new requirements were identified as critical to a successful census implementation. One fundamental change included redesigning the census form to handle six people in a household versus five, which reduces form tracking through the data capture process. Because the data capture period was fixed these requirements were implemented in parallel to deployment, taxing both requirements implementation and configuration controls. Requirements expansion was considered a major risk to a successful 2000 decennial census.

The system was deployed during a nine month period between May 1999 and January 2000 to four data capture centers (DCCs) in Baltimore, MD, Jeffersonville, IN, Phoenix, AZ and Pomona, CA. Deployment consisted of installation, checkout and certification, site acceptance test and operational test and dry-run. The DCCs average about 200,000 square feet with 800 tons of high volume air conditioning (HVAC) and require about 2000 people to operate two production shifts. During peak mail-back period over six million forms can be unloaded at a DCC from over 60 tractor-trailers. The system deployed to Jeffersonville was sized to handle 20 million forms and the systems at the other sites, 40 million forms.

The system consists of 15 commercial-off-the-shelf (COTS) products with capabilities consisting of mail check-in and sorting, paper to digital image conversion, data base management, workflow management, digital image processing, optical character and mark recognition, data review and correction, digital tape backup and recovery, system administration and some custom software. Maximum use of COTS products was required due to the short duration of the implementation period.

The products intended for form image capture, image processing, automated recognition and data correction were integrated through the Staffware workflow management product to create a forms processing cluster. Use of the Staffware workflow management software to integrate the COTS product reduced the amount of custom software development and through a unique generalized interface to the workflow COTS products, could be "plugged" into the solution allowing easy replacement of a product for a better performing one.

The cluster is capable of processing 36,000 short forms a day. The workflow management software tracks the progress of each form's images through the cluster. The workflow process consists of a series of sequential steps. However, while this simplicity is designed to contribute toward a high performance and a scalable system, the workflow system handles the complexities of rerouting a wide variety of exceptions that are equally important in achieving high performance.

Clusters are combined to form a data capture system based on each data capture center's form processing demands. The cluster as a replicable unit offered the ability to completely test the system's forms processing capability within a lab environment and to quickly combine clusters into a production system capable of processing over 400,000 forms a day.

The key motivations behind installing Staffware's workflow system

The key motivations behind installing this workflow system were:

- The requirement to track the progress of forms through digital image capture, image quality assessment, optical character and mark recognition, contextual analysis, image backup and data review and correction.
- The need to integrate multiple best of breed COTS products with minimal custom software development during an implementation period of short duration.
- To quickly improve the system through alternative products by establishing the ability, through the use of a standard workflow to COTS product interface, to easily replace a product.
- To have a system that was stable and robust and had the benefit of extended testing through its COTS product implementation in various applications.

- Flexibility to easily add or modify processing steps to meet late breaking requirements.
- Ease of administration
- Cope with the rerouting required for handling a wide variety of exceptions.

THE OVERALL BUSINESS INNOVATION

The Bureau has a long history of technological and business innovation, having introduced punch cards and electric tabulating equipment in 1890. In the 1940s the universal automatic computer (UNIVAC) was designed and built specifically for the Census Bureau. As a result of the growing workload there was a need to capture data more rapidly and a need to improve response rates. This was done using a respondent friendly form; the Bureau continued this trend by embracing the move to digital imaging, optical recognition and workflow technologies.

The Bureau understood that when applying new technologies with a fixed schedule that a solution provider would have to be flexible and creative in accepting requirements late in the system implementation phase and that their proposed system must accommodate change easily. The Bureau made this clear in their data capture system request for proposal.

Lockheed Martin Mission Systems was selected to develop, integrate, deploy, maintain, administer and decommission the system. Reasons for the selection were best of breed COTS products, a proposed architecture that was scalable and where change could be easily implemented and significant experience with a similar system for the United States Internal Revenue Service workflow software had been custom developed.

In order to save costs and cut implementation cycle times, COTS products were utilized in major components, with the Staffware workflow package acting as COTS integrator. This approach was based on the understanding gained on the IRS project.

Development was staged to prove the system at each stage as it was gradually scaled up to become the world's largest ever workflow and imaging system. The deployment of a system this large and the ability to accept late requirements was a business innovation in its own right.

At the proposal stage Lockheed Martin had developed a level A demonstration of the technology that used a single scanner to process 50 forms. A level B demonstration was prepared three months after the contract award. This was for a 'cluster,' a repeatable unit, but with just one scanner, more equipment and more output functionality. Three months later, the Level C demonstration was conducted with a full forms processing cluster with three scanners and more functionality that scanned 2,000 forms. It also included site functionality.

By March 1998 a full dress rehearsal was conducted with the equipment installed at the Bureau processing site in Jeffersonville, Indiana, with two full clusters and the site infrastructure. It was part of a larger dress rehearsal that the Bureau conducted that involved mailing out forms to three cities, processing the returns and carrying out an enumeration exercise to follow up those households that had not responded.

The Bureau users gave a lot of input to the system, which resulted in changes to its 'look and feel.' However, significant requirement changes were also made that challenged the flexibility of the architecture and the process controls for controlling these changes. The following are a few of those changes.

Form Redesign

Following the Dress Rehearsal, the Bureau redesigned the forms for the 2000 census allowing the full data input of a sixth person's data, thereby eliminating a significant amount of follow-up. This increased the physical size of the short form as well as added pages to the long form. The scalability of the system permitted it to respond quickly to the change in workload presented by the increase in form size and pages.

Two passes

At the end of 1999, dry runs were conducted with the first 100 data correction personnel hired in order to test speed and accuracy. The system had been modeled to expect 8,000 keystrokes per hour (kps). This was reduced from 12,000 kps because rejects from optical character recognition are difficult to interpret. Tests showed that the keyers were keying only 4,000 characters per hour, and that the ability of the Bureau to meet their intermediate processing milestones was in jeopardy.

At this point in the deployment, it was not possible to scale the solution because the facilities were at capacity. The only alternative was to process data critical to meeting the intermediate milestones first and the remaining data on a second pass of the images. The first pass would scan all the forms and process all the data that was required to produce the deliverable to the President by the end of the year. This represents all the data on the short forms and the same questions on the long forms.

The remainder of the questions on the long forms could be processed later from the digital image captured during the first pass and stored to a large storage device. This change was accomplished 60 days prior to the start of the data capture. The first pass of the data was successful and transition plans were executed to process the remaining data in a second pass. The ability to reconfigure the system to accommodate the two-pass variation was greatly facilitated by the Staffware workflow management component.

THE OVERALL TECHNOLOGICAL INNOVATION

Although digital imaging, optical recognition and workflow technologies are a technical innovation for the Bureau, these technologies have been effectively proven in other areas. However, the sheer size and daily production of more than 1.2 million forms make this the largest workflow and automated data capture system in the world and a technological innovation. This is the equivalent of 1.5 billion 8.5" x 11" pages processed for the United States 2000 decennial census. This aside, other more subtle technical innovations where workflow improvements were made that played a role in the success of this application.

Generic application interface

Staffware is used as the integrating architecture for the COTS products that are utilized in the forms processing cluster. A generic application interface 'wrapper' was used to integrate the workflow with the COTS products. The products vary from being just toolkits and libraries that can be compiled into the application to stand-alone applications.

The application interface can support both the synchronous and asynchronous applications. When the interface sends data to a synchronous application to work on, the executable in the interface waits for the application to return it. As soon as the application returns it, Staffware knows the task is finished.

In the case of asynchronous applications, the interface and the application are two separate executables that pass information to each other. However, there is no direct communication link when it has finished. The interface therefore polls the application periodically to ask if it has finished.

From the application side, the interface can be viewed differently, but from the workflow side all the applications look the same. This significantly reduced both the development time for interfacing the products to the workflow and reduced the support time required during operation of the system. As well as controlling the applications with simple functions like stopping, starting and pausing, it also allowed additions to the system to monitor the applications.

Windows NT

DCS 2000 is the first large image-processing project completed by Lockheed Martin Mission Systems that does not use the UNIX operating system. Windows NT was chosen because there was a greater selection of digital imaging and optical recognition COTS products. While the communication to the workflow was all done through Staffware, the communication to the interface layer services was done using Windows NT's built in administrative capabilities. The interface layer in many applications logged errors and other kinds of information in Windows NT event logs. Administrators can easily view these remotely.

System administration

Because of the sheer size of the system, software and system design were geared towards simplifying system administration. A COTS product originally part of the solution was replaced because it was difficult to administer remotely.

The workflow is superficially straightforward, consisting of a series of sequential steps with most processes passing their results to the next, with little forking of workflow cases. However, underneath it is complicated because of the rerouting that is required to handle the wide range of different exceptions.

The functionality available in Staffware is used in a complex and innovative way in order to help administrators to manage the effective handling of exception cases. The software was developed with the approach that if something fails it should do so as elegantly as possibly and it should be as easy as possible for an administrator to recover the process.

One of the key workflow innovations was to create a' fail' queue. If the unexpected occurs in any processing step in the workflow that causes it to alert an administrator, the system will fail the batch and put it into a fail queue. This might be caused, for instance, by losing a connection to the database or to an image server.

The administrators at each site will monitor the fail queues and the service that has failed the batch will log an error. It will also put a comment or error message on the workflow case, so that when the administrators are looking at the Staffware interface they can usually detect immediately what went wrong and investigate further. Once the administrators have resolved the error they can move the batch and send it back to the queue it came from or any other queue to help resolve the problem.

The system administrators find the information they are getting from the built-in Windows NT functions extremely helpful when they are trying to identify problems with the system. There is a list of each service that is running on the cluster and a count of how many form batches are being processed through that service. It gives an indication of whether the process is initialized and running correctly, if it has failed or if it is down.

One feature has proved helpful in a lot of cases, particularly with asynchronous applications. If the secondary application fails for some reason, the first application will still be waiting and would not necessarily know that the other application has failed. A monitoring function keeps track of how long those applications have been waiting and alerts an administrator if something is taking too long to process.

The theory of "elegant failure" also applies to form processing clusters. If a cluster should fail then the system is designed so that this does not affect other clusters. The system architecture maintains as much independence as possible, while at the same time being as tightly integrated as possible. Each individual application can survive without another one. Along the same lines, the interface between the cluster and the site is minimized, so if the site services fail the clusters can continue to operate and vice versa.

Quality assurance

In a data capture system of this size and providing the data for a mission critical application such as a census, it is imperative that the quality of the data being produced is continuously assessed. The data capture system continuously monitors the quality of the data produced by both the automated recognition and the manual review and correction functions.

The workflow in the forms processing cluster implements and controls the continuous monitoring. After data has been produced by either the automated or manual functions, this output stream is sampled and the digital image that was the source of the data presented to data correction personnel without their knowledge that they are performing a quality assessment function.

The original output is compared with the output from the quality assessment step to determine whether the original output was correct. If they match then the original output is considered correct. If they do not match then the process is repeated and a match attempted again with the original or the output from the first quality assessment step. If it matches the original then it is considered correct. If it matches the output from the first quality assessment then the original output is considered incorrect. After a significant sample is obtained then the overall quality of the system can be derived. The system as of this reporting has produced an overall accuracy in excess of 98 percent with 151 million forms processed.

THE SYSTEM USERS AND WHAT THEIR JOBS NOW ENTAIL

In 1990, the form marks were automatically recognized using a specially developed capability called Film Optical Sensing Device for Input to Computers (FOSDIC). The marks were recognized from the forms microfilm using a light sensing technique. Write-in fields were keyed by data input personnel from the microfilm. The forms were processed at seven processing centers.

Since the implementation of the DCS 2000, the 2000 Census operators are checking in and sorting mail using mail sorting equipment, scanning paper using high-speed optical scanners, reviewing the image quality on a personal computer display when it doesn't pass automated assessment criteria, reviewing and correcting the 30 percent of data fields that are not recognized automatically using the digital image of the field and finally using barcode wands and database technology, verifying that the Bureau acknowledged the receipt of a form's data.

THE BIGGEST HURDLES OVERCOME

Late Requirements Changes

As discussed in section 4, significant requirement changes occurred late in the deployment and final test phases. This challenge was successfully met as a result of a system architecture that was scalable and flexible that included a workflow management function that could be easily customized to accept processing flow changes.

COTS Product Substitution

An early problem was that Lockheed Martin was forced to re-evaluate its original choice of the critical image-processing package. It had been selected because it provided a lot of the functionality needed, including an interface to the Kodak scanners and full image processing capability. However, in early demonstrations it was unstable.

Just as serious for a project of this scale, it did not quite fit the overall architecture. It had its own workflow engine that controlled its functionality with which the workflow manager had to interface. After a re-evaluation, it was decided to replace the package with custom code. Lockheed Martin used a toolkit from TMS that provided some basic capability but built the software to its own design using its own code. The flexibility of the Staffware package proved to be significant, because it made the change very easy. Each of the workflow functions performed by the package was transferred to Staffware individually and the new software could interface with it at a low level.

There were also some initial performance problems. The image server and its redundant array of inexpensive disk (RAID) fault tolerant storage came from different suppliers causing problems when communicating with each other. After trying several different combinations, an integrated product was sourced from Dell, who built both.

Keying

Lockheed Martin experimented with character keying. This involves keying only individual characters to which the software has ascribed low confidence. However, the project transferred to field keying, where the whole field is re-keyed if any character within it is low confidence.

Although it may be faster for some keyers, character keying is not quite as accurate as field keying. Whereas it easy to know that something is wrong in a field, it is extremely difficult to determine exactly which character is incorrect. The potential for additional speed did not justify the accuracy lost.

Paper handling

One of the big problems in the early demonstrations was the paper handling. As paper moves through the system, it is in a batch if it has been mailed in, or a box if it has come from enumerators. Each box is processed as a batch. If a form in a batch was mis-fed so that it couldn't be automatically processed, the paper form had to be physically pulled at a later step so that it could go back for re-scanning or to be fully keyed from paper.

The system told the user which batch the form was in and where in the batch the form could be found. However, counting the sheets was very difficult and too complicated for users to do correctly each time. It was decided to completely change the way this task was performed.

After the clusters have processed them, every form is scanned with a handheld barcode scanner at site level and compared to a data receipt confirmation file provided by the Bureau. This verifies that each sheet is ready to be destroyed and identifies those that the system wants reprocessed.

The scanner actually gives a green light if it is ready to be destroyed and a red light if it needs to be pulled out for reprocessing. If reprocessing is required, it goes to a second stage where a different person rescans the bar code to find out why it has to be pulled so they can direct it either to rescanning or to be keyed from paper. This is a more labor-intensive process but has proved to ensure that every form received is fully processed.

Communications

The Bureau contracted with TRW to operate three of the four data capture centers. Due to the very aggressive schedule and the speed with which system deployment was to be executed, communications were always a challenge. Consequently, an integrated product team structure was utilized, which facilitated communications and demonstrated both Lockheed Martin's and TRW's commitment to the success of the Census.

THE NEW SYSTEM CONFIGURATION

The four data capture centers are approximately 250,000 square feet with 4,000 amp electrical service and 900 tons high volume air conditioning a located in Baltimore, Maryland, Jeffersonville Indiana, Phoenix Arizona and Pomona California. Each has a staff of approximately 2,000 people operating on two shifts, seven days a week. Jeffersonville is designed to handle 30 million forms the other three sites 40 million.

The architecture is split into site infrastructure and a number of identical forms processing clusters consisting of three high-speed scanners and supporting hardware and software. Windows NT was used as the operating system throughout the entire system. The network is 100Mbps switched Ethernet using the TCP/IP protocol.

Site hardware

Site	Sorters	Clusters	Scanners	Servers	Workstations
Baltimore	9	15	45	578	580
Jeffersonville	6	10	30	391	381
Phoenix	7	15	45	576	566
Pomona	8	14	42	545	547
Total	30	54	162	2,090	2,074

Each site has two Oracle databases, one for status and a management database with statistics on the system, such as operator keying rates, accuracy rates, etc. Docutronix is used for mail sorting and bar code reading. Data backup was performed using Legato and StorageTek tape backup and Tivoli software used for network and system management.

Each cluster has Staffware as the workflow manager to control every step. It was selected because it was a mature product that offered all the functionality needed at a cost-effective price.

Each cluster has three Kodak High Speed Scanners with Kofax scanner controllers. The scanners were the most mature and robust products available and Lockheed Martin had used them successfully on previous projects.

TMS Sequoia toolkit was used to build the image processing and image quality assessment functions to Lockheed Martin's design. Optimum Solutions Fast Accurate Questionnaire Scanning System (FAQSS) was used for optical mark recognition, as it was the most accurate available at the time.

RecoStar from CGK in Germany was used for optical character recognition (OCR), as it was the most accurate and offered contextual functionality. It was used in conjunction with custom code for contextual analysis written by Lockheed Martin to improve accuracy.

Data correction software from Captiva was used for both keying from image and keying from paper. It offered a lot of flexibility for different ways of keying that affect performance and user-friendliness.

Each cluster has an Oracle database to record the file location of each form. This is held as an image file on a RAID server with each page of the form in the same file. The data processed from it is held as an adjacent text file. Lockheed Martin had tried storing the images in a database, but it became so large it was unmanageable.

Cost Savings, Increased Revenues, and Productivity Improvements

Due to the length of time between the decennial censuses, it is difficult to make direct comparisons. Better comparisons can be made between the decennial census plan and its subsequent performance.

The decennial census has been extremely successful. As discussed earlier, the data capture participated in several majors thrusts for 2000 decennial census: the capture of census data faster within accuracy objectives using a respondent friendly form designed to increase response rates. The planned 2000 decennial response of 61 percent was exceeded at 65 percent. All intermediate processing milestones were met early with data that exceeded accuracy objectives of 98 percent. Certainly significant savings from these improvements were experienced throughout the Bureau; however, the direct cost savings are difficult to quantify. Certainly, the elimination of the data review and correction workload through the use of the digital imaging, optical recognition and workflow technologies produced a savings in manual labor that was at least $50 million.

During the implementation of the data capture system several productivity and cost savings were realized. A cost/benefit analysis showed that replacing the imaging software saved the project $3 million. The toolkit used was cheaper than the packaged software licenses, support costs were considerably reduced and fewer servers were needed. The vendor had recently rewritten the product, so the project was effectively a beta site, so considerable time was saved in testing.

Because the system was designed to be easy to administer, Lockheed Martin estimates that it would otherwise have required twice as many system administration staff. This saved four people per site over two shifts, which has saved $1 million, plus the cost of training them.

Lockheed Martin estimates that the use of commercial off-the-shelf packages, compared to writing the software from scratch as they did with the IRS, saved $1 million. The generic application interface has saved development time through reuse and reduced administration. The company has estimated this savings at $200,000.

COMPETITIVE ADVANTAGES GAINED

Whereas workflow and automated processing are in widespread use, the unique advantage of the DCS 2000 system is driven by the enormous scale of the program it had to support, which involved processing up to 17.5 million pages per day. The size and short time-scale forced the system to be made very robust, with features like failure queues and administrators moving batches, as there was little time to recover from problems.

Lockheed Martin has already won the United Kingdom contract and is investigating other opportunities. Other countries have visited the four US sites and have seen the scale of the processing. Many companies around the world stand to get more accurate and faster censuses as a result of this project.

IMMEDIATE AND LONG-TERM PLANS TO SUSTAIN COMPETITIVE ADVANTAGE

Lockheed Martin is already developing the system for the United Kingdom Census, which is using the same system as utilized in the United States. It is also proposing several other census processing systems on different scales, although none are on the same scale as the United States Decennial Census.

The constraint is not only the population to be counted, but also the speed in which the US decennial census needs to be completed. Other censuses have longer schedules enabling processing to be carried out over several more months.

Clearly, Lockheed Martin Mission Systems is considering improvements to the system. These improvements can be grouped into two categories: (1) extend the census form data capture to downstream census data processing and (2) continue to reduce errors and the number of required operators by reducing reject rates from the automated capture.

Census data is post-processed using statistical analysis and coding. The workflow system will permit the easy extension of the system for these additional processing steps. Different paths a form can take when it is coded complicate the workflow process. An additional complication is created when forms may travel through different operators; however, the Staffware workflow system permits and manages these complicated processes.

Coding can also improve accuracy and reduce reject rates. Even if something is low confidence from the automated capture, the automatic coding takes into account fuzzy logic and other techniques to avoid sending it to a keyer. These types of techniques require a complicated workflow configuration, because of the different ways of avoiding manual processing. If it still cannot be coded automatically, it may be sent for character keying, which should be faster than field keying. It can then be sent back to the automatic coder.

If it still does not code, to improve performance, just the numeric fields can be sent to a keyer. This allows the keyer to stay on the numeric keypad, rather than switching continuously to the alphanumeric portion of the keyboard. That hand movement actually slows down the keyer significantly.

After numerical keying the image may then be sent it to an automatic coder. Then it may go for alpha keying and then go back to an automatic coder. If all those steps fail, the image has to go back for manual coding.

Because keying is so labor intensive, automation can save hundreds of keyers at each site, resulting in a smaller site and smaller workload. Workflow innovations can reduce a lot of the risk and costs. In particular, merging field keying and character keying into the same system could generate major benefits.

Section 4

Directory and Appendices

Global Excellence in Workflow Awards

ACTION TECHNOLOGIES
1301 Marina Village Parkway Ste 100
Alameda, CA, 94501
Marcy Carnerie
Customer Relations Manager
Tel: 510-478-1020
Fax: 510-769-0596
marcy_carnerie@actiontech.com

ANOVA INSURANCE
PO Box 19, 3800 Amersfoort, Netherlands
Ton de Wit
Project Director
Tel: [31] (33) 445 5242
Fax: [31] (33) 4456547
witt@anova.nl

CITY OF SALZBURG
Hubert-Sattler-Gasse 7a, Postfach 63
Salzburg,, A-5024, Austria
Berthold Rauchenschwandtner
CIO, City of Salzburg
Tel: [43] (66) 28 07 22570
Fax: [43] (66) 28 07 22079
berthold.rauchenschwandtner@stadt-salzburg.at

DUBAI POLICE G. H.
Al Ethad rd., Box 1493
Dubai, United Arab Emirates
dubaipolice.gov.ae
Captain Khalid Alshamsi
Tel: [971] 1-42014208
Fax: [971] 1-42014110
kshamsi@emirates.net.ae

EISTREAM WMS INC (PREVIOUSLY EASTMAN SOFTWARE)
Funding Member
296 Concord Road
Billerica, MA, 01821, United States
http://wms.eistream.com
Ken Mei
Director, International Sales Support
Tel: [1] 978-313-7266
Fax: [1] 978-313-7566
ken.mei@eistream.com

GIGA INFORMATION GROUP
One Longwater Circle
Norwell, MA, 02061, United States
www.gigaweb.com
Connie Moore
Vice President
Tel: [1] 781-982-9500
Fax: [1] 781-878-6650
cmoore@gigaweb.com

IJET TRAVEL INTELLIGENCE
900 Bestgate Rd., Suite 400
Annapolis, MD 21401
www.ijet.com
Greg Meyer
CTO
Tel: 410-573-3860
Fax: 410-573-3869
meyerg@ijet.com

FUJITSU SOFTWARE CORPORATION
3055 Orchard Drive
San Jose, CA, 95134, United States
http://www.i-flow.com/
Paula Negron
Product Manager
Tel: 408-456-7809
Fax: 408-456-7821
pnegron@fs.fujitsu.com

GENER-X (ORDIPLAN INC.)
825 Boul. Guimond Bureau 200
Quebec J4G 2M7, Canada
Francois Roy
Vice President
Tel: 450-442-2379
Fax: 450-442-7911
froy@ordiplan.com

GOVERNMENT OF NEW BRUNSWICK
P O Box 600, Fredericton
New Brunswick, E3B 5H1, Canada
Jean-Eudes Levesque
Dir of Translation Bureau
Tel: 506-453-5363
Fax: 506-459-7911
jean-eudes.levesque@gnb.ca

KAISHA-TEC
c/o G. Long, Kaisha-Tec,
Mitaka Sangyo Plaza Annex,
3-32-3 Shimo Renjaku,

Mitaka-shi, Tokyo 181-0013, Japan
Tel: [81] 422 47 2397
Tel: [81] 422 47 2396
glong@kaisha-tec.com

R.R. DONNELLEY & SONS CO. GRAPHICS MANAGEMENT
200 World Trade Center, Suite 2000
Chicago, IL, 60654-1003, USA
David Oberst
IT Manager
Tel: 312-527-7402
Fax: 312-527-6240
david.oberst@rrd.com

STAFFWARE BV
Kraspolderweg 10
Alkmaar, 3800 HA, Netherlands
www.staffware.com
Jasper Kloos
Marketing Manager
Tel: [31] (72) 5120728
Fax: [31] (72) 5129175
jkloos@staffware.nl

STAFFWARE CORP
19 Crosby Drive, Suite 130
Bedford, MD, 01730 United States
Bonnie Morrissey
Marketing Specialist
Tel: 781-271-0003
Fax: 781-271-0066
bmorrissey@staffwarecorp.com

TAYLOR-NELSON SOFRES
16 Rue barbes
Montrouge, France, 92129, France
Arnold Haine
Information System Manager
Tel: [33] 1 40 92 29 51
Fax: [33] 1 40 92 32 26
arnold.haine@fr.thsofres.com

TRIUMPH INTERNATIONAL JAPAN
Tokyo Ryutsu Center Bldg.,
6-1-1 Heiwajima, Ota-ku
Tokyo 143-6555, Japan
www.triumphjapan.com
Dinesh Kumar
System Consultant
Tel: [81] (035) 4937-732
Fax: [81] (035) 4937-766
d.kumar@triumphjapan.com

UNISYS
Donau-City-Str. 6
Wien, A-1221, Austria
www.unisys.com
Wolfgang Grundei
Project Manager
Tel: [43] (12) 60 64 297
Fax: [43] (12) 60 64 490
wolfgang.grundei@unisys.com

US CENSUS BUREAU
4700 Silverhill Road
Gaithersburg, MD, 20879, United States
Bonnie Hopper
Tel: 301-457-8238
Fax: 301-457-4714
bhopper@census.gov

W4
4 Rue Emile Baudot
Palaiseau, 91873, France
Nathalie Genieux
Marketing Manager
Tel: [33] 1 64 53 19 12
Fax: [33] 1 64 53 28 98
nathalie.genieux@w4global.com

Contributors and Authors

RONALD S. ALEPIN (RALEPIN@FS.FUJITSU.COM)
General Manager, Enterprise Products Division
Fujitsu Software Corporation
Chief Technology Consultant
Fujitsu Limited
3055 Orchard Drive, San Jose CA 95134-2022, United States
Tel: [1] 408-456-7963 Fax: [1] 408-456-7821

Ronald Alepin is General Manager, Enterprise Products Division, Fujitsu Software Corporation and Chief Technology Consultant, Fujitsu Limited. As General Manager, he is responsible for FS' e-business products and services including INTERSTAGE and i-Flow. He has worked with Fujitsu Limited for more than fifteen years in a variety of capacities. He became General Manager at FS in January of 2000. Mr. Alepin has more than thirty years of industry experience in all areas of the computer business and on all major platforms. He is the author of several software products.

JOERG BECKER (ISJOBE@WI.UNI-MUENSTER.DE)
University of Muenster, Department of Information Systems
Leonardo Campus 3, 48149 Muenster, Germany
Phone +49 (251) 833 8100 Fax +49 (251) 833 8109

Prof. Dr. Joerg Becker is full Professor for Information Systems and Information Management and head of the Department of Information Systems at the University of Muenster, Germany. Prof. Becker has published 7 monographies and numerous papers and articles in the field of information systems, logistics, retail information systems, data and information management, neural networks, information modeling, and executive information systems. He is editor of monographies in the field of integrated information systems, business process engineering, and workflow management. As a consultant Prof. Becker has over 20 years of experience in management consulting in the areas of information strategy, business reengineering; strategy and implementation projects in the retail, manufacturing and distribution industry. He heads his own consulting practice, located near Muenster, Germany.

JUSTIN C BRUNT (JBRUNT@STAFFWARE.COM)
Research Director
Staffware plc
4 Apple Walk, Kembrey Park, Swindon, SN2 8BL, United Kingdom
Tel: +44 1793 441300 Fax +44 1793 441333

Justin Brunt has worked for Staffware since 1994 initially as VP of UK Product Development but more recently as VP of Research. He also represents Staffware on the Technical Committees of the WfMC and other bodies. Prior to joining Staffware, Justin held leading software engineering roles in a high profile European IT organization.

BETSY A. FANNING (BFANNING@AIIM.ORG)
Director, Standards
AIIM International (www.aiim.org)
1100 Wayne Avenue Suite 1100, Silver Spring, MD 20910, USA
Phone: +1.301.755.2682 Fax: +1.301.587.2711

Betsy Fanning is the manager of the ANSI/ISO Standards Program for AIIM International. In this position, she is responsible for the standards and technical reports produced by AIIM as ANSI (American National Standards). She is also the secretary for ISO TC 171, Document Imaging Applications Subcommittee 2, Application Issues. In addition to this, she is the administrator for the U. S. Technical Advisory Group to TC 171 that represents the United States at the international meetings. Betsy has experience in the development of standards as the chairman for the Electronic Imaging standards committee for 10 years. She has also served as a member of the United States Technical Advisory Group (TAG) to TC 171, Document Imaging Applications as a member of the TAG for the last 5 years. Prior to coming to AIIM, Betsy has held positions with DynSolutions, a Correspondence, Document and Records Management Company and Westinghouse Electric. In both of these positions, she has implemented imaging and document management systems. She holds a master's degree from the University of Pittsburgh and an undergraduate degree from Clarion State University.

LAYNA FISCHER (LAYNA@WFMC.ORG)
General Manager, Workflow Management Coalition (WfMC)
CEO, Future Strategies Inc. (WfMC Secretariat)
2436 North Federal Highway #374, Lighthouse Point, FL 33064, USA
Phone +1 954 782 3376, Fax +1 954 782 6365

As General Manager of the WfMC Secretariat, Layna Fischer works closely with the WfMC Steering Committee to promote the mission of the Coalition and is tasked with the overall management of membership logistics, meetings and conferences.

She also serves as Executive Director of BPMI.org, the Business Process Management Initiative and is Chair of the Workflow And Reengineering International Association (WARIA). Her responsibilities include directorship of the annual Global Excellence in Workflow Awards, cosponsored by the WfMC, WARIA and Giga Information Group.

As President and CEO of Future Strategies Inc., Ms. Fischer is editor and publisher of the business book series, **New Tools for New Times**: which includes *The Workflow Paradigm* and *Electronic Commerce*, and the annual **Excellence in Practice** series, starting with *Excellence in Practice, Innovation and Excellence in Workflow and Imaging* in 1997. She also edits and publishes the annual *Workflow Handbook* in association with the Workflow Management Coalition.

Her experience in the computer industry includes being the president and CEO of a multi-million dollar high-technology export company for seven years, during which time she also founded an offshore franchise distribution company. Ms. Fischer was a senior editor of a leading computer publication for four years and has been involved in international computer journalism and publishing for over 18 years. She was a founding director of the United States *Computer Press Association* in 1985. She serves on the boards of several organizations, including the Black Forest Group.

NATHALIE GENIEUX (NATHALIE.GENIEUX@W4GLOBAL.COM)
W4

4, Rue Emile Baudot, 91873 Palaiseau Cedex - France
Tel: +(33) 1 64 53 19 12
Fax: +(33) 1 64 53 28 98

Nathalie GENIEUX joined W4 in January 2001, when she became the French Workflow Editor's Marketing Manager. In this position, she is in charge of the development of the company's marketing corporate (communications, press relations, events, co-marketing with partners, follow-up of customer relations, professional organizations), the development of W4's position on the workflow market, and she helps the Sales Team by providing them with the appropriate tools.

Nathalie graduated from Paris University with a Master degree in International Relations. The subject of her dissertation was: "The European automobile industry in front of the Japanese challenge" (300 pages).

Prior to W4, Nathalie used to work for American and Australian companies specialized in EDM. She has an international profile, and is fluent in French, English, and German.

MARC GILLE (MGILLE@CARNOT.AG)

CARNOT AG
Niddastr. 98-102, 60329 Frankfurt am Main, Germany
Tel: +49 69 351 02 100 Fax: +49 69 351 02 199

Marc Gille holds a Ph.D. in computer science and an MSc in engineering (Dipl.-Ing.) from the Department of Electrical Engineering and Information Technology, Ruhr-Universität Bochum. He is Vice President Engineering for the Frankfurt-based CARNOT AG, vendor of the workflow management system CARNOT Process Engine. At CARNOT, Dr. Gille is responsible for all engineering operations and standards activity at CARNOT AG. Over the last ten years, he has been involved as a manager and/or architect with many, mostly architectural software projects in Germany, Europe and the US. He is a well-known member of the European Software Community and has contributed to several magazines and conferences. As a member of the Object Database Management Group, Dr. Gille has conceived and specified parts of the ODMG 2 Standard. Prior to founding CARNOT AG, Dr. Gille worked as the Vice President Engineering of MICRAM AG, a leading provider for complex Web solutions and distributor for the ODBMS Objectivity/DB in Germany.

DAVID HOLLINGSWORTH (DAVID.HOLLINGSWORTH@ICL.COM)

ICL Pathway
Forest Road, Feltham, Middlesex, TW13 7EJ, United Kingdom
Tel: +44 181 730 4112 Fax: +44 181 730 4161

David Hollingsworth is a Systems Architect with ICL, a part of the Fujitsu Group specializing in e-Business Solutions and Services. His interest in workflow systems dates from 1992 and as the ICL architect working on future office architecture he helped establish the Workflow Management Coalition as the industry standards body for workflow. He is currently chairman of its Technical Committee and has authored several of its reference documents. He holds an honors degree in Economics from the London School of Economics and also the ICL courtesy title of Distinguished Engineer.

DINESH KUMAR (D.KUMAR@TRIUMPHJAPAN.COM)
Triumph International Japan, 10F Ryuutsu Centre,
Heiwajima, Ohta-ku, Tokyo 143, Japan
Phone +81 (3) 5493-7730 Fax +81 (3) 5493-7766

Dinesh Kumar is a workflow consultant at Triumph International in Japan, working from the business perspective in order to achieve process efficiency.

He had been instrumental in the implementation of novel workflows for e-commerce in particular, with I-mode phone integration. He has also introduced a complete "No-touch" order system from website capture to product shipment. These workflows have put Triumph at the forefront of workflow technology in Japan.

Dinesh is an "international" person and has spent time in Brunei, Jamaica, Japan, Myanmar and India. He has a degree in Commerce from the University of Delhi, and obtained a Masters degree in Japan. He is perfectly fluent in Japanese.

HEINZ LIENHARD (HEINZ.LIENHARD@IVYTEAM.CH)
Chairman and Co-Founder of ivyTeam
Alpenstrasse 9, Zug, 6304, Switzerland
Tel: [41] 71 0 80 20 Fax: [41] 71 0 80 60

Heinz Lienhard lives and works in Switzerland at the lovely lake of Zug. As co-founder and head of ivyTeam he is trying hard to bring together the web application and the workflow world. He received a Master's degree in electrical engineering from the ETH (Switzerland), a Master's degree in mathematical statistics from Stanford University (California, USA) and the Dr. h.c. from the informatics department of ETH, Lausanne (Switzerland). For many years he headed the central R&D labs of Landis&Gyr Corp., now part of the Siemens group, where he built up important R&D activities in system theory, automatic control, informatics and microtechnology.

MIKE MARIN (MMARIN@FILENET.COM)
Software Engineer
FileNET Corporation
3565 Harbor Boulevard, Costa Mesa, CA 92626, United States
Tel: 1 714 662 5134 Fax: 1 714 662 5076

Mike Marin is the architect for the FileNET workflow technology. He has more that 15 years experience developing software, and has a Master on Computer Science. He is a vice-chair of the WfMC Technical Committee and chair of the WfMC Interoperability working group. Mike has contributed to the definition several workflow standards, and has received the WfMC Excellence Award, for his technical contributions to the WfMC standardization efforts.

B. JOHN MASTERS (JMASTERS@IMC.COM)

Subject Matter Expert
Information Management Consultants, Inc.
7915 Westpark Drive, McLean, VA 22102, USA
Tel: 1 813-805-6931

John Masters has over 14 years of experience in the document and information management industry. During this time he has managed both public and commercial document imaging operations, and has been involved in numerous technology assessment and operations improvement initiatives. John has been involved in all aspects of document imaging from analog to digital imaging, and has managed operations from small startups to one of the largest document processing centers in the U.S.

John has served the industry in various capacities, and in 1999 was awarded the Distinguished Service Award by the Association for Information and Image Management International (AIIM). His service has included serving on the Advisory Committee on Electronic Records for the North Carolina Department of Cultural Resources, Division of Archives and History, and a legislatively mandated committee on the development of imaging standards for public records in North Carolina. He has served as an ex-officio member of a legislatively mandated Document and Information Management Committee for the North Carolina Association of Registers of Deeds. John is the incoming Chair of the AIIM Accreditation Committee.

John is a frequently invited speaker at local, national, and international events. He has delivered presentations as part of the University of California-Berkley Continuing Education Program in conjunction with Seminarium in South America, has spoken at numerous AIIM Conferences including a number of AIIM Leadership Conferences. He has provided training programs for staff at the Bowman Gray School of Medicine of Wake Forest University and the Northwest Area Health Education Center of North Carolina.

He facilitates programs at all organizational levels including Executive Management Teams and Boards of Directors. He has been published in various circulations. John holds a Bachelor of Sciences Degree in Business Administration from Appalachian State University as well as AIIM's Master of Information Technology designation.

CAROLYN MCGREGOR (CAROLYN@IT.UTS.EDU.AU)

University of Technology, Sydney, Faculty of Information Technology
PO Box 123, Broadway, NSW 2007, Australia

Carolyn McGregor is a postgraduate researcher for the University of Technology, Sydney (UTS) and has worked as a part-time lecturer at the University of Western Sydney (UWS). She has published research, and is an industry specialist consultant, in the areas of Business Intelligence, Online Analytical Processing, Data Warehousing, Workflow and e-Commerce. Carolyn has been involved with numerous industry-based projects. Currently completing her PhD in Computing Science in the area of Intelligent Workflow Monitoring Systems, Carolyn was the first Australian to complete a PhD research internship at the IBMs TJ Watson Research Center in Yorktown, NY. Carolyn is a member of the Australian Computer Society (ACS), the Association of Information Systems (AIS) and the technical committee of the Workflow Management Coalition (WfMC).

Paula Negron (pnegron@fs.fujitsu.com)
Product Manager
Fujitsu Software Corporation
3055 Orchard Drive, San Jose CA 95134-2022, United States
Phone: 408-456-7809

Paula Negron, product manager for FS' i-Flow workflow engine, has responsibility for coordinating product releases, gathering customer feedback and working with product marketing, development and engineering to produce i-Flow's Market Requirements Documents and product roadmaps. Previously, Ms. Negron worked on systems engineering for i-Flow and a business process-modeling tool. Ms. Negron joined Fujitsu in 1995 as a management consultant at Fujitsu ICL in Finland, providing her expertise in process design and analysis. Assignments included: orchestrating process reengineering projects at large corporations, delivering training, and fulfilling speaking engagements on process management and intranet technologies. Ms. Negron is an active participant in process management standards bodies such as BPMI and WfMC.

Charlie Plesums (cplesums@csc.com or charlie@plesums.com)
Principal Consultant
Computer Sciences Corporation
Chair, External Relations Committee, WfMC
Computer Sciences Corporation Financial Services Group
www.csc.com or www.csc-fs.com
200 West Cesar Chavez, Austin Texas 78701, USA
Tel: +1 (512) 275-5554 Fax: +1 (512) 349-0742

Charlie Plesums has been involved with work management and document imaging since 1982. As one of the pioneers of the technology, he was responsible for the design and implementation of the first large-scale system, installed in the insurance industry, which has grown to now support over 20,000 users. In 1995 he joined Computer Sciences Corporation as their principal consultant in image, work management, call centers, and e-commerce. In this role he assists numerous project teams, addressing special issues such as interfaces, standards, and conversions. Charlie represents CSC as a member of the Workflow Management Coalition, and currently chairs the External Relations Committee of the WfMC. He served two full terms on the AIIM standards board, and remains active in the standards program as a member of the National Standards Council. He has spoken on technology subjects in 14 countries, to over 15,000 people. He is an AIIM "Master of Information Technologies," was an

Information Services Fellow at USAA, and served on the IBM Image Customer Advisory Council.

Charlie has a Bachelor of Electrical Engineering degree and an MS degree in Computer Science from Union College in Schenectady, New York. Many of Charlie's papers are published on his web site, www.plesums.com

JON PYKE (JPYKE@STAFFWARE.COM)
Executive Vice President and Chief Technology Officer
Chair: Workflow Management Coalition
Staffware Plc (www.staffware.com)
3 The Switchback, Gardener Road, Maidenhead, Berkshire, SL6 7RJ UK
Tel: +44 (162) 878-6800 Fax: +44 (162) 878-1654

Jon Pyke has worked in the IT industry since the mid 1970s and has a wide range of skills covering just about every aspect of software development, systems analysis and design, project management, consultancy, product management and marketing. He holds the equivalent of an MsC in computer science and is a Chartered Information Systems Practitioner. Jon is a founding member and current Chair of the Workflow Management Coalition. He is an AIIM Laureate for Workflow, and vice chair of AIIM's Emerging Technology Advisory Board (EmTAG).

MICHAEL ROSSI (MROSSI@CSC.COM)
PM JCALS (CSC Supply Chain Services)
304 West Route 38, P O Box 1038, Moorestown, NJ08057, USA
Tel:[1] 856-983-44004911 Fax:[1] 856-983-3941

Mike Rossi is a Senior Computer Scientist at Computer Sciences Corporation in Moorestown, New Jersey. He is currently assigned to the DoD's JCALS project. He holds a Bachelor's degree in Computer Science from LaSalle University and has over ten years experience involving development, pre-sales, consulting, training, documentation and project management. He has worked in the areas of defense, publishing, document/content management, workflow and systems integration, but specializes in the application of markup technologies such as SGML and XML. Mr. Rossi has served as the editor of the WfMC's Wf-XML specification versions 1.0 and 1.1 and provides continued input to the specification's evolution.

RAINER WEBER (RAINER.WEBER@SAP.COM)
Developer
SAP AG
Neurottstr. 16, 69190 Walldorf, Germany

Rainer Weber has worked for SAP since 1994 in the area of workflow development. He also represents SAP at WfMC meetings.

MICHAEL ZUR MUEHLEN (ISMIZU@WI.UNI-MUENSTER.DE)
University of Muenster, Department of Information Systems
Leonardo Campus 3, 48149 Muenster, Germany
Phone +49 (251) 833 8080 Fax +49 (251) 833 8109

Michael zur Muehlen is working as a lecturer and research assistant at the Department of Information Systems of the University of Muenster, Germany, in the fields of information modeling and workflow management. Mr. zur Muehlen has participated in numerous industrial BPR and workflow projects and has published several articles on the topics of meta modeling, process and workflow management. His main research interests include organizational aspects of workflow management systems, process-oriented controlling and resource management. Together with Prof. Yvonne L. Antonucci, Widener University, USA, Mr. zur Muehlen has received the SAP University Alliance Curriculum Development Award for the establishment of an international curriculum teaching inter-organizational business processes between Germany and the USA.

Mr. zur Muehlen is a member of the German Computer Society (GI), the IEEE Computer Society and the Association for Information Systems (AIS) where he co-chairs the special interest group on process automation and management (www.sigpam.org). As a member of the Technical Committee of the Workflow Management Coalition Mr. zur Muehlen chairs the WfMC working group "Resource Modeling" and acts as WfMC country chair for Germany.

WfMC Structure and Membership Information

WHAT IS THE WORKFLOW MANAGEMENT COALITION?

The Workflow Management Coalition, founded in August 1993, is a non-profit, international organization of workflow vendors, users, analysts and university/research groups. The Coalition's mission is to promote and develop the use of workflow through the establishment of standards for software terminology, interoperability and connectivity between workflow products. Comprising over 250 members spread throughout the world, the Coalition has quickly become established as the primary standards body for this rapidly expanding software market.

WORKFLOW STANDARDS FRAMEWORK

The Coalition has developed a framework for the establishment of workflow standards. This framework includes five categories of interoperability and communication standards that will allow multiple workflow products to coexist and interoperate within a user's environment. Technical details are included in the white paper entitled, "The Work of the Coalition," available at www.wfmc.org.

Achievements

The initial work of the Coalition focused on publishing the Reference Model and Glossary, defining a common architecture and terminology for the industry. A major milestone was achieved with the publication of the first versions of the Workflow API (WAPI) specification, covering the Workflow Client Application Interface, and the Workflow Interoperability specification. The Audit Data specification was added in 1997, being followed by the Process Definition Import/Export specification.

A further version of WAPI covers Application Invocation APIs, completing the Coalition's initial deliverables across the five interface functions. Further work includes the completion of a common object model with object bindings for IDL and OLE, interoperability extensions for security, and additional interoperability models.

The Coalition has validated the use of its specifications through international demonstrations and prototype implementations. In direct response to growing user demand, live demonstrations of a workflow interoperability scenario have shown how business can successfully exchange and process work across multiple workflow products using the Coalition's specifications.

The Wf-XML specification was promoted to beta status at the WfMC meeting in December 1999, and version 1.1 was released as an official WfMC standard in January 2002

WORKFLOW MANAGEMENT COALITION STRUCTURE

The Coalition is divided into three major committees, the Technical Committee, the External Relations Committee, and the Steering Committee. Small working groups exist within each committee for the purpose of defining workflow terminology, interoperability and connectivity standards, conformance requirements, and for assisting in the communication of this information to the workflow user community.

The Coalition's major committees normally meet three or four times per calendar year for three days at a time, with meetings usually alternating between a North American and a European location. The working group meetings are held during these three days, and as necessary throughout the year.

Coalition membership is open to all interested parties involved in the creation, analysis or deployment of workflow software systems. Membership is governed by a Document of Understanding, which outlines meeting regulations, voting rights etc. All membership material is available at www.wfmc.org.

COALITION WORKING GROUPS

The Coalition has established a number of Working Groups, each working on a particular area of specification. The working groups are loosely structured around the "Workflow Reference Model" which provides the framework for the Coalition's standards program.

The Reference Model identifies the common characteristics of workflow systems and defines five discrete functional interfaces through which a workflow management system interacts with its environment—users, computer tools and applications, other software services, etc. Working groups meet individually, and also under the umbrella of the Technical Committee, which is responsible for overall technical direction and co-ordination.

REFERENCE MODEL

In order to progress the Coalition's objectives, the following working groups have been established:

Working Groups	Objectives
Reference Model & Glossary	Specify a framework for workflow systems, identifying their characteristics, functions and interfaces. Development of standard terminology for workflow systems.
Process Definition Tools Interface (1)	Definition of a standard interface between process definition and modeling tools and the workflow engine(s).
Workflow Client	Definition of APIs for client applications

Application Interface (2)	to request services from the workflow engine to control the progression of processes, activities and work-items.[Activities completed.]
Invoked Application Interface (3)	A standard interface definition of APIs to allow the workflow engine to invoke a variety of applications, through common agent software. [Activities completed.]
Workflow Interoperability Interface (4)	Definition of workflow interoperability models and the corresponding standards to support interworking.
Administration & Monitoring Tools, Interface (5)	Definition of monitoring and control functions. To develop the Coalition's policy on product conformance against its specifications and agree an approach to vendor certification.

WHY YOU SHOULD JOIN

Joining the Workflow Management Coalition gives you the opportunity to influence the creation of the standards for the workflow industry as they are developing. Because the Coalition has members who come from all sides of the industry, it provides a first class forum for the exchange and evolution of ideas.

Being a member of the Coalition will keep you abreast of developments in the rapidly changing and expanding workflow sector. One of the benefits of your membership is to be listed on the WfMC website where you will have access to the 'members only' area where we have work-in-progress and beta documents available to members.

Membership Categories

The Coalition has currently two classes of membership:

1. **Funding general members**, who pay an annual contribution to cover the Coalition annual operating expenses. These members have voting rights in the Coalition's committees, and vote on policy, budget and election of officers.

2. **Guest and academic members** who pay an annual fee that includes meeting attendance. Guest and academic members have no voting rights, although they may participate in the working groups developing standards and interfaces.

Funding Members have the following additional benefits:

1. Participate in the working groups developing standards, interfaces, helping to shape the future of the industry

2. Have increased corporate visibility, enhancing their customers' perception of them as an industry authority

3. Sponsor Coalition workshops/tutorials at major events around the world and host a Coalition meeting

4. Display the Coalition logo on corporate collateral materials and own web site

5. Have a corporate entry with product description in the Workflow Handbook and a free copy of this Handbook

6. Be listed on the Coalition Web site, with an active link to their own Web site

The Steering Committee is currently reviewing the membership structure and may introduce some changes during this year, such as new categories and additional benefits. For the most current information, please visit the WfMC website.

How to Join

Complete the form on the Coalition's website, or contact the Coalition Secretariat, at the address below. All members are required to sign the Coalition's "Document of Understanding" which sets out the contractual rights and obligations between members and the Coalition.

THE SECRETARIAT
Workflow Management Coalition (WfMC)
2436 North Federal Highway #374,
Lighthouse Point, FL 33064, USA
Phone +1 954 782 3376, Fax +1 954 782 6365
email: wfmc@wfmc.org   http://www.wfmc.org

WfMC Officer Positions Year 2002

STEERING COMMITTEE

CHAIRMAN	Jon Pyke	Staffware Plc
VICE CHAIRMAN (Europe)	Jean Faget	W4
VICE CHAIRMAN (Americas)	Ronald Alepin	Fujitsu Software
VICE CHAIRMAN (Asia-Pacific)	Hideshige Hasegawa	Hitachi Ltd

TECHNICAL COMMITTEE

CHAIRMAN	David Hollingsworth	ICL/Fujitsu
VICE CHAIRMAN (Europe)	(open)	
VICE CHAIRMAN (Americas)	Mike Marin	FileNET
VICE CHAIRMAN (Asia-Pacific)	Ryoichi Shibuya	Hitachi Ltd

EXTERNAL RELATIONS COMMITTEE

CHAIRMAN	Charles Plesums	CSC Financial Services
VICE CHAIRMAN (Europe)	Martin Ader	W&GS
VICE CHAIRMAN (Americas)	Betsy Fanning	AIIM International
VICE CHAIRMAN (Asia-Pacific)	Yoshihsa Sadakane	NEC Soft
SECRETARY / TREASURER	Cor Visser	Work Management Europe
INDUSTRY LIAISON CHAIR	Betsy Fanning	AIIM International
USER LIAISON CHAIR	Charles Plesums	CSC Financial Services

WfMC Country Chairs

AUSTRALIA & NEW ZEALAND

Carol Prior
MAESTRO BPE Limited
Tel: +[61] 412.188934
Fax: + [61] 297 733664
caprior@ozemail.com.au

BRAZIL

Alexandre Melo
Officeware Ltda
Tel: +55 11 816 3439
Fax: +55 11 816 3895
officewa@embratel.net.br

CANADA

Susan Bird
Flying in Formation
Tel: +1 416 441 9985
Fax: +1 416 441 0989
sjbird@sympatico.ca

FRANCE

Martin Ader
Workflow & Groupware Strategies
Tel: +33 1 42 38 08 02
Tel: +33 1 42 38 08 02
ader@wngs.com

GERMANY

Michael zur Muehlen
University of Muenster
Tel: +49 251 83 38 080
Tel: +49 251 83 38 109
ismizu@wi.uni-muenster.de

ITALY

Paolo Zocchi
Savvion
Tel: +39 348 9351165
pzocchi@savvion.com

JAPAN

Hideshige Hasegawa
Hitachi Ltd
Tel: +81 45 862 8766
Fax: +81 45 865 9549
hasega_h@soft.hitachi.co.jp

KOREA

Yank Deuk Han
HandySoft Corporation
Tel: +82 2 3474 5410
Fax: +92 2 3479 5583
ydhan@handysoft.co.kr

NORDIC REGION

Thomas Skovsted-Andersen
Staffware A/S
Tel: +45 4582 4096
Fax: +45 4582 4296
tskovsted-andersen@staffware.com

SOUTH AFRICA

Mark Ehmke
Staffware South Africa
+27 11 467 1440
+27 82 600 8059
mehmke@staffware.co.za

THE NETHERLANDS

Fred van Leeuwen
DCE Consultants
Tel: +31 20 44 999 00
Fax: +31 20 44 999 99
leeuwen@dceconsultants.com

UNITED KINGDOM

Jilli Walker
Staffware Plc
Tel: +44 1628 786 800
Fax: +44 1628 786 874
jwalker@staffware.com

UNITED STATES

Carl Hillier
FileNet Corporation
Tel: +1 714 427 5707
Fax: +1 714 662 5076
chillier@filenet.com

Betsy Fanning
AIIM International
Tel: +1 301 755 2682
Fax: +1 301 587 2711
bfanning@aiim.org

WfMC Technical Committee

Working Group Chairs

WG1—Process Definition Interchange Model and APIs

Chair: OPEN

Vice Chair: Robert Shapiro
Email: rshapiro@capevisions.com

WG2/3—Client / Application APIs

Chair: Raul Medina-Mora, ATI

Email: Raul_Medina-Mora@actiontech.com

Vice-Chair: Marc-Thomas Schmidt, IBM
Email: mts@uk.ibm.com

WG4—Workflow Interoperability

Chair: Mike Marin

Email: mmarin@filenet.com

WG5—Administration & Monitoring

Chair: VACANT

WG on OMG

Chair: Marc-Thomas Schmidt, IBM
Email: mts@uk.ibm.com

Conformance WG

Chair: VACANT

WGRM—Reference Model

Chair: Dave Hollingsworth, ICL
Email: david.hollingsworth@icl.com

WG9—Resource Model

Chair: Michael zur Muehlen,
University of Muenster

Email: ismizu@wi.uni-muenster.de

SWAP

Chair: VACANT

WfMC Fellows

The WfMC recognizes individuals who have made sustained and outstanding contributions to WfMC objectives far and above that expected from normal member representation.

WfMC Fellow—Factors:

- To be considered as a candidate, the individual must;
  - Have participated in the WfMC for a period of not less than two years.
  - Be elected by majority vote within the nominating committee.
- Rights of a WfMC Fellow member:
  - Receives guest member level of email support from the Secretariat
  - Pays no fee when attending WfMC meetings
  - May participate in the work of the WfMC (workgroups, etc)

CHAIRMAN EMERITUS: DAVE SHORTER, USA

Robert Allen
United Kingdom

Mike Anderson
United Kingdom

Wolfgang Altenhuber
Austria

Richard Bailey
USA

Emmy Botterman
United Kingdom

Katherine L. Drennan
USA

Michael Grabert
USA

Shirish Hardikar
USA

Paula Helfrich
USA

Nick Kingsbury
United Kingdom

Klaus-Dieter Kreplin
Germany

Dan Matheson
USA

Sue Owen
United Kingdom

Emma Preininger
Austria

Harald Raetzsch
Austria

Michele Rochefort
Germany

Robert Shapiro
USA

David Stirrup
United Kingdom

Keith Swenson
USA

Tetsu Tada
USA

Austin Tate
United Kingdom

Alfons Westgeest
Belgium

Marilyn Wright
USA

Workflow Management Coalition
Membership Directory

The WfMC's membership comprises a wide range of organizations. All members in good standing as of December 2001 are listed here. There are currently three classes of paid membership: *Funding Members, Academic Members* and *Guest Members. Fellows* are elected by the voting members for outstanding contributions to the WfMC and pay no membership fee. They are listed separately under the **Officers and Fellows** Appendix. Each company has only one primary point of contact for purposes of the Membership Directory, but has the right to appoint a representative to the Steering, External Relations and the Technical Committees. Within this Directory, many Funding members have included information about their organization or products.

The current list of members and membership structure can be found on www.wfmc.org.

ACTION TECHNOLOGIES INC.
Guest Member
1301 Marina Village Parkway, Suite 100
Alameda, CA, 94501, United States
Raúl Medina-Mora
Senior Vice President and Chief Scientist
Tel: [1] 1-510-748-1030
Fax: [1] 1-510-769-0596
Raul_Medina-Mora@actiontech.com

ACTIVE TELECOM & TECHNOLOGY LTD
Guest Member
2007 Fortress Tower, 250 King's Road
North Point, Hong Kong, Hong Kong
Benjamin Tse
Tel: [852] (2960) 0032
Fax: [852] (2960) 0033
btse@active.com.hk

ADVISOR TECHNOLOGY SERVICES, LLC
Guest Member
900 West Trade Street, Suite 700
Charlotte, NC, 28202, United States
www.atsllc.com
Buddy Dukes
Director of Technology
Tel: [1] 704-330-2000
Tel: [1] 704-330-2350
buddy.dukes@fmr.com

AGILENT TECHNOLOGIES INC.
Funding Member
101 Parkshore
Folsom, CA, 95630, United States
www.osi.com
Eric Calhoun

Product Manager, Service Delivery
Tel: [1] 916-353-2400
Fax: [1] 916-353-0371
eric_calhoun@agilent.com

AIIM INTERNATIONAL

Funding Member
1100 Wayne Avenue, Suite 1100
Silver Springs, MD, 20910, United States
www.aiim.org
Betsy Fanning
Director, Standards
Tel: [1] 301-755-2682
Fax: [1] 301-587-2711
bfanning@aiim.org
AIIM is the global authority on Enterprise Content Management (ECM). ECM technologies are used to create, capture, customize, deliver, and manage information to support business processes. AIIM promotes the understanding, adoption, and use of Enterprise Content Management technologies through education, networking, marketing, research, standards, and advocacy programs.

ALPHAWEST 6

A business within the Solution 6 Group
Guest Member
Alphawest (Pty) Ltd
Level 21, 456 Kent Street,
Sydney NSW 2000
Suzanne Burmeister
Manager Marketing Communications
Tel: (61 2) 9278 0887
Fax: (61 2) 9283 8776
Suzanne.Burmeister@solution6.com

AP ENGINES

Funding Member
Five Clock Tower Place, Suite 250
Maynard, MA, 01754, United States
www.apengines.com
Roberta Norin
Principal Software Engineer
Tel: [1] 978-823-1052
Fax: [1] 978-461-5012
rnorin@apengines.com

ARMA INTERNATIONAL

Guest Member
4200 Somerset Drive, Suite 215
Prairie Village, KS, 66208, United States
Peter R Hermann
Executive Director & CEO
Tel: [1] 913-341-3808
Fax: [1] 913-341-3742
phermann@arma.org

ARTECH CONSULTORES SRL

Guest Member
Av. 18 de Julio 1645 P4
Montevideo, CP 11200, Uruguay
www.artech.com.uy
Rafael Mon
Product Manager
Tel: [598 2] 402 2082
Fax: [598 2] 408 0313
rafael@artech.com.uy

ASCENTIAL SOFTWARE

Guest Member
300 Lakeside Drive, Suite 2700
Oakland, CA, 94612, United States
www.ascentialsoftware.com
Ilya Klebaner
Senior R&D Manager
Tel: [1] 510-466 4919
Fax: [1] 510-466 4877
klebaner@ascentialsoftware.com

ASKANIA SRL

Guest Member
Via S. Vittore, 34
Milano, 20123, Italy
www.askania.it
Maxime Sottini
Senior Consultant
Tel: [39] 246 1778
Fax: [39] 246 1749
sottini@askania.it

ASPEN GROVE

Guest Member
220 Reservoir Street, Suite 25
Needham, MA, 02494, United States
www.aspengrove.net
Eric Patrick
CEO
Tel: [1] 781-449-9089
Tel: [1] 800-638-5051
info@aspengrove.net

AVAYA

Funding Member
2000 N.Naperville Road, Room 2B-513A,
Holmdel, NJ, 07733-3030, United States
www.avaya.com
James Knight
MTS
Tel: [1] 732-817-5434
Fax: [1] 732-817-5627
jlknight@avaya.com

AXS-One Inc.
Guest Member
301 Route 17 North
Rutherford, NJ, 07070, United States
www.axsone.com
Ken Reich
VP Workflow Technology
Tel: [1] 201-372-6320
Fax: [1] 201-935-6355
kreich@axsone.com

BancTec / Plexus
Funding Member
1310 Chesapeake Terrace
Sunnyvale, CA, 94089, United States
www.banctec.com
Bill O'Neill
Tel: [1] 408-743-4403
Fax: [1] 408-743-4318
Bill.Oneill@banctec.com

BEA Systems
Funding Member
2315 North First St.
San Jose, California, 95131, United States
www.bea.com
David Orchard
External Standards Coordination
Tel: [1] 408-570-8000
Fax: [1] 408-570-8901
david.orchard@bea.com

BOC GmbH
Funding Member
Baeckerstrasse 5/3
Vienna A-1010, Austria
www.boc-eu.com
Dimitris Karagiannis
Tel: [43] 1 513 27 36 0
Fax: [43] 1 513 27 36 5
boc@boc-eu.com
BOC Ltd was established in Dublin in 1998 to introduce high quality BPM products and services into the English speaking markets. Our head office, BOC GmbH, was founded in 1995 as a spin-off from the Department of Knowledge Engineering at the University of Vienna. Today, a network of BOC companies in Vienna, Berlin, Madrid, Athens and Dublin comprise a European organization that supplies specialist BPM products and consultancy advice to a wide variety of clients.

BrainWare Strategies Consulting GmbH
Guest Member
Sonnengasse 15
Grafenstein, Carinthia, A-9131, Austria
www.brainware-at.com

Roel Kragten
Managing Director
Tel: [43] .64.3070865 / +43.4225.300210
Fax: [43] 4225.300299
brainware@brainware-at.com

CACI
Guest Member
14151 Park Meadow Drive
Chantilly, VA, 20151, United States
Joseph De Fee
Sr. VP
Tel: [1] 703-679-3100
jdefee@caci.com

CAMILION SOLUTIONS, INC.
Guest Member
8500 Leslie St., Suite 100
Thornhill, ON, L3T 7M8, Canada
www.camilion.com
Ilan Levy
President & CEO
Tel: [1] 905 709-2224
Fax: [1] 905 709-8842
info@camilion.com

CAPITAL ONE
Guest Member
4801 Cox Road, MS 12035-0118
Glen Allen, VA, 23060, United States
Vaidyanathan Balasubramanian
Analyst/Capital One Financial
Tel: [1] 804-762-7475
Fax: [1] 804-762-7425
coleen.neary@capialone.com

CARNOT AG
Funding Member
Niddastr. 98-102
Frankfurt am Main, DE-60329, Germany
www.carnot.ag
Mark Gille
VP Engineering & CEO
Tel: [49] 69-35102-100
Fax: [49] 69-35102-199
mgille@carnot.ag

CENTRO RICERCHE FIAT
Guest Member
Strada Torino, 50
Orbassano 10043, Italy
www.crf.it
Sanseverino Marialuisa
Electronic Engr

Tel: [39] 0113083953
m.sanseverino@crf.it

CEYONIQ
Funding Member
13900 Lincoln Park Dr
Herndon, Virginia, 20171, United States
www.treev.com
Steve Stoner
Product Manager Marketing
Tel: [1] 703-904-3201
Fax: [1] 703-904-3261
s.stoner@ceyoniq.com

CHANGSONG NETWORK
Guest Member
18 fl. Penthouse, 50 Zhourong road
Chongqing, 400010, China
www.csnetwork.com.cn
Wang Daojun
CEO
Tel: [86] 23-63763366(77,8
Fax: [86] 23-63763636
enjouh@nttdata.co.jp

CHINA SYSTEMS CORPORATION
Guest Member
89 Nanking East Road, 11th floor, Section 5
Taipei, Taiwan, Taiwan
www.chinasystems.com
Joseph Scarpelli
Product Manager
Tel: [886] 2 2766 6289
Fax: [886] 2 2768 5837
Joe_Scarpelli@chinasystems.com

COMPUWARE EUROPE B.V.
Funding Member
Hoogoorddreef 5, P.O. Box 12933
Amsterdam, n/a, 1100 AX, The Netherlands
www.compuware.com
Robert Mol
Product Manager
Tel: [31] (20) 3116222
Fax: [31] (20) 3116200
robert.mol@nl.compuware.com
Compuware Corporation provides software tools and professional services to boost business productivity. Our market-leading products and skilled IT professionals provide business value in distributed, enterprise and e-business environments:
- reduced costs across the application life cycle
- improved quality
- easier integration
- enhanced performance

A multi-billion dollar corporation with more than 12,000 employees, and 110 offices in 47 countries, Compuware can meet the rapidly changing needs of businesses of all sizes. Our 7,500 professional services employees provide real-world, on-site assistance to many of the world's largest companies. Our corporate staff develops, markets and supports more than 130 software products, with more than 70 used in distributed computing environments.

CONCENTUS TECHNOLOGY CORPORATION
Guest Member
5115 Parkcenter Avenue, Suite 150
Dublin, OH 43344, United States
www.concentus-tech.com
Rajiv Ramnath
Tel: [1] 614-792-9993
Fax: [1] 614-792-0998
ramnath@concentus-tech.com

CORPORATE ARCHITECTURE ASSOCIATES
Guest Member
Laan van Weltevreden 18
Rotterdam, 3062 ZP, Rotterdam
Anton A.Soetekouw
CEO
Tel: + 31 10 453 2836
Fax: +31 10 453 2835
aas@attglobal.net

CSC FINANCIAL SERVICES GROUP
Funding Member
200 West Cesar Chavez
Austin TX 78701, United States
www.csc-fs.com
Charles Plesums
Principal Consultant
Tel: [1] 512-275-5554
Fax: [1] 512-275-8116
cplesums@csc.com

Computer Sciences Corporation (CSC) provides a wide range of consulting, outsourcing, and computer system products and services worldwide. The CSC Financial Services Group (www.csc-fs.com) brings special industry expertise to insurance, banking, and other financial institutions. Business Transformation Services is a group within CSC-FSG that offers services in Customer Relationship Management, Work Management, and e-Business.

Workflow is typically implemented with the Automated Work Distributor (AWD) product, integrated with your legacy systems and 3r call center support, document imaging, COLD, fax, OCR/ICR, and other technologies to provide a comprehensive, integrated customer service and fulfillment process. AWD is the leading workflow product in the financial services industry, providing flexible workflow services, quick implementation, and user control. CSC Teams work with the clients to share their years of experience with these products, to help the customers to quickly become self-sufficient. This professional expertise, quality products, and proven techniques provide rapid implementations with an attractive return on investment.

DASSAULT SYSTÈMES
Guest Member
9 quai Marcel Dassault
Suresnes, 92150, France
www.dsweb.com
Cédric Wahl
Research & New Technologies Engineer
Tel: [33] 1 40 99 40 99
Fax: [33] 1 40 99 43 90
owl@ds-fr.com

DCE CONSULTANTS
Guest Member
Wallaardt Sacrestraat 405
1117 BM Schiphol-Oost, The Netherlands
www.dceconsultants.com
Fred van Leeuwen
Managing Consultant
Tel: [31] (20) 449 9900
Fax: [31] (20) 449 9999
Leeuwen@dceconsultants.com

DELPHI GROUP
Guest Member
Ten Post Office Square
Boston, MA, 02109, United States
www.delphigroup.com
Mark E. Tucker
Tel: [1] 617-247-1511
Fax: [1] 617-247-4957
met@delphigroup

DOCUMENTUM INC.
Funding Member
6801 Koll Center Parkway
Pleasanton, CA 94566-7047 United States
www.documentum.com
Darlene Knafelz
Marketing Manager
Tel: 925-600-6800
Fax: 925-600-6850
darlenek@documentum.com
Documentum is the industry's leading enterprise content management provider, automating the production, exchange, and personalization of all types of content, making it easier for the Global 2000 to gain competitive advantage by connecting employees, business partners and customers, worldwide. Built on an Internet-scale, XML-enabled and standards-compliant platform, Documentum products manage Web content, power portals, enable collaborative commerce, and solve regulatory content challenges. Over 300 partners across all major industries, including high tech, pharmaceutical, healthcare, consulting services, government, manufacturing, financial services, automotive, retail, and consumer goods, build and implement specialized applications using Documentum's content management infrastructure.

DRAFTWORLDWIDE

Guest Member
919 3rd Avenue
New York, NY, 10022-3902, United States
www.draftworldwide.com
Sharon Marts
DraftWay Project Director
Tel: [1] 212-546-8000
Fax: [1] 212-546-8100
smarts@draftnet.com

DRAKE CERTIVO

Guest Member
3991 MacArthur Blvd., Suite 300
Newport Beach, CA, 92660, United States
www.certivo.net
Jamie Graham
President
Tel: [1] 949-798-6000
jgraham@certivo.net

DRESDNER BANK AG

Guest Member
Juergen-Ponto-Platz 1
60301 Frankfurt am Main, Germany
www.dresdner-bank.com
Anja Syri
Head of Workflow Management
Tel: [49] 69 263 6279
Fax: [49] 69 263 11166
Anja.Syri@Dresdner-Bank.com

DST SYSTEMS, INC.

Funding Member
330 W. 9th Street, 7th Floor
Kansas City, Missouri 64105 United States
www.dstsystems.com
Tracy Shelby
Systems Officer
Tel: (1) (816) 843-8194
Tel: (1) (816) 843-8197
twshelby@dstsystems.com
The Automated Work Distributor (AWD) from DST Systems is a robust workflow and customer management solution designed to improve productivity, enhance customer loyalty, and reduce operating costs. DST utilizes AWD in our own financial services operations, so we understand what's best for ultimate performance. AWD delivers the latest in business process management, e-commerce, automation, and customer service technology to transcend traditional imaging and workflow. AWD empowers you with the knowledge you need to better manage your business processes and take care of your most valuable asset: your customers.

DUBAI POLICE

Guest Member

Al Etehad Rd.
Dubai, United Arab Emirates
www.dubaipolice.gov.ae/
Khalid A. Alshamsi
System Administrator
Tel: [971] 4 2014105
Fax: [971] 4 2014110
kshamsi@emirates.net.ae

eiStream WMS Inc
Funding Member
296 Concord Road
Billerica, MA, 01821, United States
http://wms.eistream.com
Ken Mei
Director, International Sales Support
Tel: [1] 978-313-7266
Fax: [1] 978-313-7566
ken.mei@eistream.com
eiStream has a long history of innovation in streamlining structured processes for high-volume back-office operations. Today, eiStream continues to help organizations manage data, create new revenue opportunities and take advantage of the benefits of an e-business operating model. We are the leading provider of business process management services with proven experience, award-winning technology, worldwide partnerships and superior customers.

Enterworks, Inc.
Funding Member19886 Ashburn Road
Ashburn, VA, 20147-2358, United States
www.enterworks.com
Steve Nguyen
Executive Director, Product Marketing and Management
Tel: [1] 703 724 4799
steve.nguyen@enterworks.com

eVisory
Guest Member
29 Edgewood Run
Amherst, NH, 03031, United States
www.evisoryconsulting.com
Robert Wilson
Principal
Tel: [1] 804-342-7400
rob.wilson@evisoryconsulting.com

Fabasoft R&D Software GmbH & Co
Guest Member
Karl-Leitl-str. 1
A-4040 Linz/Puchenau, Germany
Leopold Bauernfeind
Tel: [49] 811 600 510
Fax: [49] 49 93540
Leopold.Bauernfeind@fabasoft.com

FILENET CORPORATION

Funding Member
3565 Harbor Blvd.
Costa Mesa, CA, 92626, United States
Carl Hillier
Product Manager, Business Process Management Technologies
Tel: [1] 714 327 5707
Fax: [1] 714-327-3490
chillier@filenet.com
FileNET Corporation (NASDAQ: FILE) provides The Substance Behind eBusiness by delivering Business Process Management software solutions. FileNET enables organizations around the globe to increase productivity, customer satisfaction and revenue by linking customers, partners and employees through efficient and flexible eBusiness processes. Headquartered in Costa Mesa, Calif., the company markets its innovative solutions in more than 90 countries through its own global sales, professional services and support organizations, as well as via its Value-NET(r) Partner network of resellers, system integrators and application developers.

FISERV SOLUTIONS LTD

Funding Member
2601 Technology Drive
Orlando, FL, 32804, United States
David Mitchell
Tel: [1] 407-513-5391
Fax: [1] 407-523-5332
david.mitchell@cbs.fiserv.com

FLYING IN FORMATION

Guest Member
16 Firthway Court
Toronto, ON, M3B 2K2, Canada
Susan Bird
President
Tel: [1] 416-441-9985
Fax: [1] 416-441-0989
sjbird@sympatico.ca

FRAMEWORK, INC.

Funding Member
303 South Broadway
Tarrytown, NY, 10591, United States
www.lendware.com
Jim Meyers
Chief Technology Officer
Tel: [1] 914-631-2322
Fax: [1] 914-631-3121
james.meyers@lendware.com

FRAUNHOFER-INSTITUT FÜR ARBEITSWIRTSCHAFT UND ORG

Guest Member
Nobelstrasse 12
D-705669 Stuttgart, Germany
www.iao.fhg.de

Christoph Altenhofen
Tel: [49] 7 119 70-01
Fax: [49] 7 119 70-22-99
Christoph.Altenhofen@iao.fhg.de

GENAISSANCE PHARMACEUTICALS

Guest Member
5 Science Park
New Haven, CT, 06511, United States
www.genaissance.com
Ted Kalbfleisch
Associate Director, Process Development
Tel: [1] 203-773-1450
Fax: [1] 203-562-9377
t.kalbfleisch@genaissance.com

FUJITSU SOFTWARE CORPORATION

Funding Member
3055 Orchard Drive
San Jose, CA, 95134-2022, United States
www.i-flow.com
Ronald Alepin
General Manager
Tel: [1] 408-456-7963
Fax: [1] 408-456-7821
ralepin@fs.fujitsu.com
Fujitsu Software Corporation, based in San Jose, California, is a wholly owned subsidiary of Fujitsu Limited. Fujitsu Software Corporation leverages Fujitsu's international scope and expertise to develop and deliver comprehensive technology solutions. The company's products include INTERSTAGE(tm), an e-Business infrastructure platform that includes the INTERSTAGE Application Server and i-Flow(tm); and Fujitsu COBOL. i-Flow streamlines, automates and tracks business processes to help enterprises become more productive, responsive, and profitable. Leveraging such universal standards as J2EE and XML, i-Flow delivers business process automation solutions that are easy to develop, deploy, integrate and manage. i-Flow has a flexible architecture that seamlessly integrates into existing environments. This allows you to leverage your IT infrastructure investments and allows you to easily adapt to future technologies.

GIGA INFORMATION GROUP

Guest Member
One Longwater Circle
Norwell, MA, 02061, United States
www.gigaweb.com
Connie Moore
Vice President
Tel: [1] 781-982-9500
Fax: [1] 781-878-6650
cmoore@gigaweb.com

HANDYSOFT CORPORATION

Funding Member

United States

1952 Gallows Road
Suite 200
Vienna, VA 22182
Tel: 1.800.753.9343
info@handysoft.com

South Korea
1708-2, Seocho-Dong, Seocho-Ku
Seoul 137-070, South Korea
Yang Deuk Han
Executive Vice President
Tel: [82] (2) 3479-5410
Tel: [82] (2) 3479-5593
ydhan@handysoft.co.kr

HandySoft (www.handysoft.com) is a global software company offering open, scalable, business process and workflow management solutions. With over 10 years of proven experience and profitable business growth, HandySoft is the dominant market leader for e-business solutions. We develop cutting edge process and forms automation systems to meet the unique requirements of companies and organizations everywhere. HandySoft's Web-enabled, enterprise-level workflow engine, BizFlow®, meets industry demands for a collaborative workflow product that is accessible to anyone, anywhere, at anytime. By defining, managing, automating and streamlining best practices, HandySoft's enterprise-level workflow solution, BizFlow® empowers companies to transform value to their partners, vendors, customers and organization team members. Our software integrates with any legacy database, application or data so that clients can maximize their current IT infrastructure investments. HandySoft currently has over 380 client sites worldwide, and is rapidly expanding their business. In a world in which the only constant is change, BizFlow keeps you up-to-speed, with its full package of advantages including quick, off-the-self implementation, security, ease-of-use and adaptability. BizFlow®...Work By It.

HITACHI LTD. SOFTWARE DIVISION

Funding Member
5030 Totsuka-Chou
Titsuka-Ku, Yokohama, 2448555, Japan
Hideshige Hasegawa
Senior Manager Marketing
Tel: [81] 45 862 8766
Fax: [81] 45 865 9549
hasega_h@itg.hitachi.co.jp

Hitachi offers a wide variety of integrated products for groupware systems such as e-mail and document information systems. One of these products is Hitachi's workflow system Groupmax. The powerful engine of Groupmax effectively automates office business such as the circulation of documents. Groupmax provides the following powerful tools and facilities: A visual status monitor shows the route taken and present location of each document in a business process definition Cooperative facilities between servers provide support for a wide area workflow system Groupmax supports application processes such as consultation, send back, withdrawal, activation, transfer, stop and cancellation. Groupmax is rated to be the most suitable workflow system for typical business processes in Japan and has provided a high level of customer satisfaction. Groupmax workflow supports the WfMC Interface 4.

HONEYWELL LABORATORIES—SOFTWARE SOLUTIONS LAB

Funding Member
151/1, Doraisanipalya, Bannerghatta Road,
Bangalore, Karnataka, India 560076.
www.hiso.honeywell.com/rtg &
www.honeywell.com/ssl
Thirumaran Ekambaram
Software Architect
Tel: +91-80-6585751
Fax: +91-80-6584750
Thirumaran.Ekambaram@honeywell.com

Software Solutions Lab (SSL) is part of Honeywell Laboratories, with operations at Bangalore, Minneapolis and Phoenix. We are a global software center for Honeywell's businesses, providing value through world-class software research, technology development, product development/support, digitization support and consultation. inetFlow is a dynamic Collaborative Workflow solution that leverages Honeywell's expertise in control and data management. inetFlow is built using open standards such as EJB and XML. It is aimed at enterprises, supporting business process integration and custom application development requiring workflow. It provides a bunch of server components and client utilities to rapidly build workflow-based applications. It can also be used for integrating one or more applications in an enterprise often termed as Enterprise Application Integration (EAI) or used in integration across enterprise, Business Process Integration (BPI). Some of the applications built using inetFlow include: Flight Maintenance Applications, Defect Tracking, Action Item Tracking, Requirements Tracking, Self help-Knowledge Management System, General call handling, Warranty Returns Tracking, Test Defect Tracking, Audit Tracking, Risk Management, Customer Relationship Management.

IBM CORPORATION

Funding Member
Mail Point 206, Hursley Park
Winchester Hampshire, SO21 2JN, United Kingdom
www.software.ibm.com/ts/mqseries/workflow
Klaus Deinhart
Worldwide Brand Market Management
Tel: [44] (196) 281-6788
Fax: [44] (196) 281-8338
dei@de.ibm.com

ICL/FUJITSU

Funding Member
ICL Pathway, Forest Road
Feltham
Middlesex, TW13 7EJ, United Kingdom
www.icl.com
Dave Hollingsworth
Systems Architect
Tel: [44] (181 730 4112
Fax: [44] (181) 730-4161
david.hollingsworth@icl.com

IDENTITECH INC.

Funding Member

780 South Apollo Blvd
Melbourne, FL, 32901, United States
Madeline Pagan
Tel: [1] 321-951-9503
Fax: [1] 321-951-9505
Madeline.pagan@identitech.com

IDS Scheer AG

Funding Member
Altenkesseler Strasse 20
Saarbrücken, 66115, Germany
Dieter Tramer
Tel: [49] 681 99 21 876
Fax: [49] 681 99 21801
d.tramer@ids-scheer.de
IDS Scheer: Solutions for Business Process Improvement. Around 1,500 employees at IDS Scheer advise companies in all sectors as to how they can configure their business processes in a more efficient, cost-effective and thus more competitive way. The software solutions ARIS and Process Performance Manager developed by IDS Scheer are world-wide brand leaders. IDS Scheer software is used for the analysis and improvement of business processes. The Fraunhofer Institute evaluates ARIS as the best software in this market. Analysts from the U.S. Gartner Group see IDS Scheer as the most innovative company world-wide for business process management. Indeed, IDS Scheer is internationally unique in offering one-stop solutions in respect of both consultancy and software for business process management. Apart from business process engineering, the primary activities of IDS Scheer also embrace supply chain management and customer relationship management.

ILOG, Inc.

Funding Member
1080 Linda Vista Avenue
Mountain View, CA, 94043, United States
www.ilog.com
Jean Pommier
Vice President
Tel: [1] 650-567-8000
Fax: [1] 650-567-8001
wfmc@ilog.com

IMC (Information Management Consultants, Inc.)

Guest Member
7915 Westpark Drive
McLean, Virginia, 22102, United States
www.imc.com
Suresh Shenoy
EVP
Tel: [1] (703) 394-9605
Fax: [1] (703) 893-3489
marketing@imc.com

INDUCTIS

Guest Member
392 Springfield Avenue

Summit, NJ, 07901, United States
www.inductis.com
Sudip Chakraborty
Vice President, Technology
Tel: [1] 908-598-9250
Fax: [1] 908-598-9259
sudip@inductis.com

INFOBAHN LIMITED

Guest Member
5th floor Business Plaza, 33 Gazdar Bandh Road
Santacruz West
Mumbai, Maharashtra, 400054, India
www.infobahnlimited.com
Govind Jagtiani
chief technical officer
Tel: (91)2266 03055
Fax: [91] 2266 08961
govindj@infobahnlimited.com

INTEGIC CORPORATION.

Guest Member
14585 Avion Parkway
Chantilly, Virginia, 20151, United States
www.integic.com
Scott Grzybowski
Senior Technology Consultant
Tel: [1] 703-222-4954
Fax: [1] 703-222-2840
scott.grzybowski@integic.com

IPI CORP

Funding Member
18 E 41st St, 18th Floor
New York, NY, 10017, United States
www.ipicorp.com
Seth Osher
CSA
Tel: [1] 212-213-5056
Fax: [1] 212-213-5352
seth@ipicorp.com

IVYTEAM

Guest Member
Alpenstrasse 9, P.O. Box
Zug, 6304, Switzerland
www.ivyteam.com
Heinz Lienhard
Chairman & Co-Founder
Tel: [41] 71 0 80 20
Fax: [41] 71 0 80 60
heinz.lienhard@ivyteam.ch

KABIRA TECHNOLOGIES

Guest Member
1 Mcinnis Parkway
San Rafael, CA, 94903, United States
Conrad Bock
Tel: [1] 415) 446-5052
Fax: [1] (415) 446-5199
conrad.bock@kabira.com
Kabira provides infrastructure software for the delivery of Next-Generation Services made possible by the convergence of telecommunication networks, the Internet, and traditional enterprise networks. Example Next Generation Services include: delivery of multimedia content and personal services to wireless devices, delivering online stock trading services ranging from quote information to transaction capabilities to customer alerts via the web or wireless communications, and so on.

KAINOS LIMITED

Guest Member
Kainos House, 4-6 Upper Crescent
Belfast, Northern Ireland, BT7 1NT, United Kingdom
www.kainos.com
Graham Lyttle
System Architect
Tel: [44] (28) 9057-1100
Fax: [44] (28) 9057-1101
g.lyttle@kainos.com

KAISHA-TEC

Funding Member
c/o G. Long, Kaisha-Tec,
Mitaka Sangyo Plaza Annex,
3-32-3 Shimo Renjaku,
Mitaka-shi, Tokyo 181-0013, Japan
Tel: [81] 422 47 2397
Tel: [81] 422 47 2396
glong@kaisha-tec.com
ActiveModeler/ActiveFlow is a unique workflow combination product based on the No.1 selling process modeler in Japan. Process Visualization is used to create optimized workflows and to speed well-defined development. ActiveFlow provides industrial strength workflow in a Microsoft-centric platform again with some unique features. The workflow suits well the demanding Japanese workflow market including back-office and e-commerce integration.

KANAGAWA INSTITUTE OF TECHNOLOGY

Academic Member
Dept of Information & Computer Sciences, 1030 Shimo-Ogino
Atsugi-Shi, Kanagawa, 243-0292, Japan
www.kanagawa-it.ac.jp
Haruo Hayami
Tel: [81] (462) 9132-46
Fax: [81] (462) 4284-90
hayami@ic.kanagawa-it.ac.jp

KPMG CONSULTING INC
Guest Member
100 Matsonford Road, Suite 500
Radnor, PA, 19087, U.S.A.
Terry Kaminski
Senior Manager
Tel: [1] 610-517-3770
Fax: [1] 610-263-8008
tkaminski@kpmg.com

LINCOLN REINSURANCE
Guest Member
1700 Magnavox Way
Fort Wayne, IN, 46801, United States
www.lincolnre.com/Stephen J. Harris
Lead Consultant
Tel: [1] 219-455-2630
Fax: [1] 219-455-6860
sjharris@lnc.com

LIQUIDLOGIC LTD
Guest Member
Thorpe Park, 1200 Century Way
Leeds, Yorkshire, LS15 8ZA, United Kingdom
www.liquidlogic.co.uk
Ted Brierley
Managing Director
Tel: [44] 113 251 5105
Fax: [44] 113 251 5100
enquire@liquidlogic.co.uk

MAAG HOLDINGS LTD.
Guest Member
Hardstrasse 219
Zürich, ZH, 8005, Switzerland
www.maagholding.ch
Oliver Goh
CTO
Tel: [41] 1278 7662
Fax: [41] 1271 9204
oliver@maagholding.ch

MAESTRO BPE PTY LTD
Guest Member
17 Bingara Drive
Sandy Point, NSW, 2171, Australia
Carol Prior
President
Tel: [61] 412.188934
Fax: [61] 297733664
caprior@ozemail.com.au

MC2
Guest Member

4 Chemin de Malacher, Zirst 4401
Meylan Cedex, 38944, France
Francois Olleon
Tel: [33] 4 76 05 50 34
Fax: [33] 4 76 04 50 01
francois.olleon@mc2.fr

MCALLISTER MANAGEMENT INTERNATIONAL

Guest Member
49 Jalan Pemimpin, #05-11 APS Building
Singapore 577203, Singapore
Chris Seow
Software Manager
Tel: [65] (96) 541-860
Fax: [65] 3567279
chris@mcminet.com

MEDIASURFACE PLC

Funding Member
The Tannery, 55 Bermondsey Street
London, SE1 3XG, United Kingdom
www.mediasurface.com
Jonathan Ewing
Principle Research Engineer
Tel: [44] 20 7939 7100
Fax: [44) 20 7939 7199
research@mediasurface.com

MEGA INTERNATIONAL

Funding Member
10 Boulevard du Montparnasse
Paris 75015, France
www.mega.com
Jacques Mercey
Vice President Development
Tel: [33] 142 75 40 21
Fax: [33] 142 75 40 95
jmercey@mega.com
MEGA International is a leading provider of Modeling tools and associated consultancy services. The company operates in the areas of Business, Process, Component & Object and Data modeling, as well as modeling for EAI/eBusines platforms. MEGA International's MEGA Suite integrated modeling product offers a
component based approach to modeling, with each component being available
separately or bundled in combinations to suit the user.

MENTISYS, INC.

Guest Member
1545 Peachtree Street, Suite 340
Atlanta, GA, 30309, United States
Wendy Davidson
Operations Manager
Tel: [1] 404-888-1060
Fax: [1] 404-888-1061
wendy.davidson@mentisys.com

MERCATOR SOFTWARE, INC.
Guest Member
45 Danbury Road
Wilton, CT, 06897-0840, United States
www.mercator.com
David Smiley
Director of Standards
Tel: [1] 203.761.8600
Fax: [1] 203.762.9677
dsmiley@mercator.com

METASTORM INC
Funding Member
836 Ritchie Highway, Suite 16
Severna Park, MD, 21146, United States
www.metastorm.com
Neil Hudspeth
Director of Product Management
Tel: [44] 208 971 1500
Fax: [44] 208 971 1501
NHudspeth@metastorm.com
Metastorm is the leading supplier of BPM software to the government and commercial markets. Its flagship product, Metastorm e-work, allows organizations to combine people and information systems via flexible, automated processes. Staff are empowered to do more in less time, and with fewer resources, so they can replace time spent on administrative, paper-based tasks in favor of higher-value activities. Headquartered in the U.S. with offices in Europe, Metastorm has more than 300 customers. These include national, regional and local governments, and commercial entities with needs for automating human resource, financial and mission critical processes.

MILESTONE GROUP
Guest Member
Level 7, 9 Hunter Street
Sydney, NSW, 2000, Australia
www.milestonegroup.com.au
Mike Kossenberg
Director - Advisory & Execution
Tel: [61] 28-2242-600
Fax: [61] 28-2242-601
mike.kossenberg@milestonegroup.com.aur

MINDWRAP INC
Guest Member
664H Zachary Taylor Highway
Flint Hill, VA, 22627, United States
James A. Small
Tel: [1] 540-675-3015
Fax: [1] 540-675-3130
Small@mindwrap.com

N-TIER TECHNOLOGY LLP
Guest Member
14 Greenway Road

Windham, NH, 03087, United States
Bob Smith
Tel: [1] 603-432-3404
Fax: [1] 603-432-3404
bsmith@ntiertech.com

NEC CORPORATION

Funding Member
Daito Tamachi Building 14-22, Shibaura, 4-Chome
Minato-Ku
Tokyo 108, Japan
Takashi Kojo
Vice President
Tel: [81] 978-742-8032
Fax: [81] (334) 5628-88
tkojo@nectech.com

NEC SOFT LTD.

Funding Member
1-18-6, Shinkiba, Koto-ku
Tokyo, 136-8608, JAPAN
Yoshihsa Sadakane
Marketing & Product Planning Manager
Tel: +81-3-5569-3399
sadakane@mxw.nes.nec.co.jp

NETWORK PROGRAMS

Guest MemberB-1-C Sector 10
Noida, UP, 201301, India
www.networkprograms.com
Sanjay Ambardar
Team Leader/Software Engineer
Tel: [91] 102 4536622
Fax: [91] 102 4536625
sambardar@npi.stpn.soft.net

NEW WORLD CYBERBASE SOLUTIONS, LTD.

Guest Member
3/F Jin Zhong Building, 680 Zhad Jia Bang Road
Shanghai, 200031, China
Craman Ip
General Manager
Tel: [86] (2) 164-668238
Fax: [86] (2) 164-335139
Jetcoip@public.sta.net.cn

PEACE SYSTEMS INTEGRATION CO., INC.

Guest Member
10F, Number 566, Chung-Cheng Road
Hsintien City, Taipei, Taiwan
www.peace.com.tw
Peter Pan
Tel: [886] (22) 219 6555
Fax: [886] (22) 219 6550

peterpan@peace.com.tw

PEGASYSTEMS INC.
Funding Member
101 Main Street
Cambridge, MA, 02142-1590, United States
www.pegasystems.com
Bill Byrn
Tel: [1] 617-374-9600
Fax: [1] 617-374-9620
byrnb@pegasystems.com
Since 1983, Pegasystems (NASDAQ: PEGA) has been a pioneer in rules technology and is now a leader in the industry. Business rules are the practices, processes and procedures that define how a company does business and are an important asset that differentiates enterprises in the marketplace. Pegasystems' patented rules technology allows companies to aggregate their diverse business practices and lets business managers rapidly implement change across the enterprise and over the Web. Leading companies in financial services, healthcare and communications turn to Pegasystems' rules-driven process automation technology and multi-channel service and support solutions to enhance their Customer Relationship Management (CRM) strategies. Headquartered in Cambridge, Mass., Pegasystems has regional offices in North America, Europe and the Pacific Rim.

PIRONET NDH AG
Guest Member
Josef-Lammerting-Allee 14—18
Cologne, 50933, Germany
Thomas Grota
VP Product Development
Tel: [49] 0221-770-0
Tel: [49] 0221-770-1005
einkauf@pironet-ndh.com

PM JCALS
Funding Member
SFAE-PS-CAL, Myer Center
Fort Monmouth, NJ, 07703-5626, United States
https://www.jcals.army.mil/jcals/index.cfm
Charles Peck
Tel: [1] 732-427-6256
Fax: [1] 732-532-3482
Charles.Peck@mail1.monmouth.army.mil
Joint Computer-aided Acquisition and Logistic Support (JCALS) system is a distributed computing environment that serves the U.S. Department of Defense Military Services and Defense Agencies: Army, Air Force, Navy, Marine Corps and the Defense Logistics Agency (DLA). JCALS was an outgrowth of the Army CALS, or A-CALS, initiative of the early 1990s that developed an innovative, distributed computing solution to link together legacy data and applications in a single virtual enterprise. One key feature of A-CALS was the design and development of an enterprise-wide workflow product and engine prior to their introduction in the private sector. This pioneering workflow capability initially focused on logistics data and applications but was later discovered to be key to automating any business process. Later, the A-CALS solution was recognized by senior DOD man-

agement as being applicable to the Department's overall automation solution. Army CALS was converted into a Joint Project and began introducing workflow capabilities throughout DOD. Today, JCALS is an active member of the WfMC (since 1995), contributing its pioneering workflow and XML work experience to workflow community through the standards committee work of the WfMC. The current version of the Wf-XML , the XML-based workflow interoperability standard, is on the WfMC web page and represents a collaborative effort between Project Manager (PM)JCALS, Computer Sciences Corporation (CSC) and the members of the WfMC.

PRICEWATERHOUSECOOPERS LLP
Guest Member
12902 Federal Systems Park Drive
Fairfax, VA, 22033, United States
Harrison Schultz
Tel: [1] 703-633-4686
Fax: [1] 703-322-6686
harrison.schultz@us.pwcglobal.com

PRICEWATERHOUSECOOPERS UK
Guest Member
1 Embankment Place
London, WC2N 6NN, United Kingdom
Adrian Samuels
Principal Consultant
Tel: [44] (207) 804-5000
Fax: [44] (207) 213-2442
adrian.samuels@pwcglobal.com

PROCTER & GAMBLE
Guest Member
Temselaan 100
Strombeek Bever, 1853, BELGIUM
www.pg.com
Paolo Cinelli
Corporate Databases Architecture
Tel: 32-2-456-6301
Fax: 32-2-456-2155
cinelli.p@pg.com

PROMATIS INFORMATIK
Guest Member1
Badhausweg 5
76307 Karlsbad, Germany
www.promatis.com
Thomas Karle
Senior VP Process Implementation
Tel: [49] 7248-926-0
Fax: [49] 49-7248-926-1199
thomas.karle@promatis.de

QUALIWARE
Guest Member
P.O. Box 60, Skovlytoften 9 B

DK-2840 Holte, Denmark
Kuno Brodersen
CEO
Tel: [45] 47 07 00
Fax: [45] 47 07 70
kuno@qualiware.com

ROBERT E. NOLAN COMPANY, INC.

Guest Member
17746 Preston Road
Dallas, TX, 75252, United States
Greg Robinson
Sr. Consultant
Tel: [1] 972-248-3727
Fax: [1] 972-733-1427
greg_robinson@renolan.com

SAP AG

Funding Member
Neurottstrasse 16
69190 Walldorf, Germany
www.sap.com
Rainer Weber
Tel: [49] 6227 744 844
Fax: [49] 6227 741 775
rainer.weber@sap.com

As the market leader of inter-enterprise software solutions, SAP (Systems, Applications, and Products in Data Processing) is leveraging its strength in industry-focused business software and the world's largest enterprise software customer base to deliver mySAP.com. mySAP.com provides an open collaborative business environment of personalized solutions on demand. This enables companies of all sizes and industries to fully engage their employees, customers and partners to capitalize upon the new Internet economy. mySAP.com allows people to harness the power of the Internet to work smarter, better and faster by optimizing supply chains, managing strategic relationships, reducing time to market, sharing virtual information, and increasing productivity and shareholder value.

SBB SOFTWARE GMBH

Guest Member
Haupstrasse 3C
Wolfsgraben, A-3012, Austria
www.UC4.com
Andras Pogany
Tel: [43] 2233 7788 0
Fax: [43] 2233 7788 99
andras.pogany@sbb.at

SCC SOFT COMPUTER

Guest Member
34350 US Highway 19 North
Palm Harbor, Florida, 34684-2149, United States
www.softcomputer.com
Kim Allen
Product Manager

Tel: [1] 727 789-0100
Fax: [1] 727 789-0110
kima@softcomputer.com

SeeBeyond Technology Corporation

Guest Member
404 E. Huntington Drive
Monrovia, CA, 91016, USA
www.seebeyond.com
Stephen White
Director—Standards
Tel: [1] (626) 471-6000
Fax: [1] (626) 471-6021
swhite@seebeyond.com

SEFIRA spol. s r. o.

Guest Member
Pocernicka 96
Praha 10, 108 00, Czech Republic
www.sefira.cz
Daniel Albrecht
Sr. Analyst
Tel: [420] (2)-67 02 17 00
Fax: [420] (2)-67 02 16 99
albrecht@sefira.cz

SharpSource

Guest Member
1240 Central Blvd., Suite A
Brentwood, CA, 94513, United States
www.sharpsource.com
Michael Sharps
President/CEO
Tel: [1] 925-240-8515
Fax: [1] 925-240-8516
michael.sharps@sharpsource.com

Shell Services International

Guest Member
1500 Old Spanish Trail, Room 7A36
Houston, TX, 77054, United States
John P. Buckley
Tel: [1] 713-245-3345
Fax: [1] 713-245-3107
jpbuckley@shellus.com

Siebel Systems

Guest Member
2207 Bridgepointe Parkway,
San Mateo, CA, 94404-5009, United States
Kaushik Roy
Tel: [1] 650-295-5000
Fax: [1] 650-295-5111
kroy@siebel.com

SIEMENS MEDICAL SOLUTIONS HEALTH SERVICES CORPORATION
Guest Member
51 Valley Stream Parkway
Malvern, PA, 19355, United States
www.smed.com
Jan DeHaan
Product Manager
Tel: [1] 610-219-3594
Fax: [1] 610-219-3124
jan.dehaan@smed.com

SIEMENS ENTERPRISE NETWORKS, INC.
Guest Member
1700 Technology Drive MS 171
San Jose, CA. 95110, United States
www.icn.siemens.com/enterprise
Tom Miller
Principal Engineer
Tel: [1] (408) 492-2343
tom.miller@icn.siemens.com

SOFTWARE TRADING VERTRIEBS-GMBH
Friedrichstrasse 23
A-2500 Baden, Austria
www.swt.at
Thomas Kutny
Tel: +43 2252 21741-0
Fax: +43 2252 21741-30
sales@swt.at

SOLCOM, INC.
Guest Member
617 W. Algonquin Street, Suite 201
Souix Falls, SD, 57104, United States
www.solcominc.com
Marv Addink
CEO
Tel: [1] 605-357-8212
Fax: [1] 605-335-7366
marv@solcominc.com

SPATIAL DYNAMICS CORPORATION
Guest Member
3195 Diablo Shadow Drive
Walnut Creek, CA, 94598, United States
www.spatialdynamicscorp.com
John Steensen
President & CEO
Tel: [1] 925-413-6379
jsteensen@spatialdynamicscorp.com

STAFFWARE PLC
Funding Member
3 The Switchback, Gardener Road

Maidenhead, Berkshire, SL6 7RJ, United Kingdom
Jon Pyke
CTO
Tel: [44] (162) 878-6800
Fax: [44] (162) 878-1654
jpyke@staffware.com
Staffware is a founder of the process workflow industry. Independent studies such as Gartner and Strategy Partners confirm Staffware's leadership position. Staffware is one of the top 50 software companies in Europe, and operates from 25 offices in all the major business regions of the world. In addition, its extensive partner channel covers all the countries where there is a demand for business process automation today. Over many years, Staffware has helped major organizations transform their business processes. Today, there are approximately a million licensed users of Staffware around the globe, in 5000 customer sites. These are across all main industry sectors including retail banking; wholesale banking; insurance; telecommunications; utilities; government—both federal/central and state/local; transport; professional consulting organizations and general commercial.

STANDARD LIFE ASSURANCE COMPANY LTD
Guest Member
19a Canning Street
Edinburgh, EH3 8EG, United Kingdom
John Sharp
Tel: [44] (131) 245-1014
Fax: [44] (131) 245-1020
john_sharp@standardlife.com

SUN MICROSYSTEMS
Funding Member
1800 Harrison Street, 24th Floor
Oakland, CA, 94612, United States
www.sun.com
Ken MacKenzie
Software Development Director, Forte Tools
Tel: [1] 510-869-2105
Fax: [1] 510-834-1508
ken.mackenzie@sun.com
Since its inception in 1982, a singular vision—The Network Is The Computer[tm] —has propelled Sun Microsystems, Inc. (Nasdaq: SUNW), to its position as a leading provider of industrial-strength servers, workstations, software and services that power the Internet and allow companies worldwide to dot-com their businesses. With $14.2 billion in annual revenues, Sun can be found in more than 170 countries. Forte Fusion is Sun's solution for Enterprise Application Integration (EAI). Fusion is a suite of integration tools that includes a process automation engine, reliable messaging, data transformation, and packaged application adapters. Fusion is built around industry standards such as XML and Java. For more information, see www.sun.com/forte/fusion.

TELCORDIA TECHNOLOGIES
Funding Member
445 South Street
Morristown, NJ, 07960-6438, United States
www.telcordia.com

Josephine Micallef
Chief Scientist
Tel: [1] 973-829-4227
Fax: [1] 973 829-5981
micallef@research.telcordia.com
Telcordia Technologies, Inc., an SAIC company, is one of the world's largest providers of operations support systems, network software and consulting and engineering services to the telecommunications industry. The Telcordia software organization, comprises Operations Support Systems and Service and Business Management Systems, has been ISO 9001-certified and has been assessed at Level 5, the highest level of the Capability Maturity Model®, an industry standard for measuring software development processes that was developed by the Software Engineering Institute at Carnegie Mellon University. A leader in the development of Next Generation Network technologies, Telcordia employs more than 6,500 professionals and has revenues of more than $1.5 billion. Telcordia (www.telcordia.com) is headquartered in Morristown, New Jersey, US with offices throughout the United States, Europe, Central and South America and Asia Pacific.

TELSTRA
Guest Member
Office of the Chief Architect, Level 32, 242 Exhibition St.
Melbourne, VIC, 3000, Australia
Greg Fidler
Chief Architect
Tel: [61] 39-6344-775
Fax: [61] 39-6621-604
greg.fidler@team.telstra.com

THE KEN ORR INSTITUTE
Guest Member
5883 SW 29th Str.
Topeka, KS, 66614, United States
www.kenorrinst.com
Randy Hester
Director of Advance Technology
Tel: [1] 785-228-1200
Fax: [1] 785-228-1201
hester@kenorrinst.com

THE TECHNICAL RESOURCE CONNECTION
Guest Member
12320 Racetrack Rd.
Tampa, FL, 33626, United States
www.trcinc.com
Mary Ellen Moore
Marketing Manager
Tel: [1] 813-891-6084
Fax: [1] 813-891-6138
memoore@trcinc.com

THE VANGUARD GROUP
Guest Member
P O Box 2600

Valley Forge, PA, 19482, U.S.A.
Edward Isaack
PM Workflow Services
Tel: [1] 610-503-1518
Fax: [1] 610-669-1715
Ed.Isaack@vanguard.com

TIBCO SOFTWARE, INC.
Funding Member
4 Cambridge Center, 4th Floor
Cambridge, MA, 02142, United States
John Appleton
Product Manager
Tel: [1] 617 499 4491
Fax: [1] 617-499-4409
appleton@tibco.com
TIB/InConcert(tm), in the TIBCO ActiveEnterprise line of products, is a real-time enterprise workflow engine that graphically models and proactively monitors the critical processes of today's most competitive business environments. TIB/InConcert provides the unique ability to dynamically adjust complex processes on-the-fly (any task, at any time). This incredible flexibility allows users to react faster to changing business conditions and to provide higher qualities of service and customer satisfaction. TIB/InConcert's patented Design by Discovery(r) enables businesses to immediately gain the advantages of a managed workflow process, even if they have not fully defined the entire process.

TIMOGEN SYSTEMS INC.
Guest Member
1937 Landings Drive
Mountain View, CA, 94043, United States
Yeh-Heng Sheng
CTO
Tel: [1] 650-903-9888
Fax: [1] 650-903-9327
sheng@timogen.com

TOGETHER TEAMLÖSUNGEN GMBH
Guest Member
Elmargasse 2-4
Wien, A-1191, Austria
Manfred Schwoiger
Geschaftsfuhrer
Tel: (43) (1) 31334 122
Fax: (43) (1) 31334 8960
m.schwoiger@together.at

TOSHIBA CORPORATION
Funding Member
1-1 Shibaura 1-Chome
Minato-Ku, Tokyo, 105-8001, Japan
Yosuke Terashita
Tel: [81] 3 3457 8397
Fax: [81] 3 5444 9292
yosuke.terashita@toshiba.co.jp

TOWER TECHNOLOGY, INC.
Guest Member
800 Boylston St.
Boston, MA 02199, United States
www.towertech.com
Diane Marsili
V.P. of Marketing
Tel: 1 617-236-5500
Fax: 1 617-236-1113
dmarsili@towertech.com

TRIDION B.V.
Guest Member
Burgemeester Strawanweg 101
1101 AA Amsterdam, The Netherlands
Otto de Graaf
Product Manager
Tel: [31] (20) 2020055
Fax: [31] (20) 2010501
otto.degraaf@tridion.com

UBS WARBURG
Guest Member
100 Liverpool Street
London, EC2M 2RH, United Kingdom
David C. Morris
Architect
Tel: [44] 20 7567 4409
Fax: [44] 20 7567 6867
david.morris@ubsw.com

UNISYS CORPORATION
Guest Member
One Unisys Way, MS-B121
Blue Bell, PA, 19424-0001, United States
Gregory T. Barnowsky
Sr. Architect & specialist
Tel: [1] 215-986-4004
Fax: [1] 215-986-2558
greg.t.barnowsky@unisys.com

UNIVERSITY OF MUENSTER
Academic Member
Department of Information Systems,
Leonardo-Campus 3
Muenster, 48149, Germany
Michael zur Muehlen
Research Assistant
Tel: [49] 251 833-8100
Tel: [49] 251 833-8109
ismizu@wi.uni-muenster.de

UNIVERSITY OF TECHNOLOGY, SYDNEY
Academic Member
Faculty of Information Technology, PO Box 123
Broadway, NSW, 2007, Australia
Carolyn McGregor
PhD Researcher
Tel: [61] 41-2702-940
Fax: [61] 29-3478-359
carolyn@it.uts.edu.au

URUDATA BUENOS AIRES SA
Guest Member
Florida 537 p3 of 518
Buenos Aires, Capital Federal, 1005, Argentina
www.urudata.com
Pablo García Briosso
Research Manager
Tel: [54] 511 4326 4552
Fax: [54] 511 4322 7283
pcgarcia@urudata.com

VERSATA
Guest Member
Unit 13, 663 Victoria Street
Abbotsford, VIC, 3067, Australia
www.versata.com
Sean Woodhouse
Director Engineering
Tel: [61] 39 428 0788
Fax: [61] 39 428 0786
seanw@verveinc.com

VEST-META TECHNOLOGY
Guest Member
Kolomensky Proezd, 1a
Moscow, 115446, Russia
Maria Camennova
President
Tel: [7] 095 115 60 01
Fax: [7] 095 112 23 33
mariaC@vest.msk.ru

VIGNETTE CORPORATION
Funding Member
1601 South MoPac Expressway, Building 2
Austin, TX, 78746-5776, United States
www.vignette.com
Clay Johnson
Staff Engineer
Tel: [1] 512-741-1133
Fax: [1] 512-741-4500
chjohnson@vignette.com

VISIONEST S.P.A.

Guest Member
Via Porciglia, 14
Padova, Pd, 35131, Italy
www.visionest.com
Bruno Stefanutti
Partner
Tel: [49] 661 877
Fax: [49] 876 1156
bruno.stefanutti@visionest.com

VITALZ

Guest Member
816 Congress Avenue, Suite 1460
Austin, Texas, 78701, United States
www.vitalz.com
Charles A. Canning
Sr. Software Engineer
Tel: [1] 512 615-3861
Fax: [1] 512 615-3850
ccanning@vitalz.com

VITRIA TECHNOLOGY, INC.

Funding Member
945 Stewart Drive
Sunnyvale, CA, 94086, United States
www.vitrea.com
Larissa Leybovich
Product Manager
Tel: [1] 949-857-4233
lleybovich@vitria.com

Vitria's BusinessWare is the only e-business platform that can address the full range of capability required by enterprise users-from process automation to w o r k f l o w, from monitoring to process optimization, from internal integration to external integration. Vitria's BusinessWare provides a unified environment to manage the flow of critical information among enterprise business systems-both computer-based and human-based-and beyond company boundaries to partners, suppliers and customers. The Business Process Management (BPM) component of BusinessWare seamlessly supports both process automation and manual operations out of one single platform. The workflow functionality extends the existing BPM architecture and utilizes BusinessWare's most efficient and reliable technologies such as process execution, message communication and application connectivity and is supporting WfMC standards.

W4 (WORLD WIDE WEB WORKFLOW)

Funding Member
4 rue Emile Baudot
91873 Palaiseau Cedex, France
www.w4global.com
Jean Faget
Chairman
Tel:+ 33 1 64 53 19 12
Fax: + 33 1 64 53 28 98
jean.faget@w4global.com

Created in 1996, W4 is now a leading company on the European market with an installed base of more than 80 major accounts in France and worldwide. Founded by Jean Faget, Chairman of the French Chapter of the WorkFlow Management coalition, W4 edits the native Internet W4®Enterprise solution.

W4®Enterprise provides our clients with the means to enhance their reactivity and competitiveness, to master their work organization and to optimize their processes aiming at productivity, quality, tracking and agility.

W4®Enterprise combines the edition of a workflow solution, the expertise, the advice and the related services to gain a better mastery of the work processes' evolution and of the urbanization of the company's information system. Therefore, it globally meets the market's requirements.

W4®Enterprise is used to create any application requiring the mastery of process engineering and of business processes, and becomes naturally integrated into the new e-business solutions: CRM, e-business, e-procurement, market places...

With **W4®Enterprise**, you have at your disposal a stable, performing, and scalable workflow product, which enables you to capitalize the investments already made. W4's references include France Telecom, Sofres, Groupama.

WARE2 SOFTWARE CORPORATION
Guest Member
2600 Skymark Avenue, Building 12, Suite 103
Mississauga, ON L4W 5B5, Ontario, L4W 5B2, Canada
www.ware2.com
Mark Andress
President
Tel: [1] 905-238-5750
Fax: [1] 416-994-6747
mandress@ware2.com

WAVESET TECHNOLOGIES
Guest Member
6850 Austin Center Blvd, Suite 205
Austin, TX, 78731, United States
www.waveset.com
Darran Rolls
Director of Technology
Phone: 1 512 338-1818
Fax: 1 512 338-1138
darran.rolls@waveset.com

WORK MANAGEMENT EUROPE
Funding Member
Hardwareweg 7F
Amersfoort, 3821 BL, The Netherlands
www.wmeonline.com
Cor H. Visser
Tel: [31] 33 4508530
Fax: [31] 33 4508531
cvisser@wmeonline.com

Work Management Europe supports customers and partners in BPR, Workflow Application Design and Development. Areas of expertise include Finance and Insurance, Publishing and Trade and Government. As a full service provider we accept project responsibility for implementing the designed solutions. Our approach is based on Benefits analysis and Rapid Process Prototyping and Rapid

Application development. Work Management Europe is the Benelux distributor and training Center for Action Technologies products.

WORKFLOW & GROUPWARE STRATEGIES

Funding Member
37 rue Bouret
75019 Paris, France
Martin Ader
Analyst
Tel: [33] (1) 42 38 08 15
Fax: [33] (1) 42 38 08 02
ader@wngs.com

W&GS provides consulting services to assist enterprises in deploying the proper work management technologies (Workflow, Groupware, Knowledge Management) according to their activity profiles and corporate priorities. Assistance covers projects from initial opportunity analysis up to product selections and project planning and auditing. Clients include France Telecom, l'Oréal, Danone, Bouygues Telecom, and regional government. Martin Ader, the W&GS founder, has 16 years of workflow experience including research, development, marketing, and application deployment. He works both on consulting and as an international industry analyst in the workflow area. He is the author of the Workflow Comparative Study (comparing 12 workflow engines in detail) that was sold in more than 25 countries from continents. He has conducted several missions for workflow vendors related to product positioning, requirements analysis, and development strategies.

WORKTIVITI

Guest Member
8805 Governor's Hill Drive, Suite 100
Cincinnati, OH, 45249, United States
Robert Weiss
Vice President, Engineering and General Manager
Tel: [1] 513-583-5680
Fax: [1] 513-583-8885
robert.weiss@worktiviti.com

ZÜRCHER KANTONALBANK

Guest Member
Abt. LIXA, Postfach
Zürich, CH 8010, Switzerland
Walter Haas
Tel: [41] (1) 27 5 79 46
Fax: [41] (1) 27 5 86 46
walter.haas@zkb.ch

Index

EXCELLENCE IN PRACTICE SERIES

By Layna Fischer

What makes a winner? The answer lies in the *Excellence in Practice* series by Layna Fischer, General Manager of the Workflow Management Coalition (WfMC) and Chair of the Workflow And Reengineering International Association (WARIA). To be recognized as winners, companies must address three critical areas: excellence in innovation, excellence in implementation and excellence in strategic impact to the organization.

Featuring the winners and finalists of the annual Giga Excellence Awards, with guest chapters from leading industry analysts and experts, this series profiles case studies providing considerable detail regarding the issues of implementation:

- How these companies managed both their overall technological and business innovations.
- Their system application, the system use, the users; what the job entails
- What were their key motivations
- Their system configuration (number, and type of software, servers, scanners, printers, storage devices, etc., including the vendors and integrators involved)
- How the company has been impacted by their new system; cost savings, ROI and increased productivity improvements, competitive advantage gained, etc.

INNOVATION & EXCELLENCE IN WORKFLOW AND IMAGING 1997

232 pages US $50.00. Quality laminated hardcover. Size: 7" x 10" Illustrations, charts, references, appendices, bibliography, index. ISBN: 09640233-5-0

VOLUME II 1998: INNOVATION & EXCELLENCE IN WORKFLOW AND IMAGING

354 pages US $50.00. Quality laminated hardcover. Size: 7" x 10" Illustrations, charts, references, appendices, bibliography, index. ISBN: 09640233-6-9

VOLUME III 1999: WORKFLOW PROCESS AND KNOWLEDGE MANAGEMENT

360 pages US $50.00. Quality laminated hardcover. Size: 7" x 10" Illustrations, charts, references, appendices, bibliography, index. ISBN: 09640233-8-5

WORKFLOW HANDBOOK 2001

The definitive and one-stop reference work on workflow, standards and business processes; published in collaboration with the *Workflow Management Coalition*, the industry's standards-setting body. Includes Wf-XML Binding Specification and WfMC workflow glossary. Edited by Layna Fischer

420 pages. US $95.00. Size: 7" x 10" Illustrations, charts, references, appendices, bibliography, index. ISBN 0-9703509-0-2

ORDER

- [ ] The Workflow Paradigm, Second Edition $34.95
- [ ] Electronic Commerce $29.95
- [ ] Excellence in Practice $50.00
- [ ] Excellence in Practice Volume II $50.00
- [ ] Excellence in Practice Volume III $50.00
- [ ] Excellence in Practice Volume IV $50.00
- [ ] Workflow Handbook 2001 $95.00
- [ ] Workflow Handbook 2002 $95.00

SHIPPING INFORMATION

Name: _____

Title/Occupation: _____

Company: _____

Address: _____

_____

Phone: _____ Fax: _____

Email: _____

PAYMENT INFORMATION: (Make copies of this page for additional titles)

No.	COPIES	@ $ each	= $
		FL state tax 6%	= $
		Subtotal	= $
No.	Shipping	(see rates below)	= $
		TOTAL	= $

- [ ] Check (Please make check in US Dollars drawn on a US Bank to Future Strategies Inc.)

- [ ] VISA   - [ ] MASTERCARD   - [ ] AMEX   - [ ] DINER'S CLUB

Credit Card No. _____ Exp. Date _____

Name on Card _____ Today's Date: _____

Signature _____

Mail or fax this order to:

Future Strategies Inc., Book Division
2436 North Federal Highway, #374,
Lighthouse Point, FL 33064 USA
Tel: +1 954 782 3376 Fax: +1 954 782 6365
email: waria@waria.com

AIRMAIL SHIPPING CHARGES **PER BOOK**: USA Priority Mail $5.95; Canada/Mexico $9.00; UK/Europe $14.00; Pacific Rim $17.00; Africa/South America $19.00

Overnight Courier: USA $17:00 and Global Express $95.00

(Distributors/Bookstores/Libraries/Educational Institutions, please call for special discounts and shipping schedule.)